Praise for *Albert Kahn's Daylight*

"With *Albert Kahn's Daylight*, Chris Meister gives us a meticulously researched professional biography of the Detroit designer—a thoroughly engaging read that will appeal to both the curious layperson and academic alike. It's an invaluable addition to the growing literature on the often-overlooked architect who created Henry Ford's revolutionary 'daylight factories,' industrialized the early Soviet Union, and built many of Detroit's iconic skyscrapers. Along the way, Meister explodes myths that have been passed down through the ages and sketches fascinating, short portraits of key architects and industrialists who populated the Motor City in the first half of the twentieth century. In sum, this is architectural history at its best—a book that illuminates the man, his city, and his times."

—Michael H. Hodges, author of *Building the Modern World: Albert Kahn in Detroit* (Wayne State University Press)

"A deep dive into the life and work of one of the most productive architects of the twentieth century. Chris Meister's book is not only an insightful biography of Albert Kahn, but it is also a careful and commonsensical mapping of the prolific output of Albert Kahn, Inc. It hits the mark with its emphasis on Kahn's enlightened pragmatism, expressed primarily in his signature 'daylight factory' designs yet also evident in many of his other projects."

—Terry Smith, author of *Making the Modern: Industry, Art, and Design in America*

"Architectural historians once shamefully neglected the art and influence of Albert Kahn. More recent studies have started to correct that, and now Chris Meister's splendid new study of Kahn's work and career, anchored in astonishing archival research, brings us closer to a fuller appreciation of this remarkable man and his career."

—John Gallagher, author of *Yamasaki in Detroit: A Search for Serenity* (Wayne State University Press)

"Chris Meister's *Albert Kahn's Daylight* is a well-researched, clearly written, and insightful study of Albert Kahn's life and work, including his impact on twentieth-century architecture globally. This is a valuable addition to the titles Wayne State University Press has published on Detroit architects and architecture. Well done!"

—Charles K. Hyde, professor emeritus of history, Wayne State University

ALBERT KAHN'S DAYLIGHT

Great Lakes Books

A complete listing of the books in this series can be found online at wsupress.wayne.edu.

Editor

Thomas Klug
Sterling Heights, Michigan

Previous page: Albert Kahn, December 12, 1926. Photographer unknown. Photograph courtesy Burton Historical Collection, Detroit Public Library.

Albert Kahn's Daylight

An Architect Reconsidered

CHRIS MEISTER

Wayne State University Press
Detroit

ISBN 9780814352731 (hardcover)
ISBN 9780814352748 (ebook)

Library of Congress Control Number: 2025932973

On cover: Interior of the Belle Isle Aquarium, ca. 1905. Detroit Publishing Company photograph collection, Library of Congress. Cover design by Ashley Muehlbauer.

Published with the assistance of a fund established by Thelma Gray James of Wayne State University for the publication of folklore and English studies.

Published with the assistance of the Albert Kahn Legacy Foundation, a nonprofit membership organization supporting architectural education and preservation. Visit www.AlbertKahnLegacy.org for more information.

Wayne State University Press rests on Waawiyaataanong, also referred to as Detroit, the ancestral and contemporary homeland of the Three Fires Confederacy. These sovereign lands were granted by the Ojibwe, Odawa, Potawatomi, and Wyandot Nations, in 1807, through the Treaty of Detroit. Wayne State University Press affirms Indigenous sovereignty and honors all tribes with a connection to Detroit. With our Native neighbors, the press works to advance educational equity and promote a better future for the earth and all people.

Wayne State University Press
Leonard N. Simons Building
4809 Woodward Avenue
Detroit, Michigan 48201-1309

Visit us online at wsupress.wayne.edu.

In memory of Sister Euphemia,
for her stern edge and high expectations

It is quite possible to do interesting and modern work with due respect for good tradition.

—Albert Kahn, "The Approach to Design" (1932)

Contents

Preface

The genesis of this book lay in my desire to find historical justification to leverage against the announced 2005 closing of Detroit's Belle Isle Aquarium (more accurately identified as the aquarial component of the Belle Isle Aquarium & Horticultural Building), which opened in 1904. With it being the oldest purpose-built aquarium in North America, and one of the oldest in the world, closing such a unique, architecturally appealing municipal asset simply seemed a remarkably short-sighted thing to do. Inherently unique and irreplaceable, it was designed by the city's celebrated architect Albert Kahn, whose career began in the early 1880s as an unpaid office boy in a Detroit architectural office and ended in 1942 as he headed his own large and highly successful firm.

To tell the aquarium story, I initially thought I would only need to repeat the familiar Kahn story in a perfunctory manner as background, it seeming to be so widely accepted. I was left, I believed, with simply having to find justification in the aquarium structure itself to build an argument for its preservation. I turned my attention to a near contemporaneous, but no longer extant, industrial structure attributed to Kahn in hopes of finding some noteworthy relationship. This was the 1900 Boyer Machine Company Shop in Detroit, long thought to hold significance as Kahn's first industrial commission. While examining brittle, century-old newsprint caringly preserved within a box stored in the Burton Historical Collection of the Detroit Public Library, I was surprised to discover that the shop was actually the work of St. Louis architect Louis Christian Mullgardt. If the scholarship on this attribution—widely accepted as a milestone in

Kahn's career—could be in error, perhaps there were other significant inaccuracies in his legacy as it came down through later generations. Likewise, further investigation into the misattribution led to my realization that Joseph Boyer, the client for the machine shop, had a major role in Kahn's success that both chose to play down in public.[1] If one key figure was missing from the Kahn story, there could be more. While continuing my efforts, along with others, to save the aquarium, I began to investigate the architect further. Before long I came to realize the story was far larger than I imagined—to the point where I came to doubt the Allies would have won World War II without Kahn. Not that he would have said so himself, even if he had lived to see the victory.

Discerning an overall theme for such a long, prolific, diverse, and historically impactful career is a challenge. Working in many styles in collaborative efforts where outcomes were shaped by many factors, the Kahn portfolio resists pigeonholing. Many profilers have found it convenient to concentrate on his industrial work, but even that is multifaceted—there's automotive, aviation, defense work, and newspaper publishing, to name just a few. The ultimate, unifying constant in my understanding of Kahn has been his devout advocacy of natural light in any workplace. This revelation was a direct result of an unexpectedly powerful experience in connection with my efforts surrounding the Belle Isle structure, where—I am convinced—it began.

Concurrent with my research were continuing efforts on behalf of the aquarium, then a disheartening victim of official neglect. It was closed in 2005 despite community objection, but through an unlikely alignment of factors, including political scandal, municipal financial crisis, and grassroots activism, it was reopened in 2012. I was among the group of volunteers spearheading that effort as we struggled to reboot the exhibits. Finding myself spending much of my free time in the aquarium, I pondered the wisdom behind its original design. Now knowing that Kahn's famous work with so-called daylight factories *followed* this structure, I wondered if perhaps natural lighting, obscured since at least 1954 at the aquarium when skylights were boarded up, was integral to its function. My research into the building type indicated it was, but by the 1950s, the thinking behind aquarium design shifted to artificial illumination. (William Alford Lloyd's nature-inspired solution to this problem, which Kahn had adapted, as discussed in chapter 5, was long forgotten by this time.) Closing off the skylights resulted in the public corridor of the aquarium becoming a dark, inanimate place. Our unique situation, operating a public aquarium on a totally volunteer basis, required much outside-the-box thinking and I pressed for uncovering and restoring the original skylights despite the commonly held belief that natural sunlight and aquaria are incompatible. While we struggled to revive tanks, a donor appeared, as if by providence, with an interest in restoring the skylights.

On July 24, 2014, plywood covering was pulled from one of the skylights and natural light shone in the public corridor of the aquarium for the first time in some sixty years; the result was stunning. For me, Kahn's coherent vision was suddenly revealed. Where direct sunlight fell on tank glass, fish came forward, preferring it to the artificial illumination of the rest of the tank. When the building was open to the public, before diffuser glass was reinstalled, children danced in the circle of light cast upon the floor. The place was infused with a vitality that had lain dormant for years. It was a powerful affirmation of the value of the daylight that Kahn would insist upon from that design on, a consistent feature of his work that runs through his changing architectural styles. The experience led to further inroads into a return to Kahn's original aquarium vision in which I remain proud to have played a part (including my hand-washing the entire Opalite glass tiled ceiling).[2] The result of this limited restoration of Kahn's remarkable, functional vision has been stunning and did much to resurrect the aquarium as the significant, acclaimed, and well-attended cultural asset it once was. Hopefully this work will continue.

Having an opportunity for intimate and literally hands-on interaction with this unique structure from Kahn's early career afforded a singular experience that focused my research. Kahn's problem-solving abilities were on full display in the Belle Isle Aquarium & Horticultural Building, executed with artistic command. This complex structure was designed at a time when there was no suitable contemporary model to emulate. The architect had to study and apply lessons learned decades earlier while he consulted with experts to merge that knowledge with current requirements.

My research continued with this appreciation and, as I dug deeper into the past, the scope of Kahn's historic impact continued to loom larger in my estimation. The story of a job-trained architect of such humble origins rising to dominate his profession with an international footprint seems remarkable enough, but that was just the beginning. During his rapid rise in the early years of the twentieth century, he built a remarkable firm capable of keeping pace with the unprecedented demands of many of America's great industrialists during a time of explosive growth in production.

Earlier biographers have struggled to reconcile Kahn's famously humble nature with his herculean achievements—a formidable task made more difficult by the self-effacing reminiscences that the architect shared with journalists. It is perhaps predictable that Kahn's personal story came to dominate as the march of history consigned his remarkable accomplishments to the past. Some biographers, notably Christy Borth, dubbed "a walking encyclopedia of automobile legend and anecdotes," interviewed the architect and those around him and presumably recorded conversations faithfully. Memories can be faulty, however, and it seems Kahn was not overly careful in setting down the record of his career, even contradicting himself on occasion.[3]

In relatively brief conversations and interviews destined for general audiences, Kahn routinely dropped the names of two clients who would likely be readily recognized: Henry Ford, the People's Tycoon, and Henry B. Joy, president of the luxury brand Packard Motor Car Company. He might mention his travels with Henry Bacon, who Kahn or his interviewers were always quick to identify as the designer of the well-known landmark Lincoln Memorial. Reminiscences from these associations were woven into human interest articles accepted as accurate due to their source—usually the architect himself. These became fodder for later biographies.

While Kahn repeatedly focused on a few associations for the sake of simplicity, it should not be inferred that he devalued others. The pages ahead provide documentation of his acknowledgment of the contributions of his many clients and their employees, along with his family and his own employees, without being able to name them all. While I could not hope to name all of them either, I have endeavored to shed more light on the complex matrix of Kahn's associations to more fully grasp his truly historic career. In the process, I consider it a privilege to be able to flesh out, sometimes only in an admittedly minor way, the memory of some who played noteworthy roles in Kahn's success, such as Julius Melchers, George Nettleton, and Ernest Wilby. Along the way, depth is added to our understanding of the architectural community in Detroit in the late nineteenth and early twentieth centuries. Many threads of scholarly inquiry are exposed in the pages that follow; it is my hope others will find some worthy of further study.

With clients come commissions, and again Kahn was selective in his reminisces of individual projects. Given their sheer number, it is inevitable that many notable works were quickly upstaged by others. I have endeavored to reconsider Kahn's voluminous portfolio and give renewed attention to works that stood out in their time as milestones, either for their artistic merit, cultural impact, feats of engineering, or representations as building types. While the selection is ultimately my own, I have leaned on the insight of W. Hawkins Ferry, a critic and author as well as a connoisseur and collector of art who deeply impacted Detroit's cultural scene into the 1980s. Ferry also conversed with Kahn and others in the architectural community. As recounted by critic and historian Marsha Miro, Ferry "kept track of much of this city's past which would otherwise have been erased and has gently recorded its architectural scars and successes."[4]

I would not characterize inaccuracies traced to Kahn as lies on his part, as they tend to downplay—rather than unduly enhance—aspects of his career. "Sloppy" seems a more fitting term, but the resulting popular impression of this historic figure has rested largely upon folklore that crept into later profiles, possibly with writers taking their own license with the story.[5]

Grant Hildebrand did much to revive an appreciation of Kahn's work with *Designing for Industry*, published in 1974. New ground was broken therein by his interviews with Kahn's daughters and research into family correspondence, but the book falls into familiar traps such as identifying the 1900 Boyer Machine Company Shop as "his first industrial work" and Packard Number Ten as "the first automobile plant to be built of reinforced concrete." Understandably, he accepts Kahn's dismissal of his early partnerships as inconsequential. In drawing a distinction between Kahn and his contemporary Frank Lloyd Wright, Hildebrand identifies the former's clients as moneymakers and businessmen while characterizing the latter's as tending to be tinkerers and inventors. While Hildebrand admits the comparison is problematic, I believe he miscategorizes Kahn's most significant and loyal clients. Like Kahn, they were innovative producers and as such they bonded with the architect. They made money, but it was a byproduct of making *things* and creating jobs. Unfortunately, however, the title of Hildebrand's book seems to have done much to pigeonhole his subject as a designer of factories in the minds of a new generation of academics. Similarly, the title of Federico Bucci's valuable addition to the scholarship in the early 1990s, *Albert Kahn: Architect of Ford*, leaves an impression that the architect had just one significant client.[6] True, industrial work was Kahn's area of specialization and Ford was arguably his most key commercial client, but the pages ahead demonstrate that these were only part of a multifaceted story.

When Michael Hodges published *Building the Modern World: Albert Kahn in Detroit* in 2018, he described it as "an accessible introduction for the nonarchitect, nonacademic layperson to Albert Kahn" while noting "the world still awaits a comprehensive academic biography of the architect."[7] While hoping to appeal to both those with professional and nonprofessional interests, I have attempted to make an inroad into that void while acknowledging there is more to be written on this remarkable figure and his work.

In the present volume, the scope of Kahn's career is reevaluated, and the folkloric sources of the past are filtered with a skeptical eye. Their importance and likelihood of veracity are weighed against contemporary sources and previously overlooked events, leading to my disregarding some of them. In the early chapters, the influence of hitherto marginalized or forgotten individuals and projects is added to the architect's narrative and the relevance of the Belle Isle Aquarium & Horticultural Building becomes apparent. In recognizing the roles of clients and others, I may challenge preconceived notions of their character, but my goal is to convey the context of their relationships with Kahn as faithfully as I can.

I should note that I began my research in a time-honored way, traveling to plumb archives and libraries, searching through old newspapers, periodicals, vertical file folders, and boxes of documents. Microfilm technology enabled the photographic preservation and distribution of the content of newspapers and other material, but it needed to be visually searched, frame by frame, often on hand-cranked viewers. It was tedious but often fascinating and rewarding work as I cast my research net in new directions. Coinciding with the course of my work was an ongoing explosion of the availability of searchable databases of books, periodicals, and other documents, enabling me to explore a myriad of leads inaccessible earlier while cross-referencing information for accuracy. Utilizing new resources, I have arrived at a narrative that I believe clarifies and enhances Kahn's legacy while dispelling the folklore.

One benefit of straying from the familiar Kahn narrative is a fuller appreciation of his contributions in revolutionizing construction technology. While his use of reinforced concrete construction for industrial building has drawn much interest, his application of it in other building types has been largely overlooked. The technology itself seems underappreciated, in many cases remaining unrecognized behind the façade. It is utilized in much of America's built environment, however, and Kahn's role in the dissemination of the technology through example deserves attention, which it receives to some degree here. Although only job trained in engineering, as he was in architecture, Kahn was competent in this area and built an office that often pushed the envelope in many types of construction on his customer's behalf.

While on the topic of his customer's behalf, I layered my own experience in business onto this broader approach toward research to more fully explore Kahn's client associations. In doing so, it appears Kahn's clients may, by and large, deserve more credit for being concerned with worker welfare than has often been afforded them. I believe for Kahn this concern sprang from or was nurtured through his experience with the Belle Isle Aquarium & Horticultural Building. His clients, many rising from positions on shop floors themselves, in turn gravitated to him as they shared his values in this area. Working conditions in early twentieth century Detroit may not stand up to today's standards, but at the time they were among the best in the world.

In the post–World War I era, a movement for social change gained momentum in Europe that spread to the realm of the arts. Architecture was appropriated as an instrument for social change, where Kahn believed it should be the dutiful servant of a changing society. His opposition to the movement, surely influenced by insight gained through his work for the Soviet Union between 1929 and 1932, drove me to delve into areas not often found in architectural histories, such as politics and ideology.

During the Depression years, many considered centrally planned societies and totalitarian governments as key to brighter futures. The communist government of the USSR inspired fascist Italy, Nazi Germany, and Roosevelt's New Deal in the United States to turn toward centrally planned economies enlarging state footprints at the expense of individual liberty. Although they followed their own paths, all shared roots in socialism, and their appeal to people seeking social change in the 1930s is well-documented by cultural historian Wolfgang Schivelbusch and many others.[8] This is not stated here to provoke controversy, but because it is essential in understanding various positions and allegiances affecting Kahn's career that may be considered confusing, if not difficult to defend, today. It appears that Kahn drifted from uninformed indifference regarding socialism and communism, to optimism, then to deep misgivings and even fear for the safety of his employees in Moscow and at home. With the vicissitudes of time, once the USSR proved itself a formidable ally in World War II, this attitude merged with feelings of gratitude. Without acknowledging this elephant in the room, no firm grasp of Kahn's historically impactful career is possible.

This points to ideological motivation for Kahn's pronouncements against what became known as the International Style of Modernist architecture. Some American architects, such as Frank Lloyd Wright, perceived the style as a threat to the individuality they held dear, while it appears Kahn, as a result of his Soviet experience, saw it as a greater societal threat. Staying within the zone of his profession, Kahn limited his public comments to the movement's impact on architecture. This opposition to the style led to a marginalization of his accomplishments in academia over decades, as will be discussed in the epilogue. (Wright, to his annoyance, received token recognition within the movement that made him more difficult to ignore later.)

Working at a hectic pace up to the end of his life, Kahn had no opportunity to write a memoir that might have shed light on such matters. Instead, he left interviews and speeches responding to concerns of the moment, in which he showered credit on his clients, his employees, and luck. Looking back now, it becomes clear luck had little to do with his success, although events outside his control certainly defined his path. We see an individual of artistic capacity channeling his creative talents to functional applications, a tireless worker of remarkable mental capacity able to successfully manage multiple large—eventually tremendous—projects simultaneously and, in addition to it all, an amenable individual who opened himself to opportunity.

Kahn once said, "I don't know how to make opportunity, but I know how to make myself ready for it."[9] Of all the quotes in the error-pocked interviews left behind after his death, this overlooked side comment is perhaps most germane to understanding how an impoverished immigrant German Jew, whose formal education ended at age eleven, could rise from meager beginnings, through informal learning and on-the-job experience, to build an architectural and engineering office unequalled in scope, financial success, and historic significance.

Some architects (and their biographers) have seen themselves standing aloof, like Ayn Rand's fictional Howard Roark (clearly inspired by Wright), alone atop a promontory, laughing at those who would make them conform. It seems Kahn never saw his position as conforming or even compromising; he simply saw it as meeting his customers' needs while satisfying his own—the two being closely entwined. Where he could add beauty, he did. It was an attitude that fit well with a new generation of Detroit industrialists who had recently worked themselves up from shop floors. There may have been little art in their upbringings, but they considered themselves in trustworthy hands with Kahn, for the design of their homes and clubs as well as their factories. They would form bonds of loyalty, and together change the world while simply intending to succeed as individuals.

Howard Roark's architecture, being fictitious, owed nothing to anything that came before. Kahn's architecture drew from all that came before—with the debt being more discernable in some instances than in others. While an individual, Kahn understood that he was never alone and, as noted earlier, he strove to share credit. In telling his story as I have, perhaps a more complete understanding may be gleaned of the architect and his profession in the times in which he worked. Also revealed are some long-forgotten architect-client relationships that shaped Kahn's career and the course of twentieth-century history.

What follows is an overhauled professional biography of what is arguably the most successful (when measured by objective criteria such as the sheer number, scope, and geographic diffusion of projects) and impactful (when considered within the flow of global events) architectural career ever.

1

Lessons in Industriousness, Art, and Liberty

"Genius is a tricky word. It should be applied sparingly and perhaps only by posterity," wrote a Detroit eulogist for Albert Kahn in 1942. Nevertheless, that writer thought the architect surely rated the title as much as any composer or painter. In its obituary for Kahn, the *Times* of London considered him "a man of culture" as well as an "industrial architect and engineer." A telegram of condolence from Moscow offered that "Soviet engineers and architects will always warmly remember the name of the talented American engineer and architect, Albert Kahn." The pages of the *New York Times* brought attention to both the factories and the "outstanding examples of his work outside the field of industrial design." The newspaper's writers noted, "Both architecture and industry have lost a leader," adding, "A catalogue of the buildings designed by Albert Kahn runs to astonishing figures."[1]

"He was a creature of the industrial age and one of its creators," observed editors of the *Detroit News*. "But he never became a machine himself," recalled Grand Rapids architect Roger Allen, who knew him. The day after Kahn's passing, Allen imagined, "in a thousand drafting rooms yesterday men laid down their pencils and knew something vital and warmly human had gone out of American architecture."[2]

Few architects have received such widespread acclaim outside their profession upon their death and this is a demonstration of Kahn's impact. It was the end of a singular journey started under quite inauspicious circumstances. While the Kahn story, as it has come down through the decades, contains errors and omissions, it seems the only aspects truly embellished were the disappointments of his early career, which seem to have been unduly exaggerated. This may have been an attempt to stress that he had paid his dues on a path to success, a path remarkable to the point of perhaps being embarrassing for a humble soul.

Leaving the Old World for the New

The oft-told story that Albert Kahn had his share of struggle in early life is true, nonetheless, and it surely shaped his character. While it has been consistently reported that he was born on March 21, 1869, in Rhaunen, a town then within the German state of Prussia, this location may be subject to doubt. A 1945 biographical account by Christy Borth, a journalist author directly acquainted with the architect and his siblings, noted that Joseph and Rosalie Kahn "could never quite agree whether their son Albert was born in Rhaunen, Westphalia, or in some other of the many Saar and Rhineland communities in which they lived." Battles between the French and Prussian empires over the independent Rhineland provinces appear to have been motivating factors in the family's relocations, which included stints in Cologne and Paris. Albert's truncated formal schooling was mostly acquired in the Luxembourg village of Echternach, where he may have lived under the care of an aunt, or with his family, or perhaps both at times. His formal education ended with the family's immigration to the United States in 1881. Joseph had preceded the rest of the family by a year in an attempt to establish himself. While fatigue wrought by years in a battle zone may have been a factor in the move, the growing influence of Otto von Bismarck, with mixed policies regarding Jews, likely contributed. It seems surest to simply say the family ultimately sought more promising opportunity in America.[3]

After a stay of about three months in Baltimore, the family settled in Detroit where Joseph was an itinerate rabbi. German-born, he has been described as impractical, but was also remembered as a teacher, lecturer, and author of books on science, religion, and other subjects. He was a member of the Masonic

Order, and few would disagree that he and Rosalie begot a remarkable family, intellectual but never wealthy. Joseph tried various means to provide for his wife and ultimately eight children, but the family usually simply scraped by at best. Albert remembered his mother as "a good business woman. Several times by running small shops she made money. But father had a positive genius for getting some fine-sounding scheme that promptly lost it." Meanwhile, Albert grew up doing without the amenities enjoyed by many others of his age. Both his father's poor business choices and his mother's valiant industriousness surely provided valuable lessons for Albert and his siblings. As the oldest child and the first to learn English, he was thrust into a role of responsibility and contributed to the support of the family early on. When Rosalie worked in a restaurant at the Michigan Central train station, he waited on tables. When Joseph operated a fruit cart, Albert curried the horse that drew it and cleaned the stable.[4]

Scott's Office

Kahn had an aptitude for drawing and his mother found him an entry-level job as an office boy with the architectural office of William Scott & Company, one of Detroit's premier firms. Most biographies record this as the office of John Scott, but at the time the business was still in the father's name. This was likely in 1882 or early 1883 and Kahn worked for a year without pay (as was customary), but the job offered the promise of satisfactory income in the future. He

The Kahn Family, circa 1890. Left to right: Gustav, Felix, Mollie, mother Rosalie, Julius, father Joseph, Paula, Louis (with stick), Moritz, and Albert. Photograph courtesy Albert Kahn Associates, Inc.

simultaneously waited tables at night, possibly at the Michigan Central Station restaurant, to keep income flowing to the family.[5]

While fascinated by the process of designing buildings, he was never popular in the office and never given anything more than the most menial of tasks. Some of this treatment seems to stem from young Albert's need to tend the horse that drew his father's fruit cart before reporting to Scott's office. Kahn carried the odor of the stable with him and, as he remembered, the head draftsman "always wrinkled his nose when I went by." Although he began his second year at $2.50 per week, he was denied the aspects of the work that he found intriguing. Kahn also remembered being considered inept as well as lacking motivation or potential, which may have been a manifestation of his frustration. Feeling alienated and marginalized, at one point he became so utterly discouraged that, as he put it, "I just went outside and bawled."[6]

Reminiscing in 1929, Kahn told author Helen Christine Bennett that Julius Theodore Melchers, described simply as a wood carver, happened upon the sobbing lad and asked what was the matter. "I don't know anything and can't do anything right," was Kahn's reply. Melchers is reported to have said, "I run a drawing school Sunday mornings. Come. If you have money, you can pay; if not, alright."[7] This story has often been repeated with only slight variation, but while Kahn may well have found himself outside the office sobbing in despair at some point, this chance meeting with Melchers at that moment, as if sent by God, is surely apocryphal. Nevertheless, the involvement of Melchers in his career seems godsent, however it happened. Melchers was a much more significant figure in Detroit at the time than the Bennett account, or any of the others, suggests.

The Influence of Julius T. Melchers

According to a city history published almost three decades after Kahn's drawing lessons, it was "to the self-sacrificing efforts of Julius Melchers" that many of the city's successful architects, which would include Kahn, owed their start. He was a pillar of Detroit's German enclave; another recollection noted, "Few men have had so considerable an influence on the art education of their communities." The name Julius Melchers was, according to a *Detroit Free Press* account, synonymous "with the encouragement of art in this city."[8]

Born in Soest, Prussia, around 1830, Melchers apprenticed to the sculptor Ministerman at age fifteen and was among thousands of his countrymen forced to flee Germany following the failed rebellion of 1848, which aimed to unify the country under a republican form of government modeled after the United States. He pursued artistic studies under Jean-Baptiste Carpeaux and Antoine Étex in Paris, but political activism compelled another move, this time to England, where he worked as a modeler at the Crystal Palace at Sydenham. In 1852 Melchers arrived in New York and in 1855 joined a colony of forty-one other "Forty-Eighters" in Detroit. These recent immigrants brought with them antislavery sentiments and a strong fervor for the American ideal of liberty. Many involved themselves in the Republican Party when it formed in Jackson, Michigan, in 1854 and enlisted on the side of the Union in America's Civil War. "The German refugees of 1848 gave us great soldiers, artists, captains of finance, lawyers, editors and statesmen," the editors of the *Detroit News* later noted. "This nation is strong and great because it was settled here and there by men who dared to demand liberty, political and religious." As one of them, Melchers left his "mark on American society, and that society is glad to acknowledge its debt."[9]

Melchers held class in Arbeiter Hall, a gray, wooden structure in the city's German colony that represented a lone outpost of opportunity for would-be fine and applied artists in the American Midwest. "He was, above all, a fine master of drawing," according to a 1927 account, "an exacting but encouraging master." Another student recalled the classes, in a narrow room with arching walls and a high, beamed ceiling, as having "life and meaning and atmosphere." The *Detroit News* added, "The majority of Detroit's most successful lithographers, artists, sculptors, designers and workers in other imitative or creative arts . . . have at one time or another been pupils of Julius Melchers." Students fanned out from the city as well. Architect Dankmar Adler, later partner in the famed Chicago firm Adler & Sullivan, was a pupil. Adler's family lived in Detroit, where the father was rabbi for Temple Beth El, from 1854 to 1861. (A story that Kahn once turned down an offer to work with the Chicago firm around 1893 gains credence with the Melchers and Beth El connections.)[10]

Melchers and his drawing classes were well known, especially in Detroit's German community, so it is likely Kahn or at least his parents would have been aware of them previously. It appears Melchers was aware of Kahn as well—apart from any chance meeting when the latter was sobbing on the sidewalk. Reminiscing in a 1926 gathering that included other former employees of the Scott office and some of Melcher's former students (who might hold him to greater accuracy than journalists would), Kahn noted with characteristic deadpan humor that his presence "at the office never brought forth particular pangs of joy," before recounting how "that dear departed soul, Julius Melchers, the sculptor of bygone days . . . *had taken an interest in me for some time* and invited me to his drawing school [emphasis added]."[11]

Kahn recalled instruction under Melchers as his first drawing lessons and it appears they came with a stern edge and high expectations that descendants of German immigrants may find familiar. "I don't take boys who have not the real art spirit; I have no time to fool," Melchers was quoted as saying.[12]

His charity toward Kahn was significant given that the sculptor relied on tuition to augment his income in a city and a time where art was, in his opinion, undervalued. His desire was to sculpt, as evidenced by sculptures of his currently on the campus of Wayne State University that once graced niches in the Detroit City Hall, but there were not enough commissions to be had. To make ends meet he taught, and applied his art to industry. Melchers may have made his mark on Kahn in this respect, too. He patented a design for an improved hitching post for horses and made a business of creating popular wooden statuary known as cigar-store Indians to adorn entrances of tobacco shops—work far beneath his talent but paying the bills.[13]

Melchers's impact on regional architecture was so significant that the Michigan chapter of the American Institute of Architects made him an honorary member. Its 1908 eulogy for him recalled his

> years of modest, earnest, unselfish labor as an artist and teacher; years which he gave with generous hand and heart, to the upbuilding of technical training, and a broad appreciation of the true and beautiful in life. . . .
>
> He has left us and the city which he loved, an influence and spirit which will live on, and broaden with the years.

> The artists and lovers of art, as well as all the higher life of our city, owe to him a debt of gratitude; and we architects especially, with a deep sense of our obligation and our loss, do hereby record our grateful appreciation of his high artistic talents; his fine, earnest and helpful life, and his genuine, manly character.[14]

An Appreciation for the Poetry in Life

While Melchers provided Kahn with drawing lessons, it seems likely his influence extended beyond that. The instruction appears to have given the office boy a practical foundation particularly suited for advancing in architecture. His model for industriousness might have also rubbed off on his pupil.

That is not to say the instruction in the old Arbeiter Hall, which burned in 1895, was strictly vocational. As the midwestern city's leading fine arts advocate in the late 1800s, it appears Melchers instilled in Kahn an appreciation for such things that his siblings, oriented toward the applied arts, perhaps lacked. In a 1908 profile of Kahn and his civil engineer brother Julius, Albert is identified as the "dreamer" and "artist" of the two, seeing "the poetry in life, the embellishments and the beauties." This seems a bit over-the-top, but perhaps it captures a personality division between him and Julius, the builder "who calculated strains and strengths." Other passages of the profile douse Albert with such flowery praise that one wonders if it ever truly applied, but it does document an artistic aspect of his personality. As a child in Europe, Kahn had an interest in music that his family could not afford to nurture in America. Melchers's charity allowed him to channel his artistic talent toward a vocation.[15]

In the coming years, Kahn lectured on the Renaissance to large audiences at the art museum, served long as a member of the Detroit Arts Commission beginning in 1904, and was recognized for his personal art collection. His own sketches, drawn during trips to Europe from 1890 into the 1920s, drew praise whenever exhibited.[16]

Perhaps Melchers, the old republican revolutionary, also passed along his passion for liberty. As Kahn melded architecture and engineering in his future career, he would find ways to apply them in the defense of his adopted country.

The “Office Boy” Canard

The office boy eventually found himself dismissed from Scott’s employment. As he told it, “I was not only fired, but kicked out by the head draftsman.” One suspects the whole episode remained a chip on Kahn’s shoulder, so to speak, for he began publicly telling the story of his firing once his success was firmly established (usually without naming Scott’s firm). It seems likely to also be the root of Kahn’s oft-repeated canard about factory design being considered only worthy of “an office boy” when he started. This should not be taken literally, although many biographers have done just that. While industrial structures were (and still are) often built without the benefit of an architect, the architects of the time promoted their industrial work with just as much pride as any other job and displayed factory designs in exhibitions and newspaper illustrations. As an example of the importance they attached to this work, when Kahn’s future employer, Mason & Rice, received a commission to design the D. M. Ferry Seed Company warehouse in 1879, partner George Mason traveled from Detroit to Boston to personally study the latest trends in industrial construction. When the perspective drawings were complete, Mason & Rice proudly placed them on public view.[17] In later years, as discussed in the pages ahead, architects as a group eventually relinquished the increasingly specialized industrial work and looked down upon it, but this was not the case in late-nineteenth century America.

The notion that the design of any structure of significance would be assigned to an essentially untrained, low-paid (if paid at all) employee is absurd. It seems that as his success grew, however, “office boy” was an epithet Kahn wore with biting pride as a jab at those who drove him from his first job in architecture. After his competitors deserted the industrial field only to watch him—with the aid of his finely tuned firm—surpass them, Kahn had no qualms reminding elitists among the profession, “I’m still that office boy designing factories.”[18]

2

In the Office of Mason & Rice

The dismissal from the Scott office proved providential for soon afterward Kahn went to work for the architectural firm of Mason & Rice on a recommendation from Melchers (another example of the artist's impact on the city's architecture). Unlike his experience with William Scott & Company, Kahn's new employment proved rewarding for all concerned. Again he started at the bottom. Kahn described his position as "understudy to the office boy" without pay, but in nine months he was drafting and tracing for $30 a month. A number of sources put his start date as January 1, 1885—but according to Mason's diary, that was the day his pay began. Elsewhere in Mason's notes his unpaid tenure is recorded as beginning March 3, 1884. On July 1, 1885, his pay was raised to $35 a month.[1]

While Kahn clearly applied Melcher's lessons well, Mason keenly identified two of his new employee's greatest strengths: "I have never known anyone with such an enormous capacity for concentration and application to study. Every spare moment of the day (we worked long hours in those days) Albert would spend reading our collection of architectural books. In fact, he was often fond of saying that his only formal education in architecture was obtained in the library of Mason and Rice."[2]

Kahn's own recollections of the same period evoke a fifteen-years-old's enchantment: "What a different atmosphere I found here [the Mason office compared to that of Scott]. One of encouragement from the start. . . . Work was given to me other than mere grinding of ink and running errands. I was taught to draw lines and perspectives, to make pen and ink sketches, given a chance at working drawings, at details." In addition to drawing, Melchers may have also provided the boy with lessons in drafting, but Kahn's talents clearly bloomed with practical application. Mason had an impressive collection of architectural photographs, which he used to tutor Kahn by pointing out successful work against what was not.[3]

The Principals

George Dewitt Mason was born in 1856 in Syracuse, New York. His grandfather and father had an engine and boiler manufacturing business that was wiped out during the Civil War. The father moved his family to Detroit in 1870 where he had a job with the Michigan Machinery Depot, a factory operated by an old friend, Civil War General Grover S. Wormer, and his sons. After high school young Mason took a job with the Machinery Depot where Wormer, also on the board of directors for the Detroit Lithographic Company, recognized his drawing talent and suggested he consider a career in architecture. Mason worked one summer in Mortimer L. Smith's architectural office at Wormer's suggestion, then jumped to the office of Henry T. Brush and Hugh R. Smith in 1873, believing it offered more opportunity even though it required working the initial nine months without pay. Zachariah Rice hired on at Brush & Smith two years later. Less is known of him than Mason, but he was born in Oswego, New York, in 1855. At the age of six, Rice moved with his family to Detroit where he graduated from Detroit High School in 1872. Hugh Smith died shortly after Rice joined the firm. Brush associated with John M. Donaldson in 1878, then died the following year.[4]

Both products of on-the-job training, Mason and Rice formed their own partnership in 1878, and the firm proved to be an incubator for some of Detroit's most talented young architects. Perhaps the office environment attracted the best employees, or it brought out the best in them. It seems Mason was a natural mentor who took a personal interest in employees' development. Kahn—the most successful of them all—recalled, "How we did admire Mr. Mason . . . his enthusiasm, his nice criticisms, his general helpfulness, his keen interest in us, his innate ability and his own superior draftsmanship."[5]

An often-told story (with variations) of Mason testing Kahn for colorblindness is verified by the latter repeating it publicly in the presence of the former. Mason also told the story. According to Kahn, George Voigtlander, then head draftsperson for the office, innocently mentioned to Mason that he observed Kahn was colorblind as he watched him work. Kahn greatly admired and fondly remembered Voigtlander, who was always helpful to younger members of the staff, as an artist and a role model in the office. In this instance, however, his casual remark jeopardized Kahn's job. Mason called Kahn into his private office and advised him that if he were indeed colorblind, he should seek another line of work. Having grown up with the condition, Kahn did not understand the nature of the problem nor did he know he had a problem until he found his job at stake. Mason proceeded to test Kahn by asking him to identify the various colors of the rug on the floor. Kahn could recognize primary colors, but for others he merely guessed and by coincidence was correct. "Surely luck was with me," Kahn recalled in 1926. "I have often enough

The drafting room staff of the office of Mason & Rice at 80 Griswold Street, Detroit. According to the notation on the back of this photograph, it was made on July 30, 1888, and shows, left to right, Charles Kotting, Albert Kahn, William B. Stratton, Frances Brown, George W. Nettleton, Beden [actually Charles L. Beedon], Theo Laist, R. Arthur Bailey, Jean Hackett, Joe Webber, and possibly George D. Mason. Photograph courtesy Burton Historical Collection, Detroit Public Library.

felt it was a handicap since, but have managed to shuffle along." The condition improved with time.[6]

Of course, Kahn did more than shuffle along. The natural ability his mother perceived appears to have been exceptional when measured against his peers at the time. In 1888, his drawing of a gothic dormer was granted first place in a contest of the Detroit Architectural Sketch Club judged by Donaldson, another architect who was once a Melchers pupil. Second place went to H. J. Maxwell Grylls of the future Detroit firm of Smith, Hinchman & Grylls (Mortimer Smith's successor firm). In an 1890 contest sponsored by the *Engineering and Building Record* of New York, Kahn's entry was awarded fifth place, ahead of an eighth place for fellow Detroiter Richard Mildner, another Melchers pupil as well as a Mason & Rice employee, and future partner in the firms of Mildner & Eisen. Many years later architect and respected critic Robert Craik McLean recalled that, "Albert Kahn, as a draftsman and a designer, was notable as being a wicked hand with a pencil."[7]

George W. Nettleton

George William Nettleton joined Mason & Rice two years after Kahn's start with the firm. Underappreciated in previous Kahn scholarship, it seems Nettleton also had a significant role in Kahn's education as an architect. He was born in Medina, Ohio, in 1860 and grew up on a farm as, in Kahn's words, "a member of a cultured family" of Connecticut stock. He studied carpentry after graduation from high school and spent a few years in the trade. Nettleton then attended Cornell University, graduating from the college of architecture and engineering in 1884. He declined an offer as assistant professor and instead moved to Jackson, Michigan, where he worked as a draftsperson for Lemuel Dwight Grosvenor. He moved to Detroit and became a draftsperson with Mason & Rice sometime in 1886.[8]

Kahn remembered Nettleton as the first person he had known who had attended an architectural school, and whose "helpfulness to a young chap was second only to Mr. Mason's." It seems he had additional qualities that paralleled Kahn's; on another occasion he recalled, "Mr. Nettleton was a thoroughly practical man with a wonderful mind. He combined this with an artistic temperament besides being a splendid mathematician. He always made friends with his clients and was so thoroughly sincere that he held them to the end."[9]

One of those clients was James Edmund Scripps, owner of the *Detroit News* and other Scripps League newspapers in Cincinnati, Cleveland, and St. Louis. He was also a fervent and knowledgeable patron of the arts and a founder of the Detroit Museum of Art, presenting it with a significant collection of old master paintings in 1889. In 1891 he engaged Mason & Rice to design the $7,000, two-story brick Detroit News Building and a sprawling enlargement of his personal residence echoing a Tudor baronial estate expressive of Scripps's English birth.[10]

The client found a compatible draftsman and architect in the cultured Nettleton, whose collaboration with Scripps was slightly muddled in the account passed down to us from W. Hawkins Ferry, who later interviewed architects of the era. Without citing a specific source (although Mason seems the likely candidate), Ferry recounts that Scripps "sent draughtsmen to England to study and make drawings of fourteenth century parish churches," for use in the design of Trinity Reformed Episcopal Church in Detroit.[11] On further investigation for this volume, it seems the plural "draughtsmen" was actually the singular George Nettleton, and his mission to England was concealed within his participation in the Scripps League of American Workingmen's Expedition.

Nettleton and the Workingmen's Expedition

In May 1889, the Scripps newspaper conglomerate announced its sponsorship of an expedition with the purpose of studying working conditions in Europe's industrial centers. It was a gimmick to attract working-class readership at a time rife with self-promotion efforts by many newspapers, but the Workingmen's Expedition stood out from the competition as particularly ambitious and expensive. Scripps sent forty workers from the four cities in its newspaper league with the promise to report on the best labor trends in the Old World. Nettleton was one of the delegates and officially tasked with making "a study of the workingmen's homes, factories and shops, and the general progress in building materials, heating and ventilation."[12] Given Kahn's later success in industrial architecture and future work for Scripps and his newspaper publishing son-in-law George Gough Booth, the expedition merits discussion here.

With his background, Nettleton stood apart from his fellow travelers: there were no other architects listed in the expedition otherwise composed of tradesmen and tradeswomen, mechanics, miners, railroad workers, dressmakers, and the like. They departed from New York City in mid-July 1889, bound for Liverpool, Birmingham, London, Antwerp, Essen, Lyon, and Paris (to report on the exposition there). For many it may have been a somewhat leisurely junket, but any of Nettleton's moments not devoted to inspecting working-class sites were probably spent sketching medieval churches for Scripps. As the expedition covered some three thousand miles in four weeks, Nettleton lamented being "able to get but a superficial idea of the people, their individual tendencies or their architecture, art or science."[13]

Still, he ventured a general assessment of "the architecture of a nation as representing, in a greater or less degree, the social and political influences of the time and the temperament of the people." While he admired Old World architecture for its proportions, massing, color, and ornament, Nettleton expressed disappointment with the amount of faux finish and trompe l'oeil he found. Similar trickery could be found in U.S. buildings, but he conceded that Europeans "have even outstripped us in both the quantity and quality of deceits. . . . One often forgets to ask himself how much of this beauty and grandeur is real and truthful. Is this beautiful marble wood or stucco? Is that lovely sconce back of that bracket real carving or the fancy of some painter? How soon a building loses its interest on learning what makes it most beautiful is but a painted sham."[14]

But the Scripps League of Newspapers sent the architect to study and report on workingmen's homes, factories, and shops, not to ruminate on truth in art. Through his observations on Europe's industrial architecture, Nettleton reveals the depth of his knowledge on the topic. In his view,

> factory construction has been neglected [in Europe]. It has not received the same thought and attention, nor is it reduced to the science which the architects and mill owners of our great manufacturing centers have brought it.
>
> There is a reason for this and it comes from the fact that our mills are relatively new and of recent date, while theirs are old and have stood a

> century or more, and today are manufacturing the same goods in the same way and from the same materials that generations ago brought wealth and prosperity to the people. Therefore, no change could be expected except in the new mills or those built within the last 10 or 15 years. But even in these less thought has been given in the line of comfort and safety of the operatives than is found in our own country in way of direct and ample stairways, fire escapes, thorough heating and ventilation and good sanitary and ample lavatory conveniences.

Furthermore, Nettleton found no factories "built on the modern principle of 'slow burning construction,'" where the use of heavy timber beams (which resisted flames) and other devices were employed to limit devastation by fire as much as possible in an era of abundant combustible building materials.[15] From his account it seems the American factory work environment was, in general, the best in the world in 1889, even though it may seem unacceptable when compared to today's standards (or even those of the early 1900s).

His reports from the expedition help put flesh on the memory of the man who, by all contemporary accounts, was an exemplary individual, a talented architect, and a friend and mentor to Albert Kahn. They also provide evidence that a Cornell-educated architect could take an interest in and acquire considerable understanding of factory design, further debunking Kahn's "office boy" quip.

Groundbreaking for the new Trinity Reformed Episcopal Church took place on Easter Monday, April 7, 1890, and work was completed at the end of 1892. Scripps took credit for the design and, wishing to inspire others to follow his aesthetic efforts, published a booklet explaining its architecture. In it he details how features gleaned from specific medieval churches were meticulously incorporated in the Detroit structure. Trinity was so much a personal statement that, in his booklet, Scripps lists Mason & Rice as "consulting architects." George Nettleton is listed separately as "chief draughtsman," and it seems likely he worked directly with Scripps to meld disparate features from his studies during the Workingmen's Expedition into a cohesive whole. According to a *Detroit News* account, "the design, accessories and ornamentations" were all of Scripps's "own initiation and selection." Significant in light of the draftsman's rant on European architectural deceit is Trinity's heavy reliance on authentic medieval construction methods, resulting in a structure expected to stand five hundred years. Historian George W. Stark records it being "regarded affectionately and critically as the finest example of Fourteenth Century Gothic architecture in America."[16] Scripps was pleased enough to return to Nettleton, and Kahn, for work in the future.

Rustic Retreats

Mason & Rice promoted the eclectic, so-called Shingle Style throughout the region, often in hybrid compositions. Although occasionally employed for urban residences, it was especially popular for resort communities, and Mackinac Island's 1887 Grand Hotel is perhaps the firm's most conspicuous extant achievement. Here the architects melded shingle work, applied in a meagerly, almost token manner, and colonial styling into an expansive structure noted for its record-setting long porch. The three-hundred-room hotel overlooked the northern tip of Lake Huron and the Straits of Mackinac with three stories

Grand Hotel, Mackinac Island, Michigan (1887). Mason & Rice, architects.
Photograph courtesy Burton Historical Collection, Detroit Public Library.

running 427 feet, representing one of the largest structures in the region. According to his son, Kahn claimed to have worked on the drawings for its famed porch.[17]

Mason & Rice often melded shingle work with the wildly popular Richardsonian Romanesque style being embraced by architects across the nation. Massachusetts architect Henry Hobson Richardson pioneered the style (and his name was given to it), drawn from the Romanesque architecture of the Auvergne region of France. Even when new, his buildings had appearance of antiquity while proving pliable to modern demands. The style's robust character was widely deemed suitable to the American landscape. Kahn later wrote, "Richardson's work, massive and powerful, proved a revelation." Detroit's elegant yet resolutely sturdy 1885 Bagley Fountain is an extant example of Richardson's work standing in the city at the time. The *Detroit News* reported, "A few of our own architects have caught the new spirit."[18]

Kahn's star was rising within the offices of Mason & Rice during these years. Another significant client for the architects was Hiram Walker, owner of the renowned distillery across the Detroit River in Walkerville, Ontario (later annexed by the city of Windsor). If Scripps seems to have been particularly appreciative of Nettleton's work, Walker seems to have favored Kahn. This association led to other work in Canada, both for the firm and for Kahn in later independent practice.[19]

Walker also developed the town of Kingsville, some thirty miles away on Lake Erie's north shore, as a resort destination to rival locations like Mackinac Island. Toward that end, Mason & Rice designed the grand, 120-room, shingle style Mettawas Hotel and Casino for Walker in Kingsville. Kahn signed the delineations for this structure, and a handwritten note on the reverse side of a hotel photograph in the Smithsonian Institution's Archives of American Art suggests Kahn had much to do with it. (He and his bride Ernestine honeymooned there in 1896.) Given the stylistic and material similarities, he surely was involved with the firm's design for the railway station a few blocks away from the resort it served, as recounted in local lore. This is a splendid Richardsonian Romanesque composition in fieldstone and shingle.[20] Although only twenty years old, Kahn was already a key member of the Mason & Rice office.

Mettawas Hotel and Casino, Kingsville, Ontario, Canada (1889). Mason & Rice, architects.
Photograph courtesy Burton Historical Collection, Detroit Public Library.

Kingsville Railway Station, Kingsville, Ontario, Canada (1889). Mason & Rice, architects.
Photograph courtesy Burton Historical Collection, Detroit Public Library.

Sketching About Europe with Henry Bacon

Kahn's opportunity for study abroad came in 1890 when he received a less than extravagant but professionally noteworthy $500 travel scholarship from the journal *American Architect and Building News*. Reporting on the scholarship, editor William Rotch Ware noted that Kahn's talent and drive were worthy of the journal's support. While confident that Kahn would "derive as much benefit as possible from his studies and travels in Europe," Ware expressed disappointment and bewilderment that he was the only applicant. "It is a curious commentary on the value of the various travelling-scholarships that have been established with the view of doing good that there are so few young men who appreciate the opportunities that these foundations put within their reach." The scholarship (open to men and women regardless of race) was discontinued shortly thereafter, apparently due to lack of interest, and the episode serves as an early example of Kahn seizing opportunity simply disregarded by his peers.[21]

Mason encouraged this nine-month, self-guided excursion away from the firm, having made his own first Grand Tour in 1884. Despite his advancement within the office, Kahn nonetheless felt poorly prepared for the trip. Upon traveling to Boston to accept the scholarship, however, he received encouragement from Ware. Kahn sailed for Europe on December 6, 1890, and nine days later he arrived at Southampton. By December 22 he was sketching in Genoa. "I saw so many wonderful things I just got bewildered," Kahn recalled. "I knew nothing and nobody, but I drew and drew." It must have been quite an adventure; one account tells of his often sleeping in haylofts to stretch his funds.[22]

February 1891 found him in Florence, where the twenty-one-year-old met Henry Bacon, his fourth (alongside Melchers, Mason, and Nettleton) major mentor in his architectural education. Bacon possessed much talent, but the sad timing of his unexpected death in 1924, shortly after completion of his highly acclaimed Lincoln Memorial in Washington, DC, has caused that landmark to eclipse appreciation of his other notable work.[23]

Known to most who were familiar with him simply as Harry, Bacon graduated from the University of Illinois in 1888. Afterward he worked as a draftsperson in the high-profile, New York office of McKim, Mead & White until he departed for Europe in 1889 on a $1,500 Rotch Traveling Scholarship. Like Kahn, Bacon was the sole applicant for his scholarship, which was largely spent by the time they met. (Both formally quit their jobs to take advantage of their scholarships.) As Kahn recalled many years later, Bacon "possessed innate taste, a fine appreciation of the best in architecture and the allied arts. . . . To me he proved not only a splendid teacher but a real friend whose kindness and stimulating influence I have treasured ever since." During a eulogy for Bacon, he was remembered for "that happy flexibility and grace of personality which is made up of courtesy, simplicity and humility." It is little wonder he and Kahn got along so well. The two traveled together for three or four months, with the slightly older Bacon sharing his greater architectural knowledge and the more frugal Kahn keeping their expenses tightly budgeted.[24]

Francis S. Swales, a superb draftsman, architect, and major contributor to *Pencil Points*, the professional "journal for the drafting room," according to its masthead, studied Bacon's scholarship drawings. In his opinion, Bacon "had few peers among students in sketching architecture. . . . His sketches all record objects worthy of study, and his studies are made from the worthiest point of view." Kahn so valued Bacon's knowledge that he placed it on a level with Mason & Rice's library as a resource in his own education.[25]

Of course, given Kahn's capacity and thirst for learning, he would have gained much from his European tour regardless of his crossing paths with Bacon. In return for his scholarship, he was expected to submit articles and illustrations for *American Architect and Building News*, which alone was quite an honor for any architect—much less an office draftsperson as Kahn was at the time. Nevertheless, with his typical diffidence, Kahn recalled, "The articles I tried to write were terrible. After blue-penciling the second one, the editor wrote: 'Never mind about the articles, send more sketches!'" This may be another example of Kahn belittling aspects of his early career, for his article on the architectural study opportunities in Paris is quite informative and practically any designer or artist wishing to visit the City of Light at the time would benefit from reading it.[26] Of course, it is possible that it was totally rewritten—not just punched up—by Ware or someone else at the journal, but if Kahn's original submissions were truly terrible, his writing soon improved. Just a couple years later he was giving well-attended lectures at Detroit's Museum of Art.

The breadth of his sketches as reproduced in plates appearing in *American Architect and Building News* is striking, ranging from picturesque townscapes that included commonplace details such as laundry hanging from windows to measured and carefully rendered profiles of ornamental features. Even at this early point, Kahn exhibited his industrious nature. Sketching Europe's monuments required concentration in the face of distractions from the usual hustle and bustle of city life, interruptions from passersby, and the normal traveler's urge to simply take in the sights. He did not limit himself to sketching glorious monuments and ornamental details while abroad, however. He also studied the massing of genre architecture and the utility of rural structures, all the while capturing the play of light and shadow. W. Marbury Somerville, a Seattle architect making his own sketch tour at the time, provides an example of Kahn's diligence. He crossed paths and traveled with Kahn and Bacon, probably in northern Italy. At one stop, Kahn announced his intention to make a sketch of a cathedral before catching the next train. His companions did not think it possible in the time available. They bet that Kahn could not do it and chose a casual tour of the sights for themselves instead. Somerville recalled that he and Bacon, "looked around the town and when we got back found him sitting on the curb stone with a corking good drawing all finished in an hour."[27]

"Lamballe Peaked Structure, Oct. 11 '91." Sketch by Albert Kahn, courtesy University of Michigan Museum of Art. Transferred from the College of Architecture and Design, 1972—Gift of the Family of Albert Kahn: through Dr. Edgar A. Kahn, Mrs. Barnett Malbin, Mrs. Martin L. Butzel, 1972/2.573.

After returning to Detroit and reemployment in the offices of Mason & Rice in late 1891, 140 of Kahn's drawings from his European trip were privately exhibited to the Michigan Society of Architects. Following that, they were displayed to the public at the Detroit Museum of Art where, according to one report, they "attracted a good deal of attention." (They would continue to draw note when exhibited again in 1895.) He was soon promoted to head draftsman. Francis Swales worked for George Mason a few years later and studied the firm's old office drawings. At some point, he also discussed the traveling scholarship experience with Kahn. Swales observed in *Pencil Points* that Kahn "came back to Detroit with a fully developed style of his own, which simply increased in facility as he went on."[28]

Like the firm's library, Kahn's European drawings became an office resource. They are said to have guided fireplace and paneling treatments for the elegant Hiram Walker & Sons offices in Walkerville. Mason's diary documents that Julius Melchers provided the carving for the interior ornament.[29]

Demonstrating the eclecticism of the era, a simultaneous Mason & Rice project midway across the Detroit River involved a robust, Richardsonian Romanesque composition. In describing the firm's design for a Detroit police substation on Belle Isle, a *Detroit Free Press* report noted that its "rough and

Belle Isle Police Station, Detroit, Michigan (1982). Mason & Rice, architects. Detroit News Company postcard view, circa 1908, collection of the author.

attractive exterior of field-stone combined with its gabled roof, presents rather the suggestion of a cosy, retired suburban residence." There was a stated desire to not spoil the wooded park with a structure that overtly expressed its partial function as a jail.[30] Given Kahn's involvement with the firm's earlier and quite similar Romanesque work, it appears likely he had a hand in this superb design as well.

Kahn and the White City

Another significant professional experience for Kahn was his visit to the great World's Fair in Chicago during the summer of 1893. Zach Rice served on the decorative designs committee for the Michigan exhibits at the fair and Kahn appears to have accompanied him to assist. He was deeply impressed; forty-four years later he recalled, "No one who visited the Fair will ever forget its effect on him."[31]

Indeed, the 1893 World's Columbian Exposition was an international event whose influence would be difficult to overstate. Ever since Great Britain's Great Exhibition of 1851, with its grand glass and steel hall in Hyde Park by Joseph Paxton (dubbed the Crystal Palace), nations sought to surpass each other with more magnificent and better-attended expositions with fantastic structures. In spite of the fact that its opening coincided with the Panic of 1893, a world-wide financial depression, planners of the great fair in Chicago intended to break all records for such events—and succeeded. Paid attendance was over twenty-one million; it seemed the whole world came to Chicago that summer.

The Chicago Fair's community of exhibit halls, particularly those composing its Court of Honor, showcased the work of many of America's leading architects and affected architectural taste for years to follow. Seeking a unified, monumental impact, organizers imposed a classically ordered style mandate with consistent cornice heights and an off-white color program. Collectively and popularly known as the White City, the Court of Honor façades exemplified unity of purpose while at the same time allowed architects individual expression within the confines of the mandate. The result was a style of neoclassicism sweepingly referred to as Beaux Arts in tribute to the famed Paris school of the arts. Many of these structures were also engineering wonders with vast,

A portion of the Court of Honor at the 1893 World's Columbian Exposition, Chicago, Illinois. Multiple architects. Elevated photographic view by Frances Benjamin Johnston, courtesy Library of Congress, Prints and Photographs Division.

unobstructed spans beneath glass and steel roofs. Outside of train sheds, there were few such structures to be seen anywhere at the time.

The grandeur of the temporary setting almost overshadowed the many new products on display. These included the introduction of the horseless carriage, represented by competing versions powered with steam, electric, and gasoline-driven engines. Another impressed visitor from Detroit was thirty-year-old Henry Ford. He had been developing his own vehicle and faced criticism regarding his decision to use gasoline as his power source. The fair was his opportunity to examine and compare competing products from foreign countries side by side, and evaluate the potentials of their power sources. He returned confident in his choice.[32]

To fully grasp the impact of the fair's Court of Honor on a young architect such as Kahn, one has to, in his words, "appreciate the rather sad state of architecture up to that time." In hindsight, Kahn looked upon the years preceding the fair as a dark age of rudderless eclectic romanticism in American architecture occasionally brightened by the likes of Richardson. Architect and historian Thomas E. Tallmadge christened those years the Parvenu Period—a time of prolific construction following the Civil War that was generally unbound by precepts of what might be called good taste. European architecture experienced a similar dark age at the time.[33]

Kahn had spent long hours studying books and photographs with Mason and buildings in Europe with Bacon to understand what constituted successful architecture. To his mind, the lessons were showcased for all at the fair, particularly Americans, to see at once. The White City, employing the architectural vocabulary of antiquity, demonstrated the value of discipline and collaboration in design, particularly in monumental design. The wildly enthusiastic public response provided validation for Kahn's extensive studies while demonstrating the value of organization. It is no wonder he cherished the memory.

Of course, many different architects (and clients) drew many different lessons from the Great Fair. Too many designers would superficially apply classic ornament to buildings without the discipline that leads to a cohesive whole. As demonstrated in the pages ahead with examples such as Temple Beth El and the General Motors Building, in Kahn's hands the same ornament could produce remarkable results on a broad range of scale.

Of the individual exhibits, the most popular was the aquarial pavilion of the Fisheries Building. There seems to be no documentation that Kahn took in this attraction, but given the sensation it caused, exceeding all expectations, it seems unlikely that he would have missed it during his stint at the fair. At times the number of visitors passing through its doors averaged between a hundred and 150 per minute, sustained over a span of hours, with many thousands being turned away when attendance exceeded capacity.[34]

The Fisheries Building itself was designed by Chicago architect Henry Ives Cobb, who infused images of aquatic life into the ornamentation at every opportunity. The aquarium exhibit was planned by the U.S. Fish Commission, a division of the Department of Commerce, as part of its mission to promote aquaculture in general and its own research and hatchery activities in particular. Visitors to the pavilion marveled at fifty display tanks of various sizes set into the walls of an inward spiraling corridor. Although temporary, it was

Fisheries Building, World's Columbian Exposition, Chicago, Illinois (1893). Henry Ives Cobb, architect. Interior view of the aquarium wing. Illustration by T. de Thulstrup from *Harper's Weekly*, 1893, collection of the author.

second only to the England's Brighton Aquarium (opened in 1872) as the largest in the world.[35]

Next most popular among the Columbian Exposition's exhibits was the Horticulture Building and, again, it is hard to imagine Kahn missing it. An analysis by architect and critic Henry Van Brunt suggests its designers, Jenney & Mundie, drew upon the work of Britain's Victorian-era naturalists while designing the vast botanical conservatory with plants of similar geographic and climatic ranges exhibited in one-story, glazed galleries. These terminated in higher pavilions at the outside ends that housed taller plants, while a "dome naturally took its place in the center, and, as it was to constitute the most imposing feature, interior as well as exterior, it had to be entered as directly as possible from the main porch."[36] This would be the compositional template for many future American public conservatories.

While at the time he had no reason to expect to ever have occasion to apply any lessons from these structures, Kahn surely remembered them when competing for the Belle Isle Aquarium & Horticultural Building design seven years later.

Horticultural Building at the World's Columbian Exposition, Chicago (1893). Jenney & Mundie, architects. Photographic view from the portfolio series "The Dream City," published by the N. D. Thompson Publishing Company, collection of the author.

At some point Nettleton rose to the position of general manager of the Mason & Rice office. As he and Kahn worked together, they grew to be close friends and, in the fall of 1893, they entered the competition to design the $350,000 Milwaukee Public Library and Museum, with a proposal that clearly reflected the influence of the Chicago Fair's Court of Honor. News that "Nettleton & Kahn, architects of this city" had garnered a $500 award for being among the five finalists appeared in a Detroit newspaper and the design was published in *Inland Architect and News Record.* (The competition drew seventy-four entries, including one by Frank Lloyd Wright, whose name does not appear among the finalists.) Had they been successful, they surely would have broken away to form their own firm, but it seems unlikely they actually established a legal partnership for the sake of their entry. While some employers might frown on such activity, Kahn noted that Mason "always took delight in the success of his men."[37] Nettleton and Kahn remained where they were for the next two years while the world's economy continued reeling following the panic.

Pingree's Detroit

Concurrently, many eyes throughout the nation were turned to Detroit, where an unlikely reformer was taking on the forces corrupting its government and business community, robbing its working class and honest brokers of their

Competitive Design, Milwaukee Public Library and Museum Competition (1894). Nettleton & Kahn, architects. Illustration from *Inland Architect and News Record*, vol. 23, courtesy Ryerson and Burnham Libraries, Art Institute of Chicago. Digital file #IA23XX_1456.

earnings and dignity. Hazen S. Pingree, the Republican elected to his first public office as mayor in 1889, was a millionaire of once high standing among those he sometimes termed "the silk stocking crowd." But they considered him a brash turncoat once in office when he threatened their comfortable lifestyles built on graft. Such corruption was widespread in America's cities and not limited by political party, although Democrats had controlled Detroit since the end of the Civil War and had installed a formidable, entrenched political machine. A Union veteran and shoemaker who came to the city in late 1865 with little more than his trade skills, by the time Pingree took office he and a partner had built the largest footwear manufacturer west of the Appalachian Mountains. Appealing to the disaffected working class, of whom many were immigrants, he "began a public career which lacked no elements of sensationalism," in the words of one journal.

> He antagonized great interests, and was bitterly attacked by his political enemies. He effected reductions in the [natural] gas rate, [street] car fares, and telephone rates. . . . He also reformed the [municipal] contract system, repaved the city, started a public lighting plant, and when the hard times of 1894 came on, he threw open vacant land in the city for the poor to use in gardening.[38]

There is more to Pingree's story, but this should suffice to demonstrate that through his reforms, the cost of vital utilities and services in Detroit dropped by millions of dollars, allowing *all* its workers and businesses to reap benefit from his tenure in office—not just donors and others who paid to play. For this, opponents accused him of being a socialist, and socialists did indeed support his reelections along with union and nonunion laborers. According to Detroit's venerated newspaperman Malcolm Bingay, however, Pingree "was about as Socialist as Calvin Coolidge." The mayor believed in private property rights with free markets and only sought to challenge what he saw as an immoral status quo controlled by pirates.[39]

To create work opportunities for the unemployed during the hard times of the 1893 panic, Pingree stepped up Detroit's public works program. Improvements to Belle Isle Park requiring architectural design services were included in this initiative, and some of the work fell to Mason & Rice. A bridge design went to the firm in 1894, and in 1895 it provided designs for a rustic stable complex that were clearly inspired by Kahn's European sketches. Soon after, Kahn and Nettleton left the firm to set up their own office, but images of the Belle Isle Stables drew acclaim for Mason & Rice from architectural journals.[40]

Belle Isle Stables, Detroit, Michigan (1895–97). Mason & Rice, architects. Detail photograph courtesy Burton Historical Collection, Detroit Public Library.

3

The Partnerships with Nettleton

While Kahn and Nettleton rose to top positions at Mason & Rice, another Detroit architect, Alexander Buel Trowbridge, rode out the hard times following the Panic of 1893 as a student in Paris. With a well-heeled family lineage stretching back to Michigan's territorial period, it is difficult to imagine a better-connected native Detroit architect than he. Born in 1868, he was the son of General Luther S. Trowbridge, a locally celebrated Civil War veteran who held prominent positions in the city, and grandson of Alexander W. Buel, an esteemed attorney and state legislator. A. B. Trowbridge went through the public school system, then on to Cornell, where he graduated from the college of architecture in 1890. In a span of three years, he worked in the Boston offices of architects William R. Emerson, Edmund M. Wheelwright, and Winslow & Witherell.[1]

Mason's diary documents Trowbridge commencing work as a draftsman on March 28, 1893, at $18 per week. Trowbridge listed himself as an independent architect in city directory entries for the years 1892 through 1896, however, suggesting a penchant for putting on airs. (A 1926 newspaper article identifies him as one of the most famous of the firm's former employees. He was the architectural consultant for the Federal Reserve and living in Washington, DC, at that point.) Kahn mentions his one-time partner having worked at Mason & Rice in accounts of his own early career, but curiously, biographical profiles likely originating with Trowbridge make no mention of it at all.[2]

In the 1924 edition of *Who's Who in New York*, Trowbridge is listed as having studied under Marcel Lambert at the Paris École des Beaux-Arts beginning in 1893 and graduating in 1895. In correspondence with Kahn, it seems Trowbridge failed his first attempt at the entrance examination, so he brushed up on his mathematics and watercolor skills while remaining in Paris before reapplying. (This was not unusual; as noted in Kahn's 1891 article for *American Architect and Building News*, competition at the school was rigorous and standards high.) Through all this time in France, he remained listed in the Detroit city directory as an independent architect boarding at 609 Jefferson Avenue.[3]

Kahn had written to Trowbridge with news of the Milwaukee competition. This would have made it clear that he and Nettleton anticipated an eventual break from Mason & Rice. Seizing the opportunity, Trowbridge suggested a three-person partnership. Not mincing words on the subject of pull (in the context of behind-the-scenes influence), he wrote to Kahn that the trio could potentially "put up a pretty strong front among the architects of Detroit—I have many friends and relatives and you have many in your church." Unmentioned by Trowbridge was any mention of a need for pull on the part of Nettleton, suggesting his knowledge, talent, and skill alone constituted sufficient contribution to a partnership.[4]

Trowbridge was back in Detroit by August 18, 1895, when a rumor circulated in the financial district of Griswold Street that "a new architectural firm will shortly be formed," consisting of Nettleton, Kahn, and Trowbridge. The newspaper article reporting the rumor described Nettleton and Kahn as "architectural draughtsmen of recognized ability, who have for a long time been employed in the office of Mason & Rice." Trowbridge was described as "a competent architect," with no mention of any association with Mason & Rice. Based on this omission, which seems to have been habitual with Trowbridge, and considering Trowbridge's family connections to Griswold Street, one may guess he instigated the rumor in overeagerness.[5] Since the firm would not officially form until January of the following year, one imagines the rumor making things uncomfortable in the office of Mason & Rice for four and half months. Mason, as noted, may have taken delight in his employees' success, but this surely would have been difficult to explain to clients.

By August 26 Trowbridge was working on plans for a four-story building to house the veterinary department of the Detroit College of Medicine. This may have been an example of his family's pull: his father was the treasurer of the board of trustees for the college. Soon thereafter, a notice of his opening an office at number 38 in the Campau Building also made mention of his being the son of General Luther S. Trowbridge. October brought news that he had succeeded in winning the competition for a large, $20,000 hotel and club at Harbor Point, an exclusive resort on the northern shores of Michigan's Lower Peninsula. It would be an example of "simplified Colonial architecture with generous piazzas, a large dining room, admirably adapted to terpsichorean exercises and such other uses as may be desired by summer guests."[6]

Nettleton, Kahn & Trowbridge

Despite a still depressed local economy, Nettleton, Kahn & Trowbridge, in Kahn's words, "hung out our shingle for better or worse," on January 1, 1896.[7] Businesses often launch on the strength of one client or project, and in this case, it seems to have been the Harbor Point Hotel and Club, which became a Nettleton, Kahn & Trowbridge commission and needed to be completely built and ready to open for the 1896 summer season. With a guest capacity of four hundred, it appears to have been exceeded in the region only by Mackinac Island's similarly rapidly built Grand Hotel. The new partners initially occupied Trowbridge's office in the Campau Building as they waited for the Donaldson & Meier–designed Union Trust Building to be completed. By May they had moved into a suite of offices atop the new structure, where generous skylights illuminated their drafting room. (Also in top floor suites were the offices of Baldwin & Stratton and, later, Mueller & Mildner. Stratton and Mildner appeared in chapter 2 as Mason & Rice employees.) By year's end both Kahn and Trowbridge felt confident enough to enter into marriages. Kahn married Ernestine Krolik on September 14, 1896, in Detroit. The differing socioeconomic circumstances of the Kahns and Trowbridges is demonstrated in the fact that the former honeymooned in Kingsville, Ontario, while the latter sailed for Europe. (Nettleton appears to have married in 1888.)[8]

Kahn's memories of his first partnership are unreliable, for at times he recalled some details incorrectly and he typically dismissed the office's high points while dwelling upon the low. For instance, in his often-quoted 1937 reminiscence, "Architect Pioneers in Development of Industrial Building," he wrote: "We [Nettleton, Kahn & Trowbridge] had hard sledding in '94 and '95,

Harbor Point Club Hotel, Harbor Springs, Michigan (1896). Nettleton, Kahn & Trowbridge, architects. Postcard view of detail by Tanner Souvenir Co., collection of the author.

but we pushed along as best we could, doing small houses, alterations to stores and residences, even a club house for one of the Michigan resorts and a Methodist church."[9] There definitely appears to have been some intervals that could be considered "hard sledding," but the architect is simply wrong on the dates, perhaps confusing them with the Milwaukee Public Library and Museum competition and the premature partnership rumors circulated on Griswold Street. He is also rather cavalier about the importance of the Harbor Springs commission: it is hard to imagine Mason or Rice lumping their Grand Hotel in with small houses and store alterations when describing their portfolio.

In the same vein, Kahn ignores the firm's $20,000 rebuilding of the Detroit College of Medicine after a devasting December 1896 fire. The brick walls of the seven-year-old, four-story building were largely intact and Nettleton, Kahn & Trowbridge provided plans for its reconstruction. As noted above, the college was associated with Trowbridge's father and perhaps Kahn edited it from his reminisces because it was associated with his partner's family pull. This is not to say that such commissions were inherently objectionable. Like most architects, some of Kahn's commissions involved family ties, with the 1918 Krolik & Company Warehouse being a fine example. With the College of Medicine, however, he may have been reluctant to claim laurels for a project gained through Trowbridge's family connections. More preferable for Kahn, it seems, was to note with gratitude that Mason directed work to his former employees.[10]

Kahn was also dismissive in recalling the Methodist Church, which, incidentally, was Presbyterian. Here again, the Trowbridge family involvement in Detroit's Presbyterian community likely led to the partners' 1896 design of the nearly $21,000 Bethany Memorial Church, which merited publication in *American Architect and Building News.* Such recognition for midwest architects was no small matter. Curiously, however, when recalling the project in 1937, Kahn wrote that it "didn't turn out so well architecturally," and dwelled on Ralph Adams Cram's criticism of the church published in *Architectural Review.*[11]

These commissions may not have been prominent landmarks, but they were noteworthy and brought in respectable revenue, which the firm augmented by smaller commissions. It is hard to imagine many other Detroit architects viewing them with disdain. Nevertheless, it appears the overall

Bethany Memorial Church, Detroit, Michigan (1897). Nettleton, Kahn & Trowbridge, architects. Photograph from *American Architect and Building News*, December 18, 1897, collection of the author.

volume of work remained disappointing, and surely profits were insufficient to grow the business.[12]

As the firm crept along, Kahn himself struggled: in addition to starting a family, he was contributing as much as he could to the education of his brother, Julius. When family finances permitted, Julius attended the University of Michigan and would receive a bachelor's of science degree in civil engineering in 1899. When not enrolled, he worked as a draftsman in engineering firms in Pennsylvania and New York, which included a stint at the Brooklyn Navy Yard.[13] As will be seen, the investment, born of family obligation, paid off. Julius's expertise would contribute to Albert's future success at a pivotal point in the latter's career.

The overall economy in Detroit remained sour through these years and, despite his instigating the partnership, Trowbridge forsook the uncertain rewards of entrepreneurism for a position in academia. September 1897 found him back at Cornell as professor in charge of the college of architecture, teaching the methods of the École des Beaux-Arts, "the greatest school of architecture in the world," in his estimation. Of its methods, he believed "them to be not only the best, but the only methods which have been fruitful of successful results." It was a prestigious position and by this time Trowbridge had a son, which may have factored into his decision to leave the partnership.[14]

Nettleton & Kahn

With Trowbridge went his connections, and prospects must have seemed dim for his former partners, who struggled on as Nettleton & Kahn. Occasions of desperation during Kahn's early partnerships are documented by examples of paper reuse among the few drawings that survive from this period, now in the collection of the Detroit Institute of Arts. Drawings made on the blank reverse sides of earlier work and journal plates bear witness to a need for frugality. In a January 1898 letter asking a lender to restructure a personal debt, likely a mortgage, Nettleton wrote that Detroit's dismal architectural market was no better than the year before. Furthermore, he added, "as far as our own work is concerned the outlook is very discouraging."[15]

Business perked up a bit during the course of the year, however, with the firm winning a design competition for the Grace Hospital Nurses' Home (later named in honor of its benefactor, Helen H. Newberry). Completed in 1899, the Jacobean style dormitory was 40 by 120 feet, three stories of brick and stone, with an interior nicely finished with hardwood. A hospital journal later regarded it as "an unusually beautiful example of architecture . . . unusual in institutional buildings," and the architects proudly entered the design in architectural club exhibits about the country to increase the firm's visibility. Images of homes built to Nettleton & Kahn designs published in the *Inland Architect and News Record* in 1898 provide additional evidence that the firm was more successful than Kahn let on in later interviews.[16]

In October 1898, an enthusiastic Kahn reported to the *Detroit News-Tribune* that prospects for the firm were quite satisfactory and well ahead of where they were a year earlier. Nettleton's past work under Mason & Rice for James Scripps surely led to the firm's design of the newspaper mogul's Gothic residential library. Just as Scripps directed Nettleton to comb Europe for Trinity Reformed Episcopal Church's architectural quotations, he now had the architects crib from the British Museum's reading room and Westminster Abbey's

Grace Hospital Nurses' Home, Detroit, Michigan (1898–99). Nettleton & Kahn, architects. Photograph from *Inland Architect and News Record*, collection of the author.

chapter house to showcase his collection of books and art. The focal point of the $15,000 structure was its eighteen-foot-wide octagonal reading room with black marble columns supporting a high vaulted ceiling. Walls were deliberately thick to deaden the increasing city noises outside and rose above the bookcases where they were pierced by lancets of stained-glass windows. Still eager to vaunt his knowledge of art, Scripps claimed to have designed some of the decorative brick diaper work in the library walls as well as the mosaic of the marble floor. Nettleton & Kahn may have been experiencing an upswing, but the architects surely were in no position to deny James Scripps his eccentricities. Fittingly, the library had its public debut January 24, 1900, playing host to a meeting of the Detroit Archaeological Society.[17]

The Scripps Library is long gone, but an 1899, $10,000 residence for Joseph R. McLaughlin on Detroit's East Boston Boulevard still stands in testimony of the excellent work of the firm. In December of that year Nettleton & Kahn announced plans for a casino for the Harbor Point Club, a vestige of the Trowbridge connections. The rustic, contemporary shingle styling of the casino provides stark contrast to the historicism of the Scripps library and

James E. Scripps Library, Detroit, Michigan (1898–99). Nettleton & Kahn, architects. This battered enhanced photograph appears to be the most comprehensive surviving image of the interior. Date and photographer unknown, collection of the author.

J. R. McLaughlin Residence, Detroit, Michigan (1899). Nettleton & Kahn, architects. Photograph by the author, 2023.

Harbor Point Club Casino, Harbor Springs, Michigan (1900). Nettleton & Kahn, architects. Detroit Photographic Co. photograph courtesy Library of Congress, Prints and Photographs Division.

demonstrates the versatility of Nettleton & Kahn. Inside the 58- by 104-foot frame structure was an assembly hall to seat a thousand persons, along with billiard rooms and four bowling alleys.[18]

The library and casino shared their restriction of natural light. The narrow windows in the library reading room were placed high to protect the patron's books from the sun's rays. Skylights illuminated the adjacent art gallery but the absence of windows isolated art lovers from their urban surroundings. Harbor Point casino-goers were shaded by porches and shielded from the summer sun reflecting off the lake by expanses of shingle roof and gables, sparingly pierced by relatively small windows and dormers.

Looking back on his early partnerships, it seems curious the only project Kahn remembered with fondness was the Nurses' Home. It is unknown whether, when providing a narrative for later interviewers, he simply forgot other high points or he chose to accentuate the low spots to balance his subsequent, remarkable success. At any rate, in his 1937 reminiscence he paused after recounting miseries to add, "But how happy we were when we won in competition the Grace Hospital Nurses' home to cost $18,000, for us then an important commission."[19] Perhaps it stood out as personally rewarding, or it marked an upturn after a particularly dry spell. It may have been the largest commission for the firm of Nettleton & Kahn to that point. That being the case, one imagines the prospect of a competition for a $100,000 combined public aquarium and horticultural building must have seemed to Kahn the stuff of wild dreams.

4

The Belle Isle Competition

As the nineteenth century drew toward its close, Kahn's career, while more productive than he later let on, was still in its larval stage. He grew as an artist as he climbed through the ranks of Mason & Rice to absorb all the lessons the office had to offer its staff. Entering his partnerships, he continued to grow as he learned the nuances and responsibilities of business. While Kahn was on this path, political changes were occurring in Michigan that aligned the planets for his meteoric career and provided the opportunity for his metamorphosis.

Detroit's Mayor Pingree was elected Michigan's governor, taking office in 1897. His intent was to continue his campaign for reform on the state level, but he quickly found his efforts blocked in the legislative chambers, which were just as susceptible to the corrupting influences of the day as city hall. No more willing to back down from a fight than he had been in Detroit, Pingree set about to replace intransigent legislators via the 1898 elections. Some of them were Republicans, like himself, and party leaders objected to his efforts to replace incumbents, which threatened their control of the statehouse. He replied to their protests, "Hell, I don't care a damn for Republican majorities, it's Pingree men I want."[1]

By that the governor meant people just as keen on cleaning up government as he was, such as David Emil Heineman, a passionate advocate for the City of Detroit, whose family wealth steeled resistance to corrupting influences. His civic boosterism was his way of repaying Detroit for the opportunities it provided to his family. His father, Emil Solomon Heineman, arrived in Detroit in 1851 among the Forty-Eighters who fled revolution-torn Bavaria for the United States. Emil eventually opened a wholesale clothing store, had an active role in the underground railroad, and participated in establishing the Republican Party. The business quickly expanded into a very successful enterprise, and by his death in 1896 Emil had built a handsome fortune. David was born in the family home on the northeast corner of Woodward Avenue and Adelaide Street in 1865. He earned a law degree from the University of Michigan and was appointed to the Office of City Attorney by Pingree in 1893. Although his title was "chief assistant," according to a Republican Party history, he was "the real head of the city attorney's office," overseeing its entire court work by giving personal attention to over five thousand cases, working to refine the municipal code, and streamlining operations. He was so effective his position was eliminated in 1896 when he happily returned to the private sector.[2]

As governor, Pingree pressed Heineman and others he trusted to run for the state legislature in 1898. Heineman was resoundingly elected to the Michigan House of Representatives, taking office in 1898 and proving an ally for much of Pingree's agenda while winning praise for his behind-the-scenes leadership. It is difficult to imagine Pingree's governorship being as successful as it was without Heineman.[3]

The Heineman Act

According to the same party history, upon taking office in January 1899 Heineman also lost no time enacting into law "a long-cherished plan of his for the establishment of a great aquarium. . . . for Belle Isle Park in his native city." The seed of this long-cherished dream, as reported in a later newspaper account, lay in a trip to Italy around 1890. "Mr. Heineman became much interested in the aquarium at Naples, and it occurred to him that something of the kind would be a splendid addition to his home city." On his return Heineman lobbied civic leaders to back a similar venture in Detroit but failed to create enthusiasm and financial support for his vision. This response is not surprising, given the ignoble reputations attached to the many poorly designed aquaria around the world in 1890. This will be discussed further in the following chapter, but the Naples Aquarium that caught Heineman's eye was an exception. With works designed under the expert guidance of William Alford Lloyd (again, chapter 5), this aquarium was the public exhibit area of the Stazione Zoölogica, a marine research facility. The whole establishment was underwritten by endowments and institutional support, giving it an air of respectability, while commercial public aquaria increasingly depended upon showmanship and sensationalism having little to do with scientific enlightenment.[4]

Since Heineman's initial, unsuccessful appeal for private support, the reputation of the public aquarium, at least in the United States, received a major boost in 1893 with the wild success of the aquarial display at the World's Columbian Exposition. In 1896, the municipally funded New York Aquarium opened and proved an astounding success as it unseated Brighton's 1872 attraction as the world's largest. The idea of a municipally funded public aquarium in Detroit became quite feasible just as Heineman reentered the political sphere to assist Pingree in Lansing.

Reports of a bill authorizing Detroiters to vote on funding an aquarium began to appear in February 1899. Heineman's vision was to build an aquarium only, but other members of the Detroit delegation insisted that a botanical

Stazione Zoölogica, Naples, Italy (1872). Adolf von Hildebrand, architect. The Naples Aquarium is contained therein. Photograph, circa 1890, collection of the author.

component be added. It appears to have vexed those legislators that nearby Toledo, Ohio, had a public conservatory while Detroit did not. Memories of the grand and popular Horticultural Building at the great Chicago Fair may have motivated their insistence as well. Through his travels, Heineman may have been aware that the two building types did not combine well. The very first public aquarium, the Fish House built inside what was essentially a greenhouse at London's Regents' Park Zoo, had faced intractable problems controlling temperature and algae growth since opening in 1853. The obstinate proconservatory Detroit delegates prevailed by threatening to withhold their votes, however.[5] As will be seen, their victory would greatly impact the history of industrial architecture.

Officially designated House Bill 591 but known as the Heineman Act, the legislation wound its way through the Michigan Capitol during the spring. On May 26, 1899, Governor Pingree signed the bill into law and on November 7 Detroit voters approved the measure in a landslide of support. Responsibility for the project then fell on Detroit's commissioners of Parks and Boulevards, but details regarding the structure remained unspecified. Three days after the vote there was talk by Park Commissioner Edward C. Van Leyen, himself an architect, of holding an architectural competition for the structure's design.[6]

Heineman offered his thoughts on the subject, suggesting that, in order to meet the horticultural expectations, there should be no attempt at creating a greenhouse, but "plants and shrubs and flowers and vines should be placed here and there," with the primary goal being "to delight and interest the people." He continued, "Artificial rock should be used here and there, and there should be splashing fountains and miniature rivers and lakes and cascades." This leaves one wondering how the project could have been inspired by the Naples Aquarium, where Lloyd eschewed such fakery in favor of rational architecture.[7]

For his part, Commissioner Van Leyen believed that the aquarium would by necessity feature only freshwater displays due to the budget and Detroit's inland location. He further thought the aquarium component should be situated directly beneath the conservatory. There was an argument for this: with the conservatory placed on top, it would receive optimal sun exposure while the aquarium below grade would be insulated by the surrounding earth from seasonal temperature variation. There were arguments against it as well, not the least of which was the high water table of the island. Later, Van Leyen also admitted the obvious—that no one in Detroit had any expertise in aquarium design. In order to prevail in the contest, he noted, architects "will have to make an independent study of the subject."[8]

Independent study is a deceptively simple-sounding term in this case. The investment in time and travel involved in mastering such a uniquely challenging building type would be high—especially when considering the fact that competitors would likely never have occasion to design a similar structure and reapply the knowledge gained. Architectural libraries, such as the acclaimed collection in the office of Mason & Rice, would have no books on the subject; one would need to consult experts beyond the field of architecture to comprehend the building's requirements, and personal inspection of even the nearest examples involved traveling considerable distances. An inordinate amount of effort needed to be expended for only a chance of winning.

Mason and Kahn Pursue Independent Studies

Perhaps hoping to provide a boost to his individual practice with the design of a prominent landmark, George Mason was in Washington, DC, visiting aquarium experts at the U.S. Fish Commission's Central Station just ten days after the vote. His twenty-year partnership with Zach Rice had dissolved the previous January. According to the *Detroit News*, there was no "disagreement between the partners, but each was desirous of paddling his own canoe."[9]

Mason did not make any public announcement of his travels to study aquaria and conservatories—to do so would tip off any future competitors of his investigations. His private journal notes and diaries, however, indicate he met with L. G. Harron, superintendent of aquaria, and Tarleton Hoffman Bean in Washington. Later recommended to the Detroit parks commissioners as the best-informed person in the country on aquarium construction (by William de Chastignier Ravenel, who himself would be one of the judges in the Detroit competition), Bean had been in charge of the Fish Commission's exhibits in Chicago in 1893 and Atlanta in 1895. From 1895 to 1898 he had been director of the New York Aquarium, where he supervised the preparation for the building, grew the collection, and managed its first years. At the time of Mason's visit, Bean was back at the Fish Commission, planning for the 1900 Paris exposition.

As recalled by an associate, "At no time was his deep learning inaccessible to one who sought it . . . He had a charm of personality and a freedom from the intellectual arrogance that mars so many men of learning."[10]

While the Fish Commission represented the mecca of American large-scale fishkeeping expertise, the budget for its Central Station public display was paltry; clearly the lion's share of the commission's exhibition funds was devoted to international fairs such as the World's Columbian Exposition. In contrast to those spectacles, in Washington Mason saw a twenty-four-tank exhibit housed in a plank-floored, claustrophobia-inducing ersatz grotto fashioned out of papier-mâché to look like stone.[11]

Underwhelming in comparison with aquaria elsewhere, the display was nonetheless popular with visitors and Mason made detailed notes with roughly dimensioned sketches of the Central Station's equipment and plan. The architect sketched plumbing and aeration systems and noted the tanks were siphoned out for cleaning. His papers contain meticulous observations of this sort on other features.[12]

Mason's next stop was New York City, arriving late on the evening of November 18. He went to the New York Aquarium the following morning and

Public Aquarium at the U.S. Fish Commission Central Station, Washington, DC. Interior view of marine grotto from an 1897 photograph, collection of the author.

stayed until five p.m. Any notes and sketches he may have made on that visit are missing now, but his diary survives and records that he saw Leonard B. Spencer, the knowledgeable aquarist in charge of the freshwater collection. As a veteran of the Union engineer corps during the Civil War, Spencer was likely able to supply useful insight into the mechanical operations as well as information on fishkeeping. In the next two days Mason visited the recently opened Central Park Conservatory and the New York Botanical Garden, with its museum and its conservatory then under construction.[13]

Mason's journal also contains a cryptically isolated entry that indicates he had a discussion with someone on this trip (it includes no date or location) about specific foreign aquaria and was apparently examining photos or illustrations. The aquaria were listed as those in Amsterdam, Hamburg, Naples, Paris, and Vienna—"beautiful" was written next to "Naples."[14] This is an insightful list, because all of these aquaria were either designed by or in consultation with W. A. Lloyd. Whoever it was that Mason consulted when he made these notes, they knew their history of public aquarium design.

These journal and diary entries demonstrate the complex considerations that should be part of designing for these building types. They also provide an example of the effort required for preparing a successful entry for this competition. Further, they establish Mason as quite astute in choosing his itinerary, for close on his heels members of the parks commission followed essentially the same path when launching their own studies. Unlike Mason's, their travels were publicly announced in the commissioners' meeting minutes and local newspapers.[15] Now any architect seeking to make a similar independent study basically knew where to go and who to talk to by tracing the commissioners' steps.

In mid-February Kahn made "an eastern trip," according to the *Detroit News*. While the notice only reports that "he will observe any recent architectural features of note in his travels," it seems the purpose was to become familiar with conservatories and aquaria, likely covering the same route and learning from the same experts as Mason and the commissioners. This conclusion is based on what is known of Nettleton & Kahn's eventual entry and other information related to the structure as built. On February 22, 1900, the commission approved holding an architectural competition for the building's design.[16]

Why Kahn, and not Nettleton, made this trip is uncertain. It may have been deemed better for the senior partner to stay behind and attend to the work currently in the office. On the other hand, raising flowers was Nettleton's one passionate pastime outside of architecture; he even had a modest conservatory attached to the front of the shingled home that he designed for himself and his wife. Given this, one might assume that he would have been better suited for such a fact-finding trip—at least as far as the horticultural component was concerned. Ultimately, the reason may have been simply economic, however: expenses could be reduced by having Kahn stay with family while in New York City. (Less than a month prior, within the period that such an investigative trip may have been planned, Kahn's brother Julius wrote, "We are looking forward to the day when you will be here in New York," although the context is unclear.)[17]

At any rate, this seemingly innocuous decision had devastating and far-reaching consequences. Back in Detroit, Nettleton reportedly overworked himself in his partner's absence, leading to his catching a cold that settled in his bronchial tubes. By March his health had deteriorated, and he was diagnosed with tuberculosis, or consumption as it was then often called. Shortly thereafter, he withdrew to a sanitarium in Ashville, South Carolina, to convalesce.[18]

Kahn Perseveres in Nettleton's Absence

Kahn slogged on without the man he described as "the backbone of the firm." While some of the work involved residential and light commercial jobs of little consequence, others were more noteworthy. The office had staff, but it is not known how many.[19]

During the year 1900 Nettleton & Kahn provided plans for a spurt of education-related projects. In July the firm secured the design of a 65- by 48-foot, two-story brick science building for the Michigan Military Academy in Orchard Lake. In the fall plans were announced for a 43- by 36-foot brick school house for Grosse Isle and a 60- by 90-foot, two story brick Hebrew Free School in Detroit. The firm's Sigma Phi Fraternity House in Ann Arbor opened in October.[20] Even if Nettleton was sporadically in Detroit during the remainder of 1900, one has to assume his ability to contribute was diminished by his illness and that Kahn was carrying the office workload.

Kahn biographies previous to this volume typically list the Boyer Machine Company Shop among his designs for 1900—but as mentioned in the introduction, this is erroneous. The $75,000 shop was the work of Louis Christian Mullgardt, who had designed Joseph Boyer's previous shop in St. Louis. Kahn designed a renovation for Boyer's Detroit residence somewhere around this time, however.[21]

In addition to missing his partner, Kahn was without the assistance supplied by Nettleton's wife Nellie, who worked as the firm's office administrator. On June 8, Nettleton wrote with the announcement, which must have come as a blow, that he and Nellie would be absent at least two more months. He understood that this might force Kahn to make significant personnel or organizational arrangements, which they could sort out upon his return. While his doctor was willing to work with him on the cost of the sanitarium stay and treatment, Nettleton needed to ask if Kahn could advance him three or four hundred dollars to help with the expenses. He also thanked his partner for sending photos of recent projects, which provided a diversion on days when his illness permitted such things. In a poignant letter, Nettleton wrote to Kahn, "You have no idea what an actual treat it was for me just to look at them, having [seen] nothing architectural in two months and especially of our work."[22]

Correspondence shows that Kahn did seek help to fill his partner's shoes under a temporary contract, but he could not attract anyone under the terms he was able to offer. Nettleton and his wife returned to Detroit sometime between August and October 1900. It is entirely possible his return was simply to end the expense of the sanitarium care, and not a reflection of meaningful improvement. It is reported he never regained his strength, so it is questionable whether he ever returned to the office.[23]

For several months, the Belle Isle Aquarium & Horticultural Building competition had been put on hold by Pingree's successor as Detroit mayor, William Cotter Maybury. On February 22, 1900, Maybury revealed audacious plans for a monument designed by architect Stanford White, of the New York firm of McKim, Mead & White, celebrating the city's upcoming bicentenary. To be located at the western end of Belle Isle, its centerpiece was to be a 220-foot, free-standing Doric column, the tallest in the world. This would be topped by a natural gas flame to serve as a "beacon to the commerce of the Great West." With such change anticipated for the park, including the possibility of the monument incorporating the aquarium and conservatory in its surrounding construction, it was deemed best to wait to see how fundraising for Maybury's scheme progressed. Many thought the mayor intended to use it as a legacy to eclipse Pingree's political impact and serve as a springboard for his own campaign for governor, but in the end the project expired under the weight of its grandiosity. Having failed to meet its $1 million initial fundraising goal (total cost had not yet been established), the Bicentenary Memorial Committee announced it was abandoning its efforts in mid-July.[24]

The Competition Officially Begins

On July 30 the Parks Commission restarted the Aquarium & Horticultural Building project from where it was before the February hiatus. Advertisements ran immediately announcing a design competition that was restricted to Detroit architects, who had until August 10, 1900, to decide whether they wanted to participate and a little over two months after that to work on their entries.[25]

Seventeen architects and firms joined Nettleton & Kahn in registering for the competition by the August deadline.[26] They may have been eager to show their stuff after being slighted in favor of a New York firm for Mayor Maybury's bicentenary project. They may also have underestimated the research involved in aquarium design, as will be seen.

In September, in another civic opportunity to promote local architects, the three firms occupying the top floor of the Union Trust Building (Mueller & Mildner, Nettleton & Kahn, and Stratton & Baldwin) submitted a joint, alternative design for a more modest monument celebrating Detroit's founding, intended for Woodward Avenue. The term bicentennial was applied to this, presumably to distinguish it from Maybury's failed bicentenary scheme. In the spirit of professional camaraderie, others of the city's architects would be invited to contribute to the effort, envisioned as having a platform foundation for a 28-foot-high central shaft, surrounded by four shorter pedestals—all of light-colored granite. A bronze statue of Detroit's founder, Antoine de la Mothe Cadillac, would surmount one pedestal, with the others sporting statuary depicting three other appropriate figures, apparently never determined. While the monument never came to fruition, the project reveals a close-knit local architectural community in which Kahn was a member. In a newspaper account of the project, the firm of Nettleton & Kahn was identified as participating, but a masonry journal's listing of individual architects involved includes only Kahn while omitting Nettleton. This seems to confirm that Nettleton was unwell during the time the Belle Isle entry was being prepared, leaving Kahn on his own.[27]

Despite their initial interest in the Belle Isle contest, the city's most successful architects dropped out in the course of the next two months. All provided excuses, but five days before the October 15 deadline for submissions, *To-Day*, a city newspaper, took note of their absence and suggested something was rotten in Detroit:

> One would suppose that all the best architects in Detroit would be delighted to go into an affair of this kind, not only for the $5,000 commission, but as a matter of civic pride. Strange to say, Donaldson & Meir, Stratton & Baldwin, John Scott & Co. [successor firm of William Scott's office], E. E. Meyers [*sic*], Malcolmson & Higginbotham [*sic*], Spier & Rohns, R. E. Raseman, Mueller & Mildner and Rogers & MacFarlane are not in it.[28]

According to the *To-Day* article, it was widely believed among "the big architects" that Edward Schilling had the contest in the bag, as they say. He had been an employee in Parks Commissioner Van Leyen's private architectural practice for many years and was currently on contract as the commission's architect, receiving "many hundreds of dollars." This included the 1898 bicycle shelter on Belle Isle and superintending work on greenhouses just across Inselruhe Road from the aquarium site, being designed by the Lord & Burnham Company. While the competition, developed with the aid of the American Institute of Architects (AIA) Detroit chapter, included a plan to strip the entries of the contestants' names before handing them to outside experts for judging, it was feared that Van Leyen shared with Schilling all of the information given to the commission by the experts with whom he had consulted in his official capacity. Schilling was therefore believed by many to have an unfair advantage. Apparently, few of these architects considered leveling the playing field by consulting experts in the East and making an independent study of their own, as Mason and (apparently) Kahn had done.[29]

At the last minute, George Mason dropped out as well. He notified the parks commission on the day entries were due that he would not be submitting, citing the pressure of other work. This seems a bit disingenuous since as recently as the first of October he had traveled to New York City again, specifically to visit the aquarium and conservatory one more time.[30] Mason, having fairly consulted the experts on his own, may have held out hope that he could still prevail, only to conclude at the last minute that continuing was not worth the gamble of being publicly bested by Schilling no matter the circumstances. Kahn remained in the competition, lending further support to the likelihood that he, too, had invested time and expenses consulting experts during the time when Nettleton initially took ill. In light of his illness, the partners may have thought they had too much invested to back out, no matter the odds. At any rate, the boycott winnowed the field to the benefit of the remaining designers.

Regardless of the circumstances, the competition remained another opportunity seized by Kahn that others let pass them by.

The Award

In the end, just eight plans were submitted to the parks commission by the 1 p.m. deadline on October 15. They were assigned numbers to conceal the authors' identity and immediately placed in a specially prepared, large wooden box that was shipped to New York City. There, at the Hotel Cadillac two days later, the entries were reviewed by a secret jury composed (as later revealed) of New York architects John Galen Howard and Cass Gilbert, U.S. Fish Commission aquarist William de C. Ravenel, and horticulturalist John Francis Cowell, director of Buffalo's recently opened South Park Conservatory. They were each paid $150 for their service by the parks commission, which also covered the $23.50 room rental. The jurors issued their report on October 18, 1900, determining design number 1, submitted by Nettleton & Kahn, "to be distinctly the best."[31]

5

Kahn's Metamorphosis

Credit for the winning entry in the Belle Isle Aquarium & Horticultural Building design competition is due to Kahn, although it is possible Nettleton made some contribution despite his illness and absences. With the winning submission, Kahn disregarded the published opinions of both Parks Commissioner Van Leyen, who thought the horticultural component should be situated atop the aquarium, and State Representative Heineman, who advocated for somehow melding the two in a faux landscape. Instead, Kahn placed them alongside each other. In doing so, he sidestepped the problems experienced in London's Fish House, where the greenhouse environment spurred algae growth, choking the water in the tanks. The judges obviously saw Kahn's as the superior solution to the requirements, despite any advantage Schilling was thought to have through his association with Van Leyen.

Kahn had educated himself through his independent study of the building types to the satisfaction of the judges with their expertise in conservatories and aquaria. While he may have consulted with some of these experts during his studies, Kahn could not be sure which experts eventually sat as judges.[1] As discussed earlier, identities of the designers for the entries were hidden from the judges who may have conferred with multiple Detroit architects, including some who, like Mason, ultimately decided not to join the competition.

This chapter considers the qualities of Kahn's competition entry that appealed to the judges and set in motion his metamorphosis from a middling regional architect into an architect and engineer of international and historic significance. Understanding these qualities requires consideration of certain neglected expertise—decades-old lessons largely ignored by the architectural profession. These lessons had previously been articulated by a group of Europeans collectively known as naturalists: self-educated natural scientists who were, however, by 1900, largely dismissed by academics as amateurs and religious zealots. Those operating public aquaria and conservatories in the United States were more broad-minded, and the naturalists' lessons were imparted to Kahn, who eventually applied them to his architecture with exceptional success.

Now with the hindsight of history, it becomes clear this commission was a pivotal event in Kahn's subsequent career. As such, it merits extended consideration. Most architecture concerns ways of providing shelter for humans and their work. With the Belle Isle Aquarium & Horticultural Building, Kahn found himself responsible for the *survival* of its inhabitants—plant and animal—through his design. He would later apply the lessons learned here as he designed for people inhabiting workplaces for eight-hour shifts or more.

While on the subject of workplaces, it seems the city of Detroit was undergoing a concurrent metamorphosis into a great industrial center that would impact Kahn's future in unimaginable ways. A brief discussion of this at the end of the chapter sets the stage for what is to come.

The Horticultural Component and Architectural Associationism

The botanical portion of Kahn's entry is clearly illustrated in the one surviving image from the competition, which closely matches what was built. Its configural lineage tracing to the Columbian Exposition's Horticultural Building is readily apparent, but the general composition was also used elsewhere, including Buffalo's South Park Conservatory. Kahn apparently visited the latter, based on his referencing it in some detail as he defended the construction cost of his entry before the Detroit parks commission. If so, he likely would have spoken with John Francis Cowell, who was director of the Buffalo Botanic Garden since 1894 as well as one of the competition judges. Cowell was integral in making Buffalo's conservatory a reality, but it was designed and built by the long-established manufacturer of greenhouses, Lord & Burnham of Irvington,

Competition entry for Belle Isle Aquarium & Horticultural Building (1900). Nettleton & Kahn, architects. Line cut from the *Detroit Free Press*, October 23, 1900.

New York. Between Lord & Burnham's experience and Cowell's expertise, it would be hard to imagine Buffalo's conservatory in more qualified hands. Cowell made numerous trips to the tropics, bringing back literally tons of living plants for display.[2] Public and private conservatories and horticultural experts were fairly common, and Kahn's travels may have included others, as well.

In following the rational and accepted trend for botanic conservatories, Kahn worked under theoretical principles of architectural associationism as they were laid down by Archibald Alison in 1790 with his *Essays on the Nature and Principles of Taste*. While Alison was read throughout the Victorian era in Great Britain, it is uncertain whether the Detroiter had direct awareness of the Scottish philosopher or of associationism per se. He certainly was exposed to the fruits of the theory while designing the conservatory, however, and it seems to have made a lasting impression upon him. In his essays Alison argued that beauty derived primarily from an object fulfilling its function, and only secondarily through ornament. Tastefulness is satisfied when an object's appearance is expressive of, or associated with, its function. In other words, regardless of style, a house should look like a house, an office building should look like an office building, and, in this case, a botanical conservatory should look like a botanical conservatory. Straying too far from expectations for a structure created an inherent risk that it would fail to fulfill its functions or achieve beauty. More recent to Kahn's work, in 1896 Chicago architect Louis Sullivan stated the same notion succinctly and famously as "*form ever follows function* . . . where function does not change, form does not change." Kahn echoed both Alison and Sullivan when saying in 1931, "The best in architecture has always been expressive of the particular function and purpose of the building."[3]

James Claudius Loudon, an influential early nineteenth-century British landscape architect and author, imbedded Alison's architectural associationism into the design of botanical conservatories through his publications.[4] It is not known whether Kahn ever knew of Loudon directly either, but he could not have designed an effective conservatory to win the Belle Isle competition without following the path laid by the Briton. A successful conservatory entry *had* to provide a nurturing environment enabling plants to live outside their native environments. Therefore, as discussed below, its design had to follow the principles of physics involving glass and light that governed the form of the previous conservatories.

Loudon's 1817 *Remarks on the Construction of Hothouses* did much to codify design in the years that followed.[5] In it, he draws from the work of many others to describe how sunlight naturally loses some of its life-sustaining qualities as it passes through glass, but this loss is more pronounced at greater angles. Nineteenth century conservatory designers responded with curved surfaces out of functional practicality, with metal-framed domes and curvilinear surfaces comprised of many flat panes of glass set at different angles.

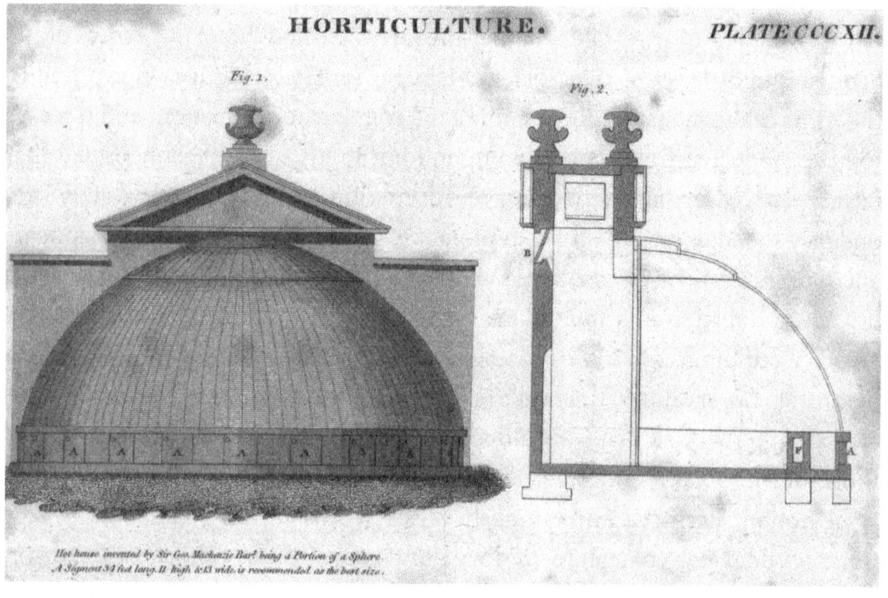

George Steuart Mackenzie's 1815 invention for a semi-dome hot house. Engraving of front elevation and side section, circa 1825, collection of the author.

This allowed the sun's rays to penetrate varying panes at as near perpendicular angles as possible during its changing tracks across the sky from hour to hour, day to day, and season to season. It also resulted in a distinctive and charming, yet highly functional, building type.

Another concern involved the position of the glass in relation to the plants on display. Sunlight's nourishing intensity diminishes with increased distance from a glass surface after passing through it, so it is also important to position the panes as near to the leaves as possible. As the height of the specimens within varies, so must the roofline—or, conversely, the floor line. Looking at Nettleton & Kahn's competition entry drawing for the Belle Isle horticultural component, the pavilion at the right side represents its southern end. Here were placed the orchids, on shelves, where they benefited from the southern exposure. Moving northward, to the left on the drawing, one sees the low tropical range, positioned where southern exposure was nearly as optimal. The roofline here is just above the tops of the plants. Next is the palm house dome, seventy-two feet in diameter and rising to fifty feet inside. Palm trees within soar above the neighboring low tropical range. To the north of that are located specimens from temperate regions whose growth is not inhibited by the translucent shadow of the dome. Where more sunlight was required, temperate plants were to be raised up off the floor. This way they, too, could be near the roofline while Kahn was able to maintain architectural symmetry when viewed from the exterior. Terminating the horticultural component at its north end is a pavilion housing the fernery. Some of these are quite tall, so Kahn, again seeking symmetry, lowers the floor so its pavilion roof is level with that of the orchid house pavilion.[6]

The Aquarial Component and Planning Around Work Flow

Analyzing the aquarial component of the competition entry is more challenging because precious little is visible in the sole surviving drawing. One sees, however, an octagonal roof that matches the roof of the center rotunda as built along with a chimney matching that of the boiler room that stood at the end of the structure. This indicates that the rest of the aquarial component was similar to what was built, only it was depicted as being accessed from the rear side of the palm house dome and extending straight to the east. Aside from a change of an east-west to a north-south orientation requiring an additional direct entrance from the outside, one can look at the final drawings to see merits of Kahn's entry that would have appealed to William de C. Ravenel as the aquarist on the panel of competition judges.

Prior to being selected as a judge, Ravenel appeared before the Detroit parks commission in November 1899 as an initial advisor on the Belle Isle project. As the U.S. Fish Commission's representative on the managing boards at all expositions held in the country, he served as its chief special agent at the Chicago fair. Speaking in Detroit to the commission, it was his opinion that perhaps the best thing the commissioners could do would be to engage an architect and send that person to Europe to study aquaria there first hand before drawing up any plans. The value of a sound design following European aquaria would far offset the travel cost. According to Ravenel, it had cost New York City $80,000 to correct the "blunders of an uniformed architect" before their aquarium was operating properly.[7]

The commissioners did not send an architect to Europe, but it is obvious that Kahn studied European aquaria nonetheless, probably through scientific journals, in preparing his entry. Safely assuming he called upon the U.S. Fish Commission in Washington, he would have learned that its work drew from the studies of William Alford Lloyd.

Sickly as a child, Lloyd became a voracious reader and at the age of ten began a job as errand boy for a London engineering concern, where he became fascinated by mechanical contrivances. By age twenty-eight he was struggling to support his wife and daughter on a meager salary working for a bookseller, but his job provided ample opportunity to read. On an 1852 visit to the Regents' Park Zoo, Lloyd stumbled upon the Fish House, then under construction. He was immediately enamored with the displays and, exhibiting an obsessive trait shared by many Victorian naturalists, he became consumed with learning all he could about aquatic life and aquarium keeping. Before long he became a highly respected author and expert on the topic, opening the first store to cater exclusively to aquarium enthusiasts. Drawing upon his penchant for engineering, he sought to stock apparatus that could be adopted to aquarium maintenance.[8]

This, in turn, led to his being hired in 1859 to design a public aquarium in Paris. Here he worked with engineers to devise a new building type, with the tanks set in walls that hid the apparatus from public view. He improved and enlarged his design with his next aquarium, in Hamburg, which opened in 1864. With fresh- and saltwater exhibits, the Hamburg Aquarium was so efficiently designed that it was soon operating at a profit with moderately priced admissions. This in turn inspired a proliferation of less efficiently executed aquaria across Europe. Abandoning Lloyd's straightforward approach, these were often designed as sensational faux undersea rock grottos that were difficult and expensive to maintain. Most failed financially or resorted to enhancing their visitors' experience with tawdry stage acts and irrelevant exhibitions. This sullied the perception of European public aquaria in general. Those in Hamburg and Naples remained exemplars of what such institutions *should* be.[9]

After ten years of successful operation, Lloyd's aquarium in Paris was destroyed in the Franco-Prussian War, but the Hamburg Aquarium, renowned for the continuing quality of its displays and respectable management, likely held a special place in the hearts of public aquaria experts such as Ravenel. As another advocate for public scientific enlightenment sarcastically put it

Hamburg Aquarium, Hamburg, Germany (1864). W. A. Lloyd with Meuron & Haller, architects. Early engraving of section view of the interior showing public corridor and flanking work area, from *Die Gartenlaube*, 1865, courtesy Kelvin Smith Library, Case Western Reserve University.

in 1876, unlike its contemporary competitors, Hamburg's aquarium had "no great hall for visitors, no rustic work [faux grotto walls], no whale or sea lion, no music, no library, no reading or smoking room; there is nothing worth mentioning besides the tanks and the animals." Upon viewing the Belle Isle competition entries with the other jurors in New York, Ravenel would have recognized Nettleton & Kahn's entry number 1 as an enlarged but faithful homage to Lloyd's Hamburg Aquarium of thirty-five years earlier and it may have brought a tear to his eye. This was not mere copying, however. The floor of the Hamburg Aquarium was below grade, with its roof just a few feet above. In the competition drawing, the position of the rotunda roof indicates it had an aquarium floor well above grade. Kahn conceived the rotunda himself, apparently as a means of relieving any visual fatigue that could result from his greatly increased number of tanks. Other differences will be noted below in the discussion of the structure as built.[10]

Following the Hamburg design, it is likely that nonsurviving documentation from Kahn's entry noted a freshwater reservoir supporting the aquarium that would also benefit the conservatory (one appears in the final detail drawings). He would have learned in his studies that Lloyd devised an economical system for successfully recycling water, salt or fresh, using dark reservoirs back when he first started aquarium keeping in his apartment in the mid-1850s. At the time, as noted in the previous chapter, the surrounding glass structure of the Regents' Park Fish House exposed the tanks to so much sunlight that they soon became choked with algae, becoming unsightly and unhealthy for the fish. Zoo personnel dealt with the problem by simply dumping the turbid water and replacing it with water brought from the sea at great expense. Financially strapped, Lloyd acquired some of the zoo's discarded sea water and devised a clever, economical, and natural method of filtering it for continual reuse. His simple solution was to place turbid water in a reservoir sealed off from light. The algae soon died in the dark and sank with other debris to the bottom. The recycled water siphoned from the top of the dark reservoir was crystal clear. An enlarged version of this system was utilized in Paris and Hamburg (and partially employed in Naples, which had the luxury of pumping seawater directly from the Mediterranean at any time).[11] With this system, the original saltwater at the Hamburg Aquarium, with minor supplementation to replace losses from leakage and evaporation, was still in use after thirty-four years. Kahn's competition entry may have noted that a parallel saltwater system, with a second Lloyd dark reservoir, could supply Belle Isle's aquarium with saltwater if desired. Regardless, Ravenel would have recognized such as feasibly inherent in the design, even though Heineman and Van Leyen both pronounced marine exhibits impractical for Detroit.

The Architectural Consideration

There were also two architects on the panel of judges, both had been educated at the Massachusetts Institute of Technology. Cass Gilbert had gained attention for designing the Minnesota State Capitol and more recently by prevailing in a fierce and controversial competition for the United States Custom House in New York City. John Galen Howard was also already successful, but his fame as a regional architect lay ahead with his move to California.[12] It seems likely they reviewed the drawings for technical competency, but it was the approval of Cowell and Ravenel that remained paramount.

From an architectural standpoint, little can be determined from the one surviving image of the competition entry except that Kahn met the challenges of the horticultural component with a symmetrical composition that manages to convey a delicate monumentality while retaining a charming intimacy. This was no small feat. While following the compositional template of previous conservatories, Kahn brought a certain élan to the ornamental elements that reflects his confidence in the Renaissance style following his scholarship and European studies.

The restraint he exhibits demonstrates an understanding, if not direct knowledge, of the doctrine espoused by Alison as channeled through Loudon. The conservatory, like those he presumably visited, presented the appearance associated with the building type. Ornamentation appears to have been considered only after functional requirements were met, and did not block the sun or obstruct ventilation to the detriment of the plants within. Some ornamentation, however, was seen as fitting for a municipal landmark welcoming the public.

Hidden behind the conservatory, little of the aquarium component's architecture is visible in the drawing. If built in that orientation it would be largely hidden from the public as well by the horticultural component, so likely it had plain brick walls punctuated with windows and skylights for the work areas. From an architectural standpoint, there was little precedent to associate with the architecture of public aquaria anyway. As noted previously, the New York Aquarium occupied a former fort. The Naples and World's Columbian Exposition aquaria were housed in ornate structures not suitable for the rustic Belle Isle Park, while some others (including Hamburg's) were buried or partially buried below ground level.

After the Award

That Schilling did not prevail does not necessarily prove that the city's leading architects incorrectly assessed their odds in the contest, and Nettleton & Kahn's victory was not yet assured: Commissioner Van Leyen apparently did hope to redirect the project to his employee, and was not deterred by the jury's decision. He disputed whether the design could be built for the stipulated $100,000, even though the expert jurors believed that it could. (Incidentally, Van Leyen was one of the William Scott & Company draftsmen when olfactory senses were offended at the time Kahn was the unpopular office boy.) Furthermore, Nettleton & Kahn had entered two separate designs, and this he argued to be a possible violation of the competition code.[13]

Kahn alone defended the firm's award before the commission in a long October 22 meeting, which again suggests Nettleton was too ill to participate. It was ultimately decided that nothing in the code prohibited a competitor from submitting multiple entries, but Kahn was asked to sign an outrageous waiver agreeing to forego all compensation if the structure, *including any changes desired by the board*, could not be built within the $100,000 budget. Kahn was confident that the aquarium as proposed and approved by the judges could be built within the amount but was unwilling to hold the firm's compensation subject to *any* changes by the commission. As a compromise, he would agree to abandoning the plans and waiving all compensation if the structure as proposed came in over budget. Ideally, Kahn explained, an architect would draw up detailed plans in good faith as to their meeting the budget. If construction bids came in high, adjustments to the plan, materials, or budget would be negotiated with the client, resulting in the highest quality building for the cost. "By this means, you will get our best ideas," but, he admitted, "if we labor under the fear all the time of getting no compensation, we, of course, will take no chances and start at a lower level. I should think it would be better to start higher and go down a little if necessary." The commission had invited architects Mason, Donaldson, and Frank Baldwin to be present and they advised accepting Kahn's position, saying it was all officials could reasonably expect. Donaldson went so far as to say he would never put his signature on a document such as Kahn was agreeing to sign but supposed it necessary when dealing with a government entity. With that settled, the plans were accepted with Nettleton & Kahn expected to "make a more extensive study of the subject" of aquaria and conservatories and with the understanding that the commissioners reserved the right to make changes adopting "new ideas."[14]

Shortly after the decision, Gustav Kahn, whose work in a construction trade surely gave him insight, confessed to his brother Albert that the award "was a great surprise for me as I did not, not for one minute, think that you would get an absolutely fair show."[15]

Gus was not the only one to feel this way. With Pingree away at the governor's office in Lansing, corruption had crept back into city administration, and it seems the Parks and Boulevards Commission was so engulfed. Concurrent with Kahn's negotiations, *To-Day* boldly asserted that "Van Leyen is enabled to make a few dollars through his clerk, Mr. Schilling, doing architectural work for the commission." During a city council investigation, it was learned that while Schilling temporarily moved out of Van Leyen's firm and into his own, separate office to draw up his entry for the aquarium and conservatory competition, he was assisted by another man who was still or had been in Van Leyen's employ. After Schilling learned he was not the successful entrant, reported *To-Day*, "he gave up the office and returned to Van Leyen's employment." Detroit's other newspapers reported examples of improprieties as well, with other commissioners rumored to be "on the rack."[16]

The Flame of Commerce

It may not be a coincidence that on the same day that the aquarium and conservatory design entries were accepted—October 15, 1900—a *Detroit Journal* headline announced, "David Heineman Is Out of Politics." The rocky 1899–1900 legislative session can be considered on balance a success for both Heineman and Governor Pingree, but neither sought reelection. Although he would later serve as a Detroit city alderman, Heineman had no love for the political process and perhaps he knew the governor, an ally, would be standing down. Pingree remained immensely popular with voters, but his eleven years battling public corruption had exacted a terrible toll on his personal life and his family. Nevertheless, it seems he was considering suggestions that he run for the presidency.[17]

Pingree and Heineman would leave state office when their terms ended in January of 1901. (Any plans the ex-governor had were cut short by his untimely death that June.) As they exited, Detroit stood on the cusp of phenomenal manufacturing growth with an outstanding generation of industrialists establishing themselves within its machining and manufacturing shops and others gravitating to the city. They may have been attracted by the egalitarian blessings, in the form of reduced costs of living, due to Pingree's efforts with municipal reform. (Civic leaders in other cities followed Pingree's example, but the fruits manifested themselves first in Detroit.)

The city's reputation as an open shop town seems to have been another related factor. Consistent with his principles, Pingree staunchly opposed monopolies of any sort, including the closed shop where workers were forced to join, and support through mandatory dues, one particular union as a condition of employment. This represented a monopoly through an arrangement, at times agreed to under duress, between union leadership and the employer. Alternatives to this were the nonunion shop, where employers forbade their workers from any union membership, and the open shop, where employers recognized the right of individual employees to belong to any union they themselves chose. Pingree's shoe factory, employing about one thousand workers, was an open shop in the late 1880s, and this seems to have been his one, nonnegotiable item in any labor arbitration. In a speech, Pingree stated that "the security of property rights does not rest upon courts and bayonets so much as it does upon a contented people." Thus while opposing what he considered union monopoly, he made a point to be responsive to their demands in his own way. And it appears other businesspeople in the city took notice. According to Detroit labor historian Richard Jules Oestreicher, many "previously nonunion firms followed his example of negotiating written contracts with trade unions, a major departure from business practices in the early 1880s and before."[18]

Pingree carried this attitude into political office, and some labor leaders found a new, effective environment for improving the lot of the working class. "Socialists and radical alternatives" within the labor movement, Oestreicher noted, became "hard pressed to convincingly present [themselves alone] as the voice of the working class." Going into the twentieth century, Detroit gained a reputation as "the national center of the open shop," according to a New Deal guide to Michigan. A survey of Detroit newspaper reports on labor strikes for this present volume suggests they were not uncommon in the city during this open shop era, but tended to be settled relatively quickly, often through arbitration, with both sides appearing eager to return to making money. Surely not every laborer was contented, but as a whole they were already among the most highly paid industrial workers nationally. It seems a significant portion of Detroit's workers were not inclined to trade their individual interests for the collective promises of forced union membership. In other cities, union and inter-union struggles over exclusive control of workers in closed shops often resulted in crippling strikes and violence that hobbled business if not driving it away. A 1905 report appearing in the *Detroit Free Press* documents many manufacturers "forsaking Chicago because of the labor difficulties" in that closed shop town.[19] No human endeavor is ever perfect, but a remarkable industrial center was built around Detroit within this more collaborative work environment.

Another factor in the city's industrial growth was its adventurous financial environment. William B. Stout, who would later build Tri-Motor airplanes in a Kahn-designed factory, offered his assessment of the attitude in Detroit that extended into its monied circles.

> Detroit is a great, growing industrial center because it is not afraid of red ink in a growing proposition. It will cease growing as a business center when it begins to look at new ideas from the viewpoint of a bank statement. . . .

> Not even the banks work that way in Detroit.
>
> Detroit is a city of vision, a group not afraid of a good gamble on their own intelligence. It is a community serving the world with its products first—and making its profits afterward in spite of itself, because of that same service.[20]

Pingree with his supporters deserve credit for their role in fostering such attitudes in Detroit, which attracted the remarkable community of industrial visionaries that followed, many of whom were Kahn's clients. Because of them, the flame of commerce would burn like a beacon into Detroit's third century, even without the symbol of a Stanford White-designed monument. And when the time came to defend the nation through the production of war matériel, Detroit would be ready, its industrial capacity facilitated by Pingree's, and Heineman's, reforms.

A Pall over the Win

After a decade of thought and planning, David Heineman's dream of an aquarium for his city now seemed poised to become reality. Perhaps fittingly, it would be designed by a scrappy local architect, at the time in the second tier, who would also play a key role in Detroit's status as a torchbearer—not only for commerce but eventually for the liberty of the free world.

Nettleton left Detroit again around November 1, 1900, this time seeking treatment in the dry, high-altitude air of Colorado. On November 26 Nettleton & Kahn's contract for the design of the Belle Isle Aquarium & Horticultural Building was finalized and approved. Design work could finally begin in earnest, with the caveat that the commission could still request changes, which they did on December 3. Kahn was presented with a list of changes, which included rotating the aquarial component ninety degrees, so that it ran from north to south like the conservatory. Thus reoriented, the skylights above the tanks and work areas on both sides of the public corridor would have equal exposure as the sun tracked across the sky, similar to the horticultural ranges. The addition of a display house separating it from the palm house changed the building from a T-shape to an H. Another public entrance, directly into the aquarial component, was now necessary. These changes imbued the two components with more pronounced individuality. As a result, their designations as aquarium and conservatory came into common usage, despite their remaining components of a conjoined structure. Some also found it convenient to simply refer to the entire structure as the aquarium.[21]

As he began the redesign, Kahn may have clung to the hope that Nettleton could soon be back in office and they could share in the detail work. On December 1, Nettleton had written a friend that although he was "suffering pretty severely and thoroughly," he was beginning "to see the light ahead and feel that I have in some ways made substantial gains already." Six days later he wrote to Kahn that "I am getting well rapidly in all but strength." Kahn had barely time to read that letter when he received the telegram stating his partner's anticipated recovery was not to be.[22]

George W. Nettleton succumbed to tuberculosis in Colorado Springs on December 13, 1900, at age forty, leaving behind his wife Nellie but no children. His body was taken back to Detroit, where the funeral service was held in his home with flowers from his beloved greenhouse. According to the *Detroit Free Press*, it was "largely attended by his friends, including a good representation of the architectural profession." George D. Mason was among the six fellow architects serving as pallbearers. Interment was in Detroit's Woodmere Cemetery.[23]

Nettleton's death cut short the career of a well-educated but plain-spoken man considered in one report as "one of the most capable architects of Detroit and Michigan." Despite the brevity of his career, many of his reported and demonstrated qualities—a passion for his work, a desire for honesty in architecture and personal conduct, concern for those in the workplace, and the ability to develop personal bonds with clients—were traits for which Kahn would become known. Undoubtedly the older architect influenced the younger, but some of these may have been shared qualities that led to their compatibility.[24] Overcoming the long odds to secure the prestigious Belle Isle Aquarium & Horticultural Building marked the zenith of the firm of Nettleton & Kahn, but Nettleton's illness and untimely death turned the moment heartrending, while leaving his partner with a daunting burden following years of sometimes difficult struggle.

While his 1937 reminiscence contains errors, Kahn was surely reliable when he wrote of Nettleton, "His passing left me in what I then believed a hopeless position."[25]

6

Mason & Kahn

Kahn had little time to mourn. As he later lamented, Nettleton died "just as things were beginning to come our way." While the partnership's business had not been as dismal as Kahn recalled when looking back, his career would soon soar in ways no one could foresee. But first he had to get through the present moment. In addition to the daunting Belle Isle project, there were other jobs needing his attention. "To keep promises meant much night and Sunday work and little rest." Kahn's wife, Ernestine, helped in the office to get the firm through this period.[1]

The previous year was likely difficult enough—pressing on now following the death of his dear friend, mentor, and partner must have been particularly dispiriting. Kahn was personally obliged to complete all the work at hand, no matter how trivial some jobs must now have seemed, and of course he needed the income. He forwarded any share of profits due Nettleton to Nellie, his widow, who was in dire need as well. The size of the office staff at this time and whether he was forced to downsize are unrecorded, but we know of at least one employee who stayed with Kahn through this difficult period. When Roland C. Gies established his independent practice as an architect in 1903, he pointed with pride to his five years of experience with Kahn beginning under Nettleton & Kahn and extending through Mason & Kahn, Kahn's next partnership.[2]

Adding to the burden was the knowledge that Nettleton contracted tuberculosis while carrying the office workload alone when Kahn was in the East, doubtless gathering information for the competition. Designing the conservatory component was surely a particularly melancholy exercise given Nettleton's passion for raising flowers. Considering all of this, it is understandable that Kahn rarely featured this project in his self-promotion efforts, despite its status as a civic landmark that was certainly the envy of his peers.[3]

Considering Mason's Offer

Park commissioners approved the redesign plan on January 7, 1901, and Kahn commenced the detail work. By the end of the month things had improved to the point that he was advertising for a draftsman, but still it must have seemed a godsend when his old employer and mentor, George Mason, extended an offer for a partnership.[4] Kahn considered the offer and sought the opinion of a former partner who knew them both.

Alexander Trowbridge responded from Cornell that he was "inclined to think it a very good arrangement. Mason has quite a following and a good reputation. He will be vigorous a good twenty years yet I should think. His business experience ought to be worth a good deal." Clearly aware of the architect's current plight, he thought Kahn "ought to have a partner right away. There might be some danger of your overworking yourself and of not giving your clients entire satisfaction by reason of the great pressures of work." Trowbridge reasoned Mason would complement Kahn's talent and he would not have extended the offer had he not valued the younger architect's abilities. Furthermore, Trowbridge thought an ideal arrangement would have Kahn running the drafting room. As for marketing the firm, Trowbridge was coldly frank in his opinion (as he had been when confidently assessing the value of his own family name when suggesting Nettleton and Kahn partner with him six years earlier): "You will naturally have a very good pull in Jewish quarters. Mason would get work in some Gentile quarters where you might find difficulty."[5]

Trowbridge's concerns over Kahn's ethnicity seem rooted in the pre-Pingree social order of Detroit, which would soon bend to the quickly evolving, results-driven ethos that came to dominate the region. While ethnic and class differences were still factors, Kahn and his brothers thrived in the chaotic whirlwind of free-market capitalism to come, their talent and industriousness trumping any anti-Semitism. Two famous examples of this are Kahn's 1915 commission to design opulent quarters for the Detroit Athletic Club at a time when the organization was perceived as barring Jewish membership, and Henry Ford's continuing, loyal patronage of Kahn despite the virulent, anti-Semitic content of his publication, the *Dearborn Independent*, in the 1920s. In both cases, Kahn had formed bonds of personal friendship that were strong enough to transcend bigotries, as will be discussed.

Business pressed on as Kahn considered Mason's offer. Parks commission records indicate he traveled to New York and Washington in early February to secure more data on aquarium buildings and fixtures. On this trip, he was accompanied by the commission's long-serving secretary and general manager, Myrtle P. Hurlbut (popularly known as M.P.). In his position, Hurlbut had considerable power in the parks department, with Commissioner Van Leyen appearing to have lost the interest he once had in the project, perhaps because Shilling did not prevail in the competition. Detroit's aquarium was clearly perceived as a serious endeavor intended to push the envelope of knowledge and technology, and experts enthusiastically lent their assistance. It was appropriate and important for a representative of the city to be closely involved, as it had been decided to have the commission, not the architect, let out the equipment contracts. Prior to the trip, the *Detroit Free Press* reported Hurlbut explaining that "in Hamburg, Germany, sea fish have been kept in an aquarium for thirty years, and he [Hurlbut] thinks it will be possible to have salt sea fish in the Belle Isle aquarium." This appears to be the first official recognition of a connection with the Hamburg Aquarium and awareness of an option for marine displays present in Kahn's design.[6]

Kahn was thrust into a situation that was rare for an architect at the time: being engaged with engineers and other specialists to design a rationalized structure alongside the client. More typically, an architect designed the structure as a shell to the client's specifications and left any equipment matters for tradesmen to deal with afterward.[7] For Alison and his disciples, architectural associationism was largely an aesthetic ideal; with the Belle Isle Aquarium & Horticultural Building it was an inescapable functional requirement. Whether Kahn possessed an innate aptitude for working in this manner or he developed it on this project is unknown, but he rose to the challenge by producing not a mere shell but a finely integrated machine.

Partnership with Mason

He accepted Mason's offer of partnership around the time of the aquarium research trip, and news of the new firm was published on February 10, 1901. Although it appears few knew it, the partnership was conceived as a one-year arrangement, with Mason moving from his longtime office at 80 Griswold Street to the suite atop the nearby Union Trust Building occupied by Kahn for nearly six years. They immediately leased additional adjoining space and expanded.[8] Although Mason had a long-established reputation, a survey of Detroit's newspapers suggests that his workload over the previous two years of independent practice (without Rice) was not notably heavier than Nettleton & Kahn's. While Kahn surely benefited from his old employer's new role as partner, it does not seem to have been a lopsided relationship. Nevertheless, the senior architect may have been motivated by kind-heartedness in making the offer and he had been close to Nettleton also, as demonstrated by being one of his pallbearers. Be that as it may, the office of Mason & Kahn proved to be a busy place. Surely work on the Belle Isle Aquarium & Horticultural Building represented a shared responsibility amid other work.

In early March, local newspapers reported a visit to Detroit by Leonard B. Spencer, the assistant in charge of the freshwater collections of the New York Aquarium, to share "the benefit of his long experience." Recognized as one of the "two or three most famous and best informed aquarium experts in the United States," he expressed the enthusiasm this project generated within ichthyological circles. He spent two or three days with the parks board and the architects discussing details. Spencer was quite optimistic about Detroit joining New York as the world's only cities to own a public aquarium, saying, "I think you are going to have a great aquarium here. There is nothing to hinder. There is plenty of room on the island, with no other buildings to shut off light and air."[9]

Other projects came into the office of Mason & Kahn as work on the Belle Isle plans continued into the summer. A Jacobean-styled, $100,000 apartment building for Frank C. Andrews, the Woodward, was announced March 31, 1901, as a Nettleton & Kahn design. This suggests Kahn had been working on the significant commission before partnering with Mason. Appreciating the pressures of designing a 200- by 216-foot, elegantly appointed building, where

The Woodward apartment building, Detroit, Michigan (1901–2). Nettleton & Kahn, architects (completed by Mason & Kahn). Photograph, circa 1902, courtesy Albert Kahn Associates, Inc.

the thirty apartments averaged seven rooms plus bathrooms and pantries, it becomes easy to understand why Kahn might need the support of a partnership while he was also completing the details of the Belle Isle building. Work commenced on the Woodward in April under the firm of Mason & Kahn.[10]

Also in April, the firm was retained to design the new, $12,000 Temple Beth El on Woodward Avenue. The Reform congregation desired a structure that would break with the tradition of looking to the Middle East for architectural inspiration for Jewish houses of worship. At the same time, the congregation also longed for a clear stylistic departure from its present location, which was a loosely gothic structure built as a Baptist church. As the *Detroit News* explained, "The problem before the architects is to design a building without Moorish or oriental features, which will be known as a place of worship by its appearance, and yet will not look like a Presbyterian, Methodist, Baptist or evangelical church of any kind."[11]

The principle of associationism was on display here: the new temple was expected to function as a place of worship, and express that in its appearance. The challenge was to achieve this without borrowing from the architecture of other religions.

Mason & Kahn's response reached back into historical precedent and delivered a façade derived from the ancient Roman Pantheon. Some Kahn biographers praise him for arriving at a bold solution for Temple Beth El, which is justified, but clearly the desire for a new direction, if undefined, originated with the client, not the architects. Regardless, Temple Beth El became a model for future synagogues.[12]

At the end of October 1901 Kahn asked the parks department to amend the Belle Isle contracts, changing the firm name from Nettleton & Kahn to Mason & Kahn. This would officially recognize Mason's authority as representing the firm in matters related to the contract and billing.[13] Although Kahn remained involved with design issues and certain other decisions, parks department records and Mason's diaries suggest the senior partner soon after assumed the bulk of the superintending duties on the project.

Dissolution of Mason & Kahn

As 1901 grew into 1902, it became known in architectural circles that the firm would be dissolving soon. Apparently not aware that it was conceived as

Temple Beth El, Detroit, Michigan (1901–3). Mason & Kahn, architects (completed by Albert Kahn). Image from the *Inland Architect and News Record*, vol. 42, Ryerson and Burnham Libraries, Art Institute of Chicago. Digital File #IA42XX_3838.

a one-year arrangement, fellow architects interpreted the dissolution as evidence of a rift. Arthur Alexander Stoughton wrote to Kahn from New York City lamenting, "I am very much concerned about your partnerial difficulties. You have been unfortunate in losing good ones and finding one not congenial." James B. Nettleton, George's younger brother and a Detroit architect himself, wrote "I have it from a reliable source that you and Mr. Mason are about to, or have already dissolved partnership. From things that have come to me from time to time I have expected this but not so soon. What led up to it I have no way of knowing nor does it concern me. Personally I thought the combination would work."[14]

Public and private documents indicate both Mason and Kahn continued to hold each other with warm regard and professional respect until the end of their lives, so any uncongeniality within the partnership, if it existed, was not personal. Judging from the known workload, it would seem the partnership was a business success that could continue if they wished. It appears, however, that both simply preferred to paddle their own canoes. On January 23, 1902, they agreed to no longer accept new work as partners, and Kahn began to advertise for an associate. (He would eventually team with Ernest Wilby from 1903 to 1918.) Notice of the dissolution of Mason & Kahn was published a month later, and a month after that it was explained that Kahn would be practicing in collaboration with his civil engineer brother, Julius, while Mason would partner with William Reed-Hill.[15]

The old firm had just completed plans for the University of Michigan's imposing, $120,000 Engineering Building, a three-and-a-half story, reinforced concrete building faced in Bedford limestone and brick and described as in the style of "an adapted Renaissance." Plans for the Century Association club building were initiated under Mason & Kahn and described as "nearly completed" shortly after the dissolution in an April 27, 1902, report. Although the club project would be scaled back somewhat by mid-1903 when Mason produced final drawings, it was remarkably true to the original vision in many of its appointments.[16]

These and other work under construction, such as Temple Beth El, the Palms apartment building (discussed in chapter 8) and the Belle Isle Aquarium & Horticultural Building, would be completed under their joint supervision. It appears that in practice, the day-to-day work for the temple and apartment

Engineering Building for the University of Michigan, Ann Arbor, Michigan (1902–3). Mason & Kahn, architects. Photograph by the Detroit Publishing Co., 1905, courtesy Library of Congress, Prints and Photographs Division.

building was assumed by Kahn while Mason oversaw the Belle Isle structure. While it might seem curious that Kahn would entrust completion of this landmark to another, perhaps its association with the memory of George Nettleton was more than he cared to bear. Mason would have understood this better than anyone else. Next to Kahn, he was also best suited for the task through his investigations for the competition and his previous experience working with the city on Belle Isle improvements. Stoughton's letter indicates the office employed eight to ten men, who presumably would have continued with one or the other of the partners or sought other opportunities. Gies, for instance, went to work in the office of Donaldson & Meier before striking out on his own in 1903. Kahn remained in the Union Trust Building while Mason returned to his old office suite on Griswold.[17]

7

The Belle Isle Aquarium & Horticultural Building

On June 1, 1901, the board of Detroit's Commission of Parks and Boulevards was disbanded as a result of a departmental reorganization and Robert E. Bolger was installed as the sole commissioner. Bolger was publicly against proceeding with the aquarium project, decrying it as an expensive luxury. Given the wording of the Heineman Act, however, he could see no escape from following through with the construction short of new legislation. Although losing his authority as general manager, Hurlbut was retained as secretary. His familiarity with the Belle Isle project already was a consideration in his retention.[1]

Construction, Equipping, and Stocking

In early 1902, Bolger anticipated the Belle Isle Aquarium & Horticultural Building being open by August of that year, but strikes by construction labor and structural iron shortages caused the work to drag out over two years beyond that prediction. When Mason and Kahn divided their office work, surely neither dreamed their commitment to the project would continue as long as it did. Mason's diary records a July 15 visit to Kahn "to see first tank frame." This is surely in regard to the decorative bronze frames that surrounded the wall tank glass in the aquarium, and the visit establishes that Kahn remained engaged in decision making as the work progressed.[2]

Photographs from late 1902 show the exterior of the aquarium largely completed and ironwork for the palm house dome underway. As work progressed, Tarleton H. Bean, of the U.S. Fish Commission, visited the aquarium worksite and observed, "The building is a very substantial and attractive one, and the work so far has been carefully done." A *Detroit Free Press* record of the visit noted, "In the matter of construction much faith is placed in the fact that an expert in such matters [Bean] has stated that no mistakes were made in the designing of the building." The statement constituted high praise for Kahn, considering the source: as director of the New York Aquarium, Bean had shepherded the institution through its initial years—and missteps—shaping it into a popular institution of research and enlightenment until he was removed from his position to make room for a political appointment. (Fortunately for the institution, its superintendent, L. B. Spencer, was able to maintain the level of quality set by Bean despite his lower status until authority over the aquarium was transferred from Tammany Hall to the New York Zoological Society in 1902.) "A strong feature of the building is the lighting facilities," Bean's report on Belle Isle continued. "The tanks are so arranged that the light falls from above and can be reduced to nothing or made so strong that it will illuminate the contents of the tanks." Bids for the aquarium equipment were received on December 7, 1903. They tipped expenditures in excess of the original appropriation, requiring the city council to tap into the budgets of other departments. This caused further delays as funding changes had to be authorized and moneys were not always immediately available. Such setbacks frustrated the project's supporters while providing some vindication for critics.[3]

Nevertheless, even naysayers found it difficult to remain negative as it came nearer to fruition. Newspaper reports indicate Commissioner Bolger overcame his initial opposition to the project and was now basking in the glow of enthusiasm it generated. In May 1903 he announced the completion of the concrete dark reservoir in the service yard between the aquarial and horticultural components, making marine displays possible. From press reports it appears Bolger shamelessly took credit for the system as a novel solution of his own invention, even though it was Kahn's design clearly following W. A. Lloyd's similarly equipped aquaria. The commissioner traveled with secretary Hurlbut about the country, consulting experts in ichthyology and botany regarding the collections. As Bolger told it, "At every point we were treated with the utmost courtesy, and the greatest interest was manifested in our aquarium due in a considerable measure to the fact that it is the second large one to be built in the United States." The advice collected enables "us to introduce the latest and best ideas in both the aquarium and the horticultural building."[4]

Installation planting had begun in the conservatory in the summer of 1903, when its structure was essentially completed and the heating and power plant operating to satisfaction. It can be assumed that Mason & Kahn's role in the project was largely fulfilled by this point. Work equipping the aquarium continued into 1904, with some freshwater fish introduced by that summer. Railroad tank cars arrived on June 28 bearing thirty thousand gallons of saltwater from the Atlantic off of Woods Hole, Massachusetts. Another ten thousand was scheduled to arrive the following week. With the saltwater in place, aquarium director R. J. Conway (formerly with the U.S. Fish Commission) headed east. His mission was to acquire marine specimens for exhibit, largely through trading freshwater fish. Travel was via a specially outfitted Michigan Fish Commission rail car riding the rails free of charge, compliments of the Michigan Central Railroad.[5]

The architecture of the Belle Isle Aquarium & Horticultural Building began drawing acclaim long before it opened. Once construction reached the point where its merits were self-evident, editors of the *Detroit News*, despite earlier grousing over cost, proclaimed the structure "the crowning glory of the island." Even while arguing tax dollars would be better spent on building a school, Rabbi Leo Franklin had to concede that "the aquarium at Belle Isle is a magnificent piece of architecture." (Franklin was typical in his choice of words; both components of the structure were often collectively called the aquarium.) It was described in a national journal as "a beautiful structure, its big glass dome being visible from long distances and easily seen from the Canadian shore of the Detroit River, glistening in the sunshine."[6]

The Visitor Experience

Finally, the formal opening ceremony was held on the morning of August 18, 1904. Featuring the third largest public aquarium in the world (behind New

York and Brighton) successfully paired with a botanical conservatory, it was an impressive feat by any measure. Bolger proudly proclaimed that it was "pronounced by the leading aquarists of this country to be second to none in the world."[7]

Kahn applied a classical, Italian-Renaissance motif to the delicate-appearing, modular steel and glass construction of the botanical component. This ornamentation, mostly of carved wood, was sparingly and judiciously placed so as not to interfere with the passage of natural sunlight through some twenty-five thousand square feet of glass, in any way that would be a detriment to the plants within. Centered on the western façade was an elegant, three-bay, projecting entrance two stories in height. The arches of the entrance, separated by Corinthian pilasters, were repeated around the drum of the palm house rising eighty feet into the air with its ventilating lantern. As the botanical

Belle Isle Aquarium & Horticultural Building, Detroit, Michigan. Nettleton & Kahn, architects, 1901–4 (completed by Mason & Kahn). Photograph of west (botanical) façade by the Detroit Publishing Company, circa 1905, courtesy Library of Congress, Prints and Photographs Division.

component stretched out from the dome to 272 feet, the overall effect was of an impressively large, yet seemingly fragile, Victorian curiosity cabinet.

The functional demands for the aquarial component were quite different from the botanical, creating an architectural challenge as the delicate-appearing expanses of glass in steel framework gave way to walls of brickwork construction, punctuated by windows and doors, topped by Spanish tile roofing. This was not a major concern in the competition design, where the aquarial component was hidden behind the botanical. With the reorientation of the redesign, however, the two components were equally prominent, with the aquarial needing its own formal entrance on its narrow north end. Unlike conservatories, there was little consensus on what an aquarium entrance should look like, and precedents ranged from the classic sobriety of the Naples Aquarium to the fantastic faux rockwork of the 1866 L'Aquarium de Boulogne (not to be confused with the present day Nausicaá Centre National de la Mer in the same French city). Such imaginative rockwork swathed interiors of sensational grotto aquaria.

Kahn chose something in between. Building upon the template arch of the conservatory's entrance bays and palm house drum, he drew from his studies to conjure an original, robust aquarium entrance surround in a Mannerist and baroque tour de force. It and the conservatory ornamentation were executed

L'Aquarium de Boulogne, Boulogne-sur-Mer, France (1866). Edouard Betencourt, architect. The entrance to this below-grade aquarium is hidden among the faux rockwork. A portion of the coastal town's casino can be seen to the right in the background. Photographic stereoview, circa 1870, by Q. V., collection of the author.

by Joachim Jungwirth, an Austrian immigrant who came to dominate the woodcarving market in Detroit and whose work in wood and other materials extended to other parts of the country.[8] Inspiration for the aquarium entrance surely came from the playful aquatic ornamentation of the Fisheries Building at the Chicago Fair and perhaps from the Brighton Aquarium as well. Banded Doric pilasters seem to drip seaweed while a conch-crowned Neptune serves as a keystone. Aquatic flora and fauna fill the spandrels framing the arch above which Detroit's city seal is supported by two spitting dolphins that would be at home as illustrations on a sixteenth-century oceanic navigation chart.

Inside the building, Kahn created what for most visitors in 1904 were vast and marvelous unobstructed spaces for the display of exhibits. The palm house offered a towering dome and 4,070 square feet of columnless floor space bathed in natural light. As a newspaper writer raved just a few months later, "Here one finds a truly tropical luxuriance. Here one feels that there is a certain majesty

Belle Isle Aquarium & Horticultural Building, north (aquarial) entrance. Construction photograph by the Baker Studio, 1904, courtesy Burton Historical Collection, Detroit Public Library.

Belle Isle Aquarium & Horticultural Building, interior of Palm House Dome. Postcard view, circa 1908, by H. L. Woehler, courtesy Burton Historical Collection, Detroit Public Library.

in the rugged strength and the peculiar beauty of these kings of the plant life."[9] Nonstructural glass walls and doors interrupted this space to provide necessary thermal barriers between the ranges.

Not requiring thermal barriers beyond the inner vestibule doors, the public area of the aquarial component presented an uninterrupted vista, 190 feet in length. This was composed of two in-line barrel-vaulted corridors separated by a twenty-eight-foot-high octagonal rotunda at the connection with the display house, where it balanced the palm dome sharing its centerline on the perpendicular to the west. For anyone moving through, the minutely undulating surfaces of the glossy, variegated green Opalite tiles seemed to shimmer like watery surfaces as they caught light in patterns that shifted with every step of the viewer. Forty-four bronze-framed display tanks lined the path. The aquarium's visitor experience was captured in a newspaper account a few months after the opening, which described the visitors' stroll past the forty-four display tanks:

> It is easy to imagine that this is some submarine art gallery with beautifully illuminated sea pictures hung on its walls of restful green. These pictures, on closer inspection, prove to be glass fronted exhibition tanks, lighted from behind, which line the sides of the corridor. With their background of shells and rock, and green things which grow in water, and their gleaming fishes that dart hither and thither, they seem, again, like miniature lakes or oceans . . . so absorbed does one become in watching the maneuvers of these curious creatures of river, lake and ocean, which quite evidently have such a peculiar interest to persons of every class and calling.[10]

Belle Isle Aquarium & Horticultural Building, public aquarial corridor. Photograph by the Detroit Publishing Company, circa 1905, courtesy Library of Congress, Prints and Photographs Division.

Behind the Scenes

There was much planning and effort to make this tropical luxuriance and submarine art gallery possible for the public to study and enjoy. While the botanical component's glazing, some panels of which opened, allowed for natural sunlight and ventilation, steam, the preferred heating since Loudon's time, was needed for the winter months. Five miles of steam piping was employed to heat the entire structure, as well as supporting greenhouses.[11] Natural light was vital to the well-being of the aquatic collection, but it needed to be controlled to avoid the problems that plagued London's Regent's Park Fish House. Kahn expanded upon the natural lighting scheme of the much smaller Hamburg Aquarium, while improving upon its ventilation with a raised structure designed to draw cooler air from the basement.

The architect would later apply lessons he learned in designing a healthy environment for plant and fish displays to advance healthier environments for workers. Those future workers, particularly in manufacturing, would also need a workplace efficiently engineered to suit its function. For the Belle Isle structure, Kahn needed to anticipate and accommodate multiple engineering

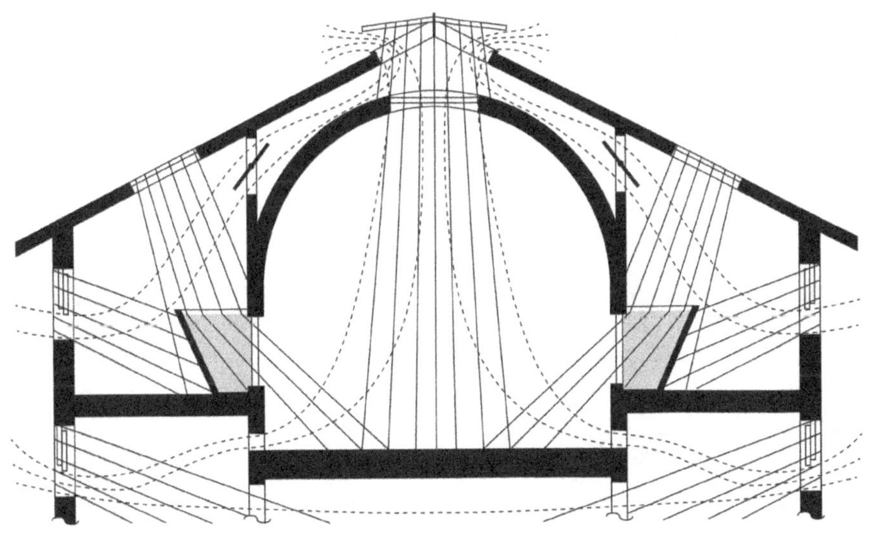

Schematic illustrating the natural lighting (solid lines) and ventilation (dashed lines) for a section of the aquarium component of the Belle Isle Aquarium & Horticultural Building. Illustration by the author based upon blueprints of the original detail drawings.

challenges that were beyond the normal expectation of an architectural design at the time. As Lloyd wrote a quarter-century earlier, "Aquarium work, being hydraulic engineering on a small scale, is essentially the work of an engineer, and not that of an architect."[12] As his career developed, Kahn would take advantage of the unusual expertise he acquired here to produce pioneering industrial designs.

The water required for the aquarium displays totaled sixty-five thousand gallons, fifty thousand gallons of which were kept in constant motion, day and night. Its journey began with two twelve-thousand-gallon dark reservoirs, of the type Lloyd originally devised, sunk into the service courtyard. One was used to filter freshwater pumped from the river, the second to filter the recycled Atlantic saltwater. From the reservoirs, the water was pumped to two separate thousand-gallon tanks located in a tower Kahn designed at the south end of the aquarial component to house them so that it could be aerated and circulated through the various service and display tanks by simply harnessing gravity. The water in the display tanks would naturally become clouded with algae

Belle Isle Aquarium & Horticultural Building, aerial view. The salt- and freshwater reservoirs are the circular features immediately to the right of the palm house dome, between the aquarial (background) and horticultural (foreground) components. The tower containing the loft tanks is visible near the south end of the aquarial component, near the right side of the photograph. Press photograph, circa 1930, courtesy R. Vance Patrick.

and debris, becoming unhealthy for fish. Turbid freshwater would be disposed into the sewer system at the end of the circuit while the precious saltwater was returned to its dark reservoir for natural filtration. Fish-keeping involved many other challenges that Kahn needed to consider. Michigan's native species, such as trout, need cool water throughout the year; ice-making machines were employed to chill the water as needed. In winter, when warm water was required for the tropical and temperate species, it was heated as an ancillary function of the hot water heating system. Aeration pumps augmented the gravity-driven oxygenation of the water. Workers in the Belle Isle Aquarium & Horticultural Building operated in three eight-hour shifts to keep the power plant running around the clock.[13]

Widespread Acclaim and Imitation

The Belle Isle Aquarium & Horticultural Building was a resounding success. In its first eighteen days of official operation, over 80,229 visitors toured the exhibits. Within a year railroads and passenger ship lines were promoting the attraction around the country. Park Commissioner Bolger—who called to cancel the project when he came into office—now boasted, "its value as a drawing card for the city cannot be overstated." In its first two years of operation, it had proven itself "popular to a degree far exceeding the most sanguine hopes of its promoters," according to the *Municipal Journal and Engineer.*[14]

The building's success inspired a reappraisal of the public aquarium as a cultural feature of the American municipal landscape. On its opening day, Bolger boasted that the country's leading aquarists had ranked it second to none in the world. This appears to have been taken as a challenge to the operators of the New York Aquarium. In 1903, while the Detroit aquarium was still being equipped, the bulletin of the New York Zoological Society stated, "As the public Aquarium is comparatively a modern institution, it may be that the ideal aquarium building has not yet been designed." Achieving *the* ideal in any building type is a lofty goal for any architect, but it seems that Kahn came closer to it than anyone else had up to then when it came to public aquaria. After publishing this statement, the Zoological Society embarked on a series of improvements to the New York Aquarium in line with the notable features underway in Detroit, including better skylighting, improved ventilation, a dark reservoir for saltwater (even though the harbor was yards away), simulated environment tankscaping (its tanks previously featured barren white tile lining), and pumped-in aeration. Described by its directors as being "a decidedly dark and dingy place," such changes may have come independently as the facility was transferred to the society's care. It is possible, however, that the shortcomings became apparent during the staff's many consultations with delegations from Detroit (Van Leyen, Mason, Kahn, Hurlbut, Bolger, and possibly others) planning the aquarium there. The work in New York continued into 1906.[15]

Public aquaria began opening elsewhere in the years that followed. Some, like Boston's South Park Aquarium (opened 1912) and the Miami Aquarium (1921) were clearly patterned as variations on the Belle Isle plan. Others, such as the Odenheimer Aquarium in New Orleans (1924), replicated its works. It was not surpassed in size until the 1923 opening of San Francisco's Steinhart Aquarium. All were dwarfed by the John G. Shedd Aquarium, which opened in Chicago in 1929. Planners for this massive endeavor visited and studied Kahn's aquarium on Belle Isle. Just as he enlarged and enhanced Lloyd's plan, they enlarged and enhanced his.[16]

The Butterfly Effect

Despite the resounding success and influence of Kahn's aquarium, he never designed another. In the years to come he would, however, continually draw from the multiple unique lessons learned with the Belle Isle structure and apply them to whatever work was at hand. Foremost among these was the value of a close working relationship between the architect, engineers, and others possessing specialized expertise (such as ichthyologists), were they the client or consultants. Designing to the aquarial and botanical building types also placed a particular burden on the architect, being directly responsible for the physical well-being of captive plants and animals on display. As noted, Kahn would take this to heart when designing structures occupied by workers for considerable portions of their days.

Apparently ingrained in Kahn's mind by the Belle Isle project was the lesson that sunlight is essential to life: while his earlier buildings were not noted for overly generous windows, his competition entry would never have prevailed had it not conformed to this reality. Daylighting became a signature feature of his subsequent nonresidential work. (For homes, small windows responded to privacy and other concerns.)

As obvious as this feature may seem, architects did not always prioritize it in their designs. In the mid-nineteenth century, the medical journal *London Lancet* appealed to British architects to admit more sunlight into building design. In its argument, the journal's editors referenced the investigations of Nathaniel Bagshaw Ward, a surgeon residing and practicing in London's dockland slums—a congested area usually overshadowed with heavy clouds of industrial smoke and soot. Like a number of other physicians, Ward was also a member of the naturalist community. With characteristic naturalist zeal, Ward gave his house and gardens over to experiments in the propagation of plants that might survive his blighted location. This activity brought him to the attention of J. C. Loudon, who featured the doctor's botanical investigations in his *Gardener's Magazine*. (Ward also originated wooden boxes with tops and sides of glass for growing plants in isolated micro environments. Popularly called Wardian cases, these were eventually adapted to become tabletop terrarium and aquarium tanks.) Beginning in the early 1800s Ward observed that lack of exposure to sunlight had adverse effects on the physical and mental health of his patients. He also found the presence of living plants to have physical and psychological benefit on patients. Drawing upon his observations and the work of others, Ward advocated that "as much light be admitted into the dwellings of both the rich and the poor as can be admitted, for I am satisfied that, *cæteris paribus*, their health would be improved."[17]

Applying Ward's medical observations to architecture, *London Lancet* editors advocated for more and larger windows. According to the journal, much of the problem rested with British taste, which seemed enamored with the buildings of southern Europe "where the intensity of light is so great that it has rather to be avoided than courted. . . . The result is, among architects a multiplicity of windows is considered a defect instead of a beauty, and studiously avoided." The editors roundly condemned such "architectural prejudices."[18]

The pleas to architectural professionals for more and larger windows were slow to take effect, but in medical circles the writings of Florence Nightingale proved influential in the late-1850s. She advocated for functionally designed, steam-heated hospital patient wards bathed in natural light and open to as much fresh air as the climate would permit. London's new St. Thomas Hospital (1868–72) embodied these principles, and an illustration from the time aptly showcases the result as visitors cheer a patient whose convalescence is aided by light from a large, operable window nearby. The scene is replete with numerous psychologically comforting, oxygen-generating plants, documenting a tradition that extends into today.[19] Ward surely would have approved.

It appears some industrial workers similarly understood the benefits of natural sunlight and ventilation regardless of architectural prejudices. An illustration from an 1879 gardening journal innocently demonstrates the positive effects of sunlight and fresh air in the workplace with a depiction of the engine room of the Waltham Watch Company Factory in Massachusetts. Here an enterprising machine operator utilized natural lighting to grow plants as it also illuminated his work. Windows are opened to allow natural ventilation to circulate the air and moderate the temperature in the room.[20]

"Visiting Day at St. Thomas Hospital, Surrey Gardens." With an attendant watering plants in the window, this scene captures Victorian-era recognition of the benefits of natural light to human health. Illustration from *The Graphic* by Edward F. Brewtnall, 1871, collection of the author.

This seemingly inconsequential scene from a forgotten day in an otherwise common work area manages to capture concepts that transcend its time and place, demonstrating life's continuing dependency on natural light and ventilation and their beneficial impact on human productivity. While the worker in this illustration may have taken such notions for granted, they have often eluded designers of industrial buildings and other structures during the course of architectural history. As demonstrated earlier, like most architects in the nineteenth century Kahn was not a proponent of noticeably large windows in his early career, and it should be noted that there were arguments in favor of fewer windows at the time. For instance, given the harshness of Michigan winters and the serious health threat of cold weather-related illness, windows were seen as undesirable sources of interior heat loss. (Equipment

A GREENHOUSE IN AN ENGINE-ROOM.

"A Greenhouse in an Engine Room." Illustration from *Gardening Illustrated*, 1879, artist unknown, collection of the author.

like that in the Waltham Watch Company engine room generated its own heat, negating that concern.)

This changed for Kahn as he entered the twentieth century and his work for the Belle Isle Aquarium & Horticulture Building must be seen as the pivotal event. Designing the conservatory and the display tank work areas for the aquarium surely imprinted the lessons of Ward and Nightingale onto the architect's psyche. As will be discussed in the pages ahead, Kahn would become closely identified with the daylight factory while he also imbued his other commercial designs with natural lighting.

Another aspect of conservatory design as it evolved in the nineteenth century was its modular construction. Repetitive units of steel frame and glass were conducive to standardization, making them economical and relatively quick to produce and install. Joseph Paxton's Crystal Palace, when it was originally built in London's Hyde Park for the Great Exhibition, was under incredibly tight constraints regarding cost and construction time. His modular glass house solution lent itself to mass production of the building components, which were made off-site prior to the start of construction. With parts premade elsewhere the huge, 1,848- by 408-foot, three-story structure was assembled in just six months.[21] Kahn followed the trend with his Belle Isle design and would apply it in his future industrial work, working in reinforced concrete and steel.

In addition to impressing the value of daylight and the concept of modularity upon Kahn, the structure on Belle Isle provided him with an introduction to the notion of designing for "flow production"—another term for the assembly line. Some production theorists identify flow production as a step in the development of mass production while others consider the two synonymous. (Today, some are applying the term to just-in-time delivery scheduling.)

It seems no coincidence that the architect who designed this conjoined aquarium and conservatory went on to master the daylight factory. To what extent the architect entered the project with innate skills and to what extent he developed them in the course of his involvement with this structure is a matter of speculation. Clearly, however, his work on Belle Isle marks a metamorphosis for Kahn, although surely no one noticed at the time. When opportunity for industrial work came his way in the future, he seized it with an insight that set him apart from his peers. To conclude the metaphor, as his career moved forward the Belle Isle structure, with its bittersweet memory of George Nettleton, was left behind like an abandoned cocoon. Carrying its lessons with him, Kahn would soon take wing.

Those familiar with the "butterfly effect" of chaos theory understand the concept that small and seemingly inconsequential actions can set in motion a chain of events producing massive repercussions. This concept is clearly illustrated in the career of Kahn, for likely no one, especially the humble, diminutive (five feet, five inches tall)[22] architect himself, could have foreseen his future destiny until it dramatically unfolded around him.

8

Underappreciated Seminal Commissions

Over two years passed between the dissolution of Mason & Kahn and the opening of the Belle Isle Aquarium & Horticultural Building in 1904. Kahn was in his thirty-sixth year at that time. When asked in 1908 for a list of his accomplishments, he emphatically responded, "No, no. I am too young. When I have completed a life work then ask me to speak authoritatively and to tell of my achievements."[1]

There is wisdom in this, for in 1908 he had no way of knowing what commissions would stand out at the end of his career, with the benefit of hindsight. Christy Borth, in one of the more enlightening biographical profiles of Kahn published three years after the architect's death, wrote perceptively of his having "commissions whose relative importance he miscomprehended at the time."[2] Furiously working until his end, the architect never had the opportunity to sit back and reflect authoritatively on his achievements, when perhaps he would himself have identified work he had undervalued in interviews earlier.

Looking back from a twenty-first century perspective, it seems apparent that four of those miscomprehended and therefore underappreciated commissions were an addition to the Chicago Pneumatic Tool Company's Detroit plant (formerly the Boyer Machine Company Shop) and its sibling in Fraserburgh, Scotland, the Palms apartment building, and the Metzger Automobile Repository. Like the Belle Isle Aquarium & Horticultural Building, these all have their origins in Kahn's earlier partnerships and are key to understanding the particularly involved set of circumstances setting the path he was to follow.

In 1900 or 1901, he designed home remodelings for Joseph Boyer, who would later bring him the factory addition, and Henry Bourne Joy, owner of the property on which the Metzger Automobile Repository was built. The apartment building was a commission that came into the Mason & Kahn office in 1901, but Kahn took responsibility for completing the job after the partnership dissolved in February 1902. It and the other three commissions required a willingness to take on engineering challenges beyond the norm for architects.[3] Nothing in his background would recommend him for such work save his success with the Belle Isle Aquarium & Horticultural Building, which was still under construction but garnering notice and acclaim. To take the symbolism of Kahn's Belle Isle metamorphosis (and perhaps the butterfly effect) a bit further, these commissions represent the first exploratory flaps of the wings of his new career.

Joseph Boyer, Kahn's Silent Association

Understanding Kahn's career trajectory requires an acknowledgment of the role played by Joseph Boyer. While Kahn was quick to shower praise and appreciation on clients such as Henry Ford and Henry Joy, he uttered nary a peep in public about Boyer. It was another matter in private, as revealed by a personal 1925 letter to the industrialist. In it, Kahn gratefully acknowledged Boyer's help in his "getting a start" and hoped he and his office had shown themselves to be "worthy of the confidence you placed in us in our early days and ever since."[4] Justification for this private gratitude and an explanation for the conspicuous absence of its public expression will be found in the pages ahead.

In addition to his confidence in Kahn, Boyer deserves much more credit for his contributions to industry and the growth of Detroit than he receives today. Indeed, as of this writing he seems all but forgotten except in annals of computer science, where Boyer's name figures large for his work related to the Burroughs Adding Machine.

Born in 1848 to a farm family in Pickering County outside of Oshawa, West Canada (later Ontario), Boyer left home around age fifteen after a few terms in the local schoolhouse. Building on his interest in repairing farm equipment, he learned the machinist trade in Oshawa, then struck out for employment in the United States in 1866, as it was still rebounding from the Civil War. Traveling and working as far west as San Francisco, he eventually settled in St. Louis, Missouri, around 1869. There he was reported to have "started a machine shop with himself as president, general manager, foreman, and hands." The business grew; its mainstay was the production of molds for glass bottles. Along the way, Boyer acquired a series of patents on his improvements to pneumatic tools associated with his work.[5]

Beginning in 1884, Boyer gave assistance to William Seward Burroughs, who was struggling to perfect his idea for a mechanized adding machine. Burroughs's declining health led Boyer to become increasingly involved in that business, the American Arithmometer Company, in addition to his own. By 1895 the growth of both companies led Boyer to build a larger facility that they shared in St. Louis, designed by Louis Christian Mullgardt. In 1898 Boyer patented a pneumatic hammer that could be held and operated by one person, which proved wildly popular. His business increased to the point that it outgrew the new facility.[6]

Boyer was ready to abandon St. Louis by 1900. In a 1922 interview he was quoted as saying, "I wanted to get away up north where the climate is not so warm and I decided to move to Detroit."[7] Given the complexity and expense of moving his established and considerable business, along with the uncertainty of valued employees relocating their families, a change in climate alone does not seem adequate motivation. It also does not explain why Detroit was chosen over other cities in similar latitudes.

A more plausible explanation was offered in an unpublished, manuscript biography, circa 1926, of Henry M. Leland, written by his long-time secretary. Formerly a repair technician who serviced Boyer's machines in St. Louis, Leland formed a friendship with Boyer before moving to Detroit in 1890, where he co-owned a machining shop. Boyer helped finance the venture with a $40,000 loan. From the manuscript, it appears the open shop labor environment of Detroit attracted Leland over closed shop cities like Chicago, where militant struggles over complete workforce control often turned violent. By 1900, the manuscript continues, Boyer was experiencing union militancy that was a compelling factor in the move from St. Louis, with the decision to move to Detroit resulting from Leland's recommendation.[8] (This explanation is bolstered by the account of American Arithmometer's similar move four years later, as recounted in chapter 10.)

Boyer's moving his business to Detroit was no small event in 1900. It was reported in the *Detroit Free Press* as "a remarkable and almost unprecedented occurrence. . . . The bringing of this great industry with its small army of employes [*sic*] to Detroit is one of the most important events in the city's industrial life, and the factory covering nearly one and one-half acres will be among the largest of the city's great industries." From the perspective of Detroiters, Boyer and his company suddenly arrived out of nowhere. He had an investment in highly paid skilled workers in St. Louis, however, and wanted as many as would come to migrate with the company. Toward that end, he dismissed offers of free or cheap property for his factory in industrial areas, instead building in the relatively pricey new Cass Farms development, paying market price for the land. When questioned, he insisted that he wanted his workers to be able to live in nice neighborhoods and still walk to their jobs.[9]

Boyer again hired Mullgardt to design the high-ceilinged, single-story 345- by 180-foot Boyer Machine Company Shop on Detroit's Second Avenue at Amsterdam Street in 1900. He turned to a local architectural firm, Nettleton & Kahn, for improvements to his residence, however.[10]

As Boyer recalled, "When I built my first building in Detroit it took all I had, but it was worth it. Detroit was indeed a wonderful mercantile town." Detroit and Boyer did well by each other: the machine shop appears to have been a catalyst for manufacturing development of the surrounding area, a railway intersection known as Milwaukee Junction. As Boyer's operation ramped up in late 1900, the *Detroit News-Tribune* reported on "a good deal of inquiry for manufacturing sites about Milwaukee Junction," and that "deals for that class of property are incubating and the results are likely to be realized soon."[11] Eventually attracting Ford, the Fisher Brothers, and others, the area would come to be considered the cradle of Detroit's automobile industry.

Kahn's Work for the Chicago and Consolidated Pneumatic Tool Companies

In January 1902 the Boyer Machine Company merged with four similar companies to form the Chicago Pneumatic Tool Company (CPT) with Boyer as a director and operating officer of the Detroit plant. As he explained, CPT's "management was most excellent and my work was to turn out the hammers." Almost immediately, the Detroit factory needed expansion and CPT hired Kahn to draw up an addition, surely on the recommendation of Boyer. Having acquired his own business training "in the school of hard knocks," as one newspaper account put it, Boyer "displayed a sincere interest in others who were treading the same path." This was likely the basis for the bond that developed between the industrialist and the architect (and inventor Burroughs, for that matter) that led to what appears to have been the Kahn's first experience in designing for industrial production, although he was essentially following Mullgardt's plan.[12]

Boyer always anticipated growth for the shop, so Mullgardt designed the original structure for westward expansion with steel columns in the curtain brick west wall. Kahn merely removed the brick and replicated Mullgardt's design in creating the addition, which included a novel variation on the sawtooth roof. Even, natural lighting from a north-facing source was considered crucial for fine machine work, and sawtooth lights on flat roofs were commonly employed to achieve it. It was a problematic solution, however, with drainage concerns, support constraints, and other issues. The Boyer roof, as it was called, overcame these by setting sawtooth lights on gabled planes that could be carried on trusses for greater spans. The roof was described in the press as remarkable for being a self-supporting span that "has in it so much glass that the immense work room that it covers will be ablaze with diffused light."[13]

While not an original factory design by Kahn, this addition work, coming as it did while his Belle Isle structure was under construction, may have started the wheels of the architect's mind spinning with regard to applying Victorian concepts of natural lighting, ventilation, and modularity to twentieth century industry.

Boyer Machine Company Shop, Detroit, Michigan (1900). Louis Christian Mullgardt, architect (shown with later additions by Chicago Pneumatic Tool Company). View of the works, circa 1938, with arrows added by the author. Black arrow indicates north. White arrows mark extremes of Albert Kahn's 1902 addition. To the east of that is the original 1900 Boyer shop structure by Mullgardt. To the west is later construction. Courtesy Fraserburgh Heritage Centre, Fraserburgh, Scotland, UK.

"Golden Rule" Policies and Kahn's First Transoceanic Design

Some twenty years Kahn's senior, Boyer likely found common ground with the architect in their humble origins. The industrialist's working-class background shaped his approach to management and surely influenced Kahn's approach to factory design. Boyer, despite his later status, "did not hesitate to throw off his coat, take a rebellious machine apart and make it right," according to one eulogy. He knew the value of ample and dependable natural light as key to precision work. He also understood the value that a contented workforce brought to any business and so he advanced what some came to call Golden Rule policies in his shops long before social reformers made it a cause. "I do not see why the men should not have as clean a place to work as those in the office, provided their work permits it. They will do better work and we can hold a better class of mechanics," he explained to a *Detroit Free Press* reporter who found the shop clean, well lighted, and airy in 1900. "Then as I expect to make this place my home for about three-fourths of my waking hours, I want things bright and cheerful myself." The building contained a gymnasium, and it appears that individual lockers and improved lavatory arrangements for employees were just as important for Boyer as the production equipment. A former employee remembered Boyer touring his factory almost every week and "greeted the workingmen at their benches, cordially and with a smiling face, and gave them great comfort by his personal interest." While Boyer vowed his company would never be a closed union shop, which would hamper his relations with his employees, he followed local machinists' union standards regarding hours and pay.[14]

Visitors from abroad observed this philosophy at work in Boyer's operation. British Member of Parliament and millionaire manufacturer Archibald White Maconochie toured the factory in October 1902 and, according to a newspaper account, said that in terms of size, cleanliness, and organization, it was probably the finest such facility he had ever seen. Furthermore, he remarked he had "never seen such care taken for the comfort of the workmen."[15]

Maconochie became chairman of the European branch of CPT, Consolidated Pneumatic Tool, and used his influence to locate its works in Fraserburgh, Scotland, the following year. Billed as a "duplicate" of the Detroit shop, Mullgardt claimed credit for the design, and this may be justified to the extent that the Boyer shop area precedent, with its Boyer roof, was followed. Archival material reveals that Kahn created the drawings for the entire Fraserburgh complex, however, and they contain much original work. This is particularly true of the two-story office building, which has no equivalent in the Detroit shop, and the glazing of the gable ends of the shop area. The latter results in a work area that looks like a greenhouse. Given this, the Fraserburgh works are significant as Kahn's first commission off the North American

Consolidated Pneumatic Tool Company Works, Fraserburgh, Scotland (1903). Albert Kahn, architect. Postcard view, circa 1902, by W. R. Melvin, collection of the author.

continent. It is also his earliest extant industrial design, although as of this writing the shop area with its Boyer roof has been demolished.[16]

The following summer, Dr. Frank Daliard, appointed by the French government to inquire into the lives and working conditions of the American workman, visited CPT and other Detroit factories. It appears that the prevailing opinion in Europe was that workers in the United States toiled under conditions that would be unacceptable in the Old World. (This is the reverse of Nettleton's 1889 opinion.) According to the *Detroit Free Press*, Daliard said "his investigations had taught him the lesson that it is not safe to rely on rumors and reports" regarding poor working conditions in America. He was "highly pleased and surprised" by the sanitary conditions and "the evident desire to provide every suitable convenience for the men." The article continued: "The feature that struck him as the most interesting and unique is the absence of the dividing line between the foreman and the workmen when it comes to social intercourse. He remarked that the American manner of treating the workingmen is such as to instill in them a degree of self-respect and independence unknown in European factories."[17]

While this Golden Rule philosophy may not have been universally implemented in all Detroit workplaces, it was often found in companies where the owner worked his way up from the shop floor and could empathize with those still there. Such opportunity for social advancement was practically unheard of in the Old World, but Detroit had an abundance of examples at the time. In addition, other companies surely found themselves needing to adopt the Golden Rule as a way to compete for higher quality employees.

Kahn would later quote John Ruskin as declaring that, while a manufacturer's duty is to always consider "how to produce what he sells in the best and cheapest form," it is also his responsibility to ensure the process is "most beneficial to the men involved." Applying this to his own business, Kahn continued, "Architecture involves the production of that which proves not only of utilitarian but also of aesthetic value; and things beautiful are most easily produced under agreeable and pleasing circumstances." He strove to operate an office environment "wherein each one, from the office boy to the chief designer, is encouraged to feel the importance of his position."[18]

As another self-made individual, Kahn may have already embraced this philosophy toward worker welfare when he connected with Boyer, but from that time on their association benefited each other, their employees, and future factory design.

The Palms Apartments and Julius Kahn's Return to Detroit

Mason & Kahn took out a building permit in May 1901 for an upscale apartment building designed for Dr. James Burgess Book. The $80,000, twenty-four–flat structure, named the Palms in recognition of Mrs. Book's original family, was reported as being "intended to be finer in every respect than anything of the kind heretofore attempted" in Detroit, and "strictly fireproof." The initial contract was let at that time and construction was expected to be completed by January 1, 1902. The project was delayed, and a new set of contracts were let in August 1901, with construction expected to start shortly thereafter.[19]

The archived drawings note they were revised from December 7, 1901, through January 21, 1902. This places revisions concurrent with arrangements for the dissolution of Mason & Kahn.[20]

It appears no reason for the delay was ever published, but it is tempting to speculate, with evidence, that it involved the fireproof construction. The threat of fire plagued urban life through the nineteenth century and builders responded with the development of fire-resistant construction, also called mill construction or heavy timber construction. While adding to the construction expense, thick timbers could span larger areas and, in the event of fire, burned relatively slowly while retaining their structural integrity longer. These qualities made heavy timber popular for mill structures, allowing for larger work areas, more time for evacuation in a fire, and greater likelihood that firefighters could prevent a total loss. The term fireproof was applied to construction with materials that were impervious to flame, such as steel frame and masonry (of course, the building's contents were susceptible to burning, which could still damage the structure). The Palms was promoted from its onset as being strictly fireproof, implying the client expected steel construction, which was expensive and difficult to obtain, or reinforced concrete, which was still considered an experimental method reserved for industrial applications. It is therefore possible that challenges surrounding the fireproof construction requirement caused the delay. In contrast, Kahn's Woodward apartments, begun at the same time and a project similar in scope but of traditional construction, was leasing by January 1902.[21]

As noted, the Palms was still under construction at the dissolution of Mason & Kahn, announced on February 23, 1902, with Kahn committed to bringing the apartment building to completion. Mason and Kahn had agreed to end the partnership a month earlier, which coincided with the return to Detroit of Kahn's brother Julius, a civil engineer who had been working abroad.[22]

Julius was born at Münstereifel on March 8, 1874, while the Kahn family roamed about the war-torn tempest that was Europe's Rhineland region. Five years younger than Albert, he attended public schools in Detroit following the family's immigration to the United States, then earned a bachelor of science in civil engineering from the University of Michigan in 1896. From there he worked as a draftsperson for the Union Bridge Company of Athens, Pennsylvania, in 1896; draftsperson for the Brooklyn Navy Yard and assistant engineer for the Bushwick Iron Works in Brooklyn in 1897; and began a position as assistant engineer for the C. W. Hunt Company of New York City, which included field work with coal handling equipment in Lake Linden, Michigan, in 1898. Meanwhile, he studied in absentia to receive a civil engineering degree from the University of Michigan in 1899. He was in New York in January 1900 when he wrote to Albert about the latter's visit to the city, but soon after departed for a position as general manager for the mining company Futayamo Shokai, in Tokyo.[23]

In January 1902 Julius was back in Detroit, where he eventually opened a practice as a consulting engineer in Albert's suite of offices atop the Union Trust Building. Working together at times, within weeks they won a contract for the design of a warehouse and elevating works for a coal and ice company. According to the March 16, 1902, announcement, Julius intended to specialize "in the design and superintendence of structural steel works, bridges, buildings, viaducts, coal handling, hoisting and general conveying machinery."[24]

Significant, but overlooked by historians, was a 1903 newspaper profile stating that Julius had been working "upon an invention covering the use of cement in building construction and reducing to a minimum the amount of steel needed . . . *for several years*" (emphasis added).[25] If true, it seems he had already given significant thought to the matter long before returning to Detroit.

This challenges the story that has come down through the decades based on Albert's interviews. It holds that the subsequent collaboration between the two brothers resulted by chance as Julius casually considered the Palms apartment building while it was already under construction, or after its completion (accounts vary). Julius is said to have asked his brother, "How did you calculate the strength of the reinforced concrete?" Albert is said to have replied, "By guess. There is no scientific data." From there, as the story goes, Julius set his mind to the task of rationalizing the process and developed the famed Kahn Bar and Kahn System of reinforced concrete—but it was too late to be employed in the Palms.[26]

It appears, however, that Julius had come to town in January 1902 with an idea for reinforced concrete ready, or near ready, to test and the Kahn brothers used the Palms as an opportunity to apply the concept. In mid-April 1902 the *Detroit News-Tribune* carried a report that the city building inspector interrupted the work on the luxury apartment building to conduct "severe tests" on the reinforced concrete floors. The inspector loaded "six tons in the weakest place he could find, where one ton is all that will ever be placed on it, in all likelihood, and noting the lack of serious result, he concluded the floors would do." The plans simply called for expanded metal reinforcement of the concrete beams, and it could be argued that the future Kahn Bar (discussed in the next chapter), or a developmental version of it, met that stipulation. Such rigorous testing would be unnecessary if accepted reinforcement methods were used, however. It therefore seems reasonable to assume that a previously untried system was being validated as a reinforcement system in the Palms, requiring field assessment.[27]

Journalist Christy Borth added a tantalizing postscript to the story. In his 1945 profile, Borth wrote that "Kahn's daring innovation in the construction of the Palms Apartments, resulted in a commission," from Henry B. Joy, "to try out the new system in building a water tank for the Packard factory." Added to this is a 1957 account of the Palms that calls its construction method "revolutionary," going on to claim, "The strength of the foundations and superstructure, of the beams, walls and ceilings, was established after careful calculations made by Albert's engineer brother, Julius Kahn."[28]

At some point, Albert and Julius may have actually had the "no scientific data" exchange, but it may have been in January 1902 or perhaps even earlier in correspondence now lost. By the mid-April 1902 load tests, at any rate, some form of a new reinforcement method clearly found its way into the structure of the Palms. Kahn may have told this inexact version of events simply because he thought it more interesting, or he did not want to reveal that the brothers were experimenting on Dr. Book's building. As will be seen in the next chapter, the story crept out but apparently few cared, and the "no scientific data" tale prevailed until now.[29] As of this writing, over 120 years later, the six-story structure is still in use as an apartment building, providing further validation of the construction method. Indeed, the rigorous load testing may have been intended to prove the technology for uses beyond residential application.

An unsung aspect of the Belle Isle Aquarium & Horticultural Building is that it also was fitted with reinforced concrete floors concurrently with the Palms construction. The Belle Isle structure's contract for the "fireproofing and concreting" was put out to bid in September 1901. The available blueprints call for concrete floors with expanded metal reinforcement, resting on steel beams supported by brick walls and cast iron columns. A construction photograph taken around early June 1902 shows that the floors were not yet in place, so they would have been laid after the floors in the Palms. While George Mason superintended construction, he worked in concert with Kahn for the completion of the Belle Isle work and the exact manner of its concrete reinforcement is not known.[30] Like the Palms, it still solidly stands. Afterward, the Kahns returned to mill construction in building design while Julius perfected and patented his concept.

The Palms apartment building, Detroit, Michigan (1901–2). Mason & Kahn, architects. Photograph by the author, 2012.

The Metzger Automobile Repository

On April 27, 1902, the *Detroit News-Tribune* reported, "The most up-to-date automobile building in the country is that now being erected on the northeast corner of Jefferson Avenue and Brush Street, by Henry B. Joy, after plans by Architect Albert Kahn." Joy's tenant, William E. Metzger, explained that "the front and side walls of the first story and much of the second floor, will be taken up by plate glass windows, so that much light may be provided and an opportunity given for the display of automobiles."[31]

The automobile, an outgrowth of the cresting bicycle craze and an exclusive luxury of the wealthy, was capturing the interest of nearly everyone and appearing in urban landscapes around the globe. Everything about it seemed energized and entrepreneurs grappled for ways to find a profit in their manufacturing, sales, or service. Even the name of Metzger's new establishment was in flux as it opened August 18, 1902: it was alternately called a depot, an exchange, a repository, and a store. (Repository is used here as it seems the term Metzger preferred.) It and others like it would be the forerunners of automotive dealerships, but they dealt in vehicles from multiple manufacturers.[32]

Metzger was Detroit's leading bicycle merchant and a pioneering automobile enthusiast. He had traveled to Europe in 1895 to study the fledgling industry and within a few years began selling Waverly Electric Carriages in a Detroit shop. Other makes quickly followed that were powered by steam and gasoline engines. Sales soon demanded he find a larger space tailored to the unique demands of the business. Metzger toured similar establishments in America's large cities to determine the features he wanted in his repository, and these were communicated to Joy's architect, Kahn, to somehow accommodate within the 66- by 100-foot lot.[33]

Promoted as the best-lighted building in the city, the expansive window bays on its sixteen-foot ground floor and its thirteen-foot second floor were as impressive as any being heralded as progressive architecture in Chicago. Indeed, the windows of neighboring buildings seem almost medieval in comparison. This represents a noteworthy engineering achievement as the building was of traditional mill construction designed to bear an additional six stories. While only four (plus an attic) were added the following year, such forward vision for growth was typical of the automobile industry and

Metzger Automobile Repository Building, Detroit, Michigan (1902). Albert Kahn, architect. Line cut illustration from the *Detroit Free Press*, February 15, 1903.

Detroit. The architectural treatment was austere, brick with minimal limestone trim, providing little to distract from the vehicles displayed on the first floor. A galvanized steel cornice added once the expansion was completed was far removed from the merchandise at street level, so it did not compete for buyers' attention.[34]

Accommodating the infrastructure considerations was as challenging as the structural concerns. Heralded as the most up-to-date building for its purpose in the country, it was a bit of a technical wonder inside, with the first floor given over to the display of forty automobiles of assorted makes and models ranging from roustabouts to heavy family carriages. A large turntable in the floor facilitated arrangement of the automobiles. The largest electrically powered elevator in the city, 18.5 by 14 feet and designed to accommodate any automobile then on the market, transported vehicles vertically (a smaller elevator accommodated passengers). Automobiles were cleaned utilizing a wash rack with the latest accessories in the basement, where tires were also stored. The second floor featured a club room suite along the Jefferson Avenue front, separated from ten of the largest modern rheostats for charging electric vehicles in the area behind. A machine shop and service areas for gasoline vehicles were on the third floor and the fourth was given to servicing electric vehicles. The two additional floors were available for storage and light manufacturing. The structure was acclaimed in national automotive journals.[35]

According to *Cycle and Automobile Trade Journal*, in 1903 Metzger was recognized as "one of the most successful and widely known cycle and automobile dealers in the United States." Known in some circles as "the Amazing Billy Metzger," he was a master salesman who understood his clientele, being one of the founders of the recently formed Automobile Club of Detroit—all motoring enthusiasts frankly described in a history of the organization as a collection of "rich men's sons." Metzger offered the second-story club room as its headquarters. After a long automobile jaunt or one of the competitive races in their open-air vehicles, members could avail themselves of the suite to shower the dust and oil away before changing into fresh attire stored in their personal lockers. It was reported that "members find it a splendid lounging place in case anything is wrong with their car and the repair men at Metzger's are working on it." Overlooking Jefferson Avenue, the spacious windows made the quarters "bright in daytime. While at night the many clusters of incandescent bulbs make the appearance even more cheerful." Henry Joy was a member and so were others he would soon persuade to join in investing in the Packard Motor Car Company.[36]

There appears no significant prior connection between Kahn and Metzger, so one assumes this commission came through Joy, who owned the property and was building the structure for his tenant. As noted above, it seems Kahn's only previous work for Joy was a home remodeling—hardly an indicator of the capabilities demanded by the design for what became one of the largest automobile repositories in the country.[37] Joy's faith in Kahn was well placed, and the repository proved a harbinger of a new age that was dawning. Detroit would supply its metaphorical horizon.

9

Another Class of Architects Must Arise

Earlier chapters have discussed Kahn's informal mentorships in art and architecture, augmented by his own studies and on-the-job education. Looking back later in life, Kahn also recognized that "my education was furthered by association with men of high attainment."[1] These associations were numerous, so it is risky to attach too much importance to any single client, with the exception of Joseph Boyer, who was introduced in the preceding chapter.

The architect spoke little of Boyer publicly, perhaps because their financial interests were intertwined, as will be discussed. Boyer also may not have wanted to advertise his record of assisting promising entrepreneurs such as Burroughs, Leland, and the Kahns lest it trigger a greater flood of assistance-seekers. Another possible explanation is that while Boyer was well-known and highly respected among industrialists, he did not receive the public attention showered upon the so-called auto barons. While Boyer's signature products—pneumatic hammers and, later, adding machines—were revolutionary, they failed to capture public imagination in the way the horseless carriage had.

When speaking to journalists, Kahn shrewdly highlighted two high-profile automobile manufacturers in nearly every account of the start of his career: the Packard Motor Car Company, which dominated the luxury end of America's automotive field, and the Ford Motor Company (FMC), whose economy-priced Model T became ubiquitous on the nation's roads. He often expressed his indebtedness to those companies' heads, Henry B. Joy and Henry Ford, respectively. Kahn's largest customer was unquestionably FMC, but his office likely would still have been one of the nation's largest without any of that automaker's voluminous business. As for Joy, he himself once corrected Kahn's effusive praise for him by affably stating, "You would have been just as big as you are if I had never been born!"[2]

Of course, Kahn had a multitude of other clients and valued associations, some of which will be discussed in the pages ahead. Key roles were also played by family members, beginning with brother Julius after his return to Detroit. In newspaper mentions over the following few years, Julius was variously described as an engineer, a consulting engineer, an architect, an associate of Albert, and as a partner of Albert.

Superior Match

News of a totally original factory design for Albert Kahn, working with Julius, was published in February 1903. It was the works for the Superior Match Company, of which Boyer was president. It may be difficult today to appreciate how competitive and technically challenging wooden stick match manufacturing was at the time, but they were used everywhere, and production relied on a combination of machine and hand work. With low-cost matches much in demand, the efficiency of the process largely determined the success of a business. Superior Match was touted as having the patent on a new automated process and its new Detroit operation promised to be one of the best of its kind in the world. Kahn surely worked closely with the inventor of the process and the production manager as the single-story factory, totaling 18,400 square feet of floor space in several structures, were planned.[3] Some aspects of the design are echoed in Kahn's original work for Fraserburgh.

All of the buildings were exceedingly fire resistant—a key consideration given the highly combustible materials that went into the product, combined with heated paraffin. Their steel structures were enclosed with vitrified tile, built upon cement floors with steel trussed roofs. The main factory building was 60 by 200 feet, with heavy walls separating the match-making room and box-making department. A boiler house and fuel room powered the work.[4]

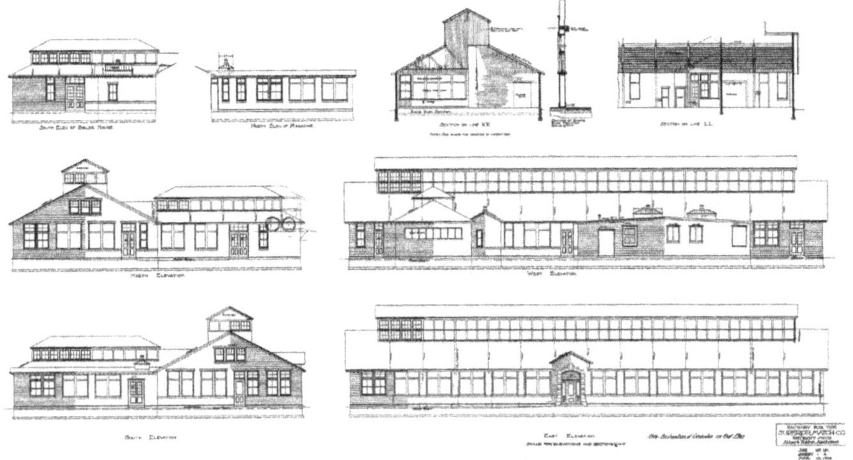

Superior Match Company Plant, Detroit, Michigan (1902). Albert Kahn, architect. Office drawing courtesy Albert Kahn Associates, Inc.

In the words of a business journal a few years later, exterior walls were "pierced by broad and deep windows, glazed with rough wire-reinforced glass, furnishing abundant light." Generously large lights designed into a monitor atop a gabled roof provided natural illumination and ventilation for the main building. Like the Belle Isle structure, the Superior Match main building was a long structure on a north-south axis, allowing the sun to illuminate both sides of the monitor as it crossed the sky during the day. In Boyer's spirit of the Golden Rule, the works featured individual lockers for each employee and modern, improved lavatory facilities. Figures on its employment vary, but at the business's 1909 dissolution the workforce numbered 60.[5]

Packard

Enthusiasm for the automobile led Henry Joy to assemble a group of Detroit investors in October 1902 to purchase controlling interest in a Warren, Ohio, automobile company started by the Packard Brothers. Most of Joy's fellow investors were, like him, young, second-generation Detroit millionaires known as the Princes of Griswold Street. Some were brothers and, like Joy, former students of the Michigan Military Academy in Orchard Lake. Representing Metzger's prime early automobile customers who lounged in the second-floor club room of his new automobile repository, they were eager to establish their own business legacies separate from those of their fathers.[6]

The one exception in their ranks was Joseph Boyer. The oldest among the investors, this son of a none-too-successful Canadian farmer and a recent migrant to the city appears to have been an odd fit with the princes: he was described in a 1906 profile as "a plain man, very plain [but] with a lot of horse sense." He had already managed to quickly make a favorable impression in Detroit, however. For example, in January 1901 Mayor Maybury formed the Detroit Industrial Bureau (with himself as the president) to attract more manufacturing. Although it had only been a year since Boyer announced he was moving to Detroit, the city's other manufacturers voted to make him the bureau's vice-president.[7] Joy did well in attracting him to Packard; while the other investors brought funding and enthusiasm for the product, Boyer brought solid production and production management experience.

According to Kahn, it was Boyer and Joy who championed his selection as architect for the new Detroit plant of the Packard Motor Car Company. Again, this was quite an expression of confidence in the newly independent architect, for they planned to build one of the largest automobile factories in the country.[8]

In April 1903 Albert and Julius Kahn began designing the plant, working with Packard's manufacturing manager, Charles J. Moore, and perhaps Boyer. Like many in the nascent automobile industry, Moore came from a background in bicycle manufacturing and produced his own steam car before signing on with Packard. Given his experience, it is difficult to deduce how much of the resulting plant was Moore's concept, or either of the Kahns, or a full collaboration. That said, the plant's design, utilizing natural lighting and ventilation, reflected attributes of the architect's recent work. Although the vehicles would be hand-assembled, some sort of flow production was envisioned. A newspaper account reports that in "planning these buildings the skill of the engineer has been drawn upon in order that there may be a no time lost in handling the material from the time that it enters at one end of the plant, in the rough, until it is turned out at the other end a finished product."[9]

The initial plant was a hollow square measuring 400 by 400 feet and, for the most part, two stories in height. Traditional mill construction enclosed two acres of floor space and maximum clearance spans within the work areas were typical for the day, 16 by 25 feet. Nevertheless, it drew praise for the abundant natural lighting of the relatively narrow production wings and an aggressive heating and ventilation system that augmented double-hung windows and provided a complete exchange of air every thirty minutes. Also noteworthy were the lavatory and locker facilities for six hundred workers, allowing them to store their clothes and lunches in a well-ventilated area while on the job. Given the ambitious nature and size of the undertaking, construction was remarkably swift. A mere ninety days lapsed between signing the construction contract and turning the property over to the owners.[10]

The die of Kahn's career seems to have been cast with the commission for the Packard Plant. Its construction ran $117,000, establishing it as Kahn's first project to exceed the Belle Isle Aquarium & Horticultural Building in building cost. Even before the construction contract was let the Kahns announced they would be "making a specialty of heavy factory and mill construction, paying especial attention to working out the details of difficult engineering and architectural propositions." With the addition of the giant Packard plant to a pool of smaller enterprises, Detroit became home to 60 percent of the automobile manufacturing in the United States. The potential growth of the infant industry captivated minds in Detroit, and Kahn's name was now directly associated with it as the designer of its most prominent factory. Kahn later described Joy as "my patron saint"—but the automaker certainly had company.[11]

Packard Motor Car Company Plant, Detroit, Michigan (1903). Albert Kahn, architect, and Julius Kahn, engineer. Photograph of original construction courtesy National Automotive Collection, Detroit Public Library.

Packard Motor Car Company Plant interior photograph showing original construction. While using traditional mill construction, attention was given to significantly increasing natural light and ventilation. Courtesy National Automotive Collection, Detroit Public Library.

Designing for Industry

Declaring specialization in factory and mill construction proved to be a decisive pronouncement: at the time Detroit was in the throes of radical change that bifurcated its architectural market. A new generation of factories approaching the scale of Packard was becoming more common, consuming the lion's share of building materials and construction labor and driving up building costs. As a result, projects between $3,000 and $50,000 that were considered medium-priced and the bread and butter of the profession began to dwindle despite the prosperous times. Detroit was experiencing a construction boom, but, as one prominent (yet sadly unnamed) Detroit architect lamented, "it is just the sort of building that does not benefit the local architect or contractor. . . . The construction of these immense buildings requires a knowledge of engineering which many of our contractors do not possess, making it necessary to bring men here from other cities who make a specialty of this kind of work."[12]

Albert was competent at engineering, and he allied with Julius at a crucial moment to make industrial architecture his specialty and himself an exception among his peers. (Kahn brothers Moritz, Louis, and Felix also became civil engineers. Moritz and Louis would have significant roles in Albert's office in the future. Felix found his destiny in California construction.) It should be noticed that there were other architects and firms, such as George D. Mason, and Smith, Hinchman & Grylls, that also managed to secure industrial commissions in the years ahead, but they were among the outliers in their profession.

Kahn later blamed the architectural profession, on the national level, for abandoning this lucrative—but increasingly challenging—field in the early 1900s. It required a collaborative design effort responding to distinct demands in workflow, utility, material, structure, labor, and other areas. To meet the challenge, Kahn began building a multidisciplinary office around himself. A seminal early hire, in 1903, was Ernest Wilby. Born in Yorkshire County, England, and brought by his parents to Canada at the age of four in 1872, Wilby returned to Yorkshire for his education at Wesley College and gained experience in architectural offices in England and Canada. His value in the highly proficient Kahn organization was recognized by his being designated an associate beginning in 1905. Years afterward, Kahn remarked, "Possessed of the highest ideals, excellent judgement and a rare sense of the practical, such acclaim as our work subsequently received was in large measure due to Mr. Wilby."[13]

Midwives to modernity, Kahn, his employees, and their clients found themselves increasingly on the cutting edge of society's trends due to the demands of their work. The architect balanced the pragmatic needs of his clients with aesthetic considerations, causing his employees to continually reevaluate the parameters of their craft.

Looking back at this time, Kahn explained in 1918,

> Architects, as a class, failed to heed the trend of the times. Only grudgingly would they allow the utilitarian to enter into the building program. Modern ideas were all right if they did not trespass upon artistic concepts. Modern requirements had the unhappy habit of interfering with preconceived ideas of beauty. But the new methods were economically sound and practically sane, so they advanced under their own impetus,

> and if conservative Architects would not adapt themselves to new conditions, then another class must arise who would.[14]

As Kahn embraced the changing demands of his times his firm became the model of this new class.

The Kahn Bar and the Kahn System

Meanwhile, Julius continued efforts related to his system of concrete reinforcement. His design augmented reinforcing bar with angled struts to prevent shear—the tendency for the steel bar to move once it inevitably separates from the surrounding matrix. After applying for a patent in December 1902, he traveled east the following June and July to explore a way of receiving revenue from it. His correspondence with Albert back in Detroit makes it clear the two were partners in the venture. While traveling, he continued to develop his ideas and sent Albert a sketch of a concept for a system of concrete flooring utilizing rows of hollow terra cotta tile alternating with rows of his reinforcement bar. These would be set into shallow forms and covered with concrete to form sturdy slabs of flooring that were 30 percent lighter, with reduced material cost, than solid, reinforced concrete floors of equal strength.[15]

From the investigations during his travels, Julius concluded that the surest way to protect his intellectual property while generating revenue was to form a company that worked with clients to engineer and build reinforced concrete structures. He was granted a patent for his Kahn Bar on August 2, 1903, and soon the Kahn brothers were employing it in a storage shed for the Great Northern Portland Cement Company in Marlboro, Michigan.[16]

Trussed Concrete Steel Company

Julius separated from his somewhat nebulous association with Albert's architectural firm in October to form the Trussed Concrete Steel Company, which incorporated on October 7, 1903, with $200,000 in capital. Julius naturally became the company's president. Albert was a director. Bringing valuable

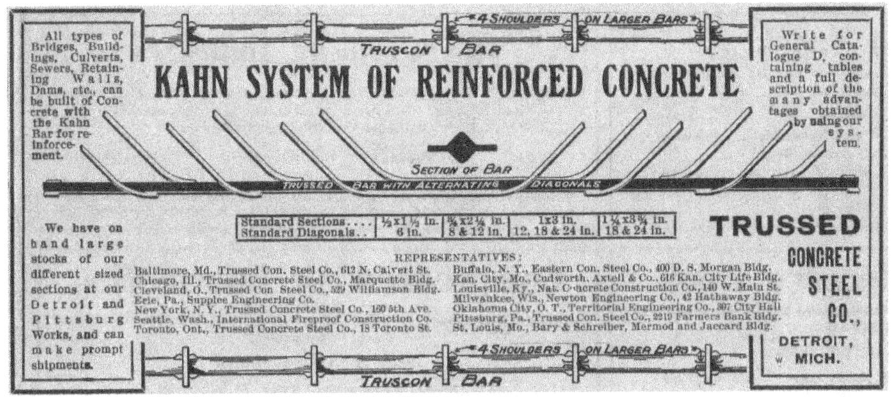

Detail of an illustration of the Kahn Bar from an advertisement for Trussed Concrete Steel Company, circa 1905, collection of the author.

expertise, Joseph Boyer served as vice-president for the next seventeen years. According to a 1922 history of the city, while Boyer was noted for his mechanical talent and accomplishments as an inventor, "it has been the force of his initiative and administrative as well as his great executive ability that has brought him to his position of prominence in the business world." The Kahns would greatly benefit in their ventures from his involvement.[17]

In February 1904 Julius received a patent for the Kahn System for flooring based upon the idea presented in the sketch he sent to Albert from the road. Uses for the Kahn System of reinforced concrete construction were swift to arise. A March 2, 1904, announcement of a three-story building in Cleveland may signal its first publicized use. Interestingly, the architect was not Albert Kahn but a Cleveland practitioner, George H. Smith, codesigner of the charming 1890 Cleveland Arcade.[18] The Kahn System was heavily advertised and soon other architects in Detroit and other cities were specifying its use.

The system surely played a role in Albert Kahn's prevailing in the competition for a post office in Battle Creek, Michigan, where he bested John Scott & Company and five other firms. Submissions were judged by James Knox Taylor, Supervising Architect of the United States Treasury, and two others in Washington, DC. Kahn's entry featured the Kahn System in the reinforced concrete construction with steel trusses supporting the roof over the work area.[19]

The Trussed Concrete Steel Company was off and running. So much so, by 1907 the company could claim projects such as the world's longest railway

United States Post Office, Battle Creek, Michigan (1906–8). Albert Kahn, architect, and Ernest Wilby, associate. Postcard view of workroom by Tom Jones, circa 1912, collection of the author.

viaduct (twenty-eight hundred feet) in Richmond, Virginia, and had four agents abroad, two in Europe and two in South America. The London office was headed (from 1907 to 1923) by Moritz Kahn, brother to Albert and Julius. Two years later, Julius's products were being used for the principal floors and roofing (carried on forty-foot arches) of the National Gallery in London.[20] Albert was not involved in these projects beyond his role as a director in the company, but he had been generating applications in Detroit and elsewhere as an architect. Significant among these was another major industrial gift conferred upon the city by Boyer.

10

Revolutionizing the Art of Building

Chapter 8 showed how Joseph Boyer single-handedly bolstered Detroit's status as an industrial power in 1900 by relocating his large, thriving manufacturing concern, with its hundreds of well-paid, skilled workers, there. In March 1904 Detroit newspapers jubilantly reported that he was about to do it again.[1]

Boyer had been an influence in, if not directly responsible for, all of Kahn's commissions in industrial architecture so far. In bringing a second, burgeoning St. Louis business to Detroit, Boyer handed Albert Kahn an opportunity to display his capabilities, while showcasing Julius's concrete reinforcement technology in which all three were now invested.

The American Arithmometer Plant

The American Arithmometer Company (AAC) began producing the Burroughs Adding Machine in St. Louis. As mentioned in chapter 8, Boyer provided crucial support to William S. Burroughs, a bookkeeper who, in the early 1880s, conceived an automated mechanism for accounting tasks. There was a major challenge in making it both reliable and relatively easy to use by office workers, however. At the time, it seemed a quixotic quest, but Burroughs quit regular employment to pursue his dream, renting workbench space in Boyer's first machine shop in St. Louis. Long after Burroughs's funds ran out and his health waned, Boyer continued his support with shop space, equipment, and skilled assistance. Burroughs secured patents in 1885 and AAC formally organized in 1888 with Burroughs as president. Boyer joined the board of directors as vice-president in 1898. Later that year, Burroughs died at the age of forty-one following a long battle with tuberculosis, but he managed to leave the company on sound footing and his family well compensated. When Boyer moved his pneumatic tool business to Detroit in 1900, AAC took over the whole St. Louis factory site that the two businesses had previously shared. Boyer was elevated to president of AAC in 1902 and the business outgrew its location two years later.[2]

According to a 1922 account, "In 1904 conditions seemed to favor removal of the plant from St. Louis. Trade union domination in that city was a restriction upon the proper development of the concern. Also, Joseph Boyer used his influence to accomplish this removal to a more advantageous location." The move was made despite the company's having already purchased land in St. Louis for expansion, so the labor situation seems a significant issue in Detroit's favor. The directors also agreed to hire Albert Kahn to design a 1.6-acre plant to cost approximately $100,000.[3]

Work began in May 1904, and the plant became the most publicized use of the Kahn System up to then. An article in *American Architect and Building News* reported, "All parts of the shop are flooded with light, saw-tooth roofs making this possible. The general construction and sizes of these saw-teeth have proved very satisfactory." With fine machining a large part of the production, Kahn utilized a traditional sawtooth roof featuring seven-foot-high sashes where every other sash could swing on center pivots for ventilation when operated by geared apparatus. The 320- by 126-foot main block offered maximum spans of twenty feet, nine inches on their centers. These were smaller than the Packard plant's mill construction spans, but adequate for the company's products. The Kahn System showed promise with its fire resistant, vibration-deadening, and sound-deadening qualities.[4]

Reinforced concrete was becoming more attractive as suitable timber for mill construction was becoming scarce and the availability of structural steel, a cause of delay on the Belle Isle structure, was unsteady. According to a newspaper report, "The building is declared absolutely fireproof and it is said the company will carry no insurance." This statement surely caused other industrialists to take note of the technology: in 1901 the traditionally constructed

American Arithmometer Company Plant, Detroit, Michigan (1904). Albert Kahn, architect. The L. C. Mullgardt-designed portion of the Boyer Machine Company Shop is visible in the distant right in this photograph, circa 1905, courtesy Charles Babbage Institute, University of Minnesota.

Olds Motor Works plant in Detroit, less than a year old, was destroyed by a fast-moving fire resulting in a total loss, save one prototype Oldsmobile vehicle. The report on the AAC Plant continued, "This class of construction is of recent date and is said to be revolutionizing the building industry in the larger class of works."[5]

Another noteworthy aspect of this venture was the commitment to employee welfare. Like Boyer four years earlier, AAC general manager Alvan Macauley was charged with relocating a successful business from St. Louis to Detroit, which involved inducing valued employees to migrate along with it. Creating an attractive production environment at AAC was key, as it had been for the Boyer Machine Company Shop, just across Amsterdam Street from the new construction. (Macauley would become president of Packard in 1916 and commission Kahn to build his grand Grosse Pointe Shores residence in 1928.) According to the same *Detroit News-Tribune* report,

> The interior finish also carries out a comparatively new idea in factory buildings, presenting a shining surface of white enamel brick. Everything about the plant will be kept as spick and span. . . . Extensive arrangements will be carried out looking into the health, comfort and pleasure of the employees. The system adopted is similar to that in vogue at the Boyer plant of the Chicago Pneumatic Tool Co. There will be a large locker room

> with individual enameled lavatories and a gymnasium with shower baths in connection.

American Architect and Building News also mentioned AAC's Golden Rule approach to business, noting that the attention paid to employee "comfort and health has in this case proved itself of direct benefit to the owners as it has in most similar cases: good workmen from many other plants are continually seeking employment here. All are eager to become associated with this concern."[6]

They joined workers who had moved with the company from St. Louis, like the employees of the Boyer Machine Company, four years earlier. For the AAC move, the 1922 account continued, "Special trains brought the machinery, together with 253 families, to Detroit, arriving here in the afternoon. By means of arrangements made through the real estate committee of the board of trade, most of the people were comfortably housed the same night, many in places which they afterwards bought. This was one of the most remarkable 'hegiras' in manufacturing history."[7]

The Concrete Steel & Tile Construction Company

Despite examples of reinforced concrete being an effective and, in many ways, preferable alternative to mill and steel structures, many construction company owners balked at embracing the new building method. It involved an investment in training and equipment while posing unfamiliar risks if improperly employed. In order to prod acceptance of the new technology by builders and their clients, the Concrete Steel & Tile Construction Company organized on October 29, 1904, "to do general engineering and construction business." Among the incorporators, the largest shareholders were Albert, with 548 shares, and Julius, with 242. Among the other participants were Boyer and Mason, with 50 and 10 shares, respectively. Boyer sold his Packard stock at a loss in 1904, and the story has endured that he was unsatisfied with the company's performance (its value skyrocketed shortly thereafter).[8] It is also possible the sale was to eliminate any conflicts created by his involvement with the Kahn companies that were building reinforced concrete structures for other automakers going forward.

Through his support, Boyer's role in both the success of the Kahns and the advancement of reinforced concrete was significant. Completed in mid-November 1905, George Mason's addition to the Cadillac Motor Car Company Plant was likely Concrete Steel & Tile's earliest building project. (Henry Leland, who suggested Boyer's original move to Detroit, was one of the Cadillac's directors and managing its production.) The construction firm followed it with building Albert Kahn's addition to the Packard plant and his new plants for George N. Piece and Ford Motor Companies (all discussed below). Concrete Steel & Tile's customer base was not limited to its investors, however, nor to industrial work. For instance, the firm executed a reinforced concrete restructuring for the interior of Detroit's Board of Trade Building in 1905 under Zach Rice as the architect.[9]

Boyer continued to reinvest his capital in other Detroit companies, expanding his part in fueling the city's tremendous industrial growth.[10]

Packard Number Ten: Reconstructing the Narrative

Packard continued to grow and in late 1905 Henry Joy, now in full control of the company, again turned to Kahn when it came time to design a building that became known as Packard Number Ten. Of all of Kahn's commissions, this may be the most misrepresented, suffering through alternate narratives. Typically, these suggest that reinforced concrete represented an untested technology that Kahn, based on his faith in his brother, daringly proposed to Packard. In his problematic 1937 memoir, Kahn recalled that Joy gave him and his brother "our first chance to try out both [the Kahn Bar and the Kahn System]. . . . The Packard building led to the construction of the Burrough Adding Machine Co. plant." A 1940 account appearing in the *Detroit Free Press* tells of the "misgivings Kahn suffered when he presented the finished draft [when to] the amazement of the directors, Kahn's plans called for a building of reinforced concrete." Somehow, the directors overcame their amazement and approved what, as the story goes, was an unprecedented construction method.[11]

The name Burroughs was not in use as the business name yet, but nonetheless, AAC's plant was already complete so *it* led to the construction of Packard Number Ten—it was not the other way around. Neither was this the first chance for the Kahns to try their bar or system. Then there was the matter of a reinforced concrete tank that Joy had Kahn build to test the Kahn Bar or a prototype of it. Both Helen Christine Bennett (in 1927) and Christy Borth (1945) cite Kahn as saying the bar had been tested on a tank for Joy prior to its use in Number Ten. Borth places this as being after the load tests on the Palms apartment building in April 1902; Bennett puts it after the patent award in August 1903. "Then we had to get a chance to try it out," Bennett quotes Kahn as saying. "I had done work for Henry B. Joy, and he gave us a chance to try it in a tank. It seemed to hold all right, and Mr. Joy ordered me to build the Packard Building."[12] Assuming these mutually supportive accounts are essentially accurate despite their slight variation, the tank was in use and performing to Joy's satisfaction for over a year prior to Kahn's October 1905 presentation of the Number Ten plans to the Packard directors. With the acclaim of the AAC Plant and a direct competitor in the luxury automobile market, Cadillac, in the process of building a Kahn System addition nearby, it is clear that Joy, if not the entire board of directors, went into the meeting *expecting* to see a design for a reinforced concrete structure, rather than being surprised by it.

As noted, traditional mill construction was used on the Packard plant built in 1903, after the Palms test. Perhaps the Kahns were not ready to use the not-yet-patented methods in such a high profile commission as the Packard plant. It is also possible that Joy wanted to let others (AAC and Cadillac, as it turned out) prove its viability before committing to the new technology—but was willing to experiment with it on a water tank in the meantime.

So it seems that there was no particular drama surrounding Number Ten, at least no more than for any other pitch before a big client. There are other versions of the meeting that seem to have details confused with other projects, such as the Ford Highland Park Plant, or give faulty sequences of events. Multiple sources attest to Kahn's remarkable memory when it came to architecture, enabling him to ferret out inconsistencies in details between drawings or call up a precedent from a particular page in a particular book in the office library.[13] It is hard to reconcile this with the faulty and inconsistent accounts of the erection of Number Ten. Perhaps Kahn simply did not value accuracy in reminiscences as much as he did in matters related to work before him on the office drawing tables.

Despite inconsistencies regarding the Number Ten backstory, and some false claims—not by Kahn—of its primary status over the years (as the first reinforced concrete factory building; Kahn's first factory building, concrete or otherwise; the first reinforced concrete automobile factory building; etc.), there is one area where Number Ten did represent a significant milestone: its clear spans between columns. The Packard board showed laudable faith in approving the design with its daring, thirty-two-foot clear spans for a multistory manufacturing building. (As noted above, AAC's maximum spans were twenty feet, nine inches. The Cadillac addition featured twenty-four-foot spans. Maximum spans with mill construction, like the original Packard construction, were twenty-five feet.) Transverse girders made it possible to eliminate every other column in Number Ten, creating then remarkable 30- by 60-foot clear floor spaces in a multistory building. In this respect, Number Ten was truly groundbreaking and an expression of confidence in the Kahn System by the architect, engineer, and client. According to Bennett, Kahn confided, "I was scared stiff when I tackled it."[14] If true, his fears were surely over the width of the clear spans that made Number Ten noteworthy, because everything else had essentially been done before and proven sound.

Packard Motor Car Company Plant continuing construction. Interior photograph showing construction utilizing the Kahn System, 1910. Image from *The Packard*, July 29, 1910, courtesy National Automotive History Collection, Detroit Public Library.

In addition to the generous clear spans, Number Ten featured large window openings, which Kahn filled nearly to the ceilings with double-hung glazing to minimize obstruction, flooding the work areas with natural light and ventilation. A short skirting of brick rising from the floor level to the window sills cast minimal shadow as it carried steam piping and other utilities around the periphery of the work area.[15]

It seems the architectural and engineering journals paid slight notice to Number Ten initially, but the business community was captivated. The benefits of the Kahn System were so readily apparent that Packard started replacing the majority of its earlier, mill construction buildings with new, higher, more fire-resistant and more spacious structures of reinforced concrete. Joy wrote that in the next two years Packard "added to our factory upwards of 250,000 sq. ft. of floor space of the Trussed Concrete Steel Company's construction," and in 1907 had "in process upwards of 100,000 sq. ft. more." Among the benefits, "shop light conditions are much better with the Kahn system of concrete construction than with brick work, because the piers are smaller."[16]

Hundreds of manufacturers visited Detroit after the completion of Number Ten to marvel at the Packard plant and plan their own new buildings. By 1908 the Packard Plant grew nearly six times larger than its original construction to contain over fourteen acres of floorspace. Joy's company had the largest

Packard Motor Car Company employees in a courtyard of the plant. A portion of the original 1903 mill construction is still standing on the left side of this retouched photograph, 1915, with newer reinforced concrete construction visible in the center distance and on the right. Courtesy National Automotive Collection, Detroit Public Library.

automotive plant in the world and Kahn was its architect.[17] Now the pace was quickening even more.

The industry itself was accelerating. Previously, proponents of electricity, gasoline, and steam vied to make theirs the preferred mode of powering automobiles. No sooner had gasoline essentially won out than Henry Ford democratized what had been a high-end, luxury market item by producing dependable but less expensive products for the masses. Not only was the automobile being continually redefined, so were the methods of producing it. Innovation and change were the watchwords, and Packard was not unique in continual reinvention of its manufacturing facilities. Some automakers began taking orders for more vehicles than they had the capacity to make, hoping they could use the revenue to build more efficient or greater capacity facilities in time to meet delivery promises. Where just a few years earlier a manufacturer might be content producing ten vehicles a day, in many cases success now required producing over a hundred.[18]

These factors combined to make the automotive industry a fertile source of repeat work for the right sort of architect. Some of Kahn's peers were still pursuing industrial work, but he was doubtless rare in his ability to cope with the volatility and demands of automobile manufacture. This created almost limitless opportunity for Kahn, but he needed to continue building a responsive organization around himself. Choreographing design and material availability with fast-paced construction was becoming imperative in the success of large projects.

George N. Pierce Company

As an example of the need for flexibility, the George N. Pierce Company in Buffalo, New York, was in the process of separating its new automobile venture from its core bicycle business. It had engaged the long-established architectural and engineering firm of Lockwood, Greene & Company, with experience in mill construction dating back to the 1830s, to design the new automobile works. It appears the Packard work inspired the Pierce building committee to reconsider its plans. In April 1906 the committee essentially ordered the architects to work with Albert Kahn as associate architect with equal status going forward on the project. The subsequent work was a collaboration of Lockwood, Greene & Company, Kahn and Trussed Concrete Steel, with Buffalo architect George Cary designing the eclectically ornamented administration building. Trussed Concrete Steel was responsible for the structural engineering and superintendence of construction for the entire plant. Beyond that, it becomes difficult to determine who was responsible for what on the project. The Concrete Steel & Tile Construction Company served as the general contractor, erecting the buildings in six months, about one-third of the time quoted for doing the work in steel or mill construction.[19]

It is regrettable that attribution is so muddied, since this fascinating plant was significantly different from most anything before it, including the Packard plant. Set on fifteen acres of the former Pan-American Exposition grounds, the eight buildings of the works had room to expand. The three-story, barrel-arched administration building also served as the "welfare building" and connected to the other structures through underground tunnels, ensuring that commerce between the buildings would not be impeded by the notorious Buffalo winters. Kahn Bar reinforced the concrete arches, forming the sixty-seven-foot width of the building, demonstrating the versatility of Julius's invention.[20]

Beyond the administration building, the mostly one-story walls of the plant structures contained remarkable amounts of glass. The assembly building was 327 by 402 feet with its roof supported by reinforced concrete bents. Unencumbered by the need to support live loads on floors above, these bents formed vast, sixty-one-foot clear spans with a sawtooth roof providing ample natural lighting from above. Double-hung sashes and rooftop globe ventilators provided natural ventilation.[21]

Fire-Resistant Offices

In 1905 Kahn proclaimed, "Reinforced concrete is revolutionizing the art of building," while the growth of industry drove all sorts of construction in Detroit: "A better class of building than heretofore constructed is the demand generally, and fire-proof construction is becoming much more general. The advent of reinforced concrete, with its wonderful fire-resisting and non-corroding

George N. Pierce Company Plant, Buffalo, New York (1906–7). Lockwood, Greene & Company, architects, and Albert Kahn, associate. Interior image of the assembly building by Trussed Concrete Steel Company, collection of the author.

properties, has much to do with this." Without mentioning the Kahn System by name, he crowed,

> Detroit boasts the invention of a system of reinforcement for concrete which is now being used far and wide, and which has been acknowledged by engineers throughout the world as the most scientific and practical ever designed.
>
> Undoubtedly Detroit will become one of the principal homes of concrete construction.[22]

The fact that Albert and Julius Kahn called the city home had much to do with fulfilling this prophecy, but there were other significant factors. Michigan's old-growth lumber resources for mill construction were dwindling and new material and methods were needed. While steel was a popular material, prices were high and sources were undependable at the time due to high demand and labor issues. Beneath the soil throughout Michigan, however, there were deposits exceptionally rich in the ingredients for superior concrete.

Detroit's construction market came to depend on reinforced concrete once builders acquired proficiency with the material. Work extended elsewhere, as well: in 1906 Kahn spoke of being able "to keep a large force of draughtsmen busy, almost exclusively, on plans for concrete work in Detroit and other cities."[23]

This included the eight-story Trussed Concrete Building in Detroit. The latter served as the headquarters for Julius Kahn's engineering and construction material company until he relocated to Youngstown in 1914. It was home to Albert's architectural firm from 1907 until 1916 and renamed the Owen Building in 1914.[24]

Another fine illustration is the reinforced concrete Palmer Building from 1910, with a façade of ornamented glazed white terra cotta and generous glass frankly expressing the grid of the Kahn System construction within. It is as effective in expressing its structure as the more celebrated steel-supported creations of the so-called Chicago School architects. The first floor of the 100- by

Palmer Building, Detroit, Michigan (1910). Albert Kahn, architect, and Ernest Wilby, associate. Photograph courtesy Albert Kahn Associates, Inc.

100-foot, six-story structure was trimmed with limestone and ornamental ironwork with a marquee for its storefronts. Its two light courts provided natural illumination and ventilation for the interior spaces.[25]

Verticality is stressed with Kahn's tallest skyscraper from this period, the eighteen-story Kresge Building built in 1913–14. Reinforced concrete construction was usually considered not cost effective above eight stories, so this building was designed with a steel frame and concrete floors clothed in white glazed brick and white lustrous glazed terra cotta. The first two floors of the Adams Street façade were designed with ornamental iron to announce their retail function; the third floor is set off with horizontal banding. Above that base, a pronounced verticality takes over the design as structural piers rise uninterrupted to the arcade beneath the cornice. Balustrades of iron fronting the windows on the fourth-floor level and masonry on the seventeenth are elegant touches that relieve the repetitious nature of the façade. Upper floors housed the offices of the S. S. Kresge Company and Kahn designed the lower floors to be occupied by physicians and dentists with enhanced plumbing and compressed air service. Large amounts of glass and an east side light court assured plenty of natural light and ventilation. As the *Michigan Technic* described it, the Kresge Building "illustrates thorough going modern design in an office building of to-day."[26]

Louis Sullivan's influential solution to skyscraper design, treating it as a column with a base, shaft and capital, was by this time over twenty years old and only partially embraced by Kahn. The Kresge structure has a definite base and shaft, but their elegant streamlining increases the delicate, soaring nature of the thing. In the pages of the journal *Architecture*, where the Kresge structure was deemed the most interesting of Detroit's tallest buildings, Kahn was credited for addressing "the real problem in every skyscraper, namely, how to stop it, in an unusual and interesting manner."[27] Where Sullivan relied on heavy, horizontal cornices serving as exaggerated capital abaci to visually terminate the upward thrust of his skyscrapers, Kahn allows his to simply transition into the air above with an attic level marked by the decorative diaper work and a relatively shallow relief band of molding for the low-pitched gable. This was a more rational solution since cornices, originally conceived to shield the windows and entrance below from rain, became ineffective at such heights. Kahn

Kresge Building, Detroit, Michigan (1913–14). Albert Kahn, architect, and Ernest Wilby, associate. Photograph from Albert Kahn, Inc., *Industrial and Commercial Buildings* (1925), collection of the author.

applied this solution to other tall buildings, such as the twelve-story Vinton Building in 1916–17.

In addition to offering generous natural lighting and exceptional fire resistance, the technology allowed for expansive interior spaces, just as it had in factories, which could be flexibly sectioned off with curtain (non–load-bearing) walls as desired.[28] This held special appeal for businesses involving rooms filled with large drafting tables, such as those Albert and Julius headed. The same qualities appealed to retailers.

Daylight Stores

In the first decade of the twentieth century, retail customers exhibited an increasing preference for natural lighting as they shopped. A well-lit store allowed for closer scrutiny of merchandise, which created an impression of honest dealing. Retailers were advised to consider this when building a new establishment while manufacturers of artificial lighting strove to approximate daylight as closely as possible. The term "daylight store" became "an advertising

Grinnell Brothers Building, Detroit, Michigan (1907–8). Albert Kahn, architect, and Ernest Wilby, associate. Photograph, circa 1913, courtesy Albert Kahn Associates, Inc.

distinction often used to catch trade," as reported in a 1909 retailing journal.[29] Reinforced concrete construction clearly held a functional advantage here—but could it be made to appear elegant for retail? With the Grinnell Brother's Building of 1907–8, Kahn clearly demonstrated it could.

Like the Metzger Automobile Repository, the 60- by 100-foot, six-story plus basement Grinnell structure was designed after a study of the nation's leading examples of music stores. Some $200,000 was invested in the results. The white terra cotta façade was divided into an arcade of three bays with green metal framing the ample glazing. Stories were taller than normal (the six floors brought the building to the typical height of seven), so the windows admitted an abundance of light. Elegant exterior ornamentation included green copper detailing.[30]

Listening rooms for auditioning the increasingly popular phonographs, along with recorded disks and cylinders, populated the basement. Business offices shared the first floor and mezzanine with an offering of instruments and sheet music for sale. A recital hall that could accommodate five hundred

Grinnell Brothers Building interior photograph of first floor and mezzanine by Manning Brothers, courtesy Burton Historical Collection, Detroit Public Library.

audience members occupied the second floor and featured a stage large enough to hold two grand pianos and a pipe organ. The floors above were divided into rooms and promenades displaying various instruments. The fifth floor was devoted to the sales and rentals of player pianos and music rolls. Elegant woodwork and merchandise were in abundance and were, of course, combustible. The structure itself was not, however, and unobtrusive fire-resistance measures, such as steel doors for the stairwells and elevators, were in place to prevent a fire, should it occur, from spreading.[31] Surely few patrons realized the building's construction shared much with the architect's concurrent industrial structures.

Natural sunlight may have instilled confidence in the retail customer in general, but it was also considered optimal when marketing goods where color was a key factor, such as dry goods and upholstered furniture. (Different sources of artificial light yield differing, marked effects on human color perception. Natural light was considered the standard condition for evaluating color.)

An entry in the furniture emporium arena for Kahn was the store for the Owen & Company, plans for which were announced in January 1909. As with the Grinnell Brothers store, a sense of verticality was created by white terra cotta and brick piers framing expansive glass with minimal iron trim. A rounded corner facing the intersection lent additional verticality to the composition and the eighth story

Owen & Company Store, Detroit, Michigan (1909–10). Albert Kahn, architect, and Ernest Wilby, associate. Linecut illustration from *Detroit Free Press*, May 23, 1909.

was treated as a cornice at little expense to the upward thrust of the composition. The vertical piers seemed to vanish at the level of the first two stories, save narrow strips of white masonry marking the rounded corner and ends of the façade. The mass of the building seemed perched above the base floors and their near-continuous expanse of glass, iron, and granite. A simple marquee projected from Gratiot Street side to announce the store entrance.[32]

Fulfilling his client's wishes, Kahn delivered a reinforced-concrete edifice that was "at once commodious and artistic," with ninety thousand square feet of floor space. At the store's February 1910 grand opening, the *Detroit Free Press* proclaimed, "The building well deserves its title 'daylight store'. Every one of the eight floors has 24 huge windows; in effect, only the south wall escapes being made of glass."[33]

Kahn's store buildings and other commercial structures would evolve on a track parallel to the path of his factories; some were likewise landmarks in architectural and engineering achievement. This subcategory of the vast output of the Kahn architecture and engineering office is deserving of further scholarship.

Association with George Gough Booth

Kahn's association with newspaper magnate James E. Scripps dated back to his employment in the firm of Mason & Rice and continued with his partnership with George W. Nettleton. This association was passed onto Scripps's son-in-law, George Gough Booth, who became president of the Evening News Association in 1906. Booth established a newspaper in Grand Rapids and engaged Kahn, working with the local firm of Williamson & Crowe as supervising architects, to design a building that would house its editorial, composition, and printing departments. In addition, nearly half the structure was given over to a unique and rather remarkable feature: a school featuring a classroom, library, a one thousand–seat theater, and a pool with lockers for the education and benefit of the newsboys who delivered the paper to subscribers and sold it on street corners. (The welfare of the newsboys, whose occupational hours were not conducive to normal schooling, was a passion of Booth's.) It was Kahn's job to encompass these functions in a 61- by 100-foot building that would be an

Grand Rapids Press Building, Grand Rapids, Michigan (1907). Albert Kahn, architect, and Ernest Wilby, associate. Unidentified, early postcard reproduction of office drawing, collection of the author.

ornament to the city in its downtown business district. In a journalistic precursor to flow production the various departments were "so arranged that not a moment will be lost in the process of turning written items into newspaper print." Half of the exterior walls, including a light well with a skylight-covered base, were given over to natural lighting. While four stories, the building was equal in height to a five-story structure due to generously high ceilings. Its Kahn System flooring was engineered to support three hundred pounds per square foot in critical press areas. Formal public areas inside were trimmed with marble and mahogany, while the exterior was given a simplified Doric treatment in Bedford limestone. The Grand Rapids Press Building opened January 1, 1907, and served as the confident first entry into a notable subcategory of the Kahn firm's output: newspaper plants.[34]

As soon as George G. Booth's Grand Rapids Press Building opened, Kahn was at work designing Booth's Cranbrook House in the hills of central Oakland County, north of Detroit. Like his father-in-law, James E. Scripps, Booth was an anglophile, and his manor house is a stately expression of the English Arts

Cranbrook House, Bloomfield Hills, Michigan (1908). Albert Kahn, architect, and Ernest Wilby, associate. Courtesy Albert Kahn Associates, Inc.

and Crafts movement. Kahn's proclivity for large windows to harness natural sunlight recedes in his residential designs for the sake of privacy and thermal insulation in an era of single-pane glass. Coupled with this, presumably, was an assumption that residents could venture outside and into the sunlight at will, unlike factory and office workers. (Cranbrook House and many other Kahn residences were surrounded by stately gardens; apartment houses often had garden courts). As a result, Kahn found the relatively few homes he and his firm designed to be welcome diversions with opportunity to dabble in historical architectural tradition.[35]

Taking Comfort in Tradition

This suited his residential clients, who often were captains of industry ushering in the modern world through their work. When they built their homes,

Albert Kahn House, Detroit, Michigan (1906). Albert Kahn, architect, and Ernest Wilby, associate. Photograph made prior to 1928 addition, courtesy Albert Kahn Associates, Inc.

however, many retreated to traditional styles. For them, Kahn "covered acres of suburban Detroit with Italian villas, medieval cottages, Tudor mansions and colonial houses," as one historian noted, adding that the architect "felt more comfortable in the past." While the facts are true, the conclusion is accurate only if one equates comfort with relaxation. While at work, Kahn and his clients were constantly on the cutting edge of modernity. Revolutionizing industry and building was surely taxing, and it is understandable that they sought the stability of traditional surroundings during their off hours. Kahn found such escapism in his own home, inspired by the English Arts and Crafts movement, where he listened intently to music recordings in the company of his art and book collections.[36]

The desire to relax in traditional surroundings extended to country clubs and Kahn designed and belonged to several, although, according to Borth, he never addressed a golf ball in his life. One club where Kahn conspicuously did not hold a membership was the Detroit Athletic Club (DAC). That club was formed in 1887 to promote amateur athletics and it achieved national renown, but the organization was in decline a quarter century later. This was in part due to the relatively remote location of its track and field facilities and the aging of its core membership. At the same time, Henry Joy felt a place was sorely needed where the city's business leaders could gather socially "to get them out of the saloons of Woodward Avenue," where many deals were sealed. The old club was dissolved in January 1913 and was replaced by a hybrid organization, combining an exclusive club with athletics, with an objective of building a grand clubhouse near the city's center to address both elements.[37]

For Albert Kahn, or any architect, it was a plum opportunity. Indeed, architects from New York and Los Angeles sought the work. Once assigned to Kahn, the design process stretched over eight months while he and the DAC's building committee inspected successful clubs around the country. Challenges in coordinating the schedules of the city's business leaders on the committee surely had a significant role in drawing out the process, but their same limited availability left Kahn with unusual autonomy. When the architect was designing factories for the same people, their attention was focused on the project with keen expectations. Designing the DAC, on the other hand, involved aesthetic sensibilities they relied upon Kahn to provide. It seems that the client organization was not too concerned about the cost, either. When the initial, million dollar design was rolled out it was stated that no expense would be spared. By the time it was completed the figure was double that. Kahn stated dryly, "The amount of money available, while not superabundant, was adequate for the results required."[38]

Kahn strove to give members a refuge from the hustle of the city, something with "the character of a fine private home" along the lines of an Italian villa, as opposed to an overtly public building like a hotel. Towards that end, the Indiana limestone exterior and ornate interior were modeled after Renaissance palaces—the work of Bramante and Peruzzi in particular—to thoroughly mask the Kahn System and structural steel construction that made possible impressive thirty-six-foot clear spans inside. Other areas in the building offered the most modern facilities for athletics. Kahn delivered a club building where Detroit's business could be conducted in surroundings

Detroit Athletic Club, Detroit, Michigan (1915). Albert Kahn, architect, and Ernest Wilby, associate. Photograph by the author, 2012.

equal to those found on the East Coast. (The DAC's first manager was lured from Boston's Algonquin Club, touted as perhaps the most exclusive club in the East.)[39]

Postscript: Kahn and DAC Membership

Before leaving the DAC, it is perhaps well to address a longstanding controversy regarding the club's membership policy. A draftsperson captured the story as he heard it in 1942, which seems close to what has circulated until this writing. As the story went, Kahn addressed a large banquet celebrating completion of the building by announcing, "I would like to join the club." To this, the tale continued, the DAC's embarrassed president had to respond, "I am sorry, the club has a policy of admitting no Jews!"[40]

Apparently, this urban myth has been deemed credible enough to linger well over a century without being discredited by the simple question, "If the club was so thoroughly anti-Semitic as to have a no-Jews-allowed policy, why did it turn around and have its showcase clubhouse designed by one?" After all, there were plenty of competent, non-Jewish architects available.

The basic claim that the club barred Jews as official policy is refuted by the fact that when it was reorganized in 1913, one of its charter members was David Heineman. Nevertheless, it appears the club's membership included an anti-Semitic element in a position to blackball new Jewish candidates. With its reorganization, the DAC took on a mantle of exclusivity and, according to the *Jewish Chronicle*, soon Jews found themselves "ineligible to membership in that organization *just because they happen to be Jews*" (emphasis original). The publication's editors added that, as a result, "no self-respecting Jews are knocking for admission at the doors of the Detroit Athletic Club."[41]

Given the discord of the times, one may naturally wonder how Kahn came to design the clubhouse, costing in the vicinity of $2 million. The explanation is that his services were championed by his patron saint, Henry B. Joy, and surely other Kahn customers, such as Joseph Boyer, who were also members. As the club's directors considered their choice of an architect, Joy put in writing his support for Kahn. In a private letter to DAC president Hugh Chalmers, he detailed many reasons for his support, including that "Mr. Kahn is the only architect with whom I have dealt where bitter differences did not arise."[42]

It appears Kahn knew nothing of Joy's behind-the-scenes advocacy until later, when the architect expressed his appreciation in a note. Joy stirringly replied, "It is indeed most gratifying to have such a note, but you owe me no thanks. I never did anything for you. You compelled me to do what I did by reason of what your record is in this community. If you don't want me to advocate for you, why then you should not do things so well—with so much ability and talent. It's all your fault, not mine."[43]

As reported in the *Detroit News*, Kahn was the center of attention during "the first big get-together meeting of the reorganized Detroit Athletic club" on December 16, 1913. The architect's stereopticon presentation giving some thousand attendees the first peek at the design of the new building spurred a run on memberships and donations. As reported in the *Detroit Free Press*, the crowd was electrified. Noticeably absent were any reports of anyone having issue with the architect being Jewish. While the *Jewish Chronicle* surely had reason for reporting that Jews were denied membership, it seems a blanket judgment that the whole organization was anti-Semitic would be inaccurate.[44]

As the building neared completion, DAC secretary Charles A. Hughes wrote in the *Detroit News*, "To Albert Kahn, one of Detroit's most distinguished architects, belongs the credit for adding so much to the city's beauty by contributing this imposing structure." On Saturday, April 17, 1915, the new DAC building opened its doors for a public tour and thousands attended. In the spotlight of attention, Kahn proclaimed, "The new D.A.C. home has come about through the earnest, close co-operation and fellowship of the great body of Detroit's best citizens and most representative men." The architect said the club's officers, directors, and building committee "worked with me in a manner of which I cannot speak too highly, and which is, in great part, responsible for what resulted."[45]

Within such enthusiastic good fellowship, Kahn was privately offered an honorary membership in the DAC. Some have viewed its honorary designation as somehow demeaning, but with an already years-long waitlist for membership it could simply have been a way of moving Kahn to the head of the line. Of course, it cannot be completely ruled out as a maneuver to avoid the chance of the architect being blackballed as a Jew, although such an act by an anti-Semitic faction would surely be seen as particularly reprehensible by other members at that moment of pronounced good will. Ultimately, Kahn declined—possibly as a protest to anti-Semitic influence within the membership, possibly bending to ethnic peer pressure as expressed in the *Jewish Chronicle*, or possibly a combination of both with some measure of regret.[46]

Division sowed by what appears to have been an anti-Semitic minority (based on the fact that it failed to obstruct the hiring of Kahn) within the club dragged on for years. One might argue that Joy and any others who objected to the discrimination should simply have resigned their membership, but that would mean giving up the struggle and handing victory, and the club, to the anti-Semitic minority. By remaining members, they had shown that earnest, close cooperation and fellowship between Jews and Gentiles could produce a noble landmark as an enduring monument that possibly helped inspire change over time. At any rate, the architect continued to enjoy the friendship of members and was a familiar guest at the club (William Knudsen's sixtieth birthday celebration for close friends and family serving as one example).[47]

11

Henry Ford and Highland Park

In 1909 there were eleven automobile companies in production in Detroit. By that year, Henry Ford's Piquette Avenue plant had been enlarged to 2.65 acres plus a satellite building—up from 1. 4 acres of floorspace as originally designed in 1905 by Field, Hinchman & Smith. With Joy's expansion and rebuilding (using the Kahn System) of the Packard plant, it is a toss-up whether he or Ford had the city's largest automobile plant that year. Ford was about to move his production to the suburban community of Highland Park, however, where land was cheaper and taxes lower (although tax savings was offset somewhat by the company investing in upgrading the community's infrastructure). He purchased 62.5 acres of land along Woodward Avenue, where he erected a sign declaring that he would build the largest automobile factory in the world.[1] Clearly, he foresaw remarkable expansion of his business.

Kahn had many consequential associations that played off of each other in various and often unpredictable ways to propel his career forward. Some, like Boyer, played such a key role that it is hard to imagine Kahn's career without them. Ford deserves a place in their coterie for the sheer amount of work his company sent to Kahn's office, but also for instigating Kahn's working relationship with William S. Knudsen, who—as told in the pages ahead—would become a dear friend and the organizational genius behind the Arsenal of Democracy in World War II.

Henry Ford's story has often been told: the son of an Irish immigrant farmer in Springwells Township, Michigan, whose name became identified with the automobile industry and mass production. Similarly to Boyer, he left the family farm at age seventeen to become an apprentice mechanic (in Detroit, in Ford's case). His spare time was devoted to developing motor-driven transportation and in 1892 he completed his first rudimentary, gasoline-driven motorcar. Over the following decade he refined his design and managed to make a name for himself and publicity for his automobiles by racing his vehicles and, in 1903, formed the Ford Motor Company (a forerunner to the company that now bears his name). Ford broke with his peers by investing heavily in the finest machining tools to produce parts consistently to precise sizes, eliminating filing-to-fit and other time-honored craft processes long considered vital to quality product assembly. In doing so, the company drastically shortened production time, enabling it to offer a line of increasingly dependable vehicles at higher volumes. This mass production lowered individual unit costs, so the manufacturer could lower retail prices while still making a profit realized by greater sales volumes. Stressing affordability and dependability over luxury, the early Ford product line culminated in the wildly popular Model T. One morning in 1909 Ford announced that, from that moment on, the company would only produce variations on the Model T. He audaciously predicted he would soon produce ten thousand vehicles a year at prices common people could afford. By staking his future on the working class, from which he came, and seeking his return on volume rather than price, Ford captivated the minds of his era and gained notoriety around the world.[2]

Kahn's Association with Henry Ford Begins

As Christy Borth told the story, likely drawn from primary sources, Kahn's business relationship and personal friendship with Henry Ford began with a telephone call by the automaker's partner, James Couzens. Malcolm Bingay, who drew from conversations with Kahn over their forty years of acquaintance, said the call came from Ford himself. At any rate, it led to the architect's first meeting with Ford, whose success with the Model T had overwhelmed the existing production facilities of the Ford Motor Company (FMC). The Bingay version had Ford telling Kahn, "Couzens has had an architect design our new building. I do not like it and they both agree that the kind of building I want to put up is impossible." As Ford attempted to explain it, Kahn was not sure it was possible either but did not want to admit that at the moment. The architect went back to his office and produced some initial rough drawings, which Ford reviewed and said, the story went, "You've got only part of the idea. Now if you do this, and then do that. . . ." According to Kahn, it was through this type of interaction that he and his most famous private client brought great things to fruition. In his typical fashion, the architect dismissed his role by saying, "All I ever did was to take his instinctive hunch and reduce it down to a working formula." Perhaps, but it was a method Kahn followed with other clients before and after. For instance, while he was reported being awestruck by Ford's vision for expanding the works across FMC's vast Highland Park tract, such vision was not unique in the architect's experience.[3] Boyer anticipated expansion of his machine shop years before hiring Kahn to design its addition, planners for the George N. Pierce plant positioned their buildings for growth, and Packard was adding to its works before and after the architect's first meeting with Ford. Ford certainly took it to new extremes, however, and thus began what was surely the most productive architect-client relationship in history.

On June 16, 1908, FMC announced that it had accepted Kahn's plans for the ambitious factory. While it would eventually consist of several connected structures on the large land tract, its initial building alone would be "865 × 75 feet and four stories high . . . of reinforced concrete, glass and steel," with total floor space of 6.25 acres beneath its roof.[4]

Kahn developed the plans working closely, as usual, with the client's production experts. One FMC engineer provides a glimpse of the process from the perspective of the client, recalling that Kahn "was extremely quick in grasping his client's needs. He would be sitting there sketching almost as fast as anybody could talk as to what was to be." Kahn's listened and responded, letting the needs drive the design. The next morning, they would be reviewing more refined sketches. Some Ford employees later expressed bitterness over Kahn receiving credit for the plant's design when they were part of the development process, but this may be a product of greater frustration working anonymously in Henry Ford's public relations shadow. Ford's image as the people's tycoon was carefully maintained, with the corporate publicity mill reserving virtually all credit for every company success to him. It is remarkable, therefore, that as early as 1909 the company journal *Ford Times* identified Kahn by name as "our architect."[5] While Kahn was consistently quick to give Henry praise, as he did all his clients, he faithfully acknowledged the collaboration of others in the planning process.

Henry Ford surely appreciated Kahn as self-educated and self-made, in addition to his rapidly acquired expertise in factory design. Furthermore, they shared an appreciation of natural light and ventilation, as evidenced by the industrialist's declaration that "one point that is absolutely essential to high-capacity, as well as to humane production, is a clean, well-lighted and well-ventilated factory."[6]

According to the *Detroit News*, as the ground was broken for the first building—the assembly structure—it was "already spoken of as the crystal palace, from the ample arrangements made for perfect light." This association with the grand exhibition hall in Sydenham seems to be clear acknowledgment of the debt Kahn owed to British naturalists and conservatory design. (The Crystal Palace's designer, Joseph Paxton, was a gardener who designed the Great Conservatory at Chatsworth prior to the 1851 Exhibition Hall.) The Highland Park Plant's identity as Kahn's first bona fide daylight factory appears to rest on his profuse use of a product originally marketed as Fenestra: a natural lighting system with panes of glass set in steel frame panels, some of which pivoted for natural ventilation. The product originated in Germany around 1880 and spread to England from where Kahn ordered it for the FMC plant. (It was later manufactured domestically by Detroit Steel Products, which in one advertising campaign promoted the product as "The Conservatory Idea.") The initial construction of the new FMC plant had 52,453 square feet of the window, "enough to make a strip one foot wide ten miles long." As reported in the *Detroit Free Press* upon its completion, "The sides and ends of the building are almost one solid mass of glass supported by steel window frames." The saturation of natural light reaching toward the center of the seventy-five-foot-wide structure was almost double that found in mill construction.[7]

The main assembly building was completed by July 1909 and initially used for storage while work began on an essentially one-story, skylit manufacturing section immediately behind it, again utilizing the Kahn System. The heaviest equipment was placed here, where it could rest directly on the ground. Flooring varied from dirt to concrete to woodblock as appropriate for the work to be done. It ran the 865-foot length of the main building and was 135 feet

Ford Motor Company Highland Park Plant, Assembly Building, Highland Park, Michigan (1909). Albert Kahn, architect, and Ernest Wilby, associate. Construction photograph, 1909, showing back side (opposite Woodward façade) and illustrating natural light penetration. From the collections of The Henry Ford. Gift of the Ford Motor Company.

wide. Work proceeded simultaneously on the powerhouse that stood along Woodward Avenue. FMC's Highland Park Plant officially began operation on January 1, 1910, with initial expectations of producing five hundred vehicles a day. A little over a year later the new administration building on Woodward Avenue was finished and the move from the Piquette plant was completed. The two-story brick and reinforced concrete office building was generously glazed, and glass partitions allowed light to penetrate far within. A newspaper account noted it was also an easy matter "for one to look the whole length of the building through these glass partitions and see your next door neighbor as easily as if he were in the same room." The second floor included the office of Henry Ford.[8]

As with FMC's competitors, employee welfare and productivity were of high concern in the design of the works, which relied on natural light augmented with artificial lighting for nighttime hours. While the Fenestra windows opened for natural ventilation, such voluminous spaces required mechanical blowers as well. Fresh air was drawn from the outside by immense suction fans, then washed by a continuous spray of water that removed impurities. Temperature of this water was adjusted to heat or cool the circulating air and control humidity. Air was forced through ducts into the work areas, achieving a complete change of air every twelve minutes. The plant included a first aid hospital for the immediate treatment of workplace injuries, and FMC provided

English language classes for workers who were recent immigrants for safety and efficiency.[9]

Meanwhile, the phenomenal sales of the Model T fueled FMC's growth. The company built and shipped 17,601 finished vehicles in January 1913 alone. It was estimated that half of all automobiles sold in the country that year would be Model Ts; the company's nationwide workforce equaled the population of Columbus, Ohio. Demand drove expansion of FMC's Highland Park Plant and by 1914 there were three four-story buildings and total factory floor space represented more than twenty-eight acres. While the product remained essentially the same, the flow of production was continually redesigned to gain efficiency. This resulted in holes being punched through walls and floors to accommodate shifts in the assembly lines that began to dominate the process.[10]

In May 1913 the company, with a capacity of two hundred thousand cars per year already, announced a major expansion that was as bold as what had come before: two six-story structures that would increase capacity by a factor of 50 percent. The structures followed the design cues of the four-story buildings and were 845 by 60 feet, separated by a 40-foot wide, rail-served craneway extending their length and height. The craneway was given a glass roof and in time the entire expansion was known collectively as simply the six-story building.[11] The atrium created by roofing the craneway was literally large enough to hold a battleship within (a full-scale wooden model of the Eagle Boat was built there during World War I).

Construction continued. Also in 1913, the roof of the administration building was raised and two more stories were inserted. A $1 million enlargement (including $600,000 in equipment) to the power plant came online in 1915. In 1916 Henry Ford announced plans to double the size of the plant to meet the seemingly insatiable demand for Model Ts. Production flow at the Highland Park Plant was in a near-constant state of experimentation, reevaluation, and redesign that eventually yielded assembly line mass production. As production costs lowered, so did prices for customers. At the same time, workers' pay increased and by 1915 the company had a profit-sharing program. FMC employees were now averaging 61 cents an hour at a time when most manufacturing workers were averaging less than half that.[12]

Many praised the Highland Park Plant as an exemplar of the daylight factory. *American Architect*, in an article illustrated with photographs of Kahn's

Two-image photographic montage view of the Ford Motor Company Highland Park Plant as it appeared from Woodward Avenue around 1915. From the left: the enlarged power plant with its five smokestacks (1909–15), the administrative building as enlarged to four stories (1909–13), the four-story assembly building representing the original construction (1909). An additional four-story structure and one of the six-story buildings (1913) at the far right marks the end of the plant. Unseen are the massive works filling the reentrant angle created by these structures. Shortly after this image was captured, work began again to double the size of the plant. Courtesy Albert Kahn Associates, Inc., with perspective correction by the author.

recent buildings for Packard, stated, "Daylight and fresh air are vital to our very existence. The health of factory workers is immeasurably affected by the abundance or dearth of both."[13] This was considered a new concept by many twentieth century observers despite its presence in the work of Victorian naturalists—a precedence suggested to some degree by the Crystal Palace nickname. By treating this observation as a fresh idea, the journal overlooked the championing of healthier architecture by Nathaniel Ward, Florence Nightingale, and the *Lancet* over sixty years earlier. Its felt novelty at the turn of the century was at the core of Kahn's post-Belle Isle success.

Growing Pains

Prior to the initial groundbreaking for the Highland Park Plant, Kahn and associate Ernest Wilby were already designing structures for automotive concerns such the E. R. Thomas Automobile Company of Buffalo, the Chalmers Motor Company in Detroit, and the Garford Company of Elyria, Ohio, in addition to those already discussed. As the Highland Park Plant grew, the firm was simultaneously at work expanding facilities for Packard and designing Detroit area plants for clients such as Continental Motors, the Dodge Brothers, the Lozier and Hudson Motor Companies, and the Grabowsky Power Wagon Company. All this, and more, was in addition to satellite work for Packard and FMC, discussed in chapter 12. Nonautomotive work included expansion of the former

AAC Plant (now operating under the Burroughs name) and many other commercial projects, such as those touched upon in chapter 10.[14]

Most customers, particularly the repeat ones, appear to have been quite pleased, but it is rare for any business venture to operate for very long without some instances of customer dissatisfaction. Kahn and his firm were not immune to this, although it seems he preferred to speak only of those occurring in his early partnerships. For instance, he told an anecdote of losing a prospective residential client at the beginning of his career when a disgruntled commercial customer intruded upon his sales pitch to complain of warped baseboards.[15]

A later instance involved the Dodge brothers, who formed a partnership in 1900 to machine and build engines. As its business (which included supporting FMC) grew, its principals, John and Horace Dodge, engaged a series of architects to design initial construction and enlargements for its Monroe Avenue works: Harry W. Chamberlain (in 1902), Malcomson & Higginbotham (1904), and Field, Hinchman & Smith (1904, 1907). They turned to Kahn, however, to design their new automobile parts plant, consisting of five buildings, in the suburban village of Hamtramck, in mid-1910. At the time boasting to surpass even FMC, its U-shaped main building, closely resembling FMC's Highland Park works, rose four stories and encompassed six acres of floor space. Kahn also designed Horace Dodge's Grosse Pointe residence (completed in 1911). As chronicled by historian Charles K. Hyde, John Dodge was dissatisfied with Kahn's proposal for the plant's brass foundry, turning that work over to Smith, Hinchman & Grylls (as that firm became known after the departure of Henry G. Field.)[16]

Dodge Brothers Company correspondence reveals that the dissatisfaction continued with Kahn's supervision of the work contracted to Bryant & Detwiler. Established in 1904, the contractor specialized in reinforced concrete construction and, like the architect, was responsible for much notable building (including many structures chronicled in these pages). Problems with this commission represent exceptions to a laudable work record.[17] While the rollicking Dodge Brothers were evidently quite fickle, architects can fall short of customer expectations for a number of reasons. It seems probable in this case that the problems were associated with internal or external growing pains that routinely impact business performance. The Detroit area's boom in reinforced concrete construction taxed resources. Kahn was at the center of it, with a sizable portion of his large staff already devoted to meeting demand. Bryant & Detwiler was also working to capture market share at a time when there was much competition for labor and materials. At any rate, the work seems to have fallen behind schedule, below quality, or both, and Kahn lost the contract.

Smith, Hinchman & Grylls recaptured the Dodge Brothers' business (which began producing its own automobiles in 1912) and successfully held it for more than decade.[18] For Kahn, there were plenty of other clients to fill the void left by the loss of the Dodge work. It seems few of those others were disappointed, for Kahn's firm enjoyed much repeat business over decades as its presence continued to extend over a widening geographic area.

12

Kahn's Office and the Cauldron of an American Style

Within twenty years of hanging out the shingle of his first partnership, Kahn had clearly established himself as a regional architect of note in a wide variety of building types. His industrial work, for a broad assortment of industries and their suppliers, extended his range further. With the success of Packard and FMC, and their loyalty toward Kahn as their architect, his work spread across the land. His prime automotive clients had needs beyond the purely industrial; they also developed satellite networks of ancillary structures. These were sales and service buildings dedicated to single manufacturers which, as the business matured, increasingly replaced multibrand automobile repositories such as Metzger's. Before the term "automotive dealership" entered the popular lexicon, they were referenced under a variety of names including sales and service buildings, branch buildings, garages, and stores.

Since the World's Columbian Exposition, the process for becoming an architect had been changing as well. In many offices, the principals acted as salespeople while the work of designing buildings emanated from drafting rooms operating with varying degrees of autonomy. The great Chicago Fair placed a spotlight on the École des Beaux-Arts and a college degree in architecture increasingly became requisite in the field. Depending on the principal, the office may have drawn its inspiration from the security of historical precedent as taught in the colleges by the likes of Trowbridge. Kahn led his office along an eclectic path as set by Mason & Rice, with its library that drew from surrounding current trends as well as precedent in response to the clients' needs and desires. Because of the demands of its industrial work, engineering and its technical advances became integral components also driving design for the Kahn office.

Thomas Eddy Tallmadge, a professor of architectural history in the 1920s who was also a Chicago architect of note, observed a yearning for a recognized "American" style of architecture that he dated going back at least as far as 1879. Believing the uniqueness of American culture deserved a unique architecture, a number of designers, including himself, endeavored to create one. As witnessed by Tallmadge, "The search for this pot of gold makes one of the most entertaining and tragic romances in art," in which those who set forth upon the quest returned, "years later, battered and defeated without their prize." He was looking back, in 1927, upon his experience as part of the Chicago School of Architecture (the name for which he coined nearly twenty years earlier) and its mostly residential subcategory, the Prairie Style.[1]

If the United States failed to yield a pot of gold for architects seeking an American style, it did provide a melting pot of cultures from which they could draw. This begot a cauldron of architectural inspiration whose contents, comprising a myriad of influences and traditions, roiled and bubbled. Societal, economic, and technical changes attending the growth of industrialism added themselves to the mix. Architects working in the industrial arena found themselves dealing within particular restrictions of practicality, utility, and budget that, according to Tallmadge, "often result in the best work. Useless cornices were thrown over-board; so were architectural columns, pediments and towers; so were all historical styles in general."[2]

These results were added to the cauldron, where the contents heaved and subsided, eddies came and went. As Kahn's work for the American automobile industry spread across the land, his contribution to the brew increased significantly, seeding communities with his passion for natural light in workplaces. It surely influenced local architects, especially as they turned to reinforced concrete construction. Future scholarship may trace Kahn's impact on indigenous American architecture of the early twentieth century just as it has been documented in the nearly contemporaneous European Modernist movement (see chapter 16). Likely the influence worked in multiple, overlapping directions.

Packard's Sales and Service Network

As long as there was no single American style, regional styles served local needs and Kahn ably obliged when given the opportunity. For instance, he catered to the expectations of well-heeled Packard buyers in an older, established Eastern city by integrating the locally entrenched Beaux Arts classicism into his design for the automaker's New York showroom. Set on an acute corner of New York's Broadway and Sixty-First Street, classical ornament enhanced an elegantly thin, matte white terra-cotta arcade rounding the turn of the intersection. Kahn System technology enabled the architect to provide a spacious showroom, two stories in height, to create an impression of stylish openness surmounted by two floors of service bays.[3]

With some twenty-five hundred Packard vehicles in the New York area, the company needed a service facility with much greater capacity, however. Kahn again obliged, stacking seven stories of glazed service floors atop a 96- by 150-foot sales floor and basement along Long Island City's Thompson Avenue. Ornamentation was minimal and little of the reinforced concrete structure was visible as most of the surface territory was ceded to twenty-five thousand

Packard Sales and Service Building, New York City (1907). Albert Kahn, architect, and Ernest Wilby, associate. Photograph from Albert Kahn, Inc., *Industrial and Commercial Buildings* (1925), collection of the author.

square feet of glass. This placed various aspects of Packard's service program on prominent display along the thoroughfare connecting Long Island to the rest of the metropolis. An automotive journal reported that from a distance, three sides of the building appeared to be almost entirely of glass. It was stunning, especially considering the minimalist direction some architecture would be heading in in the following decades. Clearly happy with the result, the client proudly showcased it with a stylishly dramatic nighttime rendering on the cover of its corporate magazine for enthusiasts. The artwork depicts fashionable customers on the surrounding grounds, seemingly drawn like moths to the abundant lighting emanating from the glass. Kahn later said, "Modern architecture is always at its best when there is a special reason for its being modern." It surely had special reason here, serving as landmark and a nighttime beacon. The original floorspace of over 2.5 acres was enlarged to over seven acres, with an eight-story addition following the same style in 1917.[4]

Packard Motor Car Company of New York, Service Building, Long Island City, New York (1907). Albert Kahn, architect, and Ernest Wilby, associate. Artwork from the cover of *The Packard*, January 7, 1911, courtesy the National Automotive History Collection, Detroit Public Library.

The following year Packard tapped Kahn for another sales and service building, this time a $250,000 landmark on Philadelphia's tony "automobile row," North Broad Street. Employing a bit more exterior structure than in Long Island City, he responded with a remarkably elegant structure of concrete and steel sheathed in matte cream terra-cotta, measuring 75 by 165 feet and eight stories tall. As in New York City, the architect utilized ornamental iron and expanses of glass to light a two-story showroom and surmounting work floors, but in this case the building's shallow arches, terra-cotta spandrels, and squared corners create the impression of a grid rather than an arcade.[5]

It is evident that Packard and Kahn perceived luxury car buyers in the Midwest as responding to, and perhaps preferring, less elegant expressions in architecture than those in the East in the first decade of the century. For

Packard Sales and Service Building, Philadelphia, Pennsylvania (1908). Albert Kahn, architect, and Ernest Wilby, associate. Photograph, following the building's conversion to loft apartments, by Michael Spain-Smith courtesy Reinhold Residential.

the company's 1910 Chicago sales and service entry, the firm embraced some precepts of the Chicago School and its kindred Prairie Style, but continued the Philadelphia first floor showroom's sense of being an enticing, glazed void.[6] The structural geometry as expressed in this three-story structure, while evocative of Kahn's industrial work, is also reflective of the Chicago School.

The public persona of the automobile company, as communicated in its corporate publication *The Packard* beginning in 1910, was one of sophistication and self-confidence bordering on cockiness as it promoted the lure of the open road. This seems to have been well-conveyed to Kahn and disseminated throughout his office. The versatile Kahn team adroitly responded with the elegance of Packard's Manhattan sales and service building balanced by its stark, prominent, and surely head-turning Long Island City service center. As shown in Chicago, other equally noteworthy entries fell between the two. As the automaker's position in

A Packard dealership, this enterprise was officially known as the Chicago Motor Car Company Headquarters, Chicago, Illinois (1910). Albert Kahn, architect, and Ernest Wilby, associate. From *The Packard*, July 1, 1910, courtesy National Automotive History Collection, Detroit Public Library.

the marketplace stabilized in the following decades, Kahn responded with more staid but consistently fine designs.

Architecture for Ford's Expanding Footprint

As Packard expanded its share of the luxury motor car market, FMC was busily seeking to build and hold the large market of middle-class automobile buyers it created with its Model T. Like the Chicago Packard showroom, the Ford Branch Building in Omaha similarly illustrates Kahn's sensitivity to middle America's utilitarian expectations. The two-story brick structure utilizing the Kahn System surely stood out from its neighboring structures in the eyes of the public. Reporting on the $40,000, 60- by 132-foot structure in 1910, *Motor Age* reveals what the architect's contemporaries considered a signature aspect of his style: "In keeping with Kahn's ideas, the building is a mass of windows." Work on other Ford branch buildings was underway in Cincinnati and Atlanta, with plans for more in Cleveland, Dallas, Houston, and Pittsburgh.[7]

Back in Detroit, FMC purchased land at the northeast corner of Woodward Avenue and Grand Boulevard in 1910 for a Kahn-designed, three-story

Ford Branch Building, Omaha, Nebraska. Albert Kahn, architect, Ernest Wilby, associate (1910). Image from *Motor Age*, December 29, 1910, courtesy National Automotive History Collection, Detroit Public Library.

sales and service building. The firm designed a $333,000 enlargement in 1913, expanding the building to eight stories tall and extending 321 feet along Grand. What little that was not glass was nearly all sheathed in terra-cotta with relatively austere, geometric ornamentation. In 1943, critic and historian W. Hawkins Ferry praised the structure as still being "as clean-cut a piece of architecture as one could find anywhere." Piers of uniform width ran uninterrupted, from the pavement to the cornice, with uniform spandrels establishing an imposing yet accessible modular composition. As Ferry noted, "Such advanced logic was frequently neglected in the roaring twenties."[8]

The Ford Assembly Plants and Kahn's Association with William S. Knudsen

Meanwhile, in the FMC factory, the scene surrounding the advent of the Ford assembly line was much too turbulent and with too many players to credit any one person, but William S. Knudsen unquestionably played a key role. A Danish immigrant who arrived at New York's Ellis Island in 1900 with $30 in his pocket and barely passible English communication skills, Knudsen labored building

Ford Sales and Service Building, Detroit, Michigan (1910, 1913). Albert Kahn, architect, and Ernest Wilby, associate. Photograph courtesy Albert Kahn Associates, Inc.

ships and repairing locomotives before moving to Buffalo and a position as bench hand at the sprawling John R. Keim Mills in 1902. At the time, the mill stamped metal parts for various products, including bicycles and telephones.[9]

Knudsen's natural genius for streamlining production coupled with job-acquired management skills led to his rise to assistant superintendent of the six-hundred-person plant when Keim began making all rear axles for Model Ts in 1908. Knudsen applied his expertise to FMC's parts production and was noticed by the automaker. Satisfied with the work but needing more axles than the Buffalo manufacturer could produce itself, FMC bought Keim in 1910 and planned major expansion to its shop. Knudsen's services were acquired as well. Like Boyer, Knudsen won the hearts of many a worker on the factory floor by his willingness to get his hands dirty, even descending into a grease pit if that was what it took to fix equipment or solve a production problem. An imposing six foot, three inches tall, he was affectionately known as Big Bill.[10]

It was Henry Ford's original intention to keep the casting business in Buffalo, as it would take eighteen months and half a million dollars to duplicate the plant in Michigan. When a wildcat strike occurred at the mills in 1912, however, a piqued Ford reconsidered and announced he would close down the Buffalo works. Knowing he was not bluffing, Knudsen pleaded with the workers to return to their jobs. When they jeered Big Bill and refused, Ford followed through by ordering all Keim tooling and management moved to Highland Park. By acquiring Knudsen, his colleagues in management, and the Keim tools, FMC made a tremendous leap forward on its path toward mass production.[11]

Knudsen's first assignment was managing the growing network of assembly plants the company had initiated in 1909. To reduce shipping costs for customers far from Highland Park, it was deemed cost-efficient to ship densely packed Model T parts to rail-served satellite plants where they could be assembled into vehicles for regional sales. The first was built in Kansas City and the business model proved so effective it was eventually implemented abroad while competitors sought to imitate it. Kahn designed nearly all of the assembly plants for FMC and a good deal of those that followed for other manufacturers. Knudsen is quoted saying Kahn "subscribed to the principle that if you want to build a factory, the thing to do was make a layout of your machinery, and the flow of the material, and then build a building around it." Kindred spirits, the two made a fine team. Knudsen was promoted to FMC production supervisor though never given a formal title, typical for the company under Henry Ford's management.[12]

Traveling extensively to manage the satellite production, Knudsen soon gained a reputation across the country as a solid production man respected by workers and management alike. According to his biography, Knudsen worked directly with Kahn on 14 FMC assembly plants, but the number was probably about twice that.[13] Typically, four to six stories with vast amounts of glass and sash, the early iterations of Ford assembly plants looked like the spawn of Highland Park that they were.

In the process of expanding the network of FMC assembly plants, Kahn and Knudsen became close friends, and the historical impact resulting from their collaboration was huge. Like Kahn's interaction with Boyer, it has gone remarkably unnoticed in his biographies. Proof of their friendship, however, can be found in a celebration held in recognition of Knudsen's sixtieth birthday in 1939. A formal luncheon drew many dignitaries, including Henry Ford, who had driven Big Bill from FMC in 1921 (as discussed later). Nevertheless the two continued to hold each other in great respect; Ford's presence was particularly

Ford Sales, Service and Assembly Building, Omaha, Nebraska (1916). Albert Kahn, architect, and Ernest Wilby, associate. Photograph after its conversion to apartments by the author, 2023.

noteworthy given that Knudsen was president of General Motors when he turned sixty. Kahn, however, attended a later dinner at the DAC that was limited to Knudsen's family and close friends. In 1942, Kahn spoke of his long association with Knudsen as "one of my most precious experiences."[14]

Managing Success and Architectural Style on a Large Scale

The preceding pages recount Kahn's rise in personal success and the coincident phenomenal, unprecedented growth and reach of his architectural firm. It was, of course, a business generally considered to be among the arts. As Francis Swales observed from his drafting room perspective, however, the largest firms tended to produce such impersonal work that their leaders were more properly considered businesspersons, not architects. Kahn and his firm were exceptions to this stereotype in Swales's mind. Having seen Kahn at work and spent time studying drawings made by his hand, Swales understood him to be an architect of exceptional talent "who can do something besides turn the handle of a money-making machine." Kahn managed to systematize the business side of the practice and relieved himself of that burden to the extent possible in order to reserve "to himself the guidance of the designing," Swales noted. Continuing to sketch and design despite his remarkable success and its accompanying demands, Kahn seems to have kept the respect of those in the drafting room in much the same way that a Boyer or a Knudsen kept the respect of those on their shop floors.[15]

Given the sheer amount of work in the office, however, it stretches credulity to take too literally Ferry's 1970 assertion that "Kahn either designed himself or closely designed every building he built." But he seems to have been personally involved with shepherding major projects, of which there were plenty, through the process. Some architects, like Wirt Rowland, seem to have been used to working in offices with a more hands-off management style, leaving them with more autonomy. (By all accounts, Rowland did great work under Kahn, but he did shop his services around to other firms.) In the Kahn office, it seems to have been more of group effort, with Kahn ultimately at the helm. As Kahn explained it to Bennett in 1929, "sometimes six or ten of us work on a design together."[16]

Rowland explained that, due to the repeat work brought by their clients, particularly in the automobile industry, the firm was responsible "to erect building after building, hardly varying in demands of arrangements, thereby offering the opportunity to perfect by repetition and constant experiment." This experimentation is evident in the sales and service buildings, but also other building types, such as branch banks. One imagines it being a challenge to instill variety, but "History furnishes us," Wirt continued, "a rich store of precedent for analysis which must be broad as well as minute, and the opportunity to study scale, treatment of surface, profile and line." So the past not only offered ornament to appropriate, but centuries of problem-solving lessons. The office had its own history to draw from as well. Roland added, "With 20 years of experiment behind us, we have rubbed elbows with every difficulty under the sun, and what can and what cannot be done with practical requirements is pretty well known."[17]

Kahn created a remarkable design process to meet the unprecedented demands of the office without sacrificing product quality. Past and present architecture provided both a palette and a tool box to reach into for solutions—when they were needed and could apply. It is tempting to assign credit to specific architects within the firm for designs in a specific style, such as the Prairie School or Renaissance classicism, but this may miss the bigger picture. The demand compelled the process and the process generated a style that could meet the demand. Swales believed that if Kahn had a smaller practice with more intimate commissions such as residences, he would have developed a more personally expressive style and received more recognition as an individual architect. Fate would not have it, however: the Kahn office style was already something bigger than the architect and it continued to grow.

It was not a machine, however, although historian Henry-Russell Hitchcock attempted to denigrate Kahn's office as "a plan factory." It was a team process, but with individuals infusing the style from different directions with their individual creativity, producing a dynamic that kept it in a constant state of renewal. Kahn captured the notion in his 1931 "Architectural Trend" speech when he noted, discussing the art in general, "All good architecture is the result of cumulative effort devoted to the prime needs of the respective time." In an earlier era when human activity was geographically limited, with little academic input, national styles naturally arose, but "today, owing to modern methods of transportation to printing and photography, we may familiarize ourselves with all that has been done. Thus, we make use of all established styles."[18]

Of course, with so much to draw from, confusion could easily reign. Kahn credited the cohesive approach to design presented at the World's Columbian Exposition, with its monumental and inspiring results, as establishing the path out of stylistic chaos. Since then, he continued, "there has been a general revival in good taste. . . . Germany has led the van in cutting away from the debased in vogue. In the work of [Alfred] Messel, we see perhaps the first serious attempt at abandonment of prevalent tradition and establishment of a new type of work expressive of the modern trend."[19]

The Influence of Alfred Messel

Clearly, the Kahn office had many influences, and Messel's legacy had a strong impact on much of its freely derived gothic, commercial work outside the automobile industry. An *Architectural Record* article appearing just after Messel's 1909 death promoted his approach as a needed counterbalance to the doctrinaire influence exerted by the École des Beaux-Arts on American practitioners. The author, École-educated Chicago architect Alfred Hoyt Granger, reported a stylistic thread running through the best of current German buildings at the time, with origins in Professor Messel. It marked the development of an "art which has not thrown aside tradition, but which, to the contrary, has absorbed whatever the builders of the past can teach the present, has copied their spirit rather than their form of expression, and which produces buildings thoroughly adapted to the twentieth century, with its complicated needs and yet full of a beauty and vitality all their own."[20]

The International Studio, another influential journal of the day, declared, "In Messel's art Gothicism, Renaissance and Barock [*sic*] have undergone an ennobling rebirth," offering "distinguished simplicity and harmonious monumentality." The 1896–1904 Wertheim Department Store in Berlin is perhaps Messel's best-remembered composition. Its 1904 Leipziger Platz annex employed restrained and straightened German Gothic window tracery combined with classic arcade under a mansard roof. As it was described by Fiske

Haus Wertheim, Berlin, Germany (1904). Alfred Messel, architect.
Postcard view, circa 1900, collection of the author.

Kimball, while historic forms "furnished the suggestions, all have been so transformed that the impression is predominantly modern."[21]

Following Messel's death, this torch was carried by the likes of Peter Behrens, Paul Bonatz, Ludwig Hoffman (Messel's contemporary, not to be confused with Josef), and, when opportunity across the Atlantic made it appropriate, Albert Kahn. This presented an alternative, more evolutionary approach to modernity than the extreme break with the past being formulated by Walter Gropius, Antonio Sant'Elia, and others. Prior to the Great War, the Messel circle simply represented one stylistic trend and the Gropius circle another, coexisting as differing niches within their craft. This would change as the latter became politicized, causing some later critics to dismiss Messel's legacy as being historicist. Structures like the Wertheim store created quite a stir when they were new, however.[22]

The Detroit News Building

Kahn's customer for the Grand Rapids Press Building was Evening News Association president George Booth, whose passion for the culture of his English heritage ran deep, as evidenced by his Cranbrook estate. He also held a passion for the traditions and art of printing; one of its manifestations was his Cranbrook Press—a labor of love, hand printing books in the spirit of William Morris and the Arts and Crafts tradition. (It is touching to note that Booth employed Nellie M. Nettleton, widow of Kahn's earlier partner, in a key position of responsibility for this altruistic venture.[23]) When it came time to build a new home for the *Detroit News*, Booth again turned to Kahn, with the requirement that he design a modern building suited to modern printing that would, at the same time, project an image of the newspaper as an established fixture within the city.

The Detroit News Building represented a cutting-edge rethinking of newspaper production-house design utilizing the latest equipment. With 148,000 square feet of floor space, it was the world's largest building devoted exclusively to newspaper publication. Kahn considered it to be "a factory, pure and simple"—but it was hardly simple, and the styling of his contemporary industrial work would not do in its downtown setting. The solution commemorated the cultivation of the client while allowing the architect to demonstrate his awareness of recent trends in Europe as instigated by Messel and his followers.[24]

The Detroit News Building was recognized in the newspaper's pages as "an amplification of a style of architecture which for the last few years has been the vogue in Europe, with severe lines and stately arches but a new sense of proportion." As described by Rowland, it suggested "a medieval prototype, although really and essentially American—locally middle western. . . . Its structural expression, like much of the modern German work, forms one of the chief and striking features of its design. The concrete frame of its construction is clearly shown by its series of piers and spandrels." George Harold Edgell, dean of Harvard University's school of architecture, said of the building, "The proportions of arcades, windows, and attic are exceptionally fine. The ornament, classic in feeling, but modern in design, is sparing and appropriate. One senses immediately the lightness, airiness and functional practicality of the work, while one delights in its proportions and refinement. It avoids any archæologising and lavish parade and attains the finer art."[25]

Detroit News Building, Detroit, Michigan (1915–17). Albert Kahn, architect, and Ernest Wilby, associate. Exterior photograph, circa 1917, courtesy Albert Kahn Associates, Inc.

The modernized Gothic of the exterior bore an Arts and Crafts imprint, with statues honoring four luminaries from the history of printing amid decorative displays of medieval printers' marks. This reflected the extent of Booth's bibliophilia, which also fired support of his Cranbrook Press.[26] Although it especially suited the client in this case, such mixing of cultures and eras were in the spirit of Messel's and Kahn's rummaging of history for the right effect.

While the building exuded a rather solid appearance, in keeping with the factory concept very little natural lighting was sacrificed for the sake of the architectural design. The many windows, lightwell, and skylights were placed for the most productive benefit in illuminating and facilitating the rhythmic production of a major newspaper on a daily basis. The first floor was largely devoted to the presses and a drive-through shipping court. Presses operated in proud, full view from the street through an arcade of large, round-arched windows. A first-floor public entrance area was treated in what the office described as "a modified Renaissance manner," while second-floor offices for administration, editorial, and reporting were treated in "a modified Elizabethan style." On the third floor the reinforced concrete gave way to a structural steel monitor to maximize the effect of skylights illuminating the fine work of the composing, art, and engraving departments as well as a carpentry and machine shop.[27]

A decade later, George D. Mason's Detroit Masonic Temple presented an opportunity to contrast Kahn's indirect, almost impressionistic borrowing from Gothic precedent for the Detroit News Building with a more archeologically direct appropriation of the style. While still a fine product of early twentieth century mid-America, this grand edifice more dutifully acknowledges its source material, whereas Kahn was satisfied with simply capturing its essence.

Despite the pressures of his office, Kahn managed to find time to assist his old employer, mentor, partner, and friend on this, the largest Masonic temple in the world. The gracefully hulking, $3.5 million neo-Gothic edifice began

Masonic Temple, Detroit, Michigan (1920–26). George D. Mason & Company, architect. Photograph, circa 1928, courtesy Burton Historical Collection, Detroit Public Library.

to rise along the north side of Cass Park near the end of 1920 and would be dedicated six years later. As he visited the work in progress, Malcolm Bingay frequently came across Kahn scurrying about its unfinished interior. "He was as enthusiastic over the Temple as if it were his own," the journalist recalled. Kahn contributed "his time and energy, his magnificent artistic genius and his boundless enthusiasm, merely in the joy of friendship."[28]

A Mirror Reflecting a Mirror to Create an American Style

For Kahn, as with most other things, his rummaging through the past and present was a team effort. He provided or approved the overall vision for individual projects, with the wide-ranging office product bearing his signature in terms of practicality, quality, and a reverence for natural light. This resulting office style was subject to the shifting of architectural trend and customer desire, so it was more democratic than autocratic at its core while still under the guidance of Kahn's intuitive judgement of good taste as drawn from his mentorships, experience, and continuing self-education. As such, Kahn's architecture was not so much a personal style as it was an office style, with many architects, engineers, and others contributing. With its fate based on merit and Kahn firmly and personally responsible, however, the office maintained an individualist character amid its collaborative operation. Survival depended on its ability to respond to customer wants and changing external factors, including cultural trends. This entwined Kahn's office within the American fabric. With its work distributed across the country it had an undeniable role in shaping the American architectural landscape. At the same time, the office was continually responding to external stimulus, and the American architectural landscape helped shape its product, like a mirror reflecting a mirror.

Writing in a 1915 essay for the journal *Architecture*, Princeton-educated New York architect Aymar Embury II wrote of Kahn's architectural offerings in Detroit as "spick and span in their newness, absolutely commercial in design, and yet with such a clever air of practicality and cleanliness and comfort and efficiency, that there is, after all, something beautiful about them." The result is expressive of the unyielding, straightforward Detroit spirit as recounted by

William Stout. Embury continued with observations noting Kahn's "interesting combination of concrete piers supporting glass and steel," and found something "*which might be copied with advantage* [emphasis added]."[29] As will be discussed, it has been documented that the European architects of the later, so-called International Style were influenced by Kahn's industrial work. Although the subject awaits further scholarship, it seems reasonable to assume his prewar commercial work was also an influence. After all, like his industrial offerings, this commercial work was touted in architectural and automotive journals, making it highly visible to visitors to the United States.

When later considering what might constitute a national style for architecture in the United States, Kahn had this to say:

> A purely American style is no more possible nor required than a strictly American vocabulary. Just as the American people is a composite of many nations, just so its architecture must be a composite; but just as American characteristics influence American life, so they influence American architecture. . . . Those who so deplore the non-existence of an American architecture need merely to look about. It has been here for years only they don't know it.[30]

13

Rapid Response During the Great War

On April 16, 1917, the United States declared war on Germany, foremost among the Central Powers, placing itself on the side of the opposing Allied Powers in a colossal conflict that had grown since 1914 to encompass much of the globe. Just the previous November, President Woodrow Wilson had been reelected after a campaign that boasted "he kept us out of the war," and popular sentiment had been strongly against involvement. So much so, leaders were deliberately unprepared to enter the fray under the notion that readying for war increased the likelihood of going to war. Now there was tremendous, sudden pressure to train troops that would soon be shipped to battle zones and to produce matériel to send with them.

Before entering the war, the United States enjoyed a period of prosperity as the world's single largest civilian economy. Now, emergency wartime restrictions essentially put an end to activities such as automobile production and civilian construction, but there was a surge in federal construction as the military establishment swelled. Troops needed housing and factories for matériel were in demand. It was suddenly a desperate time, and the Quartermaster Corps, responsible for military buildings, was overwhelmed. The U.S. government needed to look to the private sector, and the architect to whom it first turned was Albert Kahn, for his experience in both residential and rapidly executed industrial design.[1]

An Architectural Office Ready for the Task

During the civilian economic surge, Kahn's office swelled with work such as the Detroit News Building and the various automobile plant expansions. His organization outgrew its suite in the Trussed Concrete Building and in May 1917, just after the U.S. declaration of war, he moved his office to a 14,000 square foot space on the upper floor of the ten-story Marquette Building (briefly called the Congress Building). This was a 1902 Donaldson & Meier–designed structure that was enlarged and remodeled in 1916. It was a move long in planning: over the course of five to six months, Kahn remodeled the skylit tenth floor to his needs utilizing glass partitions to spread natural light and create a sense of openness. Here were two large drafting rooms, separate rooms for structural and mechanical engineering, a room for specification writers, and another for typing and correlating the documents, along with executive offices, conference rooms, a library, vault, and other support spaces. It housed a considerable business staffed by about eighty people. Wilby would withdraw from the firm in 1918 due to ill health.[2]

Few architects went to Kahn's lengths to share with his competition his successful business model. In 1918 an article on the organization of his office, complete with floor plan, was published in *Architectural Forum*. It even reproduced the job tickets used to track workflow and detailed how drawings were consigned to and retrieved from the office vault. There were photographs of an oak-paneled conference room lined by shelves with the more important books from Kahn's library. Bound architectural journals and technical treatises were kept by the drafting tables in the skylit design rooms for handy reference. All the books were tools just as were triangles, compasses, and French curves. (Borth reported that, when Kahn thought designers needed to be pointed in a certain direction, he drew upon his "amazingly retentive memory and could tell his associates exactly on what page in what book they could find a picture of some architectural detail they were seeking.")[3]

Training Airfields for the Great War

When the U.S. government turned to Kahn for the design of urgently needed military training airfields, it was a historic first—never before had the U.S.

military turned to a civilian architect for such work. Architect Alfred H. Granger served as Captain of Engineers during the war and wrote frankly of "the fact that architecture, as a profession, does not stand in high repute with the heads of the various departments of the Government." He lamented that architects had acquired reputations for being overly concerned about how a structure should look at the expense of caring how it was built. The engineering prowess and reputation for speedy dependability of Kahn's office had much to do with turning this bias around in his case.[4]

The army and navy had entered the war with only four airfields between them and those were poorly equipped. On May 24, 1917, Kahn was designated Architect of the Aviation Section of the Signal Corps of the United States Army, charged with quickly creating plans for a self-contained community for training combat pilots. The plans would be used for building similar facilities across the country. Speed was of the essence, both in providing the plans and getting the structures built, so Kahn's office designed the structures for fast construction with readily available material—primarily wood and concrete. Building types included a 60- by 60-foot hangar capable of housing twelve airplanes, a hospital, an airplane repair shop, officers' quarters, barracks, a supply depot, school buildings, utility structures, a machine shop, and latrines. As a representative example of the task, an estimated $1 million was spent developing a single property for combat pilot training, Selfridge Field north of Detroit, which was somewhat primed for the use beforehand. (Henry Joy had previously purchased the property and began preparing it for aviation use. With the declaration of war, he sold it at cost to the army.) Actual construction was estimated to "cost in the neighborhood of $600,000," as reported in the *Detroit News*.[5]

With its staff working day and night, and probably supplemented by additional hires, the Kahn office produced the drawings in ten days. Cadets were being trained within months and by the war's end there were thirty-one such fields across the country and seven in France. Permanent bases built to Kahn's designs were under construction for Langley Field in Virginia and Rockwell Field in California at the time of the armistice.[6]

Payne Field, West Point, Mississippi (1918). Albert Kahn, architect, and Ernest Wilby, associate. This aerial photograph shows some of the template building designs that Kahn's office created for temporary combat pilot training airfields during World War I. Collection of the author.

Hangar 9, Kelly Field, San Antonio, Texas (1918). Ernest Wilby, associate. The only extant structure from the training field project, this hangar has been restored in its original location for use as an event venue as part of the Brooks City-Base Development. Photograph by the author, 2021.

The Eagle Boat Plant

Kahn's largest single client was FMC, and Henry Ford was an ardent pacifist who, in 1915, launched a highly publicized private-sector junket called the Peace Ship to raise civilian opposition to the expanding war. Clearly it failed to change the course of events and, once the United States entered the conflict on the side of the Allies, he committed all the resources of FMC to providing matériel to arm the American forces. For Ford and other manufacturers, the war work, with the government setting prices, represented a loss in overall revenue compared to their normal civilian production. Most, like Ford, voluntarily and enthusiastically answered the call, but the government applied pressure and coerced any who declined.[7]

While the war against the Central Powers was primarily fought on land and in the skies elsewhere in the world, German U-boat submarines posed an immediate, menacing threat along U.S. seaboards. The navy saw an urgent need to quickly build a fleet of shallow-draft battleships specifically designed to patrol coastal waters, but traditional shipbuilding facilities were already overloaded with other work. Officials turned to FMC and Ford, who proposed using unskilled labor to mass-produce the navy-designed vessels dubbed Eagle Boats (even though their size actually qualified them as battleships). The navy approved, and the task of making it happen fell to Knudsen, who was in charge of FMC's war production. A totally new manufacturing facility was required and it was built from scratch on undeveloped FMC property along the River Rouge in the Dearborn area of southeast Michigan. Kahn worked with Knudsen, and their respective engineering and production experts worked together to design and build the plant with remarkable speed, especially considering that it involved what was believed to be the largest building in the world at nearly a third of a mile long and covering nearly twelve acres.[8]

The speed of this unprecedented project was phenomenal. The secretary of the navy sent FMC a telegram on January 1918 with instructions to proceed with the project—promising a formal contract would follow. For Knudsen and Kahn, planning was a juggling act as the navy was still evolving the ship's design. Their teams continually updated the production process and the facilities around it while scheduling the supply chain requirements attending such a huge construction project in an emergency situation. Work on the shipyard began on February 20, even though the contract was not signed until March. Manufacturing began at one end of the plant on April 20, with the construction at the other end of the building still underway.[9]

The fabrication building was 150 feet wide and 450 feet in length. It led to the colossal assembly building, 305 feet wide by 1,700 feet long. The roofline rose to fit the ship as it trekked through the building, growing during production. For 1,400 feet beginning in the assembly room clearance stood at 36 feet, 5 inches. The ship's superstructure was added in the remaining 300 feet of the assembly line, so the clearance there rose to 50 feet, 9 inches. Twenty-one of the Eagles could be under construction at one time, moving along three sets of railroad tracks through the building. Once in operation, the structure was characterized in *Popular Mechanics* as a "Vast Conservatory," and "not unlike an enormous train shed of great height," with "many

Ford Motor Company "B" Building (the Eagle Boat Plant), Dearborn, Michigan (1918). Albert Kahn, architect, and Ernest Wilby, associate. This May 16, 1918, construction photograph shows only a portion of the structure, with glazing being added to the assembly room. Railroad cars near the crane on the right provide scale. From the collections of The Henry Ford. Gift of the Mow Family.

thousand rapid-fire workmen building real fighting ships in an amazing 'greenhouse.'"[10]

Kahn and Knudsen's role in designing a plant to get the Eagle Boat quickly into production amid a national emergency was nothing short of exemplary. The first ten Eagles were delivered for performance evaluation on schedule, but the process slowed from there as the challenges inherent in mass-producing ships became manifest. The signing of the armistice in November 1918 brought an abrupt end to the project, and the navy's order for 112 ships, initially expected to rise, was cut to sixty. At the end, FMC was able to set an Eagle Boat in the water a mere ten days after laying the keel. This was remarkable, but that was short of Ford's early, optimistic boast of building one a day. FMC bought the building and began converting it to civilian production as soon as the last Eagle rolled out. It became the nucleus of the Rouge Plant, with Kahn designing additional structures.[11]

Launch of the first Eagle Boat, July 11, 1918, with finishing work to be completed once afloat. Workers on the track establish scale. Photograph from the collections of The Henry Ford. Gift of the Ford Motor Company.

The Architectural Profession Reconsiders Industrial Work . . . Too Late

As mentioned earlier, many architects shied from industrial commissions as the increasingly complex work required greater collaboration. All large commissions required collaboration, of course, but the perception of the architect as an artist working on some isolated plateau had taken root, as noted by Captain Granger earlier in this chapter. Statistics are sketchy, but by the eve of the First World War it appears some 90 percent of all building in the country was accomplished without the benefit of an architect.[12] The profession divvied up the remaining market segment, comprising what was considered the more prestigious work.

When the United States entered the war there was an initial flurry of government construction to support the war effort. As discussed, Kahn was handed some huge war-related projects, but other architects benefited from projects suited to smaller offices. As the government work tapered off once its needs were met, however, so did the civilian construction opportunities nationwide, due to wartime restrictions. A quick end to the war was not anticipated in early 1918 and the architectural profession was in a state of near panic as its roughly 10 percent of the building market evaporated for the foreseeable future. The only work left to go around was continuing industrial work related to the war effort. Perhaps because of his conspicuous success in this area, Kahn was invited to provide the closing address when the AIA met in Philadelphia in April 1918 for its annual convention.[13]

Suddenly, it seemed every architect in the country was eager for industrial work—but Kahn knew the organization and aptitude needed to succeed in that arena were not easily nor immediately acquired, despite what others might think. Munitions factories represented the bulk of the available work, and of that, what was not going to Kahn and the handful of other capable architectural firms was now going to engineering contractors. There was talk among AIA members that the solution to their dire straits was to mount a publicity campaign to educate industrialists on the value of hiring an architect. Later in life Kahn would chalk his success up to luck (an explanation thoughtful people surely found unsatisfactory), but on this occasion he made no bones about the fact that, in general, the architectural profession had a reputation for conceited intransigence. Furthermore, the problem of this perception did not lie solely with industrial clients because it was too widespread.[14]

It was up to Kahn to break the news to his fellow AIA members, desperate for work, that a public relations effort at this late date, aimed at industrialists and merely singing the praises of the architectural profession, was unrealistic and doomed to fail. He peppered his talk with humorous exaggerations that may seem sardonic now but appear to have had their desired effect at the time. According to a convention report in *American Architect*, Kahn managed to keep his colleagues receptive and in good spirits.[15] He was, nevertheless, unflinching in his critique: factory owners were happy to have a building that was pleasing in appearance, for it presented a public face for the business and instilled pride in employees. But appearance *had* to be subordinate to function for, at the end of the day, industrial clients did not need celebrated monuments—they needed to generate profit from the work performed within. With tongue perhaps only partially in cheek, Kahn explained:

> Put yourself in the place of a man about to build a factory. Would you call upon an artistic superman, the ardent idealist who soars in the skies, discourses on beauty of design and everything else but practical requirements, or would you seek the man who would suggest a practical, commonsense layout to meet your requirements, the man who would look at the problem from your own standpoint, who would place himself, as it were, in your shoes, and strive to solve the problem with and for you? The answer is obvious. You would place the work with the man of sound judgment, rather than with the artist, even if real and not imaginary, as is so often the case. You would seek an organization composed of men competent and qualified to handle the project in its various phases of plan, design and engineering, both structural and mechanical. Now such organizations are not built in a day, but require time to bring together and perfect in team work.
>
> That any one can do a good manufacturing building, and that it requires no particular skill, has been the general impression of the profession. The owners, however, know it to be quite different and no amount of propaganda will convince them otherwise. . . .
>
> This brings me to a point which so often makes for distrust of the Architect—the eternal disposition of many to occupy a pedestal of exalted

> importance and superiority. It is their intent to make up by an air of profound wisdom what they lack of actual knowledge. Educate the client is their cry, and while they are attempting to educate him on something he knows more about than they, some saner man rightfully walks away with the work. This attitude is particularly offensive to the builder of an industrial plant, who, as a rule, has definite ideas of what he wants.[16]

Kahn closed his AIA address by encouraging architects to set their sights on the postwar building boom that he believed was to come eventually and seize it by following his example, taking the challenging but necessary steps to reclaim industrial work. "The field of plan and design is rightfully the Architects', not the Engineers' nor the Contractors." He predicted the end of the war would see the greatest era of construction ever, and industrial building would surpass all expectations. That said, "The part Architects shall play in the field of industrial building rests with themselves entirely."[17]

It was the message he felt his colleagues needed to hear, but George C. Nimmons, for one, did not seem to agree that architects needed to change their demeanor, at least at the time. With the large-scale Chicago mail order plant for Sears, Roebuck and other significant commercial work in his portfolio, Nimmons penned the first of a two-part essay on "Modern Industrial Plants" for the November 1918 number of the *Architectural Record*. In it, he seems to blame almost everyone but architects for the present state of the profession, essentially illustrating Kahn's point about widespread denial and arrogance within their ranks. At one point, Nimmons brashly states, "Many manufacturers and commercial men do not even know that there is an important relation between their pursuits and architecture," followed by a litany of key building considerations of which Kahn would likely argue successful industrial clients were already well aware.[18]

Armistice

The United States and its industry were, by political design, not ready to enter the war when it came, having hoped that it would never go to war. Once the decision was made to enter the fight, American troops were dependent on their

French and British allies for arms until the American government determined what was needed and who would supply it. Then, by and large, American industry stepped up, spending months working at all possible speed to convert their civilian facilities to wartime production. The FMC Eagle Boat project stood out for its sheer massiveness, but the company was far from alone. By June 1918, 90 percent of Detroit's industries were involved in producing for the war effort, with sixteen factories making airplanes and parts. Some companies, notably DuPont and Bethlehem Steel, saw significant profits supplying warring nations prior to the United States joining the hostilities, but overall, corporate earnings declined while the country was actually at war in 1917 and 1918.[19]

It all came to a screeching halt with the signing of the armistice on November 11, 1918, just as America's industries were hitting their war production stride. Production was closed down as quickly as possible, but the public was stuck with a staggering tax bill and visions of mountains of surplus war matériel. Excess warships of many types, including some Eagle Boats, were sold for scrap. Embarrassed politicians and opportunistic critics were quick to turn on industrialists who had answered their nation's call, decrying them as merchants of death and recipients of blood money. As one industry historian explained in 1941, "the wartime automobile man considered himself abused by the Government" during the Great War. DuPont, a chemical company that had seen great profit during the hostilities, used it to become the largest single stockholder of automaker General Motors in peacetime.[20]

With German U-boats no longer haunting American coasts, the navy had little use for sub chasers. Much of the surplus inventory of Eagle Boats were sold to other countries at a loss. During a 1919 Senate inquiry it was alleged that the Eagle Boat program was "the biggest fiasco of the war," with Ford accused of profiteering while putting the lives of sailors at risk in a patently unseaworthy craft. Key testimony hostile to Ford came from a worker on the line producing the Eagles for FMC. Harry E. Leroy, described as an organ maker who claimed to also have knowledge of boatbuilding, "wanted to clear his conscience, because he knew that some men's sons would be drowned if they went to sea in an Eagle boat." Leroy claimed that the sub chasers were "all wrong" and "cannot stand up in heavy weather." Ford was running for a Senate seat at the time, and it appears the charges crumbled when it was revealed that

Leroy's testimony was at the behest and coaching of the campaign manager to the automaker's opponent.[21]

A number of qualified experts and navy officials testified to the faithfulness of FMC's execution of its contract. Ultimately the investigation absolved Ford of any wrongdoing in connection with the contract. As reported in the *Grand Rapids Press*, FMC's performance was deemed satisfactory. "The navy did not seem to be entirely blameless in the matter," however. "The Ford company had to contend with changes in specifications, involving delay. It had no experience in shipbuilding, but was selected to do the work because the navy could find no one else to do it. [Furthermore,] the government 'could not help' losing money in cancelling contracts with the Ford company."[22]

Despite the facts or Ford's and FMC's absolution in the Senate investigation and elsewhere, the claim that the Eagle Boat project was either an embarrassing failure or a deliberate swindle has endured. Perhaps this is because the investigation shared newspaper coverage with Henry Ford's highly publicized, concurrent libel lawsuit against the Tribune Company.

An unfortunate byproduct of the controversy has been to cast a truly herculean collaboration between Kahn and Knudsen (assisted by others, of course) into history's shadows. As an example, in a discussion of the Rouge Plant's genesis structure, Grant Hildebrand wrote, "The building was designed to produce, of all things, World War I submarine chasers; Ford had convinced the government that these could be produced by assembly line methods. They couldn't."[23] Kahn scholars, including this author, owe much to Hildebrand—but respectfully, they could. Although poorly suited for anything but their intended use patrolling coastal waters in pursuit of submarines, some Eagle Boats survived the surplus scrap program to see U.S. Navy service in World War II. While serving with resolve, one was torpedoed off the coast of Maine by a German U-boat. Forty-nine crewpersons perished (thirteen survived) in the sinking of USS Eagle Boat no. 56 (PE-56), representing the greatest loss of life in New England waters during the Second World War.

14

Architecture Following the Great War

The building boom that Albert Kahn envisioned following the Great War came to pass as projects delayed by wartime restrictions were resuscitated. He reported over $23 million in construction for 1919 through his office alone. Although interrupted by a short but severe economic depression in 1920, the economy received a boost felt in Detroit as factories ceased their munitions productions and returned to making more profitable automobiles for a clamoring public.[1] While the people of Europe coped with rebuilding in the wake of war's destruction, those in the United States sought a return to normalcy. For many, that meant simply getting back to business.

General Motors Building

Originally conceived as the Durant Building in 1919, the style of the General Motors Building seems to reflect the internal politics of the corporate client more than anything else. A common misconception is that William C. Durant, the tireless marketer who founded the company in 1908 and was currently serving as its president, initiated the structure as a tribute to himself. Corporate scholarship suggests that, to the contrary, Durant saw the building as a needless extravagance foisted upon him by the company board, led by Pierre S.

du Pont of the influential, East Coast, old-money family. Board members had lost patience with Durant's aggressive (some would say reckless) one-man leadership and felt a huge administrative headquarters would better cultivate the multilayered corporate organization they preferred. The decision to name it after Durant was made by leading stockholders and officers without his knowledge and represented an effort to placate the headstrong president as they pressed their plan to restructure the company.[2] This being the case, it stands to reason that the board, dominated by Eastern investors, might feel more comfortable with an edifice reflecting the Beaux Arts classicism still entrenched in New England financial institutions over the more overtly function-driven architecture common in the Great Lakes region and points west. Du Pont's cousin, Thomas Coleman du Pont, commissioned the monolithic, Beaux Arts Equitable Building in New York City's Wall Street financial district in 1913. In proposing the style for the Detroit building, Kahn was likely responding to his client's expectations, either as stated by DuPont or supposed by the architect. (Durant resigned in November 1920 and the name of the structure was changed to the General Motors Building. Du Pont held the presidency for a short while before turning the office over to Alfred P. Sloan Jr.)

However Kahn arrived at the stylistic treatment, the results have been largely hailed as superb, unlike the Equitable Building and other buildings that were so widely panned they drove New York City government to impose a zoning law to keep anything similar from ever being built in the city again. (The Equitable Building was set at the edge of its property lot lines and rose essentially straight up for thirty-eight floors, blocking the sunlight from surrounding streets and neighboring buildings.) In Detroit, Kahn struck a balance with the General Motors Building, which is impressive without being oppressive. Its fifteen steel-framed stories, minimally sheathed in light buff-colored Bedford, Indiana, limestone with generous glazing, run 203 feet from the sidewalk to the cornice. Just below the cornice, the top two floors were reserved for executive offices and defined by 292 engaged Corinthian columns wrapping around the many corners at that lofty height. While the building seems to soar, the Corinthian arcade remains close enough to a pedestrian on the ground that it can be appreciated on a human scale. Along with its adjacent five-story plus basement research laboratory it covered two city blocks. The building contained seventeen hundred offices and, according to *Contractor's*

Atlas, a builder's journal of the day, "Every office has outside light and air, thus eliminating the inconvenience of working with artificial light, which is bound to be detrimental to employees." Many of the building's 5,148 windows opened onto one of six light courts that were larger in proportion to the building mass than most of its contemporary office structures. This arrangement infused the mammoth structure with an unexpected sense of airiness while sharing sunlight with neighbors. *Contractor's Atlas* concluded that the architect, as he had done with factories, set "a new mark in the construction of large office buildings."[3]

With thirty-two acres of floor space, the office building was thought the second largest in world (the Equitable Building claimed about forty), and the largest

General Motors Building (currently Cadillac Place), Detroit, Michigan (1919–23). Albert Kahn, architect, and Ernest Wilby, associate. This photograph shows the Grand Boulevard entrance side of the building and the penetration of natural light even into the north-facing light wells. Sunlight visible through the windows of the far wing on the right attest to the natural light exposure. The Laboratories Building is visible on the left. Photograph, circa 1923, courtesy Albert Kahn Associates, Inc.

occupied by a single business. The first floor and mezzanine levels of the building were wrapped on three sides with an arcade of generous display windows. Occupying the south side of the property, the 502- by 60-foot, limestone-faced Laboratories Building was built of reinforced concrete to minimize vibration for the work conducted within (chemical, mechanical and metallurgical laboratories and a machine shop). A massive, forty-foot-tall colonnade of six Ionic columns with diameters of five feet marked its entrance and testified to the value placed on the work within.[4]

The General Motors Building transcends its Beaux Arts trappings to exude structural honesty and virtuosic mastery of repetition integrated with its applied classical details. Organization—both in architectural composition and corporate operation—is communicated through its eight wings, fifteen stories, over three hundred columns, and thousands of windows. Ferry, looking back some twenty years later, discerned in Kahn's architecture "a directness and a mechanical precision that are a true index of the machine age," which, with the General Motors Building, was "carried to its logical climax. The principle of mechanical repetition is even found in the quadruple bays which jut out like a series of massive promontories."[5]

Detroit Police Headquarters

Concurrent with the General Motors Building were plans for a new police headquarters for which Kahn seems to have held the inside track early on. Just as he had traveled with other clients to inspect other building types, he traveled with Detroit Police Commissioner James W. Inches on a trip east in late 1919 to inspect police buildings in several large cities. Inches found little he thought worth imitating; he wanted the new facility to break from the norm. Like the Temple Beth El building committee, he had the right architect in this regard. "We don't want our headquarters building to look like a dungeon or a morgue," Inches explained on their return. "We want light and air, sanitation, cheerfulness and healthfulness, and Mr. Kahn says we're going to have it." The commissioner went on to assure Detroiters, "We're going to have a building strong enough, but we'll camouflage the forbidding exterior feature."[6]

It was over a year, January 1921, before Kahn was officially designated the architect of the police building, and the design grew significantly before its completion in late 1922, but Inches and Kahn basically achieved their initial vision.[7] Echoing the more elaborate DAC further along Madison Avenue, a sober rendering of a Renaissance palazzo was adapted to project seriousness without looking ominous. It rests on a rusticated base featuring a two-story arcade above which five repetitive pier and spandrel office floors rise to a terminating two-story attic and pronounced cornice. Placement of a single, ample light court at the rear of the building allows the structure to appear as a foursquare mass from the street elevations.

Kahn's, and the commissioner's, humanitarianism is evident in the location of the structure's approximately two hundred jail cells on the top two floors. This placement was a radical departure from the tradition of placing the cells

Detroit Police Headquarters, Detroit, Michigan (1922). Albert Kahn, architect, and Ernest Wilby, associate. Photograph courtesy Burton Historical Collection, Detroit Public Library.

in basement levels where, in order to be removed from the public, prisoners were usually relegated to areas where it was difficult to provide sunlight and ventilation and sanitation was a challenge to maintain. Inches condemned this practice as a "crime against humanity." The Detroit structure's upper floors were set off by an ornamental railing and treated as the attic on the façade, with two floors of windows covered by patterned grills, making them appear two stories in height. This is a pleasant departure from the cliché of iron jail bars. The arrangement of the detainment area on the top floors reflects Kahn's rational approach to problem solving: the prisoners were high above the public's view, where escape was near impossible, yet the cells, in the words of one newspaper account, were "as bright, sanitary and airy as any hotel." The superintendent of police quipped, "it will almost be a pleasure to be arrested."[8]

First National Bank Building

Yet another prominent Kahn structure with its origin in 1919 was the First National Bank Building, located on a nearly half-acre, polygonal site previously occupied by George Mason's 1907 Hotel Pontchartrain. The initial plan was to strip down the elegant but outmoded eleven-story hotel to its steel structure and rebuild it as a bank and office building to Kahn's design. In the following year the decision was made to completely raze the hotel and build a new, twenty-five-story structure to a new design by Kahn. Construction began June 21, 1920, and the building's formal grand opening was March 17, 1922.[9]

Exhibiting judiciously applied Renaissance styling inside and out, it rose 312 feet above the sidewalks to be the tallest building in Michigan, with 10.5 acres of floorspace. More closely adhering to the Sullivan model for skyscraper design than the earlier Kresge or Vinton Buildings, Kahn's exterior here exhibited a pronounced base, shaft, and capital features. As a long-accepted architectural composition, it might have reflected a midwestern desire to return to tradition following exposure to the madness of modern warfare. It is perhaps understandable that Americans would have yearned for the past more than Europeans, who were surrounded by the destruction, but this sentimentality would diminish as the rest of the world recovered and America's civilian economy continued to flourish.[10]

First National Bank, Detroit, Michigan (1922). Albert Kahn, architect, and Ernest Wilby, associate. Photograph courtesy Burton Historical Collection, Detroit Public Library.

Ford Rouge Plant

As these structures were rising in the Detroit skyline, Kahn's office continued to grow and prosper with a steady base of industrial work. Some of these were new plants, such as the 1919 plant for Paige-Detroit Motor Car Company, featuring fifteen acres of floor space.[11] Others were the near-continual expansions of Kahn's previous plants, including those for Burroughs and Packard. Exceeding them all were the seemingly endless expansions of the Ford Rouge Plant.

Within two weeks of the armistice, rumors circulated that FMC plans involved shuttering the Highland Park Plant and moving its Model T production to the River Rouge site. The multifaceted process took nine years to complete, and it literally began as the last Eagle Boat rolled out of the colossal Rouge assembly building, followed by workers reinforcing the foundation to support a second story added to the interior. Production of automotive bodies began there by August 1919. The following February saw the first Fordson Tractor emerge from the line alongside the Model T bodies. New support structures began to rise next, with most being designed by Kahn. These included blast furnaces, textile and steel mills, and plants for the production of cement, glass, leather, paper, and rubber. By 1924 the Rouge Plant, as it came to be known, was the largest in the world, yet it was considered only half built.[12]

Knudsen Joins General Motors

In March of 1921, after converting the Eagle Boat Plant to peacetime production and opening three assembly plants in Europe, William Knudsen and Henry Ford parted ways. Samuel S. Marquis, author of a perceptive character

Partial view of the Ford Motor Company Rouge Plant, Dearborn, Michigan (1922 plus later additions). Albert Kahn, Inc., architect. The glass plant occupies the center of the photograph while the white building in the distant right is the Ford Rotunda, a welcome center constructed in 1936 using material from the FMC exhibit building for the Century of Progress Exposition. Photograph, 1937, from the collections of The Henry Ford. Gift of the Ford Motor Company.

study of Ford, wrote of his inexplicable penchant for pushing capable and loyal executives out of the corporation. Of these, Knudsen's departure was the most portentous—driving a tremendous talent away and delivering him into the hands of the competition. (As Marquis observed, Ford could be as "temperamental as an artist and as erratic.") At first, Knudsen quietly found a modestly paying position with a parts manufacturer that was clearly beneath his proven potential and previous salary. It took ten months for General Motors (GM) leadership to become aware that he was available, but on February 23, 1922, he was hired as an assistant to Charles Stewart Mott, vice-president and chairman of the advisory staff.[13]

Knudsen was given an ambiguous position, but Mott and Sloan knew that Ford had driven away an executive of rare caliber and they needed to move quickly. Big Bill spent two weeks surveying several GM units and made a number of recommendations to improve production. On the strength of these, before his first month was out, he was elevated to vice-president in charge of operations for the Chevrolet division. At the time, GM divisions were nearly autonomous, but Chevrolet's unenviable role in the corporation was to compete with the Model T for the low-price automobile market. FMC's single automotive product, the ubiquitous Model T, was outselling Chevrolet by a 13:1 ratio. The division lost $8,692,000 in 1921 and GM engineers were recommending the corporation just give up and abandon the brand. Knudsen saw potential, however, and believed Ford's intention to continue with the Model T alone and develop the Rouge Plant as its single production site was shortsighted and in denial of changing public tastes. Knudsen's vision was to decentralize Chevrolet production and make it more flexible and responsive to change. He set to work with Chevrolet vice-president of manufacturing Kaufman Thuma Keller (widely known as K.T.) to turn the division around and mount a serious challenge to FMC.[14]

The Fisher Brothers

To set Chevrolet on the right course, Knudsen turned to Kahn, his partner for the FMC assembly plants, for plant design. Through GM, Kahn secured a mutually beneficial association with the seven Fisher brothers. The Fishers were sons of a carriage shop operator in Norwalk, Ohio, where they all learned the trade of carriage and wagon building. Fred J. and Charles T. ventured to Detroit, where an uncle had established a separate carriage business. The uncle helped finance his nephews' startup of the Fisher Body Company, which was dedicated to building automobile bodies to supply the many manufacturers. A two-story, 130- by 300-foot factory building in the Milwaukee Junction area of Detroit was purchased in 1908 and soon expanded upon. Five younger brothers (William A., Lawrence P., Edward F., Alfred J., and Howard A.) moved from their home and family business in Norwalk as they successively came of age. (Their father believed it was better for his sons to find their fortunes elsewhere rather than to make room for them in his carriage shop, which would entail laying off loyal non-family employees.)[15]

Detroit journalist Malcolm Bingay may have overstated things when he wrote, "Henry Ford put the world on wheels, and the Fisher Brothers covered it," but he was not far off the mark. From an initial order of 150 units for the Cadillac Motor Car Company, Fisher Body grew to be the world's largest manufacturer of automobile bodies in 1915, with plants in Detroit and Walkerville, Ontario. The last in a series of additions to their Milwaukee Junction property had been designed by Smith, Hinchman & Grylls in 1919—just as GM purchased controlling interest in the company. GM signed a ten-year agreement to buy all of its bodies from the company, and a new expansion program began building Fisher Body plants near GM's assembly plants. With the coming of Knudsen, the Fishers' expansion and their fortunes would accelerate further. Within a few years, Fisher Body became one of the ten largest employers in American industry, with forty-four plants supplying nearby automotive manufacturers throughout the United States and Canada.[16]

By September 1922, the Kahn office was at work on a 400,000-square-foot Chevrolet assembly plant and a 200,000-square-foot plant for Fisher Body in Buffalo, expected to yield five hundred complete automobiles daily. In Norwood, Ohio, outside Cincinnati, 200,000- and 150,000-square-foot plants were built for Chevrolet and Fisher, respectively, to yield three hundred cars a day. Kahn's firm designed alterations and additions for a transmission plant in Toledo as well. More was planned as Knudsen envisioned Chevrolet achieving a daily output of two thousand cars within six months. Building would continue until Knudsen reached his goal of matching FMC one to one in production and sales.[17] Meanwhile, design and construction of FMC's mammoth Rouge Plant continued unabated.

The Riddle of Henry Ford

Two titans of American production, Big Bill Knudsen and Henry Ford, were squaring off against each other in 1922. Albert Kahn was the go-to architect for both, but the relationship with Ford would be strained by the automaker's printed attacks, beginning in 1920, on Jewish bankers he thought conspired against his success. Before it was over, the vile campaign had grown to malign the Jewish population in general, but it seems to have never occurred to Ford that any Jews he actually knew and respected would take offense. This is consistent with the observations of those around the automaker who held him in high regard overall despite being seriously aggrieved by his actions on occasion. Marquis found him continually swayed by "various and conflicting thoughts and emotions. . . . Phenomenal strength of mind in one direction is offset by lamentable weakness in another."[18]

Be that as it may, the attacks were "very much of a blow to Uncle Albert," according to one of Kahn's nephews. His reminiscence holds that Kahn did not set foot at the Rouge Plant for ten years beginning in 1920, but the accuracy of this seems doubtful since Ford publicly apologized for the vitriol in the face of widening outrage in 1927. Furthermore, Kahn's firm executed significant commissions for FMC in the intervening years that surely merited personal attention by the architect. Kahn recalled an early 1929 meeting with the automaker, stating, "I knew that he once had a prejudice against Jews." It appears the architect had by then placed it in the past but considered it still worth mentioning. At the time, however, Kahn surely *was* deeply hurt, and the situation must have been cause for considerable angst. With the DAC, Kahn had friends and valued associations in the membership and very likely wished he could accept the offer to join, but it was impossible while an anti-Semitic element in the club was blocking other Jews for being Jews. With Ford in the 1920s, the dichotomy existed within a single individual with whom Kahn had enjoyed spectacularly rewarding relationship for over a decade. "He is a strange man," the architect said of Ford. "He seems to feel always that he is being guided by someone outside himself."[19]

In a 1923 letter to his wife Ernestine, Kahn fretted over the firm's chances of holding FMC's business through the storm, which may explain his overly fawning praise for the client. An example can be found in an interview published amid the anti-Semitic episode. "The Ford Motor Company is different from any other concern in the world. . . . It is a marvelous organization," Kahn remarked. "The Ford executives always know just what they want. . . . It is really a privilege to work" for them. "We learn so much from Ford's that we are well content to follow their instructions."[20]

While it would be understandable if Kahn felt a particular need to play up to FMC's management during this period in Ford's life, it seems he was never really at risk of losing its business. Through it all, Ford continued with apparent sincerity to regard the architect as "a man who, in my opinion, is without equal," as he told the nationally influential journalist Arthur Brisbane. It may be difficult to understand how Ford could publish such opinions about Jews while holding Kahn in the highest esteem, but many close to the automaker believed he truly could not comprehend the broader, destructive, cumulative effect of the campaign until motivated to the apology. Knudsen, who never lost his deep respect for Ford even while trying to better his former employer in the marketplace, once advised, "you had better not spend your time trying to guess the riddle of Henry Ford, because that would be an all-time job with no results."[21]

Ford Engineering Laboratory

As the Great War receded in memories, so did lingering traces of the Beaux Arts. They became increasingly passé, and the flexible stylistic approach charted by Alfred Messel and others resurfaced. Austrian architect Otto Wagner characterized the trend as a sort of objective realism, bending historical precedent in service to the realities of the present. As the influential historian of modern art Sheldon Cheney wrote in 1930, their style could be "recognized anywhere as Teutonic—and yet universal in its grasp of essential honesty and modern cleanliness of mass and line."[22]

It was vividly on display with Kahn's extraordinary 1922–23 Ford Engineering Laboratory, which took what might be considered an eclectic approach, but one streamlined for a new era. In the Engineering Laboratory, Kahn tapped this

Messel-derived modernism while effectively meshing his concurrent work in one-story, skylit factory structures with an office design. Whether it was deliberately intended to be or not, this architectural gem in Dearborn is in many ways the antithesis of the General Motors Building looming north of Detroit's downtown. While both are monuments in their own right, one is the lavish, $500 million imprint of a bureaucratic corporation headquartered in New York City that forms a highly visible local landmark above the Detroit horizon. The other is a nobly restrained, yet expansive, $1.2 million engineering laboratory framed in a bucolic setting on an artificial lake and closely hugging the formerly rural landscape that the company's owner roamed as a boy. While the elevations are impressive, the true size of the building is difficult to appreciate from ground level.[23]

The tile-roofed Ford Engineering Laboratory attains monumentality through its horizontal expanse: the Bedford limestone exterior features a façade that is

Ford Engineering Laboratory, Dearborn, Michigan (1922–23). Albert Kahn, Inc., architect. Exterior photograph, 1923, courtesy Albert Kahn Associates, Inc.

near unrelenting in its repetition of closely spaced, tall narrow windows. The one-story main mass of the building, essentially a shop area, was 804 feet wide by 202 feet deep with windows separated by flat abstractions of Doric columns that almost look like they had been debossed from the wall surface. For 235 feet at the façade's center, the administrative section protruded from the plane of the building and rose to two stories for the offices of Henry and Edsel Ford and the executive engineering staff. Here four fully articulated, engaged Doric columns announced the entrance while inside the office section extended for fifty-one feet into the building with rich, wood-paneled interior appointments.[24]

Natural light for the work areas is amply supplied from above with monitor bays running the length of the building's roof. This is a Truscon variation on the Aiken, or high and low bay, roof, using crisp, unobstructed steel beams that bend upward to create the monitors instead of typical truss work. (Offering many products and services beyond reinforced concrete, Julius Kahn's Trussed Concrete Steel Company had changed its name to Truscon in March 1918.)

Work area of the Ford Engineering Laboratory. Photograph, 1923, courtesy Albert Kahn Associates, Inc.

A simple innovation, slanting vertical clerestory windows, renders them self-cleaning with exposure to precipitation. According to an account by George Nimmons, "The steelwork has been designed upon architectural, rather than structural lines," and the building is "exceptionally well lighted" by the monitors. The sixty-four thousand square feet of glass equaled some 40 percent of the floor-space. The center monitor bay is higher than the others, with the steel trusses exposed to provide dramatic flair for the interior, with stark functionality. Ventilation was augmented with blowers.[25]

The Ford laboratory was a singular structure, uniquely suited to Kahn's office at that moment. Although hand carved, the abstracted ornament approaches the appearance of mass production. Nevertheless, it was still grounded in classical traditions Kahn studied in the Mason & Rice library, sketched throughout Europe, and marveled at while visiting the Chicago World's Fair. According to a *Detroit Free Press* reporter, the architect classified the Ford Engineering Laboratory as "something of a glorified industrial construction" in a "modern Renaissance design."[26]

Nimmons also noted, "The floor is of maple from Ford's own sawmills at Iron Mountain [Michigan], and is kept as clean and polished as any ballroom floor." This floor, and the building's dimensions, make the Ford Engineering Laboratory the likely subject of a very rare example of Frank Lloyd Wright praising the work of a fellow architect. In a 1930 speech, Wright waxed eloquent over a Kahn building he described as beautiful and a very fine thing wherein men worked at wonderful machines resting on polished flooring as the sun shined in.[27]

15

Albert Kahn, Inc.

In October 1923 Kahn incorporated his office. Many architectural offices led by a principal figure simply cease to exist when that figure retires or dies. (When Henry Bacon died suddenly in 1924, Kahn assisted his widow by appealing to fellow architects to buy out his practice while personally providing a generous contribution to help her get by.) Partnerships dissolve or reshuffle with the life changes of their principals, becoming something other than what they were. Depending on their organization, corporations may be more robust and less dependent on the vicissitudes of mortality. Kahn chose incorporation while keeping his well-established name and reputation to build upon as the company's brand. Contrary to many accounts, he also kept the business in the family, at least initially. In effect, Kahn sold the business in exchange for thirty-five thousand shares of $10 par common stock in the new corporation. His brothers Moritz and Louis later obtained financial interests as minority shareholders. A reorganization would include other employees among owners, but that was not until 1940.[1] Nevertheless, it was a forward-thinking move that would, as it turned out, see the company through his death while it was playing a pivotal role in the liberation of nations.

Also in 1923, Moritz Kahn returned from London, where he was general manager for Truscon, to join Albert Kahn, Inc. The youngest of the family, Louis, had been with the architectural firm since 1909. According to Kahn, "It was Louis who minded the store."[2]

Albert Kahn, Inc., continued expanding its portfolio of a wide range of building types for a wide range of clients in the 1920s. By middecade the firm had about 250 employees, including architects, engineers (structural and mechanical), and outside superintendents (who comprised upwards of forty). Its volume of construction work totaled between $30 and $50 million annually.[3]

During this time, some of Kahn's automotive clients explored building airplanes for civilian use following the Great War. The consumer aviation market never caught on in the numbers needed to justify mass production, however, and most automakers eventually lost interest. Edsel Ford, Henry's son, maintained his enthusiasm and drew his father into a venture developing the commercial aviation industry and providing Kahn with additional opportunities to build on his experience with the U.S. Signal Corps. In the process, the architect again managed to make pioneering contributions in yet another building arena, the public airport.

Ford's Airports

A factory and hangar, both designed by Albert Kahn, Inc., were under construction on land behind the Ford Engineering Laboratory by July 1924. (This is further evidence that Henry never considered severing his business relationship with Kahn despite the contemptible contemporaneous articles in the *Dearborn Independent.*) The factory was the domain of William B. Stout's Metal Airplane Company and Ralph H. Upson's Aircraft Development Corporation (experimenting with metal dirigibles). An archival photograph of the structure, which was destroyed by fire two years later, shows it to feature large work areas bathed in natural light. A hangar stood nearby.[4]

The airport facilities were quickly expanded. A replacement factory built in 1926 was 125 by 500 feet, then expanded with a 140- by 250-foot addition in 1929. This was the incubator for the renowned, corrugated metal–clad Tri-Motor airplane. A second, larger hangar was another marvel of engineering, 360 feet by 125 feet, with the cantilevered roof trusswork supported by a row of interior braces running down the center, which were widely spaced at 62 feet apart. This allowed for portals with clear spans of 320 feet, on both long sides of the building. Serving as doors were sixty 10-foot by 20-foot-tall metal and glass

Stout Metal Airplane Company Factory, Ford Airport, Dearborn, Michigan (1924). Albert Kahn, Inc., architect. Photograph, 1924, from the collections of The Henry Ford. Gift of the Ford Motor Company.

Fenestra panels. These doors, combined with generous windows on the short ends and skylights, flooded the structure with natural light.[5]

Ford's network of connecting aviation facilities spread Kahn's work and influence over to other cities in the same manner as the automotive assembly plants, with Stout Air Services carrying freight and passengers to airports in other cities. The years 1926 and 1927 saw Kahn-designed hangars, similar to the one in Dearborn, under construction at Ford Airports serving Cleveland and Chicago.[6]

By 1929 the Dearborn enterprise could boast a Kahn-designed free-standing passenger terminal. In 1931 the architect also designed the Dearborn Inn, an early and elegant airport hotel for the airport's travelers as well as visitors to Ford's Edison Institute (later the Henry Ford Museum) and Greenfield Village. Kahn's aviation industry work was not restricted to Ford or the

Ford Airport Hangar, Lansing, Illinois (1926–27). Albert Kahn, Inc., architect. On the left is entrance to an office containing a ticketing counter with a passenger depot (waiting area) in the foreground. Photograph by the author, 2023.

Midwest, however. In 1929 the firm designed a $1 million Hartford, Connecticut, manufacturing plant for the Chance Vought Aircraft Corporation of Long Island, New York.[7]

Kahn did not make his own initial flight until August 15, 1928, when he was treated to an aerial tour of Detroit in a Stinson airplane. This provided the architect with his first airborne view of several buildings he and his firm had designed.[8]

The Detroit Free Press Building

One of the structures that surely stood out from the air, with a fourteen-story office tower, was the 1925 Detroit Free Press Building. (Kahn had designed a ten-story building for the publisher in 1913 that was notable for its steel frame construction.) The new structure varied from Kahn's plants for the *Grand Rapids Press* and the *Detroit News* by including rentable office space. It was still an industrial building in that it contained the massive presses necessary for the production of a daily, large-circulation newspaper, but these were relegated to a two-story basement under half the building. The foundation for the other half consisted of a basement and subbasement. The first floor was given to a

Detroit Free Press Building, Detroit, Michigan (1924–25). Albert Kahn, Inc., architect. Photograph, circa 1925, courtesy Albert Kahn Associates, Inc.

marble-lined lobby featuring historically themed murals, with circulation and advertising facilities along with a lobby for the connected Detroit Club (built in 1891, designed by Wilson Eyre). Second and third floors housed the newspaper's offices. The rest of the reinforced-concrete, six-story block-and-steel-frame tower were given to rented office space with light wells sunk alongside the tower. The whole structure was promoted as being "designed by the master hand and mind of Albert Kahn."[9]

Hugh Ferriss exhibited a delineation of the building before the Architectural League of New York, causing a *Town and Country* reviewer to observe, "Mr. Kahn's Detroit Free Press Building chisels out solid cube thick block forms against the sky, the handsome mass striped by the flattest and least Renaissance of pilasters, the bulk opened up in a wise and modern fashion by major fenestration."[10] The Teutonic gothicity of the limestone exterior echoed the Detroit News Building, but here it soared with the structure's greater height.

The Maccabees Building

Chapter 14 mentioned New York City's 1916 zoning law, which required building mass to be reduced and increasingly set back as it rose from the property line, in conformance with prescribed angles from the centers of bordering streets. Given his established appreciation for natural light, it is understandable that Kahn would embrace such a design protocol as reflected in the design of the Detroit Free Press Building: while its relatively narrow tower rises straight up for fourteen stories from the sidewalk along its Lafayette Street façade, it is considerably set back from the flanking six-story wings. The results of the setback code proved popular even where it was not mandated, setting a new trend in building design.

It is also on display in Kahn's design for Detroit's $2.5 million Maccabees Building, which served as the national headquarters for the fraternal organization. As recounted in the *Detroit News*,

> It makes use of the set-back idea which was born of the New York City Zoning Act and obtains the best light possible for every part of the building. Two wings, 10 stories high . . . flank the central section of 14 stories.
>
> The style of architecture in this building follows the lines which Mr. Kahn has used in most buildings he designed. So well known is it that professionals and even many laymen would at a glance recognize the building as his work.[11]

Kahn likely winced to see himself, and not the whole office, credited: there are numerous instances when he took pains to make sure a journalist did not single him out so. That said, he must have been pleased with his firm being recognized as producing a recognizable style from out of the plethora of influences the building exhibited. He said of it, "There are no illusions—no deceptions in the design of the Maccabees Building: nothing pretends to be other than it is; every line tells the frankness, the straightforwardness and the power characteristic of this Country, and the romance of American accomplishments is portrayed by the cleanliness and natural, unaffected beauty of the design found in no other recognized type of design."[12]

Maccabees Building, Detroit, Michigan (1925–27). Albert Kahn, Inc., architect. Photograph, circa 1927, courtesy Albert Kahn Associates, Inc.

For Kahn, the absence of illusion did not preclude ornament, foreign influence, or historic reference. He acknowledged the Maccabees Building was "patterned more or less after some of the modern German work of the years just preceding the Great War and nothing better has been done anywhere in the line of modern building. . . . In its detail, the Romanesque of Central and Southern France, of St. Giles, Arles and Avalon is apparent." Kahn himself had carefully sketched these inspiring sources just a year earlier, but the building was the collaborative product of the office working with the client. He explained the "decorations protruding near the cornice and suggestive of timbers are based on Spanish styles prevalent in New Mexico and Arizona. They were designed to resemble the gargoyles of Notre Dame in Paris." But such ornamental details merely served to enhance the overall composition, which he said personified "the idea of truth in architecture [with] nothing concealed by false frills." Again, verticality was emphasized, with "every office and room in the building [receiving] its full share of sunlight and fresh air."[13]

The Fisher Building

A few years before Kahn's Maccabees Building, Finnish architect Eliel Saarinen entered the highly touted 1922 competition for the design of the Chicago Tribune Building with a submission that was also inspired by New York's zoning law. Saarinen's entry drew the second-place award, but many in architectural circles considered it the best design. Kahn was quite impressed by this approach to the challenge of American tall building composition, observing, "it took a foreigner from Finland who had never built a skyscraper to show us in his remarkable competitive design for the Chicago Tribune Building, *the* real solution of the problem."[14] Saarinen moved to the United States in 1923 to teach at the University of Michigan.

Kahn's much-celebrated Fisher Building, which many justifiably see as directly inspired by Saarinen's design for the Tribune Tower, is without question the apex of Kahn's nonindustrial work, if only for its opulence. The Fisher brothers had reaped an enormous windfall through the sale of their remaining ownership of Fisher Body to GM, and they were now prepared to spare no expense as they invested in real estate. As originally envisioned, the structure would be complete unto itself as the first unit of an eventual three-part development covering an entire city block on Grand Boulevard at an estimated cost of $35 million. This first edifice, the only one realized, was placed across the intersection from the General Motors Building, with its tower effectively positioned where a jog in Second Avenue situated it at the end of a grand approach.[15]

The Fishers placed all their faith in Albert Kahn, Inc., to design the first phase as a truly grand, stand-alone structure and to build it quickly. With a virtually unlimited budget, the *Detroit News* reported, "No expense, Mr. Kahn said, has been spared to make the Fisher building the very epitome of things beautiful." Construction began August 24, 1927, on the L-shaped, eleven-story office block with a majestic twenty-eight-story tower at its corner. In a mere fifteen months, 12,000 tons of steel, 350,000 cubic yards of marble and concrete, and vast amounts of bronze and other materials were crafted into what was described in engineering circles as "a monumental example of structural beauty" ranking among the world's most ornate commercial structures.[16]

The result, according to an article in the *Evening Star* of Washington, DC, "startled the architectural world with its splendor." A reporter for the *Detroit*

Fisher Building, Detroit, Michigan (1927–28). Albert Kahn, Inc., architect. Photograph, 1928, courtesy Historic Architecture and Landscape Image Collection, Ryerson and Burnham Art and Architecture Archives, Art Institute of Chicago. Digital file #38960.

News labeled it "an outstanding example of the new American school of architecture which has arisen to typify the spirit of modern progress." The February 20, 1929, issue of *American Architect* was devoted to the singular structure, with its editors opining, "If the average building tells all its story at first glance, this building will bear looking at many times and yet leave room for further discoveries." Acclaimed architectural delineator Hugh Ferriss noted the unusual cooperation between the client, builder, and collaborating artists in achieving such stunning results so quickly and concluded "the strong qualities which this structure preeminently exhibits are precisely those which caused the rapid rise in the architectural field of this individual designer."[17]

Ferriss was of course writing of Kahn, but as noted the architect did not shy from acknowledging the contributions of those in his office. In *American Architect*, Kahn reported that Robert Hubel oversaw the exterior design while Hugo Knap was in charge of the interior. Wayne Yates supervised the working drawings and H. C. Blake served as special engineer, leading a corps of assistants vital in the swift execution of the plan. The numerous artisans were noted as well.[18]

Interior corridor of the Fisher Building. Photograph courtesy Historic Architecture and Landscape Image Collection, Ryerson and Burnham Art and Architecture Archives, Art Institute of Chicago. Digital file #38961.

A quarter of the Fisher Building's $13 million cost was reported to having been spent on the creation of pure beauty. The first three floors of the street elevations were sheathed in North Star, Minnesota, granite with a grey-green appearance, giving way above to Beaver Dam Mar Villa marble from Maryland. This delicately clouded white marble with black veining was reported to be the only marble available in the quantity needed for the massive office block and the 441-foot tower. White marble from Carthage, Missouri, lined the court areas where typically one might find tile. Sculpture and ornamentation, some quite massive and weighing several tons, further enhanced the exterior, without distracting from the unity of the composition. The Fisher Building was an elaborate, self-contained community complex as much as an office building. Three floors were devoted to retail accessed from grand arcades averaging 30 feet in width by 44 in height and featuring exquisite rare marbles in a variety of colors enhanced by bronzes and applied art. Included in the structure were a three-thousand-seat theater and an eleven-story parking garage. The sheer massiveness of the building challenged Kahn's desire for natural lighting.

Nevertheless, he still managed to provide some eighteen hundred windows, each with bronze frames. According to a booklet promoting its opening, "every office enjoys its share of sunshine and the benefit of direct daylight is secured by all." Blowers were required for ventilation, however, and the building's air was exchanged every three minutes.[19]

The Kresge Administration Building

With 1929 came the completion of Kahn's new administrative headquarters for the S. S. Kresge Corporation in Detroit, a structure that represents another underrated artistic achievement for the architect and his office.

Kresge's administration had outgrown the top floors of its tower on Grand Circus Park and turned to Kahn to design another structure, this time bucking the trend toward tall buildings. On a full block overlooking Detroit's Cass Park,

S. S. Kresge Administration Building, Detroit, Michigan (1929–30). Albert Kahn, Inc., architect. Photograph, circa 1930, courtesy Albert Kahn Associates, Inc.

and with a frontage of 372 feet and depth of 180 feet, the composition projects a massive presence while rising only four stories above grade.[20]

Kahn described the exterior as belonging to the "modern American type modeled somewhat upon German precedent, similar in character to that of the Fisher building," and indeed it owes much to the German buildings he had recently sketched. From a polished granite base, a mass of the Bedford limestone rises with fluted pilasters separating generous, double-hung windows. The fourth floor is differentiated to appear as an attic level beneath a splendid copper mansard roof with gilded terra-cotta trim. A modestly taller entrance pavilion, featuring more polished granite and bronze doors, provides a cynosure for the composition. At the rear, two ample light courts faced in enameled brick provide additional natural illumination and ventilation to the interior.[21]

Inside, the lobby featured walnut paneling accented by marble pilasters and flooring. Beyond that, a bright, marble-lined reception area provided access to the grand stair and elevators. The rest of the first floor was designated for the buying department for the company's 632 stores throughout the United States and Canada. The second floor contained executive offices and the third was dedicated to administrative functions and drafting departments. While the fourth floor contained executive rooms, the story also housed a restaurant, lounges, a library, and an emergency hospital (in case of accident or sudden illness) for employee use. As a company press release stated, "there is expressed in marble and stone, and in equipment and arrangement, every consideration that goes to make employees content, pleasant, and efficient."[22]

The Detroit Times Building

December 6, 1929, saw the opening of the new building for the *Detroit Times*, which was owned by William Randolph Hearst. The legendary publisher gathered some two hundred special guests to mark the formal opening of the imposing edifice in its fifth-floor newspaper assembly room. In attendance were Kahn, whose office designed the structure, and his brothers Louis and Moritz, along with many of their most notable clients, including Henry Ford and Henry Joy.[23]

Conforming to an irregularly shaped property, the architect again found inspiration in contemporary trends in Germany with a six-story structure of pronounced Gothic-like verticality, especially when viewed from the acute angle of the taller main entrance. This entrance led to an elegant, marble-trimmed, two-story, oval reception room. A portal off the lobby led to a bank of elevators and grand stairs paved with coral Tennessee marble. Once again for a newspaper building, production was proudly on display. "The visitor, climbing this magnificent staircase," according to an account of the day, "may pause at the press balcony on the second floor to watch the giant presses grinding out newspapers" on the printshop floor receding into the distance below. The shop was lit by two-story, beveled windows faced on the exterior with Minnesota pink granite surmounted by Indiana limestone. This was studded with sculptural elements representing the many disciplines united in the production of a newspaper.[24] Today the street name, Times Square, lingers as an orphaned reminder of the enterprise and the grand building that once stood there.

More Business Than the New York Architects

Kahn's office had certainly grown since those seemingly hopeless days following Nettleton's death. Sources vary on the size of the office staff on the eve of

Detroit Times Building, Detroit, Michigan (1928–29). Albert Kahn, Inc., architect. Unidentified press photograph, circa 1966, collection of the author.

the Great Depression, as the Kresge Administration Building and the Detroit Times Building were being designed and executed. According to the architect, employment was "on an average between 300 and 350 men and women" in the good years leading up to the notorious stock market crash, but it is possible this number included a spike in personnel connected to the Stalingrad Tractor Plant commission, discussed in the following chapter.[25]

The Marquette Building suite could not accommodate such numbers, so their ranks surely included staff assigned to job locations and branch offices. "We do not seek work in other cities," Kahn noted in 1925, "but we are now operating in about twenty different cities." This represented far-flung work for local clients, such as FMC, and out-of-town clients soliciting their services. In 1929, according to the *New York Journal*'s editor, Arthur Brisbane, the New York branch of Albert Kahn, Inc., constituted the largest architectural office in that city. As Brisbane put it, "I think that it is a very remarkable thing" that Kahn, "with a branch, would have more draftsmen and a bigger organization and more business than the New York architects."[26]

Respected British architect Howard Morley Robertson noted in 1927:

> The office of Albert Kahn is one of those great architectural organizations . . . which exist nowhere in the world on the scale found in three or four of the biggest cities of the United States . . . but what, in Kahn's office, is more remarkable than size is the quality of the work turned out, the obvious influence over so many plans and details of the directing brain of Albert Kahn, the stamp of whose personality is clearly evident in innumerable buildings of widely varying type.[27]

While one might contend, as many do, that other architects exhibited more creativity and pushed the bounds of style to a greater extent than Kahn, arguments that he is somehow only deserving of recognition as an industrial architect can only be based in ignorance of his overall impact. Chicago School architects garner justified credit for pioneering broad-windowed offices in cities that could obtain and justify costly steel framing, but Kahn's efficiently designed, reinforced concrete commissions from coast to coast set an obtainable example to inspire progressive architecture in smaller communities. In the process, his more humane working environments for successful clients surely saw imitation as production-based prosperity spread.

Kahn's innate modesty was a key element in his success. Surely it was a factor drawing his self-made clients, who recognized him as one of their own. They would have had little patience for a self-anointed artistic superman attempting to talk down to them, as Kahn explained at the 1918 AIA meeting. But when they wanted an artist to design a Detroit Athletic Club or a Fisher Building, to cite just two examples, they knew they could count on him to deliver in that arena as well. As Kahn was ever accommodating, he expected his employees to be as well. Prima donnas were not to be tolerated, not even as company president. Kahn explained, "In our offices there are no jealousies."[28]

Excellent architects who could stand the pace were drawn to the Kahn office. The talented Ernest Wilby stands as an example of an employee who had been content with this office structure for fifteen years, apparently only leaving due to health concerns. He was in the company of many long-term employees who perhaps sacrificed individual fame for the sake of the stability they could be assured of under the Kahn, Inc., umbrella. Others were more transient, but Kahn still valued their contributions. Like Mason, Kahn did not begrudge anyone pursuing their dreams and welcomed back returning employees such as Wirt Rowland. One of his departures was to study architecture at Harvard with Kahn's encouragement and letter of recommendation. Rowland wrote years later that Kahn never had an unkind word for him.[29]

The reputation, experience, and organization built by Kahn over these years are without parallel. Functioning cohesively, the firm routinely managed several remarkably large and diverse projects simultaneously—projects that by themselves were beyond the capability of most architectural firms. Instead of a project progressing in stages from one department to the next, the various areas of expertise worked in unison and in continual communication with each other to provide an incredibly fast turnaround with minimal conflict and rework. Kahn did his best to share this process with other architects, but it appears few cared to attempt to emulate his success. Perhaps they could not manage a business on the level that Kahn managed his. Or perhaps they simply did not possess the personal nature needed to lead such an organization—a nature rooted in his upbringing but also shaped by his interaction with clients of similar disposition and high attainment.[30]

16

Ideology and "Architectural Trend"

Chapter 12 included an exploration of Kahn's acknowledged debt to Alfred Messel. While Messel produced some fine work, his real contribution to architecture may have been his example, which gave those that followed license to rummage the past and apply what they found in the service of the present, free of constraints such as rules of architectural orders imposed by the long dead. A building need only serve the present, which exerts its own constraints such as utility and current taste to rein in excess. In the wake of his death, architects such as Kahn built upon Messel's precedent and the wealth of the past to meet the needs of their day in their individual manner.

Another movement for a new architectural style arose in Europe in the first decades of the twentieth century. As early as 1913 Germany's Walter Gropius reprinted images of Kahn's industrial work, without identifying its architect, to illustrate the stylistic potential for structure shorn of ornament. This was also embraced in the Futurist architecture of Italy's Antonio Sant'Elia. In a 1914 manifesto, Sant'Elia rejected all historicism, ornament, and traditions of the past in favor of a new, machine-influenced dynamism appropriate to a new society. Swiss-born Le Corbusier and German Erich Mendelsohn also drew inspiration from the Kahn illustrations that Gropius published and republished them themselves, still without credit. These were part of an ideologically driven troupe of designers who abandoned the evolving path toward new architecture trod by the likes of Messel in favor of immediate liberation from everything that came before, or so they claimed.[1]

Following the Great War, this urge for liberation took on a greater sense of urgency and a formidable burden of social responsibility. There was a drive to effect collective change so that such destruction as had been wrought by the war could never be repeated. Eventually identified as architects of the International Style, they found support among those widely considered to compose the world's intelligentsia, who were seeking a socialist world order that promised a preferable alternative to a capitalistic one that, in their minds, was unjust, predisposed to war, and had seen its day. Architecture, they believed, could provide tangible expression of their ideology by scorning tradition, with the more striking the results, the better. Because it represented such a decisive break with the past, the International Style architects and their champions tended to consider only *their* work to be truly modern, engendering the resentment of architects pursuing differing paths to modern relevance.[2]

A Dandy Time Looking Up Things

In late 1927 Kahn made another trip to Europe, which was still rebuilding from the war, and he noted the new architecture he found in abundance. Whereas Detroit's new construction, such as the General Motors Building, signaled growth through prosperity, Europeans were rebuilding from war's vast ruin on tight budgets. Much of the urgently needed recent construction was being funded by cash-strapped states, and a group of architects excelled at buildings of unadorned simplicity that suited the moment in sometimes interesting ways. They were not merely responding to budget constraints, however. They were part of an ideological movement leveraging architecture to clear a path for a new society then being envisioned.[3] Kahn, however, seems to have been only interested in the new construction he encountered.

In a letter on his return voyage dated January 28, 1928, Kahn wrote of visiting Stuttgart, Leipzig, Dusseldorf, Cologne, and Berlin. "Architecturally there is more of good modern work in these towns than in all the other non-German cities put together. I had a dandy time looking up things." Commenting on the progress being made he observed, "Germany is coming back. . . . My next visit to Europe will certainly devote a good portion of the trip to Germany." It seems that he felt he had seen enough of Italy's classic architecture by this juncture, but added, "many changes have taken place under Mussolini."[4]

This is not an indication that he no longer valued his accumulated knowledge: in later lectures and essays he stressed the importance of understanding historic precedent despite changing tastes. There were new trends drawing his curiosity, however, proving that as he neared sixty years old Kahn was still educating himself and willing to consider new directions.

Ideological Architecture in the Soviet Union, Italy, and Germany

Examples of ideologically driven architecture could be found scattered about Europe and it is not certain which Kahn visited in person or whether he had any initial awareness of the theoretical underpinnings. It was truly an international movement, although three countries—the Soviet Union, Italy, and Germany—stand out for their state support at a time when private sector clients were, by and large, slow to embrace its most ideologically strident practitioners. Soviet architectural historian Salim Omarovich Kahn-Mahomedov claimed the USSR as home to "the first truly socialist architecture," with architects wishing "to create a new form of architecture, free from conservative Tsarist traditions" following the 1917 Revolution.[5] The movement was multinational in scope, however, with stalwart manifestos issued by its architects promoting an unmistakable socialist agenda. Three projects illustrative of state-supported construction are represented here.

Of course, in the Soviet Union individual private client support had ceased to be and was replaced by what was termed a social commission. When it came time to build again, according to El Lissitzky, architects needed to shed the old skin of their classical training, and their first act was one of complete rupture with the past. One stunning example of this effort clearly embraced the styling of industry—Gosprom (house of state industry) in Kharkov (now Kharkiv in sovereign Ukraine, where the building is known as Derzhprom). The building was described in 1931 by a temporary resident from America, journalist Eve Garrette Grady, as "a most interesting adaption of German modernistic architecture and claimed to be the largest office building in Europe." Intentionally

Gosprom, Kharkov, USSR. (1925–28). Sergi Seraphimov, Samuil Kravetz, and Mark Fleger, architects. Soviet-era postcard view, captioned "USSR in Construction," collection of the author.

at odds with the surrounding indigenous architecture of the formerly agrarian community, it was an unmistakable expression of Communist state authority. That authority and its building were so resented by the locals that Red Army sentries were posted around Gosprom to prevent bombing or vandalism.[6]

In Italy, the International Style had roots in the Futurist movement as pioneered by the drawings and writings of Sant'Elia, who was killed fighting during the Great War before he could build much. As noted above, the Futurists initially rejected traditional ornament as trappings of the bourgeois past, but this changed with the winds of politics. The multidiscipline movement's founder and emissary, poet Filippo Tommaso Marinetti, proudly boasted in the January 1, 1927, issue of *Critica Fascista*, that it was this group of artists that were the first to rally around Il Duce in his march toward dictatorship. Columbia University's Herbert W. Schneider recorded his first-hand impressions of Italy's transformation. "The stronghold of the futurists has been architecture," he wrote. "When Mussolini announced his plan of rebuilding and enlarging Rome, the futurists immediately set to work." This resulted in the many changes noted by Kahn in his correspondence. Mussolini was not as inclined to cast off *all* the vestiges of Rome's past glory, however: historical associations served his pursuit of grandeur and historic legitimacy. Futurists or not, architects obliged and, as a result, examples of "the new Fascist style," wrote Rexford Newcome in 1942, "although definitely modern in spirit, embody a feeling that reflects Italy's previous classic tradition." Marinetti also asserted that this architecture was impacting all the cities of the world, although it is arguable as to which countries were leading and which following.[7]

At this early point, Kahn seems to have been oblivious to the political appropriation of classical ornament and simply interested by its results. As observed by an author contributing to *National Geographic*, "modernity has come suddenly, if not completely, to Rome. . . . My first impression was that Fascism's public works were transforming the country's aspect completely." The new upper and middle class, he noted, comprised government bureaucrats dwelling in "ultramodern modern apartments, five or six stories with elevator," looking down upon the governed, housed in old construction below.[8]

Following the war, Germany was in social and economic tatters, making it ripe for political change. Gropius founded the Bauhaus, a publicly funded school of design that for many and complex reasons became symbolic of the upheaval springing from the socialist movement. As designed by Gropius in 1925, its campus at Dessau reflected the school's curriculum, which attempted to unite the arts under a new way of thinking endorsed by the German state. It echoed earlier industrial work by Gropius and epitomized the movement that came to be known as the International Style. Townspeople were forced to support the school through their local taxes, and they came to resent the faculty and students, who came from throughout Germany and abroad, bringing nonconformist ideals. Ideological battles between Communists and National Socialists within the campus community led to riots requiring police response, and unrest spread to the city.[9]

Local attitudes toward these three building projects were surely shaped by resentment of the governments that funded them with their tax dollars. Added to this, the International Style approach was seen as deliberately provocative, which it must be admitted was the goal of many of its champions. When the style seemed everywhere stalled in the mid-1920s due to a lack of private sector patronage, German architect Ludwig Mies van der Rohe rallied a Moscow gathering of architects by proclaiming that the movement needed to align itself with an organization such as the Communist Party for support.[10]

Entertaining Gropius

In 1928, Gropius made his first visit to the United States, touring it from coast to coast over nearly two months with a small entourage. The visit was not much publicized, and the architect was little known in America at the time, although his name was mentioned in an April *Detroit Free Press* article on the Weissenhof residential settlement in Stuttgart. This was a largely state-sponsored 1927 collaboration of several European Modernist architects, including Gropius, intended to showcase experimental architectural design for nations beginning to rebuild in earnest. Kahn surely visited it while in the city in 1927.[11]

Gropius stopped in Detroit in May 1928, where an enthusiastic Kahn played host to the then former director of the Bauhaus, treating him to an elegant dinner, a tour of the city's architecture, and a visit to Dearborn and the FMC works. According to a biography of Gropius largely shaped by him, Kahn was pleased by the German architect's admiration of his reinforced concrete industrial work. He was less happy, the story goes, when Gropius made clear his indifference to his host's nonindustrial architecture.[12] (It seems such candidness was a trait common within the profession.)

Gropius was obviously seen by Kahn as a distinguished guest. It is unknown whether Kahn yet grasped the political and ideological subtexts associated with this new architecture, however. (In Mies's speech opening the Weissenhof project to the public, he framed it as part of the great struggle to create a new way of life.)[13] Based on his admitted ignorance of the Soviet government, discussed below, Kahn probably considered the motivation of these European avant-gardists outside of his areas of concern. Coming events would cause this to change. It is clear, however, that in 1928 he was at the very least intrigued by this current architectural trend.

The Stalingrad Tractor Plant

For those seeking a socialist world order, their mecca was where it was being implemented in the 1920s: the Soviet Union. A popular misconception held that the Communist regime inherited from the tsars a nation economically and culturally backward, which was partially but not totally true. Although much of its vast territory remained rural or unpopulated, Russia had a moderate industrial base prior to the revolution and was even making automobiles, but not in mass production. In the years that followed, factories built under the deposed and executed Nicholas II swiftly fell to disuse and skilled workers and engineering personnel dispersed into the countryside or emigrated. (Factories visited by FMC representatives in 1926 were proof of this.) Communist attempts to revive the industry were for naught and eventually the need for foreign assistance was officially acknowledged. In November 1928 a delegation of thirteen engineers from the USSR arrived in New York with a daunting assignment: somehow acquire the expertise and equipment needed to implement Joseph Stalin's far-reaching plan to industrialize—essentially from scratch—their vast country in a span of five years. The engineers began a tour of U.S. industries, trying to absorb all the information they could while making the necessary business connections.[14]

By the following April they had made their way to Detroit, having come to understand the value of having the right team to design a manufacturing plant. Automakers with a long tradition of showcasing their capabilities proudly opened their plants to the delegation and sang praises of Kahn's firm. (As a high-ranking engineer in Stalin's government later divulged, "To a Soviet official long steeped in intrigue and saturated with fears, the American candor and lack of suspicion seemed almost childlike.") This led the Soviet engineers to make an impromptu visit to Kahn's office atop the Marquette Building.[15]

The delegation's members were under great pressure to expedite construction of a massive new tractor plant at Stalingrad (formerly the village of Tzaritzn, currently Volgograd), capable of producing twenty thousand tractors a year. It was envisioned as the flagship effort of Stalin's first Five-Year Plan but was stagnating due to a number of factors, including poor direction by planners, who lacked experience for such a grandiose undertaking, and an unskilled labor force.[16] At Kahn's office, the Soviet delegation found a one-stop shop that could help them satisfy the expectations of Stalin, who had a well-established reputation within Soviet borders for dealing harshly with those who disappointed him.

Kahn later recalled laboring over his decision to work for the Soviet Union. "I knew little or nothing about the Russian government, and the people behind it," as he later admitted, but "there was bitter feeling against Communists among the people with whom I had to do business." They had their reasons: in a Communist-led 1921 strike against Fabbrica Italiana Automobili Torino (Fiat), unionist workers seized its factory in Turin, Italy, locking company officers out of the building and attempting to produce automobiles on their own. Within two weeks the folly of the plan was obvious, but the movement's surrounding chaos and unrest saw Mussolini, previously an extreme socialist labor agitator, rise to power as a Fascist leader promising to restore the desperately desired order he helped disrupt. Nevertheless, in time communist activists succeeded in destabilizing industry around the continent and, to a much lesser degree, in the United States. The ideology meanwhile gained appeal among some workers and, perhaps more significantly, American intelligentsia.[17]

While Kahn's clients may have had legitimate concerns over the spread of the ideology, it is understandable that the architect himself knew little or nothing about the people behind the Soviet government in 1929. Kremlin leaders were remarkably successful in hiding the brutal oppressiveness and failures of their regime while presenting the image of being a classless workers' utopia where poverty, unemployment, and other social ills currently plaguing capitalist democracies were unknown. With much of the Western media and intelligentsia complicit in promoting this façade, knowingly in some cases, Kahn would have had little reason to refuse the commission. In addition, the peoples of the former Russian Empire had an unquestionable history of suffering under the previous rule of the tsars. "The more I thought about it," he later told Malcolm Bingay, "the more I became convinced it was the right thing to do. I said yes."[18]

Subsequent meetings resulted in a contract for Albert Kahn, Inc., to design and equip a $4 million tractor plant in Stalingrad, signed May 8, 1929, with Amtorg, a trading company set up by the Soviet government to facilitate foreign commerce. The USSR having no diplomatic relations with the United States at the time, Amtorg's headquarters in New York served as a pseudoembassy for the Soviet government, through which covert agents were admitted into the country along with legitimate business personnel. Like an embassy, it employed locals for some positions. In Amtorg's case, these employees were carefully vetted members of the Communist Party of the United States of America (CPUSA) and the Fifth Avenue address was a hotbed of espionage activity.[19]

Officially designated the Dzerzhinsky Tractorstroy, the Stalingrad plant was a formidable undertaking. Kahn's previous manufacturing projects, such as the FMC Rouge Plant, were built and equipped over several years as production was transferred from older locations. This allowed construction and its cost to be spread out over time while production ramped up through an inevitable period of adjustment. The Stalingrad plant was to rise from the fields complete and become fully operational as fast as possible. With Soviet industry not able to meet the requirements, material such as tremendous steel trusses were fabricated in the United States and Germany and shipped to Stalingrad. Albert Kahn, Inc., provided the plans, oversaw the fabrication and transport of the building material, chose the equipment, and directed the construction in conjunction with Soviet authorities.[20]

There was much excitement surrounding this flagship project and a Soviet industry newspaper proclaimed that the involvement of the Kahn firm guaranteed it would be built on schedule with the benefit of American expertise. There was excitement in the United States as well: by September 1929 the Soviet Union represented the nation's fourth largest market for machinery. (Its government was on track to becoming the world's largest buyer of machinery and equipment, even before the Black Tuesday stock market crash that came a month later.) In the USSR, as *Detroit News* foreign correspondent Philip Adler noted at the time, the *tractorstroy* was being proclaimed as "key not only to socialist Russia, but the socialization of the entire world." Throughout the Soviet Union, radio broadcasts and newspapers accounts expounded the Five-Year Plan goal to "Overtake and Outdistance the Capitalist Countries!" The Stalingrad Tractor Plant was completed in five months, while equipping it ran another seven. It was visited by an American journalist during the equipping phase, who described the plant as impressively big and modern. The assembly room, over 1,300 by 300 feet, bristled with "an endless forest of lathes, drills gear cutters and a hundred machines that only a specialist could name, all of them bearing American trade-marks."[21]

Stalingrad Tractor Plant, Stalingrad, USSR (1929–30). Albert Kahn, Inc., architect. Soviet postcard, circa 1930, collection of the author.

While the size and speed of the project was not unusual for Albert Kahn, Inc., or many of its American clients, it was remarkable for being accomplished across a tremendous distance and considerable cultural and language differences. While work was underway, Soviet chief of the plant Vasily Ivanovich Ivanov confided to a visiting Detroit correspondent, "We are trying to keep up your 'Americansky Temp.'" When the plant was completed, however, Soviet propagandists credited it all to the "Bolshevik tempo" of work, claiming that even "Albert Kahn, accustomed to the dizzy speed records of America could not believe it at all."[22] Actually, he probably could.

Kahn and the Five-Year Plan

A few months into the Stalingrad project, the Soviet government was impressed enough with Kahn's performance to offer the firm a two-year contract to provide technical assistance and training for all industrial construction in the USSR

This was signed January 9, 1930. It was a colossal, multifaceted undertaking that ultimately resulted in the design of some 570 manufacturing plants—some equal to or larger than the Stalingrad project—and the training of thousands of Soviet architects, engineers, and draftspersons. The bulk of the training was done in Moscow under the supervision of Kahn's brother Moritz (vice-president of the firm), with about twenty-five experts from the Detroit office rotating in and out over the course of the contract. Meanwhile, twenty-five rotating Soviet trainees were assigned to study at the Kahn office in Detroit.[23]

Over the nearly three years of its Soviet contracts, Kahn's office contributed greatly to the industrialization of the Soviet state, including mammoth tractor plants at Kharkov and, biggest of all, Chelyabinsk. There were other foreign architectural and engineering firms working on Five-Year Plan industrial projects, however, as well as individual engineers. It should be noted that only industrial work with clearly objective, functional requirements was entrusted to these foreigners. Other architectural work was reserved for Soviets and a small circle of outside socialist sympathizers. All were public projects, but those with arguably more subjective, aesthetic latitude than technological requirements (housing, theaters, club buildings, communal baths, communal kitchens, etc.) were designed by ideologically committed architects as demanded by the concept of *partiinost'*—Lenin's decree that all intellectual pursuit serve the revolution. Nonindustrial architecture was a vehicle for propaganda and therefore not to be entrusted to nonbelievers.[24]

Soviet Realities

Although Kahn would not visit the Soviet Union himself until fall 1931, his knowledge of the USSR soon expanded from the little or nothing he possessed before signing the contracts. As mentioned, the government of the Soviet Union was so successful in masking its true nature and conditions within its borders that tourists and workers were voluntarily flocking there. Some five thousand tourists visited in 1930, with many who otherwise faced unemployment choosing to stay and work. The number probably doubled the next year. Closely chaperoned so they only saw what officials wanted them to see and when they saw it, "Nearly all these tourists flitted lightly from one city to another and swallowed all that was handed to them," according to Fred C. Beal. An American working in Kharkov and officially "in charge of propaganda and cultural relations," Beal's duties included guiding foreign visitors and correspondents about the Kahn, Inc.–designed tractor plant there.[25]

Originally a committed communist, Beal became disillusioned by what he saw in the USSR and his role therein. This included witnessing the brutal roundups of masses of beggars to get them off the streets prior to the arrival of foreign visitors. Starving men, women, and children were all trucked off and callously deposited in distant wilderness areas in hope that they would not survive their walk back. Such actions were perpetrated to remove visual contradiction to the myth promoted abroad that there was no unemployment in the Soviet Union while the capitalist countries floundered. Staged shams were routine, such as showcase collectivist farms staffed with well-fed and robust actors while Beal had seen actual farm workers typically listless and emaciated, existing at the edge of starvation. Although segregated from the general Soviet population, Kahn's employees would eventually get a sense of the Soviet reality, as will be seen. In the meantime, according to Beal, the blinkered American tourists returned home believing themselves to be "informed enough to write a book, to give interviews, to deliver lectures on the Communist progress." In America, 210 books were published on the subject of planned government in 1930. The number jumped to 365 the next year, while magazine articles on the topic soared.[26] The scale of the ruse was vast and aided by a language barrier; it understandably took awhile for many of the foreign specialists to catch on.

Nevertheless, in 1930 a contrary narrative began to gather credence that would cause Kahn to privately express doubt about his socialist state client. For example, on September 13 a group of some 150 unarmed peasants, including women and children, made a desperate dash toward one of Poland's border checkpoints to get *out* of the supposed workers' paradise. Unable to act until the refugees actually reached the checkpoint, Polish soldiers watched as they were mowed down by Red Army machinegun fire within forty feet of their goal. The majority was killed while the wounded were dragged back to the Soviet interior. The story was reported on the front page of the *Detroit Free Press* on the next day, so it could not have escaped Kahn's notice.[27]

On September 21, 1930, the front page of the newspaper carried an accusation that some 450 Americans, workers at the Stalingrad Tractor Plant and their families, were effectively being held prisoners, unable to leave the Soviet Union, with their lives "threatened by typhoid, typhus, dysentery, scurvy, malaria, pneumonia and a number of unknown Asiatic fevers." Their communications with the outside world were being read and censored, and pay supposed to be wired to American banks was not being deposited. Given Soviet state secrecy, it was not possible to verify the story, but it was provided by Lemuel Lewis, one of the hundreds of Americans who migrated to Stalingrad to work at the tractor plant under contracts with Amtorg. He was exiled from the USSR for his role in a racially motivated confrontation, which the Soviet government attempted to leverage for maximum effect in an effort to highlight American racial strife. Ironically, the publicity served to substantiate Lewis's claims once he was outside Soviet borders and free to speak. By this time, Kahn's work at Stalingrad was completed and his employees were involved in other projects, but he felt it necessary to address the controversy. "All of our workers are now in Moscow, happy and contented," he stated through a press release. "Our men have nothing to do with the Stalingrad plant."[28]

Clearly, Kahn could not be held responsible for any client's management of its plants, but it seems he was not being forthright with his claim that all of his staff in Moscow were happy and contented. Kahn employees being debriefed by the U.S. State Department on exiting the USSR in late 1930 professed to be feeling relieved to get out. They reported that Soviet citizens lived in such fear of their government that "if there is someone missing, one knows—political prison. Fearing to raise suspicion people dare not say a word." Another employee, William H. Bruss, an architectural engineer who worked in the Moscow office that first year, regarded the ordinary Soviet citizens he encountered as "Nice people—but scared to death." He found them to be "All fatalists. You know: 'They got my brother-in-law yesterday; maybe it'll be me tomorrow.'" Such impressions had to have been conveyed to Kahn. This awareness was not isolated to the Kahn employees in Moscow. Foreign specialists contributing to other Five-Year Plan endeavors learned not to be candid about any frustrations in working with Soviet workers once they understood that their complaints could result in the imprisonment or even execution of the offender.[29]

This created a dilemma that one imagines as somewhat similar to the situation when Henry Ford's publications aired anti-Semitic rants. Should architects, or any professionals, turn away legitimate business or publicly condemn clients whose disconnected actions run against the grain of their own values? Such was not the norm in the early 1930s, especially amid the Depression, when the jobs of many valued employees hung in the balance. If Albert Kahn, Inc., lost its Soviet contracts, many would be laid off at a time when their chances of finding other architectural work was nil.

There was a significant difference here, though. While words printed in Henry Ford's name were patently offensive, they remained words. The actions committed in the name of a new socialist order resulted in calamitous misery, torture, and death, which eventually numbered in the many millions. Complicating the matter for Kahn was that several of his employees and their families were currently within the Soviet Union and outside the support of U.S. diplomatic relations. There would be little recourse should they be denied exit if Kahn reneged on his contract or appeared to be shutting down operations prematurely. While this may seem like paranoia to a modern reader, such concerns were common among foreigners in the Soviet Union who knew its true nature and wished to leave. For instance, the prominent American entertainer Paul Robeson heartily embraced the promise of Soviet state, where he was much beloved. So much so, in 1936 he enrolled his son in an exclusive Moscow school attended by children of high Soviet officials, including Stalin's daughter. Later, a top CPUSA leader, in a rare example of disobedience to the Kremlin, confidentially advised Robeson to make Paul Jr.'s enrollment highly public, to lessen the chances of the son becoming a hostage of the Soviet government (a common occurrence to keep foreigners obedient). The entertainer followed the advice, while covertly planning, beneath the ever-watchful eyes of authorities, to eventually remove his son to the safety of London under the pretense of it only being a short vacation.[30]

With the potential that his employees could become hostages, Kahn understandably kept private his thoughts about the politics of the Soviet world. Western intelligentsia, meanwhile, touted the totalitarian orders of the Soviet Union and Mussolini's Italy with increasing enthusiasm as exemplars for other countries to emulate. In contrast, they ascribed to capitalism alone the horrors of war and the expanding economic depression. Along with these governments, they also hailed the work of certain architects whose work was supposed to exemplify this ideology.[31] It appears Kahn saw the field of architecture, where he held unquestioned expertise, as the forum where he could sound a warning.

Modernism with a Capital "M"

Although not immediately adopting the term International Style, books on the subject were published in Europe in the 1920s. Supportive commentators placed this Modern architecture, often distinguished with a capital M to separate it from merely recent construction, within social and historical contexts that would not be perceived as threatening. In Europe it was promoted by its architects as a break with the past, but American critics painted it as a continuation leading to a new direction. As Anthony Vidler summarized the American narrative eighty years later: "History might lead architecture to modernity, but once there it was to be cast off." A widely influential book touting the movement and its architects was published in the United States in 1929. Its reception situated the twenty-six-year-old author, Henry-Russell Hitchcock, Jr., as America's foremost authority on the subject in the minds of many. *Modern Architecture: Romanticism and Reintegration* celebrated the work of select, mostly European architects responsible for collectivist manifestos, seeing them as New Pioneers of a New Tradition (his capitalization), while acknowledging some antecedents. He also saw reinforced concrete construction as the lynchpin of this new tradition in architecture, as acknowledged by Gropius, Le Corbusier, and others in publications that Hitchcock cited.[32]

Hitchcock seemed to be unfortunately, if not inexplicably, unaware of Kahn's celebrated work employing reinforced concrete as well as steel and glass. Had his cutting-edge designs, such as those for Packard in Long Island City and Philadelphia, been given their due, perhaps Kahn would have been regarded over the years as an initiator of the Modern instead of a merely prefacing inspiration. As it was, Hitchcock only mentioned the architect with a rather perplexing observation of which it is difficult to make heads or tails: "the Classical factories which Ford commissioned of Albert Kahn before the Finnish influence became dominant in Michigan look like factories only at the expense of the Doric order."[33]

A professor at Wesleyan University, Hitchcock was billed as "one of the most brilliant critics of modern architecture" when he spoke on the subject at the Detroit Institute of Arts on the evening of January 13, 1931. As promoted in the *Detroit Free Press*, he would be speaking on the "remarkable changes, as well as the accomplishments, of European building" during the previous decade, which "presents a strong contrast to work in the United States." Modern European architecture, particularly that of Germany, was described as "lively, intelligent and interesting work," regarding which, "Mr. Hitchcock is, of all students of architecture, the best fitted to discuss."[34] That was quite a claim that Kahn might have found hard to resist seeing substantiated, but it is not known whether he was in attendance that evening.

Hitchcock's book was on the shelves of the Detroit Public Library, however, and may have been in the Kahn office as well. Kahn might easily have read the professor's characterization of the World's Columbian Exposition architecture as "a sort of white plague," and the Gropius-designed Bauhaus campus as an example of "the possibilities of large-scale architectural development in answer to contemporary sociological needs."[35]

"Architectural Trend"

With faith in socialism as a panacea for the prevailing economic woes on the rise, and Hitchcock's touting of its architects as offering the answer to contemporary sociological needs, it seems Kahn felt compelled to speak up. Through the Moscow office, he had insight into the deceits of the Soviet order that many in the United States failed to grasp. Likely feeling only qualified to discuss architecture, he couched his comments within concerns over how the new movement impacted his profession. For him, it was time to make a principled stand for the role of tradition in the evolution of architecture and, by extension, the role of tradition in society. His choice of venue was an interesting one. While Hitchcock had ventured into the Midwest for his presentation, Kahn went to the East Coast, stronghold of the intelligentsia. He spoke before the members of the Maryland Academy of Sciences, an organization dedicated to presenting scientific and technological matters before the public and located not far from Washington, DC. It appears that Kahn understood that in the United States, as elsewhere, nonprofessional, general interest journals were used to sow support for revolutionary social change among intelligentsia through the arts. If the International Style needed the patronage of the state to survive in the United States as it did in Europe, Washington could be a key debate setting. Titled "Architectural Trend," the text was published in the April 15, 1931, number of the *Journal of the Maryland Academy of Sciences*.[36]

In his lecture, the sixty-two-year-old Kahn reflected on the wonder of the moment for an architect, liberated, as never before, from the bounds of time and geography that limited previous efforts. "Today, owing to modern methods of transportation, to printing and photography, we may familiarize ourselves with all that has been done. Thus we make use of all established styles." The cumulative wealth of the global effort to build was presently virtually available to all to tap for guidance and inspiration. Ironically if not tragically, however, "At present there is a trend to follow no style, to throw all precedent to the winds and to do the utterly new and original. But there is nothing utterly new, so, to be original, we indulge in the strange and bizarre."[37]

Ostensibly, he was speaking of architecture, but his words suggested broader meaning when he declared that "a new theory has taken hold." One senses he believed his colleagues, and perhaps much of the world, should be reveling in relative peace and growing prosperity (albeit momentarily interrupted by what at the time could still be a relatively short economic depression), but instead, "All done these past fifty years, during which we believed ourselves emancipating from a periodically recurring dark age, is to go for naught. All the work we considered fine and inspiring, the work of men we believed sincere and honest, artists of the first rank, is proclaimed archeology not architecture." Perhaps he was speaking metaphorically when he evoked the great Columbian Exposition that made such an impression upon him in his youth:

> Many of us believed the World's Fair in Chicago an epoch marking achievement in the development of architecture in this country. Now it is contended by some that more harm than good resulted in the reform. . . . If, in re-employing older forms and applying them to our newer problems, we have done wrong, than all architecture of the past is wrong for all of it is but a development of what was done before. [But new] problems make for new solutions. We have had many of both. . . . American ingenuity and resourcefulness have developed requirements never before presented the architect for solution. New materials have been found and put to use, new types of construction evolved, new problems presented.[38]

"Architectural Trend" is Kahn's defense of the past as a vast resource to be understood and drawn upon, but in the spirit of Messel it need not straitjacket the present. Even if much of antiquity might prove passé now, there were still valuable lessons to learn from it and new ways to apply them. After paying respect to the series of events and works that brought American architecture to its 1931 present, he turned to what he perceived as a threat to the profession he loved: the undue attention, in his mind, being paid to a group of European designers advancing a "new" architecture contemptuous of what came before rather than building upon it. As evidenced by his 1918 address before the AIA, Kahn was not one to shy away from expressing his opinion on professional issues about which he felt strongly, although he could season the message with humor to make it easier for the audience to digest.

He rarely named names in a negative light, but it appears he felt justified here in identifying those he saw as "the wild men of Germany": Walter Gropius, Hans Poelzig, and Eric Mendelsohn. In discussing the trend in France, he called out Le Corbusier, André Lurçat, and Robert Mallet-Stevens: "Their work is inexplicable, the more so for having found so many admirers." He accurately noted that the avant-garde of the Soviet Union was motivated to reject all tradition as "being the fruits of capitalism," and in consequence, in his opinion, produced "the most freakish results" of Modernism. Kahn found "Their new architecture is just as difficult to understand as their new economic system."[39] Apostles of this movement may have taken umbrage at Kahn's characterizations, but one can imagine his immediate audience now in stitches.

"Do not misunderstand me," he urged returning to the seriousness of the matter, "I am a firm believer in progress. . . . I am fully in accord with those who strive for a fuller expression of contemporary life and thought." He gave the new movement credit where he thought it was due, such as its presentation of the true nature of materials. As technological advances enabled reduction of wall surfaces, the embrace of natural light and ventilation he long championed could find new forms of expression. "That, however, does not mean ugly buildings entirely of steel and glass, as advocated by some."[40]

This last sentence may be construed as Kahn bemoaning the advent of steel and glass buildings, but when they came, they were not much different from his reinforced-concrete and glass Long Island City Packard Sales and Service Building, by then nearly a quarter century old. Perhaps he was not cautioning against the choice of material here, but against applying it in an ugly manner.

Graceful structures could be wrought from glass and steel, as he would demonstrate with Chrysler's Half-Ton Truck Plant a few years hence.

The Death of Pogojeff

By confining his discussion to architecture, Kahn avoided assailing his Soviet client or its ideology directly. For many Americans in the 1930s, the Soviet Union presented a sort of broad-ranging Rorschach test. Those who desperately wanted to believe in a new world delivering humankind from its lot saw only the promise of a centrally planned society and managed to look past its horrid failings. Those already opposed to it found validation by focusing on the failings and saw little, if anything, worth emulating.[41] For Kahn, who entered into the Soviet contracts with the intent of helping the people, there was a very real human dimension. While many at home were out of work, his staff members abroad were at least employed. Nevertheless they dealt with unaccustomed privations, surveillance, and—they had to know—bodily risk posed by their government hosts. The Soviet citizens working alongside them, Kahn also surely understood, experienced greater privation and lived in even greater immediate peril.

For the Soviet trainees assigned to the Kahn office atop the Maquette Building in Detroit, it was surely a surreal experience. Like others similarly assigned to the United States, it may be presumed they were carefully vetted for their loyalty, with it drilled into them that "as a Communist you are a sworn enemy of the capitalist society." They would have been instructed to learn as much as they could while divulging nothing and avoiding political discussion. Even in the Depression, Detroit offered unaccustomed temptations and challenges to their state-conditioned beliefs. All the while they would be under the surveillance of Soviet agents—perhaps overt, but presumably covert as well.[42]

At least one of the trainees, it appears, dared to stay. A twenty-eight-year-old civil engineer and graduate of the Moscow Technical Institute, Arkady I. Pogojeff may have been typical of the Soviet trainees working and learning alongside Kahn's Detroit staff. Perhaps suspected as a potential defector, however, he was called to the Amtorg offices in New York. After meeting with officials, he was ordered to board a ship, no later than March 28, 1931, and return to Moscow. As reported in the *New York Times*, he feared he would be executed once back in the USSR, so he failed to leave by the specified date. On the afternoon of Thursday, April 2, 1931, Pogojeff plummeted to his death from a hotel window. Police ruled it a suicide, but a leading anti-Communist member of New York's Russian-American community suspected assassination at the hands of the Soviet Cheka secret police. When questioned by New York police, Amtorg officials denied that he had been ordered to return home and speculated he was depressed due to ill health and took his own life. There appears to be only one account of this incident by anyone associated with the Kahn office and it dates to seventeen years later. Frank Barcus, by then a former employee who had been part of the team traveling to Moscow in 1930, said he thought Pogojeff committed suicide but clearly did so rather than return to the Soviet Union.[43] If Barcus was aware of Pogojeff's death and at least some of the details, it can be assumed that Kahn and the rest of the staff knew as well. Whether they believed the suicide story, they would have understood that the reach of the Cheka extended across oceans to U.S. soil. Perhaps this stiffened Kahn's resolve to oppose the ideology behind his Soviet government client while validating caution in doing so indirectly.

Reverberations from "Architectural Trend"

"Architectural Trend" may be viewed as Kahn simply setting straight the record of the previous fifty years of architectural history in contrast to a narrative he was watching develop at the hands of Hitchcock and others. As it was penned by one who had a significant role in that history, it would seem worthy of recognition as an important document for architectural historians to study. As noted above, Kahn may have been purposefully targeting East Coast intellectual elites in his choice of venue. He appears to have drawn the attention of at least one.

In the July 1931 issue of the popular *Scribner's Magazine*, Edmund Wilson, associate editor for the *New Republic*, published a diatribe against Henry Ford that, somewhat curiously, included Ford's architect in the crosshairs. Wilson was clearly a socialist; he would vote for the Communist Party candidate in the 1932 U.S. presidential election while adding his signature to a CPUSA manifesto calling for "a temporary dictatorship of the class-conscious workers." In an account of his travels in the USSR shortly thereafter, he concealed the oppression he witnessed. As would later be admitted by former CPUSA executive council member Benjamin Gitlow, the party was directed by the Soviet government in Moscow to discredit Ford as an enemy of labor even as he was helping build a Five-Year Plan automobile plant in the USSR and training its technicians in Dearborn. Wilson's essay appears to be part of this CPUSA campaign, and by expanding his disparagement to included Kahn's capitalism-driven architecture he conversely promoted the agenda of European socialist architecture among the U.S. intelligentsia.[44] His criticism of Ford, and Kahn, was titled "The Despot of Dearborn."

Within its pages, Kahn's Fisher Building is seemingly arbitrarily dismissed as the culmination of "a bulky herd of thick, square, Middle Western skyscrapers." With no direct connection between Ford and the Fisher Building, Wilson was going out of his way to take swipes at Kahn. Returning to FMC, he wrote that structures in Dearborn "rise block-shaped and monstrous from the plain like the monument of some barbarian god . . . they present the five and-ten-cent-store taste of America on a scale almost stupefying."[45] It is likely this ire was stirred by Kahn's remarks on the new architecture in Europe, which Wilson seems to have preferred. This new architecture would soon be showcased by New York's Museum of Modern Art, and ironically, Kahn's very industrial buildings Wilson scorned served as its inspiration.

17

"The Approach to Design"

While Kahn expressed his concerns about the totalitarian architectural trend coming out of Europe, it seems he continued to hope, as many did, that industrialization and mass production would improve the lot of the Soviet population and bring reform to its ruthless government. Contractually committed, his office in Moscow remained while the growing worldwide economic depression was definitely being felt in Detroit. Depressions were an understood part of the economic cycle, however, with the Panic of 1893 being a particularly severe example. Leaders in established businesses felt it their responsibility, as well as in their self-interest, to stimulate consumer spending. For them, the key to prosperity lay in consumer confidence, not government intrusion into the private sector. Although unemployment ran high, for a while Kahn's office was busy providing plans for new projects and expansions. Not all of these ventures were realized.[1]

The New Center Building

A notable project that came to pass began to rise literally in the shadow of the Fisher Building. Eleven months after the notorious Black Thursday stock market crash in October 1929, the Fisher brothers announced a new project: the New Center Building. Anticipating growth in the area of their Fisher Building, the brothers had earlier purchased property across Second Avenue, intending to erect an office building in the fall of 1931. They were disturbed, however, at the reaction by President Herbert Hoover's administration, businessmen, and consumers alike to the economic downturn. Sensing what they thought an unnecessary and dangerous degree of public angst, the Fishers hoped that by moving their building plans up to September 1930, they would instill confidence, which would "serve as an incentive for others to proceed with normal expansion and thus assist in the solving of the unemployment problem." By pressing on despite the naysayers, the Fishers demonstrated their faith that Detroit's industrial and financial importance would continue to expand through normal free-market capitalist activity. The project was seen as a bold, private-sector civic initiative in the face of prevailing negativity.[2]

The Fishers again turned to Kahn, this time for a ten-story, $10 million office structure with a frontage of 265 feet. The limestone and granite façade shares stylistic affinity with the Fisher Building and the Kresge Administration Building. The offices of Albert Kahn, Inc., moved onto the New Center Building's third floor after its completion in July 1931. A writer for the *Detroit Free Press* noted the style had come to be known as "modern American" by 1930.[3] The New Center Building was elegant and expensively built, but it did not possess the profuse ornamentation of the Fisher Building: the materials, craftsmanship, and economy-boosting potential of the building industry were on display.

A Detroit Store for the Richman Brothers

Like the New Center Building, the Richman Brothers Store was intended as a confident statement in defiance of the Depression. "We believe it is distinctly up to the business men of the United States to take the initiative in starting the wheels of business and industry moving," said Nathan G. Richman as he announced plans to invest some $4 million in moving into the Detroit market. "All we need is courage, vision and confidence in the United States."[4]

The eight-story store was built next to Kahn's Grinnell Brothers Building on Woodward, but its Clifford Street façade would be prominent to those coming from the downtown business district. The fifty-two-year-old client company was one of the country's largest manufacturers and retailers of men's

New Center Building, Detroit, Michigan (1931) (currently the Kahn Apartments). Albert Kahn, Inc., architect. Photograph, 1931, courtesy Albert Kahn Associates, Inc.

clothing, which it sold at discount prices. Richman Brothers wanted a building that would serve as "a token of our confidence in Detroit and the automobile industry in particular."[5] A bold, forward-looking architectural statement was in order.

Kahn responded with a composition proving he had lost none of his edge, so to speak, since designing his daylight stores of the 1910s. Now Kahn moved on from terra-cotta and iron ornamentation to simply letting the nature of the materials provide visual interest to a streamlined composition. It was described at its 1931 opening as "complete in modernity, a steel and concrete structure, trimmed with white marble and stainless steel." Perhaps most striking in its day were the horizontal bands of windows, collectively framed by steel, running uninterrupted between the corner piers above the ground floor along the Woodward and Clifford Street façades. Lettering incorporated into the façade, a functionally justified form of ornamentation accepted by the strident

Richman Brothers Store, Detroit, Michigan (1931). Albert Kahn, Inc., architect. The Grinnell Brothers Building is to the right in this 1931 photograph, courtesy Albert Kahn Associates, Inc.

Modernists, identified the business and its low prices, while custom-designed lighting accentuated the marble and stainless steel at night.[6]

Clearly, Kahn had no qualms jettisoning ornament from his nonindustrial work when the situation merited. His nonresidential work had always been of its time and, indeed, here it would be hard to distinguish between the Richman Brothers Store and some of the more enduring work of the wild men of Germany and their European brethren.

This demonstrates that Kahn's beef with the self-proclaimed Modernists was not so much stylistic, since his own work evolved in a similar vein over the years—*but it did evolve*, and he saw it as an evolution. It was descendant of tradition, not a deliberate affront to it. In the United States, he argued, the evolution of skeleton frame construction technology created opportunity for experimentation for "purely utilitarian purposes" that produced attractive results. "Since then our architects' efforts have marked a distinct advance in architecture. There has been created something akin to an individual and characteristic type." To put it another way, with ideology aside, the homespun contemporary architecture evolving in the United States, perhaps stimulated by Kahn's assembly buildings and other far-flung work, seemed on firmer foundation than the more passionate creations, unmoored by tradition, of activist auteurs.[7]

Meanwhile, Kahn was a self-made individual, wildly succeeding in a free market through his business associations with other similarly self-made individuals. He was supported by employees cohesively working in a merit-based office environment who were individually free to come and go as they pleased, as evidenced by Wirt Rowland. The European-led Modernism actively promoted a socialist, collectivist agenda through manifestos and other public pronouncements. Why would Kahn care to seriously entertain their agenda, which stood in polar opposition to his way of life? Surely, as demonstrated by his efforts to share his lessons of success with his peers, Kahn thought that they would be far better off embracing his business model than he could ever be embracing their ideology.

Staking a Second World's Fair at Chicago

Confidence in the capitalist system was to be demonstrated on a national level at the upcoming, second great World's Fair in Chicago. Titled A Century of Progress, the 1933 exposition was another private-sector initiative to inspire consumer confidence to spend a way out of the Depression—a particularly brazen and ambitious one—and two years before its projected opening, planners were desperate to sign on a major exhibitor to generate faith in the project. Kahn's long-time associate and friend, William Knudsen, now president of the Chevrolet division of General Motors, stepped up, pledging $1 million of Chevrolet money to build the fair's largest private exhibit building if GM matched the amount, which it did. (Knudsen enjoyed considerable sway with the corporation after the previously failing division outsold Ford in 1927 and 1928 under his direction. It was a feat many believed impossible.) His one condition was that GM be granted exclusive right to display a working assembly line. Henry Ford was skeptical of the fair's success and furious that his former employee outfoxed him with the assembly line exhibit, so FMC declined to participate at all.[8]

In July 1931, Knudsen turned to Kahn to design a building around the concept of an assembly line, staged as pageant yet nonetheless producing automobiles. Around this, as described in a corporate biography, were exhibits showcasing GM products, "ranging from automobiles and Diesel engines to the smallest ball bearings." Kahn was also obliged to follow the fair's own style dictates, as demonstrated in his preliminary design published in October 1931. Memories of the World's Columbian Exposition's impact on architecture were only forty years old and expectations for a similar spectacle were high. In order to create an energized ambiance generating consumer confidence, planners made the daring decision to require the fairground buildings to showcase Modernist designs. It was a bold move for an already bold and risky venture. For all its hype, capital M Modern architecture remained a hard sell, even in Europe, where it surely would have floundered without state support. With no guarantee the American public would warm to the cutting-edge architectural imagery considered key in promoting the fair, it served as the core for an aggressive marketing campaign.[9] The results are discussed in the next chapter.

Travel to the Soviet Union and Modernist Europe

In the fall of 1931 Kahn combined a trip to the Soviet Union, related to his firm's work there, with a European visit to continue his survey of contemporary

Preliminary Design for General Motors Building, A Century of Progress International Exposition (1931). Albert Kahn, Inc. office drawing, photographed by Kaufmann & Fabry, courtesy Ryerson and Burnham Libraries, Art Institute of Chicago. Digital file #40509.

architecture begun three years earlier. After spending weeks in the Soviet Union, Kahn expressed his opinion on its recent architecture. "No better example of the art of revolt may be found anywhere in the world than in the present day architecture of Russia," he declared. Kahn made plain that he deemed these architectural efforts to be clumsily forced, politically driven attempts to be different only for difference's sake and to further the propaganda needs of the state.[10]

Before returning home, Kahn made visits to France and Germany. Perhaps with an eye toward the upcoming Chicago Fair, he specifically planned to take in the work of Le Corbusier, Mendelsohn, and Gropius, experiencing it in person rather than only through photographs. He also sketched, and what emerges from surviving drawings is an image of an established, senior architect continuing to stay abreast of current developments in his art. This is exemplified by quick drawings of Philipp Schaefer's 1929 Karstadt Department Store in Berlin, which was widely considered at the time as Europe's most modern mercantile design. At sixty-two years of age, Kahn was still studying the latest architectural trends and applying them as he thought appropriate while remaining the creative force in his large Detroit office.[11]

Grappling with Soviet Tyranny

Kahn's trip was bracketed by press statements that masked his growing concern over his contract with the Soviet government. Prior to his departure, Kahn may have been feigning optimism, given the depositions of his employees as they returned from the USSR and the death of Pogojeff. "My engineers," Kahn claimed before leaving, "have almost quit grumbling now that they have completed 18 months of their two-year contracts. Food, living conditions and the working atmosphere have all changed for the better." (In actuality, few if any spent a full two years in the country; rotating out after one year was the norm.) On his return, he announced, "From the things the Russians have accomplished toward advancing their people out of semi-barbarism, observing their great new manufacturing plants, schools and public improvements, and noting the spirit and industry which everybody is devoting to his job, it is my opinion that they are going to make their system work."[12] While all arguably true, he omits any mention of state coercion and the cost in human suffering being paid for such improvements.

Perhaps Kahn actually believed he was painting an accurate image of his Soviet client rather than cautiously measuring his words—the list of Americans, mostly tourists, returning from the USSR earnestly singing its government's praises was long. It is difficult to accept that such a brilliant man could be that gullible, however, and his critical statements surrounding Soviet architecture may have marked the extent to which he felt he could freely speak. Others knew the truth but maintained the lie out of ideological loyalty, greed, or simply to save face. From what else is known of the architect's character, it is hard to imagine that he would have acted from any of these. More plausible is that he feared retribution against his employees in the Soviet Union, for reasons stated in the previous chapter. Had they outlived Stalin, perhaps Kahn or his brother Moritz might have felt safe enough to be more candid about their socialist state client.

Such was not unheard of; in 1964 Marjorie Merriweather Post confided that while she resided in Moscow as the wife of U.S. Ambassador to the Soviet Union Joseph E. Davies (from 1936 to 1938), she was routinely awakened by nocturnal screams and gunfire. They were the sounds of families being torn apart by the secret police conducting midnight arrests in surrounding neighborhoods. One night she turned to her husband in bed and said, "I know perfectly well they are executing a lot of those people." He responded by telling her, unconvincingly, that she was only hearing the noise of subway construction.[13] (Years later Davies was honored with the Order of Lenin.)

Kahn became somewhat more forthcoming in 1932, possibly as a result of comments made by a former employee, William Bruss, quoted earlier regarding the state of fear under which the Soviet people lived. Among the first group of employees traveling with Moritz to set up the office in Moscow, Bruss had toured Europe before returning after his one-year assignment ended; then he gave a public presentation across the Detroit River in Ontario. At the Windsor Public Library in November 1931, he informed his audience that the outside world was not being told the truth about the Soviet Union, explaining that the Western press was complicit in hiding the large-scale misery and oppression within its borders. During a question-and-answer session, he was asked why Albert Kahn was not making similar claims if they were true. According to the Windsor *Border Cities Star*, Bruss replied that within Kahn's Soviet contracts "there is a clause which states that he must agree to do everything possible to promote good will between the United States and Russia and thus gain further recognition and establish credit" for the socialist state. Moritz, in Detroit at the time, delivered a swift denial of this to the newspaper. It appears none of the primary newspapers in Detroit picked up the story. According to Sonia Melnikova-Raich, who has pioneered research into this aspect of Kahn's career, she could not find any such clause in the contracts archived in the former Soviet Union.[14] Bruss's claim about the contract was not accurate, but his account of the truth being hidden from the Western public certainly was.

On January 24, 1932, two months after the Bruss incident, Albert Kahn spoke about his client in Detroit with greater transparency than he had previously. "Freedom, as we know it, does not exist in Russia," he explained. "Everybody is wretchedly poor, everybody is poorly dressed. You meet unkempt beggars, itinerant street peddlers, poorly dressed women with babes in arms and drunkards in the gutters." The architect renewed his plea for normalized relations, however, still believing it beneficial to both countries. Injecting his characteristic humor, he declared "Send the most rabid American communists to Russia and they will be cured."[15]

A little more than a month later, Kahn departed on his second trip to the Soviet Union, this time with the stated purpose of negotiating a third contract as the second was expiring. Moritz was back in Detroit; likely it was thought unwise to have two of the firm's three principals (brother Louis was the third) in Moscow at the same time. At any rate, Moritz provided a briefing to the press that was on balance pessimistic, although he left the door open for the possibility of agreement on a new contract. This minor optimism might have been more of a device for leaving the door open while getting the employees safely out of the country. On March 28 Albert made the formal announcement that new contract negotiations had failed. He was able to safely close down the office and get all his employees that wanted to leave, along with their families, out of the country by April 24. Two or three of the twenty-four employees chose to stay and work independently. It should be noted that Kahn continued to advocate for American recognition of the USSR after the contracts expired and his employees had returned home, suggesting he sincerely believed it would be beneficial to all, as he had maintained from the beginning.[16]

Exhibiting the International Style

February 1932 had brought the opening of the *Modern Architecture—International Exhibition* at New York's Museum of Modern Art (MOMA). It was accompanied by a catalogue published under the exhibit name and also as *Modern Architects*. In addition, a companion volume was written by the exhibit's curators, Henry-Russell Hitchcock and Philip Johnson: *The International Style: Architecture Since 1922*.

Great significance and little humility were attached to this exhibit as the enthusiasts of European Modernism believed it would melt away American resistance to the style. MOMA director Alfred Barr proclaimed the exhibit "of extraordinary, perhaps epoch-making, importance." According to a preliminary proposal for the exhibition written by Johnson, it was intended to remedy the current state of American architecture, characterized as "a chaos of conflicting and very often unintelligent building." Believing an "introduction to an integrated and decidedly rational mode of building is sorely needed," Johnson prophesied, "The stimulation and direction which an exhibition of this type can give to contemporary architectural thought is incalculable."[17]

To be fair, Hitchcock and Johnson attempted to walk back such hyperbole in later years, but at the time their effectively aggrandized efforts found a limited but zealous audience that wielded profound influence over the teaching of architecture and architectural history in America for decades to come. The message was clear: the avant-gardist of Europe and their followers in America, as identified by Hitchcock and Johnson, were *the* true purveyors of Modern architecture. Being hard to ignore, Frank Lloyd Wright's contribution to Modernism was given token acknowledgment, but others attempting their own routes to a new style outside the ideological coterie were marginalized as being only half-modern. *The International Style* is a remarkable book on many levels, including its authors' disdain for individualism and their enthusiasm for having the state, not a client, mandate style.[18]

Albert Kahn's work was not included in the exhibit or *The International Style*, although the catalogue did provide a passing nod to his "magnificent factories." Any exhibit is subject to limitations, not the least of which are space and budget, so it seems unfair to attach too much meaning to any architect's exclusion. Much of Kahn's recent design work easily met the criteria Hitchcock and

Johnson attached to the style, however, so it seems odd he received no mention in the companion book. One would not be alone in suspecting that the thrashing Kahn gave the movement in "Architectural Trend" had something to do with it, despite the essay's limited audience. At any rate, *The International Style* became a canon text for architectural studies across the land, and its authors' snub of Kahn surely contributed to the scholarly neglect of his work over the years.[19]

"The Approach to Design"

"I have before me a catalog of an exhibition of 'modern architecture' being held at the moment in this country," wrote Kahn in an essay for *Pencil Points*, published just after MOMA's *Modern Architecture* roadshow began its nationwide tour.[20] He was one of several architects invited to ruminate on the philosophy of contemporary design, and his contribution makes "Architectural Trend" almost seem milquetoast.

Unlike that essay, which may not have been seen by many of his peers, Kahn's "The Approach to Design" was published in a journal that was key reading in architectural offices across the country. Perhaps piqued by criticism such as Edmund Wilson's, Kahn decried the International Style as a formula being applied by "a new cult" to all building types—"the working man's cottage, the factory, the power station, the hospital, the hotel, the apartment house, yea even the residence and church." Kahn's more wrathful attitude also seems likely colored by the death of Pogojeff and the miseries he had personally witnessed in the Soviet Union. He spoke with authority when he proclaimed, "I, for one, certainly disapprove of making all buildings look like factories."[21]

He questioned whether Gropius's Bauhaus school building, considered one of the movement's greatest achievements, even qualified as architecture. Kahn asserted, "We may find in this country hundreds of factory buildings, particularly the court and alley elevations where often there is no attempt whatever to design, just as uninteresting" as the Bauhaus campus. While Kahn was aware that his industrial work was considered as part of the inspiration for this cult, he protested, "I would be the last man to claim the results [of his own industrial work] as anything more than sound engineering unless the problem and the appropriation afforded a more architectural character."[22]

From his travels in Germany, he believed much of the cheap building in this style could be excused by the postwar economy. He also conceded in some cases the new style was preferable to examples of excessive ornamentation in prewar Germany, "but to extend the particular type, however well suited to Germany's conditions, to all other countries is deplorable." Again, he heaped scorn on Le Corbusier and his followers. "Only those who have actually seen the finished results can appreciate the difference between their theories and their accomplishments."[23]

In "Architectural Trend" Kahn noted that architecture periodically went through dark ages. In the pages of *Pencil Points*, he expressed fear that it was now happening again and zeroed in on the ideology behind it, borrowing terminology of the Stalin regime: "Today we appear to be working on a 'Five Year Plan' for revolutionizing the art of building." Nevertheless, he cited some Europeans, such as Dutch architect Jacobus Johannes Pieter Oud as demonstrating "what modern architecture at its best may be." (Oud was also recognized in *The International Style* and one might sincerely wonder what Kahn saw in his work that he did not see in that of Gropius.) Ultimately, Kahn counseled young architects to "neither be carried away by the present nor unduly fettered by the past."[24]

Meanwhile, Frank Lloyd Wright also had misgivings about the MOMA exhibit, perceiving the inclusion of his work as simply, and in his mind falsely, legitimizing the style before an American audience. When he discovered that the exhibit would tour the United States after closing in New York, he pointedly wrote Philip Johnson demanding his work be exempted from future showings. "There is a radical divergence between the international propaganda and the ideal of architecture I have fought for all my life," Wright exclaimed. (For his part, Johnson had admitted privately to Oud that he was indeed "making propaganda" by stressing the aesthetics of the style while downplaying the "sociology" behind it.)[25]

MOMA threatened legal action against Wright, which Wright belittled as "the Moscow of Modern Art." Wright eventually acquiesced once the institution agreed to his terms that it provide his counterstatement to the exhibit's propaganda to the public. Johnson thought this token concession of little consequence, reasoning that few of the traveling exhibit's patrons would be interested in paying for copies of Wright's essay, and its counterrevolutionary message would be lost in the architect's dense prose.[26]

Still, it seems the exhibit's cocurators must have placed high value on including Wright, who indeed lent legitimacy even though his career was in such a deep trough that his initial involvement in the exhibit was bought for $250. (His comeback commission, Fallingwater, was still in future at the time.) In his counterstatement, titled "Of Thee I Sing," Wright questioned whether man had sunk to such depths as to allow a group of self-anointed arbiters of taste to determine his preferences in architecture. He declared the International Style to be not only communistic but a highly objectionable mode of communism and characterized claims by its architects and champions of having begotten something new as akin to a eunuch's aspiration to fatherhood.[27] Kahn's comments on the style certainly seem mild in comparison, but it appears Hitchcock and Johnson had irreversibly hitched their wagon to Wright's prestige and its close association with Sullivan. They humored Wright while marginalizing Kahn within their circle of influence.

Bantering with Saarinen

Kahn, meanwhile, limited his remarks to concerns of appropriateness. According to Christy Borth, architects who knew Kahn and the artistic and technical quality of his work "accepted his acid comments gratefully."[28] That may have been true in some cases, but it seems his attacks on the Modernist movement ruffled the feathers of some respected colleagues.

Eliel Saarinen, the Finnish architect whose new approach to skyscrapers was immediately and enthusiastically embraced by Kahn a decade earlier, became president of George Booth's Cranbrook Academy of Art in Bloomfield Hills. In November 1932, Kahn, along with about 150 other architects and their friends, was a dinner guest of the academy. Emil Lorch, esteemed dean of the recently established University of Michigan College of Architecture, served as master of ceremonies. Saarinen, by now a dear friend of Kahn's, addressed the gathering by declaring,

> We need to free our buildings from stylistic chains. Styles are the death masques of true architecture. . . . We do not demand that a piece of music conform to certain styles. We simply say that the work is by Beethoven or

> Brahms [or] Bach as the case may be. Architecture should be the expression of the person himself suited to his own time, and expressive of the particular needs of the particular problem . . . traditional styles only hamper us and make for emptiness and meaningless forms.[29]

One suspects Saarinen intended to prompt a response specifically from Kahn by evoking great composers, since the latter's love of classical music was well known. At any rate, Kahn rose and countered:

> We need tradition. We need the past. Many problems have been solved admirably in the past and we are quite right to profit by past achievements today.
>
> Of course, if everyone had Mr. Saarinen's creative genius we might talk about discarding tradition. But just think of the horrors which have been committed in the name of modernism, when some architect discards the past wholly and strikes out by himself.
>
> It is one thing for a man to paint a picture according to his own ideas. If it is hideous no one has to look at it. But it is very different with architecture. A building stands up against the sky in a public street and you have to look at it whether you want to or not. If it is ugly, it is a public nuisance. Without style and without a knowledge of it, I don't see where we are going to land. People who are not highly gifted, and there are many such, need the discipline of tradition. A thorough understanding of earlier tradition is necessary for the good of the profession.[30]

This exchange places Kahn's attitude toward his work of the 1930s in context with a few tidy sentences. While architecture is considered one of the fine arts, professional business responsibilities constrain the work of an architect more than they do other artists. While timely innovation tempered by traditional norms is vital, self-indulgent novelty must be discouraged. At times the debate between Saarinen and Kahn became heated, but it remained cordial, according to a *Detroit News* account of the evening. The underlying friendship between the two architects was obvious and both found circles of support within the audience.[31]

18

Rescuing Modernism

In 1932, advocacy for the International Style approach to modern architecture was spreading among the intelligentsia in the United States, but it was not yet embraced by the general American public or the dwindling number of business leaders who were in a position to build. Meanwhile, proponents who had dreamed of linking the style under state support to a new worldwide social order were finding politics a shifting foundation. In the Soviet Union, a prime incubator for the style, it had effectively been banned on April 23, 1932, under a decree reserving architectural design decisions for the Kremlin. In Germany, the Dessau city council voted to cut Bauhaus funding in August, leading to the closure of its campus there. Its defiant current director, Ludwig Mies van der Rohe, relocated the school to a former factory building in Berlin, but its future looked bleak. New construction was down throughout Europe with the exception of Italy, where the International Style efforts of the Futurists continued as a segment of Fascist architecture under Mussolini's aggressive reshaping of the landscape.[1]

Franklin Delano Roosevelt was elected president of the United States in November. Coming to Washington with him was, in the words of a 1935 Brookings Institution publication, "a new Administration skeptical of the individualism of the past, expressing confidence in a greater degree of collective action, and heralding a 'New Deal' in terms of this belief." Opponents of the Roosevelt administration may have been motivated in their criticism by a variety of concerns and interests, but this observed faith in collective action was particularly alarming with totalitarianism on the march. Even allies in Congress had concerns, such as Democratic representative T. V. Smith, who admitted seeing in the New Deal "all the surface similarities" with "the new despotisms of Italy, Germany and Russia."[2]

As pointed out in the previous chapter, planners of the Century of Progress Exposition in Chicago hoped to spur the private sector out of its economic depression, removing temptation to follow the collectivist path that at the moment seemed quite attractive. In one of history's many paradoxes, with the 1933 World's Fair business leaders heartily embraced controversial experimental architecture similar to that promoting socialism in Europe in order to advance capitalism in America. (Contrary to some histories, the fair was never intended to promote the New Deal; it was just the opposite.[3] Planners aimed to present an alternative to it.)

A Century of Progress, 1933

In its final form, the General Motors Exhibit Building for the 1933 great Chicago Fair was the largest private building on the grounds, and tallest thanks to a decision to incorporate a tower into the initial design. Kahn delivered a smart, streamlined composition with a 454- by 306-foot base and a central tower rising 177 feet into the air, like a lighthouse along the Lake Michigan shore. The tower did much to transform GM's pavilion into a landmark within a compendium of landmark structures vying for attention. The Kahn firm's embrace of elegant streamlining for interiors was demonstrated by the structure's central entrance hall, 118 by 55 feet under a fifty-foot-high ceiling. It served as a salon featuring a sculpture of Carl Milles and other artwork. In addition to vehicle showrooms, there were also a 235-person theater and a showcase research laboratory. GM's big draw, however—and one of the true sensations of the fair—was the 420- by 90-foot Chevrolet-Fisher Body Assembly Plant. Here a thousand spectators at a time could watch from elevated galleries the assembly of twenty-five Chevrolet Master Six automobiles per day beneath a clerestory roof supported by sixteen continuous steel beam arches.[4]

Kahn admitted in the pages of *Architectural Forum* that the challenge of the fair was one of "stage setting" rather than "permanent architecture."

General Motors Exhibit Building, A Century of Progress Exposition, Chicago, Illinois (1931–33). Albert Kahn, Inc., architect. Photograph courtesy General Motors Corporation Archives and Special Collections.

Central entrance of the General Motors Exhibit Building. Photograph courtesy General Motors Corporation Archives and Special Collections.

Nonetheless, he found the exposition to be "a distinct success and a credit to those in charge of administration as well as design. A pageant of indescribable beauty has been created." Kahn had no doubt that the styling of the fair would impact future architecture. Recalling and defending the World's Columbian Exposition, he believed "it served admirably in presenting to a nation, then sadly in need of it, the beauty inherent in monumental planning and grouping." The Century of Progress, Kahn believed, met "the problem in a different, more novel, though no less successful manner."[5]

While not quite turning a profit, the 1933 season of the exposition was considered an astounding private-sector success, with 27.7 million attendees stimulating sales of automobiles and other products promoted at the fair. The public responded enthusiastically to its modernism as well. Industrial designer Walter Dorwin Teague wrote in 1934, "Pictures of the buildings have circulated everywhere in publications and moving pictures. Already the influence is manifest. Sales of modern furniture have multiplied ten times in the past year." He went on to predict the styling would soon be manifest in homes throughout America. In terms of affecting public acceptance of modern styling, the fair had far greater impact than the more elite MOMA *Modern Architecture Exhibition*.[6]

By the time it was done, General Motors spent over $2 million on its exhibit in 1933, and its directors were thrilled with Knudsen's initiative. The corporation's pavilion proved to be the most visited private-sector exhibit of any world's fair ever, with an estimated attendance of about 230,000 visitors per day.[7]

The Chrysler-DeSoto Administration Building

The impact of the fair's architecture was near immediate, as reflected in a new administration building Kahn designed for Chrysler Corporation (then being jointly promoted with its DeSoto division). Before the first season of the Chicago Fair drew to a close, ground was broken on Detroit's East Jefferson Avenue for the $350,000 edifice, sometimes called the Chrysler-DeSoto Sales and Service Building as well as the corporate headquarters. Company officials proudly pointed to the Century of Progress Exposition as its influence.[8]

Stylistically, the two-story, 550-foot-long structure would have fit nicely on the fairgrounds and was reflective of the client—a scrappy, relatively new enterprise formed in 1925. Kahn described the streamlined building as "extremely straightforward and simple," while the *Detroit Free Press* noted its being "modernistic in design." The exterior façade was faced with light buff, semipolished Mankato limestone, trimmed with black granite and stainless steel. This was bookended by two rather squat, round towers topped by three rings of opal glass and stainless steel that were illuminated at night. Within the towers were circular entrance lobbies leading, on the first floor, to a stunning 336- by 50-foot showroom, illuminated by seventeen-foot-tall show windows and uninterrupted by any supports for the ceiling twenty feet above the floor. It was a visually imposing feat of creative engineering, with the second floor, home to executive offices and an otherwise open floor plan, suspended from above by the steel trusses that also supported the roof.[9]

Chrysler-DeSoto Administration Building, Detroit, Michigan (1933–34). Albert Kahn, Inc., architect. Photograph, circa 1934, courtesy Stellantis Historical Services.

A Century of Progress, 1934

Clearly Henry Ford had made a mistake by not participating in the second great Chicago Fair in 1933, but he had an opportunity to correct it. A Century of Progress had been so well received its organizers, sensing an opportunity to turn their relatively slight net loss into a profit, decided to take the unusual step of extending it for the 1934 summer season. The decision drove a whirlwind of activity among planners and exhibitors.[10]

On December 26, 1933, Edsel Ford called Kahn to discuss his designing another exhibit pavilion. The choice lots had been taken the previous season and what was available was a long, irregular section that presented a challenge. Nevertheless, speed was of the essence; preliminary sketches were approved and working drawings started on January 16, 1934. The building, complete with exhibits showcasing the company's global breadth and technical achievements, along with artifacts from Henry Ford's museum, was ready when the fair reopened on May 26.[11]

Ford may have entered this grand bazaar late, but he did it with gusto. FMC spent $3 million, and the structure designed by Kahn exceeded the General Motors Exhibit Building as the largest building on the fairgrounds. Mostly on one level, its overall length was 860 feet, with two wings flanking a remarkable, 110-foot-tall by 210-foot diameter rotunda. "Simulating the outline of the gear mesh used in machinery seemed appropriate," Kahn explained while describing the rotunda. The overall design of the building was said to have been inspired by an automobile engine connecting rod. The eighty-six-foot diameter center of the rotunda was open to the sky, with a concentric partition of windows transmitting natural light to the surrounding interior. Teague designed the industrial exhibits, which complemented Kahn's undeniably Modernist architecture. To ease Ford's mind over the expense, Kahn designed the structure to lend itself to disassembly and partial reuse after the close of the fair. This resulted in the Ford Rotunda, which served as FMC's Dearborn welcome center beginning in 1936.[12]

Overall, the 1933–34 fair rivaled the impact of its Chicago predecessor. With nearly 16.48 million paying attendees, it outdrew the 1893 fair despite the depression—which became known as the Great Depression with the added stress of disastrous drought on the Great Plains. Of course, the Century of

Ford Motor Company Exhibit Building, A Century of Progress Exposition, Chicago, Illinois (1934). Albert Kahn, Inc., architect. Photograph courtesy Albert Kahn Associates, Inc.

Rotunda interior of the Ford Motor Company Exhibit Building. Photograph from the collections of The Henry Ford. Gift of the Ford Motor Company.

Progress enjoyed an advantage in running two seasons. The fair had its desired effect, with increased automobile sales and a boost in consumer spending credited to the optimism it generated.[13]

Front-page coverage in the *Detroit Free Press* proclaimed the fair to be

> Detroit's and America's answer to the efforts of the Brain Trusters in Washington to regulate business, to destroy competition and initiative, to standardize life into the monotony that precedes stagnation and decay.
>
> It is a war of individualism against the false dreams of security—the Marxist concept against the philosophy of Adam Smith.
>
> It [is] pagentry, yes—but the drama behind it is that of America at the crossroads.[14]

Despite such editorializing and the public's response, the Century of Progress Exposition failed to sway the policy direction of the New Deal administration. America remained poised at the crossroads as its consuming public embraced Modernist styling. In Europe, meanwhile, the International Style's state sponsors were turning against it.

The Peril of Confusing Art with Politics

Shortly after its opening in May 1933, Ralph Adams Cram saw the fair's buildings as the "outmoded" last gasp of a fad that was "being abandoned in Europe." So-called Modernism, he pronounced (without an apparent ounce of regret, being America's preeminent revivalist architect), "has had its day." Indeed, architects in the Soviet Union, who had debated so earnestly in developing an architectural landscape worthy as the legacy of Marx, Lenin, and Stalin, now found themselves forced to submit to the changing preference of a government they thought was the manifestation of *their* will. Those who did not accede to the new Socialist Realism style (sometimes called the Stalinist Style), with its often garish return to classical elements, faced arrest and consignment to the Gulag prison system. Some met execution.[15]

In Germany, the Bauhaus that epitomized the movement had just officially closed in Berlin following a period of uncertainty with Hitler's rise to power.

As George Nelson, trained as an architect but supporting himself as a writer and critic during the Great Depression, observed, "The gentlemen who held the reins made the mistake—in their case quite understandable—of confusing art with politics." In their quest to design a new world, Bauhaus administrators set a stage where Communist and Nazi faculty and students battled for artistic control. Mies's attempt at neutrality was for naught as the school acquired a reputation of leaning toward the Communist Party of Germany, which was outlawed once the Nazis came to power.[16]

For a while, Nazi authorities remained ambiguous regarding Modernism, which served to present a mask of normalcy and open-mindedness for tourists as the German press worked to quash stories of atrocities. Tradition-scorning art and architecture had been useful in undermining the old social order for the Communists and Nazis as they vied for authoritative power in Germany, but ultimately, as in the Soviet Union, tradition was seen as necessary to legitimize the regime that prevailed. Modernist architects stayed in Germany until it became obvious they would never be allowed to design another building, then those who could emigrated. By the end of the 1930s, the International Style was derided as "architecture fit only for the robot," in the words of a German Library of Information publication. It was time for yet another architecture in which ideas of the state "would determine the style" of a new Germany. In the same volume, Hitler is quoted saying of architecture, "It is a wonderful thing to participate in a work which serves the interest of no individual but belongs to all and will render service for centuries."[17]

American Consumers Discover Modernism

Looking back in 1966, Hitchcock conceded that the MOMA exhibit and books coincided with the apex of the International Style's relevance: by 1933 the prospects for the Modernism he and Johnson selectively championed were nil in the countries where previously it had enjoyed its greatest support. While not blackballed elsewhere in Europe, International Style architects were seeing their opportunities dwindle in suffering economies. As for America, Johnson wrote in 1994, "The general Public could not have cared less" about the exhibit. It drew little critical attention and relatively few visitors, but its impact, as Johnson accurately noted, "was huge in the architectural world. It caused endless discussion and fights within the profession."[18]

Chicago's Century of Progress Exposition rescued Modernist architecture by unmooring it from its ideological raison d'être. The fair showcased the trend as implemented by a more diverse collection of architects, including a larger ratio of Americans. Not every building proved memorable on its own, but together their impact was powerful. Thomas Tallmadge, in his 1936 edition of *The Story of Architecture in America*, considered it one of the country's great architectural achievements of the Depression years—"a vast proving ground for the new architecture in all its aspects."[19] Modernism as an architectural style that many considered weird before became more acceptable in the United States through the promotion and success of the fair. Americans now firmly identified the architecture, along with similarly styled consumer products, with dreams of a prosperous future—as opposed to a centrally planned one.

Never presuming to force his tastes upon his clients, Kahn seemingly effortlessly embraced the new style that had the public clamoring following the fair. Although his work had been purloined by the International Style architects without credit, he did not claim any role in the trend as he rather impartially explained in 1933 that

> people ask about the influence of the exposition buildings because they embody ideas that are new to most of the visitors, but they are not new to architects. They are merely expressions of a spirit that crystalized after the World war, spread over Europe and to America.
>
> Simplicity, directness, a frank adaptation of the exterior of the building to the function of its interior, and economy in construction are the outstanding characteristics of the new spirit.[20]

The United States even offered haven, and work, to many of Europe's refugee International Style architects as German totalitarianism continued its march. This caused Frank Lloyd Wright to later lament that American universities had become packed with left-wing Modernist architects imported from Europe whose work he termed as "Nazi."[21] With theoreticians of the likes of Gropius and Mies being appointed to influential teaching positions at schools such as Harvard and the Illinois Institute of Technology, respectively, it is little wonder *The International Style* came to be considered a canonical text for college courses (and remains in print today). This has created, for a long while, a perception that the architects chronicled within its pages somehow cornered the market on Modernism at the time. While many of them were brilliant, to claim today that there existed an ocean of difference between the International Style and American Modernism, apart from the background ideologies of designers and clients, risks accusation of splitting hairs by more dispassionate observers.

Assisting the Development of the New

In "Architectural Trend," Kahn acknowledged that "occasionally a good housecleaning is necessary, a fine stimulant. . . . It is so easy to grow complacent and self-satisfied, for which reason a new impetus is desirable." He viewed the 1893 World's Columban Exposition as providing such a stimulant in its day; on the other hand the ideologically motivated work of the 1920s that became the International Style threatened "the destruction of all established canons."[22]

It seems the 1933–34 Century of Progress Exposition, like the earlier Chicago Fair, provided a welcome stimulant. In a 1937 speech before the Adcraft Club of Detroit, Kahn recognized that "there can be no doubt that the modern trend is leading to good results." On this occasion he recognized some of his firm's "attempts along the modern. Ours has been largely industrial work, which has established us to assist somewhat in the development of the new."[23]

After citing the Chrysler-DeSoto Administration Building, he discussed the 1935–36 studios for the WWJ radio studios, a pioneering interest of the *Detroit News*, then headed by William E. Scripps. The grandson of James E. Scripps, he represented the third generation of an architect-client relationship dating back to Kahn's partnership with Nettleton and even earlier to his employment with Mason & Rice. The latest commission had Kahn again traveling the country, this time to study recent studio facilities, before starting the plans for the five-story building, where sound insulation demanded windowless studios, including one with seating for 340 persons. The result was described in the *Detroit News* as "ultra modern in equipment and appearance." While it went against his long-held advocacy of natural lighting, in this instance

Kahn conceded, “It would have been a mistake to build the front for anything but what it is—a facing for rooms from which windows must be excluded.” Therefore, the seventy-foot-tall façade presents a buff Indiana limestone promontory relieved only by vertical fluting above the second story. It seems directly descended from the General Motors and Ford pavilions for the recent Chicago Fair. Sculptural reliefs by Carl Milles framed the entrance, and windows behind the façade distinguished the office areas from the studio rooms.[24]

Following close on the heels of the WWJ Studios was a series of commissions further demonstrating Kahn’s stylistic embrace of the times. The 1937 Lady Esther Cosmetic Factory in Clearing, Illinois, featured relatively plain surfaces, simple geometric trim, and rounded corners to yield a machine-age composition. It is evocative of the appliance and home furnishing styles of its day, including ladies’ vanity tables, designed by the likes of Teague and Norman Bel Geddes. The 1937–38 office building for United Airlines at Chicago Municipal Airport (now Chicago Midway International Airport), with a curved, polished Indiana limestone veneer, suggested the streamlined excitement of commercial air travel. In contrast, Kahn relied on sharp-edged rectilinear forms for the 1938 Burroughs Adding Machine Company Factory in Plymouth—replacing the American Arithmometer plant he designed for Joseph Boyer at the beginning of his career in industrial architecture. Here a central tower remained windowless because its sole, yet critical, function was to hold a fire-suppressing water tank aloft. In “Architectural Trend” Kahn warned of “ugly buildings entirely of steel and glass,” but his 1938 Chrysler Corporation Half-Ton Truck Plant proved the material could, in the right hands, yield graceful beauty. With nearly sixteen acres of total floor space, it was estimated to contain over five acres of glass above short brick with concrete sills.[25]

In the end it seems, like other architectural trends in America, Kahn and his firm influenced the work of others and the work of others influenced them. It should be noted that Kahn’s opinion of at least some International Style designs mellowed in his later lectures. For example, in 1939 he commended Gropius for showing “the potentialities inherent in well studied factory buildings.”[26]

And his nuanced attitude did not prevent him from providing assistance to colleagues working in that vein. According to Erich Mendelsohn, writing at a time when he was a refugee from Hitler’s Germany, “One of the last favors Albert Kahn bestowed on me was his generous letter written on my behalf

WWJ Studios Building, Detroit, Michigan (1935–36). Albert Kahn, Inc., architect. Photograph from Albert Kahn, Inc., *Industrial and Commercial Buildings* (1938), collection of the author.

Lady Esther Plant, Cleering, Illinois (1937). Albert Kahn, Inc., architect. Photograph courtesy Albert Kahn Associates, Inc.

United Airlines Administration Building, Chicago, Illinois (1938). Albert Kahn, Inc., architect. Historic Architecture and Landscape Image Collection, Ryerson and Burnham Art and Architecture Archives, Art Institute of Chicago. Digital file #60304.

Burroughs Adding Machine Company Factory, Plymouth, Michigan (1938). Albert Kahn, Inc., architect. Photograph courtesy Albert Kahn Associates, Inc.

Chrysler Corporation Half-Ton Truck Plant, Detroit, Michigan (1938). Albert Kahn, Inc., architect. Photograph courtesy Albert Kahn Associates, Inc.

to the John Simon Guggenheim Foundation." The letter was in support of a fellowship award, which Mendelsohn received in 1943, enabling him to write *A Contemporary Philosophy of Architecture* (unpublished). Mendelsohn also commented, "That Albert has paid so much attention to my own work is one of my life's most cherished memories."[27]

Bantering with Wright

In his Adcraft Club speech, Kahn also stated that, "architecture today is in my opinion only about 10% art and 90% business"—a comment that has generated as much misunderstanding as the "Architectural Trend" lecture. Architect and friend Paul Cret wrote, "For me, this underrating of himself as an artist is only another proof of Albert Kahn's innate modesty." Perhaps, but Kahn was by no means belittling the artistic talent required of an architect. Rather, he was simply acknowledging the organizational demands that had grown in proportion around the profession over the many years of his practice. The days where he struggled virtually alone following the death of Nettleton were in the distant past. Handling large commissions in 1937 required expertise in many more fields—such as electrical, lighting, ventilation, plumbing, and sanitation—than any individual could be expected to master. Meanwhile workflow, cash flow, legal, regulatory, and other considerations required management. For Kahn, operating on the scale he did for the clients he served, these functions were as crucial to a successful organization as its artistic facets, although only the latter was the public face of his product.[28]

While merely recognizing the reality of practicing on his level, the quote was taken out of context in numerous publications, to the consternation of many an architect. Over a year later, Frank Lloyd Wright was addressing a Detroit audience on "The Future of Architecture" in the grand theater within the Fisher Building. During a question-and-answer session with the audience, Wright opined, "I think Henry Ford's factories are very fine. When your Albert Kahn builds factories, they're good, even if they're 90 per cent business and 10 per cent art."[29]

The relationship between Kahn and Wright was an interesting one, and the two may have considered each other friends, if judged from their public banter. Kahn unambiguously considered Wright one of the country's leading architects, but it is unsure how the latter even interpreted the designations "friend" or "architect." Several years earlier Wright told a gathering of Grand Rapids architects of being chauffeured through the streets of Detroit by Kahn. "I had seen the industrial buildings that he designed and for which I have always had a great respect. But when I saw him self-consciously 'putting on' architecture [presumably through examples such as the Fisher Building] I could only tell him I wished to God he would forget about architecture and stick to industrial buildings."[30]

That was in 1931, a rather low period when a financially desperate Wright and his third wife, Olgivanna, conceived of forming the Taliesen Fellowship, which might be described as a hybrid of an architectural office and a commune, where vetted members paid for the experience in addition to working the farm and other upkeep. Fearing opposition to the unconventional idea, Wright reached out to "ten worth while architects," seeking letters of reference endorsing his self-described "radical architect's venture." Kahn was one of the ten and became a supporting Friend of the Fellowship.[31]

During his 1938 Fisher Theatre appearance, Wright again aired a qualified—to the point of being uncomplimentary—compliment: "Albert Kahn is one of the most valuable men in America today as a builder, but I wish he'd stick to his knitting." Wright then offered Kahn, who was in the audience, an opportunity to stand and defend himself. He declined. Surely Kahn's refusal was affable and accompanied by a smile on his face, notwithstanding the possibility he was also muttering something less than flattering under his breath.[32]

Afterward, during a luncheon attended by the press, Kahn took his turn. From his seat at the speaker's table, he stood and addressed the gathering to express great admiration for Wright. Then he asked the guest of honor to share an example of outstanding modern architecture, but "not a factory and not done by yourself." Wright was notoriously stingy in acknowledging the accomplishments of competitors, and now Kahn placed him on the spot, turning the tables from the lecture earlier that day. Kahn surely assumed Wright would duck the question by praising a factory if he had the opportunity, as this was one area where they did not compete. Denied that dodge, Wright was nevertheless evasive in his reply, saying he knew of many little buildings around the country "that grew out of circumstances, common sense and a feeling for the ground," but did not identify any or point out a specific one for particular merit. According to George Nelson, those around Wright considered him scary.[33] Kahn's challenge was a public display of good-natured, if perhaps pointed, gamesmanship and one imagines few architects besides Kahn having the self-confidence to engage Wright in such a manner.

Architectural Forum and Rexford Newcomb

The August 1938 issue of the influential *Architectural Forum* was largely devoted to an account of Albert Kahn, Inc. Such a prominent, lengthy profile on Kahn and the firm in an esteemed professional journal understandably seemed a solid source for later historians to rely heavily upon—and they did. Unfortunately, its discussion of the origins of the founder and firm was fraught with much of the inaccurate folklore and errors that have been repeated over decades. For instance, "the Packard job" was described as "the first reinforced concrete factory in America" when it was not even Kahn's first reinforced concrete factory.

Reporting was on firm footing as it recounted the current organization and recent work of the firm, however.[34]

The same George Nelson just mentioned was the *Architectural Forum* associate editor who managed the content for the profile of the firm, including the faulty, four-page historical account. The text exhibits little of the droll pithiness that distinguished other of Nelson's architectural essays, however, suggesting he simply shepherded what was provided by the firm through the print-production process. Even if someone else generated the text, one would assume it was reviewed by personnel in the firm. Nevertheless, the errors were approved, to be repeated over the decades.[35]

The *Architectural Forum* profile was expanded and bound as a book, *Industrial Architecture of Albert Kahn, Inc.*, released early in the following year. Authorship of the book is credited to Nelson, who would become an architect himself as well as an influential furniture designer.[36] With the focus of the journal and the book on the industrial commissions that dominated the firm's work through the Depression years, these influential sources appear to have done much to solidify in the minds of historians Kahn's identity as solely a factory architect.

Kahn's work in the 1930s earned him recognition in Rexford Newcomb's 1942 textbook *History of Modern Architecture*, however, placing him solidly in the company of Gropius, Mies, and Saarinen. Unfettered by the ideological bias apparent in Hitchcock's publications, this is one of the few academic treatments of the subject, perhaps the only one published during Kahn's life, to credit him as making "significant contributions . . . to express modern life in terms of an architecture formed of modern materials." It does so without sequestering Kahn to the field of industrial architecture, remembering the Ford Exhibit Building for the Century of Progress Exposition as giving "a fine idea of the stage that modernism had reached at that time. Notable are the strong proportions and the fine simplicity of the building."[37]

Respected as the dean of the College of Fine and Applied Arts at the University of Illinois for a decade, the well-published Newcomb was no slouch in the field of American architectural history when he stood apart in recognizing Kahn's work in this area. MOMA had another opportunity to acknowledge Kahn's contribution to architecture during his lifetime with its 1942 primer

What Is Modern Architecture? but failed to take advantage of it. Kahn was not mentioned in its pages.[38]

Scorn for the Windowless Workplace

Throughout the years and the waxing and waning of various styles, daylighting remained a consistent characteristic of Kahn's work, along with as much natural ventilation as obtainable. While he came to accept and excel at Modernism in the Machine Age, there was another trend gaining momentum in the '30s that he could not embrace: the windowless factory.

In 1930 the Austin Company signed a contract to design the first windowless, large-scale modern factory. Built for the Simonds Saw and Steel Company of Fitchburg, Massachusetts, the one-story, 570- by 360-foot, $1.5 million plant professed to artificially simulate the conditions of a June afternoon within its confines, twenty-four hours a day, 365 days a year. It was reported to embody "radically advanced ideas for scientific creation of artificial lighting, ventilation and other working conditions." To compensate for the lack of a sky or landscape for employees to view, "The nation's foremost color authorities have been consulted in an effort to obtain for the interior of the Simonds plant the exact colors to promote ideal working conditions."[39]

One can only imagine what Victorian naturalists would have thought of such radically advanced scientific ideas . . . but it is clear what Albert Kahn thought of them. His common sense understanding of the superior qualities of natural light and ventilation was imprinted upon him with the Belle Isle Aquarium & Horticultural Building at the turn of the century. In a speech given to a building industry luncheon in 1939, after more windowless factories had been built, Kahn observed, "As for day-light, several attempts have been made at excluding all such, and depending upon artificial light and artificial ventilation. This is called 'progress' by some. To me it seems rather stupid." Buttressing the nineteenth-century work of Dr. Ward and the poignant efforts of that anonymous watch factory engine operator pictured in the first illustration of this volume, Kahn continued, "to deliberately deprive the workers of God-given sunshine and a whiff of ozone is to me incomprehensible."[40]

19

Bringing Out the Best

In 1939, New York City mounted a world's fair optimistically christened the World of Tomorrow. Albert Kahn, Inc., was again the architect of record for the pavilions of both FMC and GM, but they were largely the visions of industrial designers Walter Dorwin Teague and Norman Bel Geddes, respectively, as consumer marketing and showmanship were the foremost consideration.[1] The situation likely suited Kahn since it left his architectural firm only responsible for ensuring the structures were buildable and sound while the designers, Henry Ford, and William Knudsen (now president of GM), competed with each other.

Kahn was about to be drawn into a larger, vastly more momentous fray. As a lad he stood crying outside an architect's office because he was never given any meaningful work to do. Now he was on the verge of being tasked with the lion's share of the most important architectural job in history: the design and ushering through of construction of the behemoth manufacturing facilities required to defeat the mighty Axis Powers in World War II.

Kahn's Call from Glenn Martin

It began at the start of 1939. Aircraft manufacturer Glenn Martin called Kahn to give him the heads up that a large, seemingly unfulfillable, request could soon be coming his way. The client, the Glenn L. Martin Company (GLM), was in negotiation with the frantic government of France. Desperately and urgently needed were 115 long-range bomber planes for combat against German forces, which had been massively, illegally, and as secretly as possible rearming since Hitler came to power in 1933. An existential battle between France and its perennial foe could ignite at any moment, and to meet the demand GLM would have to build a sizable addition to its plant on an extremely expedited schedule. As the architect explained somewhat dryly, "I imagine he called us because we had previously erected for him a building big enough to cover three football fields, without a pillar in it." This was a cavernous, 300- by 450-foot aircraft assembly building the firm designed for GLM in 1937.[2]

Martin was extremely anxious and asked for Kahn's home telephone number so he could call immediately if the deal closed outside of business hours. The telephone call confirming the order came at the architect's home on a Thursday night, February 2. Friday morning, he was at Martin's plant, outside Baltimore, having flown with an architectural assistant, a structural engineer, and a cost estimator. They listened to the client's needs and drew up proposals, one of which was approved on Saturday. Seventy-seven days after the telephone call and three days ahead of schedule, the 680- by 240-foot, $1,850,000, steel, glass, and concrete addition was turned over to the client. Martin now had the largest aircraft plant in the United States, and production of the bombers for France began four days later.[3]

It was a daunting effort requiring precision integration of the design, material supply, and construction processes. Kahn's team worked night and day to get the plans out to the contractors, who had only three days to provide their bids. "The suppliers and contractors entered into the spirit of the thing the same as we did," Kahn reported. "I don't think dirt was ever removed and concrete put in as fast as was done in the Martin job." This was especially impressive considering the work was done in uncooperative February weather. "Everything clicked perfectly," he said in April, praising all concerned. "I don't know whether we ourselves could do it again."[4] It was certainly a challenging record to break, but Kahn and his team would exceed the effort in other ways in the next few years ahead.

"C-Building" addition to the Glenn L. Martin Company Plant, Middle River, Maryland (1939). Albert Kahn, Inc., architect. Photograph, circa 1940, courtesy Albert Kahn Associates, Inc.

Dominoes Fall as Stalin Allies with Hitler

The sense of urgency for France came as the Nazis were backing one side in the Spanish Civil War being fought just across the French southern border. Communist partisans, supported by the USSR, were backing the other side in Spain, which lost with the fall of Madrid at the end of March 1939. In August, the population of the Soviet Union and ardent Communists around the globe were shocked to learn that the governments of the USSR and Germany had entered into a nonaggression pact. Not immediately apparent at the time was that Stalin had committed to supplying Hitler's war machine with the fruits of the Five-Year Plan industrial improvements *and* the two totalitarians had agreed in dividing up Europe between them. In September, the Germans invaded Poland from the west and the Soviets invaded from the east. World War II had begun, and the Soviet Red Army began conquests of Eastern European countries.

For Kahn, the alliance must have been particularly wrenching, knowing that the industrial buildings his firm designed and others it helped with were being used to enable this belligerence. While he apparently never publicly spoke of the subject until after Germany's Operation Barbarossa (discussed below), it was known that the tractor plants and other facilities Kahn designed for the USSR had long been converted to weapon production, and—contrary to what has been written over the years—it appears that the Kahn employees were well aware it would happen as they were designing the structures.[5]

Often repeated in Kahn biographies has been Malcolm Bingay's account of his mid-1942 conversation with the architect, who spoke of the Soviets requiring heavier foundations than were necessary for the production publicized for the facilities. "My brother Moritz and I suspected something," Kahn was reported to have remembered, but the Soviets "merely smiled when we suggested lighter construction and said we did not understand their 'weather.'" At that point, in the original telling, the Kahns both realized the factories were intended to produce heavy armament. As Kahn recalled, he and his brother (who died in January 1939) were both in Moscow for the incident. If this is accurate, it would have had to occur in late 1931.[6]

Recent scholarship suggests that Five-Year Plan factories, including those involving the Kahn firm, were initially conceived for war production, then overlayed with a public "disguise" of civilian use. This appears to have been suspected throughout Kahn's Moscow office, but whether any earlier than Kahn relayed to Bingay is unclear.[7] It might be noted, however, that any nation should be expected to build for its own defense, and it was assumed at the time that a German invasion of the USSR seemed most probable, rather than an alliance between the two. That may have been little comfort for Kahn as the world watched Germany and the USSR together divide up Europe beginning in late 1939, however.

Bases for the Naval Defense Program

The United States was still officially neutral, but there was much more work to be done. Kahn's office was covertly hired by the U.S. Navy to design bases in a massive, $63 million clandestine operation in October 1939. A number of feats in the Kahn portfolio qualified the firm for the job, but it was reported to be largely a result of the work for GLM that the firm was chosen by a special navy committee in a direct, no-bid arrangement to maintain secrecy. (The firm

U.S. Navy Seaplane Hangar, Quonset Point, Rhode Island (1939–40). Albert Kahn, Inc. architect. Photograph, 1941, courtesy Library of Congress.

was quietly approached and told what it would be paid to define and execute the work if it accepted the job.) The navy had been witnessing the progressive, brutal expansion of the Japanese Empire and it became clear that the window of opportunity for establishing effective defense against it was rapidly closing. Although Japanese military observers in ships and planes could see the work being done to fortify bases—often on tiny, remote islands—the scope and details of the plans needed to be kept secret as much as possible to avoid triggering a military response. (Partial details were released in February 1940.)[8]

Albert Kahn, Inc., was charged with preparing working drawings for all the buildings on six bases. For each project, Kahn explained, representatives of the chosen contractors and navy officials met in Kahn's New Center Building offices to "discuss each class of structure, determine the type of construction, the buildings first required, and other details, after which the plans were turned out in the order demanded." There was little room for indulging artistic license, although housing would need to be designed for significantly different climates. Under this process the firm produced some 1,650 sheets of 30- by 36-inch and 30- by 54-inch drawings in less than seven months, or a little over nine per day within six-day work weeks.[9]

In time the program became the world's largest construction venture, and the Kahn plans were reused to build further bases as additional funding became available. In such an environment, it is admittedly difficult to weigh the contribution of an architect apart from the heroics of the whole team. (In the days following the attack on Pearl Harbor, contractors were caught up as combatants defending Wake Island, with many dying and the rest taken prisoner.) Nevertheless, plans and specifications were absolutely essential, and when kinks in the project arose, Kahn's office exceeded expectations to keep work progressing. One of the contractors confided in the architect, "I can take great comfort in the fact that you will find some way in which to do a miracle."[10]

Examples from the Arsenal of Democracy

By May 1940 the Axis Powers and the USSR had overwhelmed other military forces of Europe, with the Soviet Union contributing its industry to supply Hitler's conquests. It was suddenly clear to officials in Washington that the United States was as unprepared to respond as it had been for the First World War. President Roosevelt turned to the one person recommended to him as solely capable of rallying the American industrial might required to defeat the Axis war machine: William S. Knudsen. The GM president was well liked and respected throughout industry—in board rooms, on shop floors, and even by his chief competitor and former employer, Henry Ford. FDR and his New Deal administration had roundly demonized America's industrial leaders for years, however, creating serious antagonism and trust issues on top of manufacturers' bitter memories of their treatment after the First World War. Given the poisoned political landscape, it is difficult imagine anyone other than Knudsen who could have managed as well in organizing and executing what became known as the Arsenal of Democracy (a phrase he coined).[11]

It was not clear what needed to be done and there was no set organizational structure, but Big Bill took charge after walking away from his lofty salary at GM to serve his adopted country, without compensation. Roosevelt chose well. While the United States severely lacked matériel in all areas, Knudsen first concentrated on production requiring the longest lead time: tanks and long-range bombers, which meant first building plants to manufacture them. While existing plants, including automotive, were eventually converted to smaller scale war work, nothing existed to fulfill the demand for these items. (The country already had a shipbuilding industry in place, but it needed expansion.) With action urgently needed but no funding yet authorized, Big Bill secured pledges from fellow industrialists, on the strength of his reputation and handshake, to commit their businesses to costly undertakings. Many of those to whom he turned were Kahn clients, and it was to Kahn they turned for building the massive defense plants required. The work became a deluge, and within a year Kahn's firm (reorganized as Albert Kahn Associated Architects and Engineers, Inc., and bringing nonfamily members into the fold) had the design and construction of more than fifty defense plants under its responsibility.[12]

The pace of work increased through the frantic last years of Kahn's life, which were thus monopolized by the defense effort. (After his death, the work was continued by the firm for the duration of the war with his brother Louis as president.) Just three examples of this herculean task will be discussed here, but they are representative of the firm's estimated one hundred million square feet of defense industry workspace it designed at this time.[13]

On June 7, 1940, with Germany's military might descending upon Paris, Knudsen telephoned K. T. Keller, the president of Chrysler. As later reported in the *Detroit News*, Knudsen bluntly asked, "K.T., will you make tanks?" While well-versed in automotive production, Keller had no way of assessing the scope of this commitment. Nevertheless, he immediately responded, "Yes Bill: where can I see one?" This casual cutting to the chase of such an enormous but urgent matter illustrates the unique quality that made Knudsen an indispensable figure at this moment in history. Eighteen years earlier both were vice-presidents of GM's Chevrolet division, and they understood each other's character, as well as the dire nature of the current times, quite well. After a crammed study of the mass production problem, it was agreed that an unprecedented manufacturing facility was needed. They turned to an equally indispensable figure: Kahn.[14]

Kahn's office supplied preliminary plans to get the project officially approved in mid-August 1940, followed by complete drawings. Ground was broken for the nearly sixteen-acre Chrysler Corporation Tank Arsenal in Warren, Michigan, on September 11. November 19 saw the first of the structural steel set in place and on February 10, 1941, pilot production work began in a completed section of the plant as building construction continued. More than eighty thousand individual panes of glass covered 95 percent of the building. The first twenty-eight-ton "medium" tank was delivered to the Army on April 24, followed by a second before the day's celebration was over. This was some five months ahead of schedule.[15]

In January 1941, Kahn's team was well underway with plans for what would become the Ford Willow Run Bomber Plant, near Ypsilanti, Michigan. It was another ambitious undertaking, capable of accommodating production of around ninety B-24 Liberator long-range bombers simultaneously on a mile-long, L-shaped assembly line. On April 18, 1941, ground was broken, and limited parts production began in September of that year. The first complete plane came off the assembly line September 10, 1942. Covering sixty-two acres under one roof, the manufacturing and assembly building was the largest in the world . . . until Kahn surpassed it with the Dodge Chicago Plant.[16]

Operation: Barbarossa

Through this time, the United Kingdom stood virtually alone against the Nazi onslaught in Europe, with Italy and Japan expanding their raging aggression in Africa and the Indo-Pacific region. As U.S.-made matériel became available, it, along with American food and oil, was shared with the British, who paid for it

Chrysler Corporation Tank Arsenal, Warren, Michigan (1941). Albert Kahn Associated Architects and Engineers, Inc., architect. Construction photograph, 1941, by Central Press Association, collection of the author.

Ford Motor Company Willow Run Bomber Plant, Ypsilanti, Michigan (1941–42). Albert Kahn Associated Architects and Engineers, Inc., architect. Interior photograph, 1943, showing B-24 bomber production, from the collections of The Henry Ford. Gift of the Ford Motor Company.

with land for strategic bases and cash until those options were exhausted. Then the United States supplied the Allies through its Lend-Lease Program. All the while, the Americans were building up their own defensive capability while training troops. As Germany increased its production through the acquisition of factories and slave labor, fueled with raw material under its pact with the Soviet Union, the question was whether British resistance could buy the United States enough time to fully prepare before entering the war.

Everything changed in the early hours of June 22, 1941, with Hitler's invasion of the Soviet Union under the codename Operation: Barbarossa. Just as Stalin plotted to undermine FMC through CPUSA while partnering with the manufacturer to acquire its technology (noted in chapter 16), Hitler planned to invade the USSR while partnering with Stalin to acquire its raw materials. The Soviet Union quickly aligned with the Allied Powers, although many feared the Soviet state would fall as quickly as France. German brutality against combatants and civilians alike steeled the long-suffering population's will to resist, however, despite decades of oppression by its own government. Casualties among civilians and the Red and German armies ran appallingly high across vast stretches of Soviet territory. Meanwhile, in a massive, mandatory migration, the Soviet government conscripted civilians to staff munitions factories far beyond the German reach in Siberia, such as the Chelyabinsk Tractor Plant. Kahn-designed factories within the battle zone and long converted to arms production, such as the Stalingrad Tractor Plant, became much fought-over strategic objectives. The Arsenal of Democracy worked to equip and feed Soviet resistance, which served to weaken the Nazi war machine while the United States was still readying for battle.

After years of angst over his Soviet contracts, Kahn surely found some vindication in this turn of events. It was an outcome few could have foreseen.

America Enters the War

America officially entered the war following the December 7, 1941, attack on Pearl Harbor. The already demanding pressure on Kahn and his firm only increased. The Dodge Chicago Plant would build engines for the B-29 Superfortress bomber, the design of which was not finalized until early 1942. Chrysler and Albert Kahn, Inc., presented the army with manufacturing plans that involved fifteen buildings, including a one-story assembly building covering eighty-two acres, on May 9 for approval. The plans were rejected on the grounds that they required too much precious steel; somehow, they would need to achieve the same ends with less. Keller was quoted as saying, "Mr. Kahn pondered that limitation several hours and then came up with the plan that needed less than half the steel we had been allowed." This savings was achieved by returning to a familiar technology, reengineered for the unique application: reinforced concrete construction. The structure was a seemingly endless series of 30-foot-wide vaulted bays 38 feet long. (Longer bays were possible but would have required more steel reinforcement, which could otherwise be used for building battleships.) Ground was broken in June and the plant was in use by March 1943, although the equipping process lagged behind due to material shortages.[17]

Again, these projects represent just a fraction of the firm's defense work. It was a superhuman effort that swelled the Kahn workforce to 650 as it diligently but furiously worked around the clock to design and build industrial structures with incredible speed, despite incessant labor strikes throughout the supply chain and wartime rationing of construction and tooling materials. The firm repeatedly broke engineering records for clear spans and overall size, but the pace severely taxed the health of Kahn, who was now in his seventies. "Night and day he labored," noted the *Detroit Free Press* of the architect, "getting what little rest he could while flying across the continent supervising construction from the Atlantic to the Pacific."[18]

Dodge Chicago Plant, Chicago, Illinois (1942–44). Albert Kahn Associated Architects and Engineers, Inc., architect. Aerial photograph, 1945, courtesy Albert Kahn Associates, Inc.

Albert Kahn, right, shown at a Glenn L. Martin Plant in 1942. Photograph courtesy the Glenn L. Martin Maryland Aviation Museum.

Tribute

On June 24, 1942, Kahn was honored by the American Institute of Architects with a special medal. Founded in 1857, the organization's gold medal, awarded on a somewhat annual basis, is generally considered its highest honor. It would seem, however, the recognition bestowed upon Kahn (and no one else in the history of the AIA) would hold greater distinction. Perhaps because it was simply referred to as a special award it is often overlooked by biographers, but such singular recognition seems deserving of note. An illustrious assembly of over 450 architects and dignitaries gathered in wartime to attend the event at Detroit's Hotel Statler, and the award received coverage in radio reports, newspapers, and magazines to an extent unprecedented for an architectural recognition. The event held even greater distinction as the keynote address was provided by William Knudsen. Then serving an unprecedented civilian commission as Lieutenant-General, he was charged with overseeing all wartime production for the U.S. military. That Big Bill was afforded time from a critically important, intense, and harried schedule to so honor his dear, long-time friend Kahn is significant.

The award citation read,

> **Albert Kahn**
>
> Exponent of organized efficiency, of disciplined energy, of broad-visioned planning, he has notably contributed to the expansion of the field of architectural practice.
>
> Master of steel and concrete, master of space and time, he stands today at the forefront of our profession in meeting the colossal demands of a government in its hour of need.[19]

The war effort took its toll and led to Kahn's death on December 8, 1942. The cause was listed as coronary thrombosis, with a three-year history of coronary heart disease and coronary sclerosis as contributing factors. These years correspond with the years consumed in designing for the defense effort, but just the day before his death he was able to write to a friend and former employee, "Things certainly are turning. Hitler and Mussolini will see their doom."[20]

As personal friend Rabbi Leo M. Franklin observed at Kahn's funeral, "Some say that he was another casualty of the war, in that because of the duties that the war laid upon him, he overstrained himself. Well, he would not have had it otherwise."[21]

Indeed, Kahn cherished his career as a singular opportunity to achieve great things as part of an extraordinary assemblage of individuals. The architect was not considered a vendor by his most loyal and accomplished clients—he truly was a valued member of this accomplished, egalitarian association of producers, as exemplified by the inscription on a photograph hanging on his office wall at the time of his passing. Below the sepia image of a grey-haired Henry Ford, the automaker affectingly penned:

> *To Albert Kahn*
> *Your best friend is the one who can bring out the best that is in you*
> *Henry Ford.*[22]

A year before his death, Kahn commented upon the associates laboring in his office to meet the military emergency, saying, "It has been a privilege to work with them and to have had a share in the undertakings." His myriad close business associations over the years show he cherished the same spirit of partnership and mutual admiration with them. So many were, like him, self-made individuals who rose to help create America's industrial might. They were uniquely suited to turn that might and dedicate it, along with themselves, to the urgent public need at that moment. Kahn concluded by reflecting, "The experience has been one never to be forgotten, one never afforded before in our history and one that will never offer again."[23]

Epilogue

As recounted in the preceding pages, Kahn's career as an architect spanned some forty-five years, not counting his employment as a draftsperson. His architectural office was at the top, or nearly so, of such firms in the country for over half of that period. His work spanned the nation and circled the globe. He was a pioneer in the use of reinforced concrete construction for a variety of building types and had a key role in the industrial development of the early twentieth century, along with parallel improvements of the workplace. With examples in cities and towns across America, his methods of—and insistence on—harnessing natural light in his architecture were imitated at home in the United States and inspired Modernists in Europe. On top of all this, it is difficult to imagine an Allied victory in World War II without his firm's role in the industrialization of the Soviet Union and U.S. defense industry construction.

At the time of his death, Kahn was perhaps the most well-known of American architects in the minds of the general public, as borne out by a survey of the *Readers' Guide to Periodical Literature* for July 1941 through June 1943 that reveals nine entries for Albert Kahn and two unique entries for Albert Kahn Associated Architects and Engineers. The closest competition was Frank Lloyd Wright, whose renown, it seems fair to note, extended beyond his art while Kahn was alive. (A 1928 news account described Wright as being as "internationally known for the turbulence of his domestic affairs as for his achievements in architecture."[1]) As with most persons, the public's memories of Kahn naturally faded following his death, but it seems remembrance dissipated particularly precipitously among architectural historians.

In 1991 Roxanne Kuter Williamson published an intriguing study in which she created an index for grading the fame quotient of some six hundred

American architects. It was based on the number of times they were cited in twenty-four survey volumes and encyclopedias devoted to architectural history that include the work of those practicing in the United States. In this ranking, Frank Lloyd Wright occupies the top tier, alongside Henry Hobson Richardson, Louis Sullivan, and McKim, Mead & White with twenty-four citations each. It might seem that an architect of Kahn's achievement and status on par with Wright's while alive should justifiably appear at or near that level, but with fifteen citations, Kahn ran below thirty-five other architects and firms, including the eighteenth-century Salem, Massachusetts, carpenter architect Samuel McIntire. With no disrespect intended for any of those in between, and recognizing that, as Williamson points out, "Financial success is seldom equitable with the kind of success that makes an architect famous," it still seems that Kahn has been unduly overlooked by architectural historians in the past.[2] It is fitting to explore this situation before closing the book, so to speak, on this professional biography.

Honest Humility

"Mr. Kahn was anything but the prima donna," recalled the *Detroit Times* after his passing. "He was practical and simple and friendly and reticent about his attainments, constantly deprecating his success by saying he was merely lucky." So unassuming in his personal relations, he was easy to take for granted by those associating with him.

While known for his collections of art and music, he also loved such common pleasures as "rooting lustily at baseball games."[3] This well-grounded quality endeared him with his self-made clients seeking a practical architect with whom they could relate, whether they needed a utilitarian factory, an appealing store, an efficient office building, or a comforting home. For all needs he provided rational solutions that he endeavored to package in good taste. Some have suggested he adopted factory methods in his office, but it could be argued he simply ran it as a well-managed business, and that his returning customers came to rely upon him for it. While possessing considerable artistic ability and knowledge, Kahn certainly did not presume to be an auteur of the likes of Wright or Mies. His clients looked to him for something else—quality work in which they could take pride, delivered on their schedule. This earned him much repeat business as his clients prospered in part through their association with him. Many considered Kahn a friend and peer. According to Paul Cret, Kahn's success benefited all architects by demonstrating that the "clear vision of the business man" was "not incompatible with the creative mind of the artist with his persistent quest for beauty."[4]

Holding his profession in high regard, Kahn railed against what he considered the disposition of many architects seeking to occupy a pedestal of exalted importance and superiority. His criticism could be applied to a number of architects, but one wonders whether Frank Lloyd Wright saw himself being so labeled by Kahn when he told a television interviewer in 1958 that, "early on in life I had to choose between honest arrogance and hypocritical humility. I chose honest arrogance."[5]

If Kahn was ever guilty of hypocrisy, it was in dismissing his own success as a matter of luck. This may have suited his personality, but it was not at all helpful for those attempting to construct an accurate assessment of the scope of his career. This has left biographers and historians relying on fragmented and self-effacing reminiscences that were often erroneous or in conflict with each other over details. It was natural that many turned to George Nelson's seemingly authoritative 1938 profile, as it was prepared under the eyes of Kahn and his firm, but it, too, is problematic as well as decidedly skewed in its focus toward what was then the firm's recent industrial work.

Daunting Scale

Kahn's modesty obscured a professional output that almost defies comprehension on many levels, making his career an intimidating subject to approach. As noted at the beginning of this volume, the catalogue of the buildings designed by Albert Kahn and his firm runs to astonishing figures, so that only a small representation could be discussed in this one book, with otherwise worthy entries that did not fit the narrative flow regrettably omitted. During the architect's life the firm was responsible for nearly two thousand built structures, with more from earlier partnerships where Kahn is due at least shared credit. In this flurry of activity with many overlapping projects were structures built with remarkable speed. Many were of incredible, record-setting dimension and attained historic importance through their use.[6] They ran the gamut from a conjoined public aquarium and conservatory, of which he designed only one, to industrial structure types that numbered in the many hundreds. But there were plenty of building types and satisfied customers in between.

The diversity of building types offers many potentially rich veins to be mined by future scholarship. Hopefully, these pages have increased appreciation of his career and its place in history by drawing back the veil of time for a more enlightened understanding.

Ideology-Driven Marginalization

It is undeniable that Kahn came to specialize in industrial work, however. This, and the onslaught of industrial work for defense at the end of his career, has contributed to the dismissal of Kahn as merely a designer of factories—as if designing for production was a simple matter. This dismissal served a number of self-interested purposes in others. As demonstrated in Kahn's good-natured banter with Wright, classifying Kahn as an industrial architect allowed his less financially successful peers an opportunity to minimize his achievement respective to their own. One might say, "Sure, Kahn has a larger, more lucrative practice than mine or anyone else's, but that's *only* because he designs so many factories." Implied would be the assessment that factories, for some reason, should not be counted.

This form of class distinction also enabled the champions of International Style Modernism to rationalize imitating Kahn's work without acknowledging it as a real architectural precedent. It would be difficult, after all, to claim you are creating a new architecture for a new socialist society while plagiarizing a contemporaneous and highly successful capitalist architect. It was much easier to simply not consider Kahn's work architecture in the first place.

Of course, Kahn's frank, public criticism of excesses in the name of the International Style made it easy for those needing to pigeon-hole him as reactionary, but his evolutionary approach to design was just as predestined for the memory hole of Modernist teaching after World War II as Messel's.[7] High-profile figures in the International Style movement, including their chroniclers, were too invested in establishing their exclusive claim to Modernism as the architecture of a rebelling future to give Kahn more than begrudging recognition, if any.

The smoke of battle from World War II had barely cleared when Hitchcock used an October 16, 1945, lecture at the Detroit Institute of Arts to consign Kahn's contribution to twentieth century architecture to a level somewhere beneath academic interest. He was speaking in association with a touring MOMA exhibition on contemporary architecture, which included a photograph of the 1938 Chrysler Corporation Half-Ton Truck Plant by Kahn's firm. Nevertheless, Hitchcock explained that since Kahn's work inherited traditions from the nineteenth century, he could never be considered a "truly modern architect in the sense of the European 'International Style.' "[8]

While visiting Detroit Hitchcock observed that some of Kahn's early work, in his estimation, demonstrated artistic potential of the type he said Frank Lloyd Wright possessed. In the academician's opinion, however, Kahn abandoned any hope of developing his "individual genius" by preferring "to develop what I suppose is the finest private bureaucratic architectural organization in the world." It appears that, in Hitchcock's eyes, Kahn surrendered any chance of true architectural greatness when he began building an organization destined to play an integral role in the defeat of the Axis Powers. (For his part, Hitchcock worked in a Kahn-designed Pratt & Whitney defense plant during the war.) Despite Wright's declared unwillingness to be credited as an International Style antecedent, Hitchcock continued to laud him as an individual genius, which few would argue, while maintaining Kahn's genius was only "bureaucratic." By this Hitchcock meant that Kahn headed a large, well-run office, which again few would argue with. Although Hitchcock denied it, bureaucracy has a pejorative connotation of suppressing individual achievement. Hitchcock invoked it despite his earlier expressions of contempt for individuality when a new era of collectivism seemed to be dawning during the interwar period. In later assessments, Hitchcock concluded that "Kahn was a mediocre architect considered as an individual."[9]

It is unquestionable that Kahn's legacy was linked to the capabilities of the firm he engendered, but architects ordinarily rely on the support of offices, and it is rare that any figure of historical interest achieves that status without the assistance of others. He excelled in creating an environment where talented individuals worked together as part of a team to achieve a superior work product that few other firms could match. Some employees came and went as suited their individual aspirations, but this is expected in a free society. Kahn's management system worked smoothly while avoiding the natural tendency of bureaucracies to serve themselves at the detriment of their customers. That it continued even after his death offers its own potential vein for scholarship.

In his 1947 essay entitled "The Architecture of Bureaucracy and the Architecture of Genius," Hitchcock seems to have suddenly found a postwar appreciation for individualism in architecture that was not present in his earlier publications on the International Style. Once having sung the praises of state-mandated architectural styles, he now felt it important to caution against building colossal structures planned by bureaucracies like, by implication through the use of accompanying photos, the Kahn office while drawing parallels with the "public monuments of Nazidom."[10]

While Hitchcock had some interesting and valid things to say, his linking of Kahn to Nazidom is particularly offensive given the crucial contributions of the architect and his firm in the defeat of fascism. As published in *Architectural Review*, the page layout of Hitchcock's thesis featured a two-page spread visually pitting the product of Kahn and Wright against each other. On the right side is the image of the Dodge Chicago Plant, designed by Kahn's firm for the production of B-29 Superfortress long-range bomber engines during the war. The view is a series of connected one-story, low-arched bays receding toward a vanishing point. While remarkably long, the scale is difficult to appreciate in the small photograph, and the overall impression conveyed is one of uninspired monotony. On the opposing page is a much larger image of a model of Wright's future showpiece, the Solomon R. Guggenheim Museum in New York City with its seemingly gravity-defying spiral gallery rising well above the street. Intended to illustrate the difference between the architectures of bureaucracy and genius as Hitchcock saw it, this is an extreme example of an apple to orange comparison.[11]

Differences between these two innovative structures and their construction histories could fill a separate volume, but to hit on just one, the time span from the signing of Chrysler's initial contract to completion of construction of the Dodge Chicago Plant—a single building of which covered nearly eighty-two acres—ran about sixteen months. These months transpired during a war in which construction material rationing necessitated major last-minute design changes. Once fully equipped, the finished plant surpassed expectation in the production of unprecedentedly large, complicated, and powerful aircraft engines from raw materials. In short, it fulfilled its vital purpose most excellently. In contrast, sixteen *years* passed between the initial concept of the Guggenheim Museum and its opening. These were years of peace and prosperity, with plentiful materials and labor. While an undeniably stunning landmark, the curved walls of the finished gallery make for difficulty in displaying flat art—the building's primary function. Hitchcock's collaborator for *The International Style*, Philip Johnson, said of the Guggenheim gallery after its completion, "it is totally impossible, it does not work—but what a room!"[12] To resurrect and paraphrase a common witticism from the second half of the twentieth century and with all due respect to the master of Taliesin's unquestioned genius: if the Allied nations had had to rely on Frank Lloyd Wright to design the Arsenal of Democracy, they would all be speaking German now.

Hitchcock conceded that it might not be wise to have Wright designing airplane plants while also stating it might be unwise to have Kahn design a "Modern Gallery"—although the Detroiter surely could have delivered a fitting one, based on his record across many building types. The majority of Wright's commissions were residences, and in this area, it is easier to provide apples-to-apples comparison with Kahn. Wright-designed homes, a great many of which may be toured today, are varied and endlessly fascinating. The architect demanded a lot from his clients, however, leaving some of them to wonder whether it was they or Wright who actually owned their houses. Tales of design and material failings leading to issues such as leaking roofs are legion and often owners have needed to invest heavily in corrections beyond normal maintenance. In contrast, the few Kahn homes available for tour today are steeped with tradition; perhaps they are not to everyone's taste and not as uniquely memorable as Wright's, but surely many people can more easily imagine living comfortably within them. As for International Style residences, they could be a hard sell even among mutually celebrating auteur-architects. "Mies hates this house," Philip Johnson conceded of his own home, the celebrated Glass House that he designed in homage to the German expatriate. Mies told a client that Johnson's Glass House looked like a hot dog stand when illuminated at night.[13] These comparisons are not evoked to denigrate Kahn's contemporaries, who were responsible for truly wonderful buildings, but to illustrate how myopic it was for Hitchcock to cavalierly dismiss Kahn as a mediocre architect.

As for Hitchcock's linking Kahn's work done in the service of capitalism to Nazidom, it appears to be part of a larger campaign to promote an ideological agenda that has proven remarkably durable. In the mindset of some of the New Deal coterie was the self-gratifying conviction, witnessed with astonishment by less zealous members of the Roosevelt administration, that communism and fascism were polar opposites (with capitalism ideologically aligned with the latter) rather than the revolutionary left wing and reactionary right wing, respectively, of the Marxist socialist movement. This left and right wing premise was widely recognized during the 1920s and '30s, and the simultaneous turmoil among socialists on the Bauhaus campus could be viewed as symptomatic of a feverish family squabble. At the time of the Hitler-Stalin Pact Soviet foreign minister Vyacheslav Molotov reduced the differences between communism and fascism to, in his words, a matter of taste, but history would prove them catastrophically irreconcilable. This original sibling relationship has been increasingly disclaimed since, but it helps in understanding how the two wings could affiliate in some situations while breaking into the most violent of rivalries in others.[14] While this may seem to be wandering from the topic at hand, the New Dealers' conviction that Nazism and capitalism were more closely related than Nazism and communism seems to have provided a dimension of moral justification to the marginalization of the accomplishments of Kahn and his major clients by academia. Direct linkage between Nazism and communism was supplied by no less of an authority than Adolf Hitler, however.

In December 1939, Hermann Rauschning attempted to warn the world of Hitler's closely held deeper purposes by publishing the text of his personal conversations of a few years earlier with the Führer. Ranking high in the Nazi Party, Rauschning presided over the Senate of the Free City of Danzig (now Gdańsk, Poland) from 1933 to 1934. He sought to operate the port, crucial to Germany's economy, as a free enterprise zone. This placed him at loggerheads with Nazi leaders in Berlin wanting to exert direct party control over shipping, which Rauschning feared would drive badly needed international commerce elsewhere. Ultimately, he was called to Berlin to explain his position directly to Hitler. This was one of a number of confidential conversations, and upon grasping the direction of Hitler's means and motives, Rauschning became disillusioned and left the party while it was on the rise in 1935 and fled Germany in 1937. When he published *Hitler Speaks* from London, he did not claim to be transcribing conversations exactly verbatim but reconstructing them, in English, from thorough notes he made at the time, augmented by his memory. Some doubted his veracity when the book came out, but Rauschning's 1939 documentation foreshadowed subsequent events, such as Hitler's June 1941 turn against collaborator Stalin. As evidence supporting other details has come to light, Rauschning's reliability has won respect from scholarly historians over the years.[15]

During their Berlin conversation, Hitler revealed his muddled ideological moorings. It became clear, nevertheless, that the Nazi economy and society would be centrally planned, with its benefit to the party being the supreme object. "I have learnt a great deal from Marxism," Rauschning quotes Hitler as saying. "The difference between them and myself is that I have really put into practice what these peddlers and pen-pushers have timidly begun." While Hitler thought eliminating all property rights futilely ran against human nature, he maintained the state needed to structure ownership and the economy according to its need—not the individual's. Rauschning deduced that one thing Hitler's fascism clearly was not was capitalism. "A red thread may be plainly seen through all the inconsistent, contradictory activities" of Hitler's megalomania, he added. This pattern similarly caused Hitler's later authoritative biographer, Joachim C. Fest, to conclude the Führer "was not the desperate last gasp of dying capitalism as a good many ideologists have described him." National Socialists and Communists did not battle each other over great ideological differences, Fest continued, but over political control of the vital German working class while both sought the destruction of old-world institutions and values.[16]

In the United States, the New Dealers' perspective conveniently justified using a rather tortured line of reasoning that somehow equated capitalism with fascism, since—they argued—neither were communism. The strained logic was twisted to lead to a wobbly, if not clearly false, conclusion, but it conveniently served political ends. As an example of this logic, while politicking for his boss on a national platform in 1937, FDR's Secretary of the Interior Harold Ickes condemned what he termed "big business fascist America—an enslaved

America."[17] The Hitler-Stalin Pact, followed by the post–Operation Barbarossa need to supply Allies, which suddenly included the Soviet Union, gave pause to such anti–big business rhetoric, but it resumed following the war. With Kahn's clients again cast as fascists, coupled with the architect's trashing of the International Style, the conditions were ripe for consigning his legacy to the memory hole by a postwar academia still enamored with the New Deal.

During World War II and afterward, art commentators and historians refused to recognize the actual architectural monuments of the fascist states, presumably and understandably lest they appear to legitimize the ideology. The faulty reasoning equating capitalism with fascism seems to have led to Hitchcock's Nazidom linkage. In an ironic twist, collateral damage from this ideological construct appears to have included a failure to fully appreciate the historic import of Kahn's legacy of monumental work built for the express purpose of defeating Nazidom.[18]

For decades, Hitchcock had a well-respected, if not mythic, voice in the field of architectural history and his opinion of Kahn's work suited many in postwar academia. (Hitchcock's legacy has itself become an area of study following his death in 1987, and it should be noted that Modernism occupied only a portion of his scholarship.) He, Sigfried Giedion, Nicholas Pevsner, and others characterized by Anthony Vidler as trying "to write the history of modernism in a partisan, if not propagandistic, mode" influenced generations of other authors, educators, and their students. Many were prone to receiving the message: during the Great Depression and after, legions of academicians owed their faculty positions to New Deal policies.[19]

It seems logical to assume this would result in an academic tendency to defend its social ideals as its legacy, ideals embodied in the work of expatriate International Style architects who found their way to positions in American universities, as Wright came to lament. Any recognition of the progressive nature and impact of Kahn's work, beyond engineering advances, in the service of free-market capitalism, including his designs for the New Deal–defying Century of Progress Exposition, did not mesh well with the dominant narrative developed in the postwar years.

This fate was similar to that of his work for the Soviet Union, which was written out of history books there shortly after the termination of his firm's contract. Instead, all credit for the Five-Year Plan industrialization was reserved for the Communist Party. (The process of expunging Kahn from

Soviet histories involved the state executions of those who answered their government's call to work with Kahn's staff in Detroit and Moscow.)[20]

Retrieving Kahn from the Memory Hole

Kahn went from being perhaps the most well-known architect in America to being nearly forgotten by the public outside of the Detroit area and marginalized in academia following 1947. His well-organized firm continued under his name, however, keeping the memory alive through corporate publications following his death. *The Legacy of Albert Kahn*, containing a biography penned by W. Hawkins Ferry, was published as a catalogue accompanying a 1970 exhibit at the Detroit Institute of Arts and currently continues in print by Wayne State University Press. In 1972 the University of Michigan Museum of Art exhibited a collection of Kahn's sketches from his travels over the years, accompanied by a catalogue. Thirty-two years after Kahn's death, Grant Hildebrand, an architect once employed by the firm, published the monograph *Designing for Industry: The Architecture of Albert Kahn.*

In time, the luster of the International Style faded, the Soviet Union dissolved, and generational change occurred in academia. Perhaps not coincidentally, Kahn's work has since been the subject of increasing scholarship, as illustrated in the bibliography.[21]

Tracing Kahn's Distinctive Artistic Signature

As that work is evaluated, it is my hope that this volume leads to broadened consideration of Kahn's impact on both his art and his times. It is time to retire the characterization of Kahn as a standout only as a designer for industry. While reasons for this abound—such as his press statements over the years, his industrial contracts with the USSR, the 1937 *Architectural Forum* coverage, and the glut of newsworthy defense industry work, to the exclusion of all else, during his final years—it also appears the industrial architect status was influenced by an ideological premises that is perhaps due reevaluation as well.

Returning to Hitchcock's categorization of Kahn as a bureaucratic genius rather than an architectural one, it seems the sheer length and breadth of his career contributed to his marginalization by historians. Claire Zimmerman noted that many perceive Kahn as having "authored a process, not a personal language of architecture with a distinctive artistic signature."[22] There is certainly an argument to support this perception, but it is my stance that the process was simply effective management. This unignorably effective management, with its amazingly productive yield, should not blind us to an appreciation of his contributions to design that emerged from the roiling cauldron of the American building scene. The defining design characteristic of Kahn's work, over a long and varied career during which so many architectural trends waxed and waned, is his overriding passion for natural light and ventilation for workers. It drove the form and appearance of most everything Kahn designed except residential work, where privacy held sway. For this reason, I have pointed to the Belle Isle Aquarium & Horticultural Building as the fountainhead of Kahn's subtle but enduring signature.

From there architectural trends were tapped in the process of aesthetic execution, and this, Kahn readily admitted, was shaped through group effort. Ultimately, however, the results were approved by Kahn (as well as the client) as long as he lived. With that said, based on Kahn's frequent references to Messel, I suspect any contemporary Teutonic tendencies tracible in his buildings, such as found in the firm's work for Detroit newspapers, are particularly suggestive of Kahn's individual artistic predilections. That said, they were also manifestations of an American architecture that, as Kahn noted in "Architectural Trend," had already existed for years. The question of Kahn's influence on that American style and its influence on Kahn may fall into a chicken-or-the-egg debate, with perhaps only a few clear exceptions, such as occasions where the office employed distinct Prairie styling.

Recognizing Achievement

Kahn was an accomplished architect of international scope and unparalleled success, especially when considering his underprivileged beginnings and on-the-job education. While assessing artistic success will always be a matter of subjective debate, no single professional architect approaches Kahn's business success and impact on global history. His impact stemmed from his work for industrial clients, who considered him one of their own, as well as his controversial Soviet contracts, and his titanic contribution to the war effort. All was achieved through his masterful fusion of the art of architecture and engineering. As his friend Paul Cret emphatically declared at the time of his death, "Kahn cannot be called an industrial-architect; he was an architect, without hyphen and a great one."[23]

Acknowledgments

I am indebted to Wayne State University Press, particularly Sandra Korn and Thomas Klug, for embracing this addition to its offering of publications concerning Albert Kahn. Joining that collection, which dates back decades, along with offerings by other publishers, places this volume in fine company. I would like to acknowledge the contributions of Amy Pattullo as copyeditor and thank the readers in the blind review process for their time and comments on my manuscript. Challenges and rewrites arising from that process have resulted in what I consider to be a better book.

One of the rewards in taking on a project such as this has been the interactions with so many people with whom I may never have otherwise crossed paths. Many I had the pleasure of meeting in person, often while visiting inspirational libraries and other places. Others I met through correspondence and some assisted without providing their name.

Albert Kahn Associates, Inc., was remarkably supportive of an author endeavoring an overhaul of what might be considered the organization's origin story. I should point out that the firm's personnel only offered assistance and never attempted to influence the content of this book. Kahn and his times represent a content-rich field for many scholarly disciplines, and I hope this volume will inspire more avenues of study, for the topic is too large to allow anyone to write its last word. Among those at AKA who provided support and encouragement are Donald Bauman, Alan Cobb, John Cole, Heidi Pfannes, and Caitlin Wunderlich.

Within the circle of Albert Kahn scholarship, I have benefited from the knowledge, encouragement, and assistance of Dale Carlson, Deirdre Hennebury,

Michael Hodges, Carol Rose Kahn, Sonia Melnikova-Raich, Michael G. Smith, and Claire Zimmerman. Furthermore, my associations with the Albert Kahn Legacy Foundation and the Albert Kahn Research Coalition have been rewarding.

Assistance along the way has been provided by the staffs of the Art Institute of Chicago; Ryerson & Burnham Library (J. T. de la Torre in particular); Case Western Reserve University's Kelvin Smith Library; Chicago Public Library (Evan Meszaros); Cranbrook Center for Collections and Research (Gregory M. Wittkopp, Laura MacNewman); Crystal Palace Foundation (Martin Frel); Delta Gamma Fraternity (Tiffany Tracy); Detroit Historical Society (Brendan Roney); Detroit Institute of Arts (Nancy Barr, Douglas Bulka, James Hanks); Detroit Public Library Burton Historical Collection and National Automotive History Collection (Mark Bowden, Carla Reczek); Jackson, Michigan, District Library; Fraserburgh, Scotland, Heritage Centre Adult Services Department (Robert Henderson); Eastern Michigan University's Halle Library; General Motors Archives and Special Collections (Christo Danti, Larry Kinsel); Glenn L. Martin Maryland Aviation Museum (Stanley Piet, Jr.); Google Books; Hathi Trust; Internet Archive; The Henry Ford Research Center (James Orr); Kew Royal Botanic Gardens (David Cooke); Village of Lansing, Illinois (Mayor Patty Eidam); Lawrence Technological University Library (Adrienne Alluzzo, Catherine Phillips); Library of Michigan; Michigan eLibrary; Royal Oak, Michigan, Public Library (Lori Boden, Diane McGovern); St. Louis Public Library; Selfridge Military Air Museum, Selfridge Air National Guard Base (Lt. Co. Lou Nigro, Lori Nye, Rob Sandstrom); Shedd Aquarium (Ashleigh Bragg, Alisun DeKock); Smithsonian Institution Archives of American Art (Marisa Bourgoin); Stellantis Historical Services (Brandt Rosenbusch, Danielle Szostak-Viers); U.S. Army Tank-Automotive and Armaments Command (John Daniele, Rachel Johnson); United States Fish and Wildlife Service (Lou Ann Speulda-Drews), Bentley Historical Library, University of Michigan (Michael S. Smith); University of Michigan Museum of Art; University of Minnesota Libraries, Charles Babbage Institute (Stephanie H. Crowe and Amanda Wick); Walter P. Reuther Library, Wayne State University (Aimee Ergas); and Windsor, Ontario, Public Library Local History Department (Tom Vajdik).

Others contributing by making valuable introductions, assisting with translations and images, or connecting me with resources have been Robert Alexander,

Garnet Cousins, Lisa DiChiera, Joseph Dobrzeniecki, Molly Dobrzeniecki, Tara Hernandez, William Lynch, Christine Maurer, Justin Meister, Philip Meister, R. Vance Patrick, Maria Pfeiffer, Michael Skinner, Levi Smith, and Kurt Snyder.

My deep thanks to all, including any I may have missed recognizing here. This book would not have been possible without their assistance. While I have had many engaging discussions along the way, responsibility for the conclusions that I derived from my research and this resulting volume rests with me.

Notes

Full references are given here to newspaper articles, government sources, and archival material. The latter are keyed to the archives listed in the bibliography. Shortened references are given to articles and books listed in the bibliography.

Preface

1 I first found indication that Mullgardt designed the Boyer Shop in the fragile pages of a May 26, 1900, edition of the obscure *Detroit Northside Gazette*. An example of its misattribution to Kahn can be found in a timeline appearing in Carter, *Albert Kahn*, 14. The circumstances giving rise to the misattribution are recounted in Meister, "Albert Kahn's Partners in Industrial Architecture," 84.

2 The determined, grassroots volunteers initially worked against long odds in uncertain times as the Friends of the Belle Isle Aquarium (FOBIA), which became amalgamated with other park advocates to form the Belle Isle Conservancy in 2012. Funds raised earlier by FOBIA provided seed money leading to a 2011 Michigan State Historic Preservation Fund grant for emergency work to repair the roof over the aquarium. The skylights were restored through the generous support of Trayce and Randy Fenton in 2014, and in 2015 the restoration lighting was underwritten by Joy and Allan Nachman. Another volunteer, Deborah Chandonnet, played a key role in fundraising. The 2015 ceiling restoration was funded by the William Davidson Foundation, and the Louisa St. Clair Chapter of the National Daughters of the American Revolution underwrote the restoration of the foyer in 2021.

3 "Auto Historian Borth, 80, Dies," *Detroit Free Press*, March 25, 1976, pt. 2, p. 11. Christian Carl (Christy) Borth was a reporter for the *Detroit Free Press* and established the Detroit bureau of *Time* magazine in 1937. He was surely the author of the *Time* articles on Kahn in the late 1930s and early 1940s. During World War II Borth was a member of the Automotive Council for War Production, chronicling its story in *Freedom's Arsenal* among his other books. As with Ferry, works by Borth populate the bibliography of this volume and provide unique insight while being subjected to the scrutiny described in the text.

4 Marsha Miro, "Pursuing the Newest Art with an Old-World Patron's Zeal," *Detroit Free Press*, April 26, 1981, "Detroit" section, p. 24. As recounted by Miro, W. (William) Hawkins Ferry was influenced by Eliel and Eero Saarinen as a student at Cranbrook School for Boys. He studied at Harvard University's School of Design while it was under the direction of Walter Gropius and Marcel Breuer and briefly taught architecture at Wayne State University. A noted Detroit patron of the arts, he interviewed Kahn and George D. Mason for his writings on local architecture, which include the still-definitive study, *Buildings of Detroit*.

5 "Architect Pioneers in Development of Industrial Building," written for a newsletter of his wife Ernestine's university sorority, is an example where the architect alone is responsible for the errors. The same seems true of the errors appearing in the oft-quoted August 1938 issue of *Architectural Forum*. George Nelson appears to have merely edited the text, which surely was provided by the firm. Both these sources are discussed further when they are cited in the chapters ahead.

Others who interviewed Kahn are cited in the notes to follow and include Helen Christine Bennett (publishing in 1929), Malcolm Bingay (in a series of newspaper columns and books beginning as early as 1935), and Donald M. Davies (1940). Florence Davies, an editor and art critic for the *Detroit News* from 1922 through 1947, provides some insightful accounts of the interactions she witnessed between Kahn and others.

6 Grant Hildebrand, *Designing for Industry: The Architecture of Albert Kahn* (Cambridge, MA: MIT Press, 1974), 25, 31, 86; Federico Bucci, *Albert Kahn: Architect of Ford*, trans. Carmen DiCinque (New York: Princeton Architectural Press, 1993).

7 Michael H. Hodges, *Building the Modern World: Albert Kahn in Detroit* (Detroit: Wayne State University Press, 2018).

8 Wolfgang Schivelbusch, *Three New Deals: Reflections on Roosevelt's America, Mussolini's Italy, and Hitler's Germany*, trans. Jefferson Chase (New York: Metropolitan Books, 2006).

9 Helen Christine Bennett, "You Can't Build Skyscrapers with Your Head in the Sky," *American Magazine* 108 (December 1929), 121.

Chapter 1

1 "Albert Kahn," *Detroit Times*, December 9, 1942, 22; "Mr. Albert Kahn," *Times* (London), December 9, 1942, 9; "Soviet Engineers, Architects, Cable Sympathy to Mrs. Kahn," *Embassy of the Union of Socialist Republics Information Bulletin*, December 29, 1942, 2; "Albert Kahn Dies; Famous Architect," *New York Times*, December 9, 1942, 27; "Albert Kahn," *New York Times*, December 10, 1942, 24.

2 "Albert Kahn," *Detroit News*, December 9, 1942, 26; [Roger Allen], "A.K.," *Grand Rapids Press*, December 9, 1942, 14.

3 Bennett, "You Can't Build Skyscrapers," 121; Borth, *Masters of Mass Production*, 97–98; "World Famous Detroit Architect Dies Unexpectedly at Age of 73," *Detroit Jewish Chronicle*, December 11, 1942, 1.

4 "Died," *Detroit News*, May 13, 1912, 14; Bennett, "You Can't Build Skyscrapers," 121; "Joseph Kahn," *Detroit Free Press*, July 22, 1935, 2; Davies, "Million-Dollar 'Office Boy,'" 6; "World Famous Detroit Architect Dies Unexpectedly at Age of 73," *Detroit Jewish Chronicle*, December 11, 1942, 1, 16; and Zieman, "Albert Kahn," 29–30. Rosalie (Cohn) died May 11, 1912, at age sixty-six in her residence at 74 Frederick, Detroit. Joseph died July 20, 1935, at age ninety in his residence at 26637 York, Huntington Woods. Both were interred at Woodmere Cemetery.

5 Borth, *Masters of Mass Production*, 98. Even Kahn himself routinely and inaccurately identified the firm as John Scott & Company. As an example, see "As He Is Known," 127. While John (1851–1928) lived in Detroit and surely ran the office at the time of Kahn's employment, the firm was in William's name, who resided across the Detroit River in Windsor, Ontario. The firm's name was changed to John Scott & Company following William's 1889 death, long after Kahn's employment there. The likelihood of Kahn's employment beginning in 1882 or 1883 is derived from his March 3, 1884, starting date at Mason & Rice (discussed and cited in Hildebrand, *Designing for Industry*, 7) as recorded in Mason's notes. Kahn maintained he had worked a year for Scott without pay, so he must have started there before March 1883. It is unknown how long he was paid before being dismissed and how long he might have been unemployed before being hired by Mason & Rice. *Detroit City Directory for 1882* (Detroit: J. W. Weeks, 1882), 182, 883, and 1056; "Windsor," *Detroit Free Press*, July 1, 1889, 1; Albert Marquis, *Book of Detroiters* 433; and "Eminent Detroit Architect Dead," 72.

6 "Poor as a Boy, Rich at 54," *Detroit Times*, March 11, 1923, 4; Albert Kahn, "Tribute to George D. Mason 1923 [1926]," AKA-BHL, box 1; "Eminent Architect Dead," 4; Bennett, "You Can't Build Skyscrapers," 121; and Ray Pearson, "The Power That Erring Men Call Chance," *Detroit Free Press*, February 25, 1940, pt. 1, p. 7. Typically discreet, Kahn rarely identified Scott's office as the site of his unhappy first architectural employment. He made an exception when presenting his tribute to Mason, likely because many in the audience already knew full well he had worked for Scott. After Kahn's success was well established, the Scott office boasted he "started architecture with the firm." "John Scott & Company Reorganize," 72.

7 Bennett, "You Can't Build Skyscrapers," 121.

8 Leake, *History of Detroit*, 337; Russell, *Germanic Influence in the Making of Michigan*, 219; "Death Takes Aged Sculptor," *Detroit Free Press*, January 15, 1908, 1.

9 "Death Takes Aged Sculptor," *Detroit Free Press*, January 15, 1908, 1; "The Death of Julius Melchers," *Detroit News*, January 15, 1908, 4; "Apoplexy Takes Julius Melchers," *Detroit News*, January 15, 1908, 7; "Detroit's German Colony Vanishes, Absorbed by the City," *Detroit News*, November 27, 1927, pt. 2, p. 9; Lewis-Hind, *Gari Melchers: Painter*, n.p.

10 "Art's Sake!" *Detroit News*, August 22, 1897, pt. 2, p. 1; George W. Stark, "Leipziger Cartoons in News Once Famous Around World," *Detroit News*, November 28, 1935, 17; Russell, *Germanic Influence*, 219; "Julius Melchers Retires," *Detroit News*, May 12, 1900, 5; "Death Takes Aged Sculptor," *Detroit Free Press*,

January 15, 1908, 1; Burroughs, *Retrospective Exhibition of Paintings by Gari Melchers*, v; "Through the Death of Dankmar Adler . . ." *American Architect and Building News*; Gregersen and Saltztein, *Dankmar Adler*, 1–2.

11 Kahn, "Tribute to George D. Mason 1923 [1926]," AKA-BHL.

12 "Art's Sake!" *Detroit News*, August 22, 1897, pt. 2, p. 1.

13 Lodge and Quaife, *I Remember Detroit*.

14 "Michigan Chapter," *American Institute of Architects Quarterly Bulletin*, 29. Melchers closed his studio and retired in May 1900. He died eight years later. "Julius Melchers Retires," *Detroit News*, May 12, 1900, 5.

15 "The Romantic Rise of Two Brothers Whose Achievements Have Worked a Revolution in the Constructive World," *Detroit News-Tribune*, September 20, 1908, pt. 1, p. 20; Borth, *Masters of Mass Production*, 98.

16 "Talks on Architecture," *Detroit News*, January 22, 1898, 2; "Sayings and Doings," *Detroit Free Press*, April 5, 1898, 5; "Ordered to Act" *Detroit News*, September 28, 1904, 8; "The Week in Art," *Detroit News*, March 25, 1928, pt. 12, p. 7; Florence Davies, "Notable Modern Masters in a Detroit Collection," *Detroit News*, August 31, 1930, pt. 10, p. 8.

17 "Later City Items," *Detroit Evening News*, August 9, 1897, 3: Kahn, "Tribute to George D. Mason 1923 [1926]," AKA-BHL; Hawkins Ferry, "Representative Detroit Buildings," 48.

18 Davies, "Million-Dollar 'Office Boy,' " 6.

Chapter 2

1 George D. Mason's diary for 1885, entries for January 1 and July 1, MS / Mason, George D., box 1: Diaries, DPL-BHC; Kahn, "Tribute to George D. Mason 1923 [1926]," AKA-BHL, box 1, n.p.; Louis Tendler "Under Mantle of Glory," *Detroit News*, December 10, 1942, pt. 1, p. 18; Ferry, "Representative Detroit Buildings," 51; Hildebrand, *Designing for Industry*, 23n6. As recorded by Bennett, Kahn credited Melchers's son Gari, the celebrated painter, for recommending him to Mason & Rice. Bennett, "You Can't Build Skyscrapers," 121. Most other tellings, including Tendler, quoting Mason, say it was Julius, which seems more likely.

2 Louis Tendler "Under Mantle of Glory," *Detroit News*, December 10, 1942, pt. 1, p. 18.

3 Kahn, "Tribute to George D. Mason 1923 [1926]," AKA-BHL, box 1, n.p.

4 "Last Rites Monday for Zachariah Rice," *Detroit News*, October 5, 1929, 13; Ferry, "Representative Detroit Buildings," 49, 55; and George D. Mason, "Few Facts of the Early Architectural Development of Detroit," 1, 5. The present narrative attempts to reconcile mild conflicts between these sources. A history of the firm Smith, Hinchman & Grylls has Mason starting with Mortimer Smith in the summer of 1874 and completing "two years of training in Smith's office," then spending "a short time in the office of Henry T. Brush." Holleman and Gallagher, *Smith, Hinchman & Grylls*, 37. This appears to be a result of confusion involving Mortimer Smith and Hugh Smith.

5 "Last Rites Monday for Zachariah Rice," 13; and Kahn, "Tribute to George D. Mason 1923 [1926]," AKA-BHL, box 1, n.p.

6 Kahn, "Tribute to George D. Mason 1923 [1926]," AKA-BHL, box 1, n.p.; and Swales, "Master Draftsmen," pt. 12, p. 84.

7 "Town Talk," *Detroit News*, December 30, 1888, 8; "Architectural Doings," *Detroit News*, March 23, 1890, 7; Kahn, "Tribute to George D. Mason 1923 [1926]," AKA-BHL, box 1, n.p.; Russell, *Germanic Influence*, 220; and McLean, "Albert Kahn Signs Contract with Russians," 39.

8 *Detroit City Directory for 1887*, 1047; *U.S. Census Records for Detroit, 1900*, entry for George W. Nettleton; death certificate for George W. Nettleton, December 13, 1900, El Paso County, Colorado; *The Ten Year Book of Cornell University, 1868–1908*, 399; Albert Kahn, "Architect Pioneers in Development of Industrial Building," 377; Hildebrand, *Designing for Industry*, 7. Nettleton is listed as a draftsman for L. D. Grosvenor on page 213 of the *Jackson City Directory for 1885–86*. I would like to thank the Adult Services Department of the Jackson District Library for this information.

George should not be confused with his younger brother, James Burritt Nettleton (1864–1927), who also studied architecture at Cornell. James worked for Donaldson & Meier in Detroit from 1887 to 1898. After three years in Toledo, he returned to Detroit and Donaldson & Meier in 1902. In 1907 he entered into a partnership with Alfred E. Weaver, where he continued until his death. *Detroit City Directory for 1887*, 1047; Charles Moore, *History of Michigan*, vol. 3 (Chicago: Lewis Publishing Company, 1915), 1454; and "James Nettleton Dies at Age of 53," *Detroit Free Press*, April 30, 1927.

9 Kahn, "Tribute to George D. Mason 1923 [1926]," AKA-BHL, box 1, n.p.; unidentified newspaper clipping [December 14, 1900], AKP-AAA, microfilm roll 1114, frame 64.

10 "Building Intelligence," 303; *James E. Scripps*, 44; Ferry, *Buildings of Detroit*, 133–34, 264, and plate 282. Further evidence of Scripps's promotion of the arts is found with his discourse on Norman and Gothic architectural history at the Detroit Museum of Art in 1898 (where Kahn presented on Renaissance architecture) and his participation (along with Kahn) on the city's Arts Council when it was formed in 1903. "Personal and Club News," 93; and *City of Detroit Journal of the Common Council from January 13, 1903, to January 12, 1904*, 974.

11 "Building Intelligence," 303; James E. Scripps, *Descriptive Account of the New Edifice Erected for Trinity Church, Detroit* (Detroit: Ladies Aid Society of Trinity Church, 1892), 3–4; Ferry, "Representative Detroit Buildings," 55. Elsewhere in his essay Ferry cites Mason as contributing background anecdotes.

12 "Trade Notes," *Carpentry and Building* 11 (August 1899), 170; and Baldasty, *E. W. Scripps and the Business of Newspapers*, 102–3.

13 "American Workingmen's Expedition to the Paris Exhibition," 72; "Workingmen's Expedition to Europe," 32; George W. Nettleton, "Viewing Europe with an Artist's

Eye," *Detroit Evening News*, December 29, 1889, 9; Baldasty, *E. W. Scripps and the Business of Newspapers*, 102–3.

14 Nettleton, "Viewing Europe with an Artist's Eye," 9.

15 George W. Nettleton, "European Workshops," *Detroit Evening News*, November 19, 1889, 3.

16 See Scripps, *Descriptive Account*, 3–21; Stark, *Detroit: An Industrial Miracle*, 48; Ferry, *Buildings of Detroit*, 274.

17 "Mackinac's Big Hotel," *Detroit Free Press*, January 17, 1887, 2; "A Mammoth Structure," *Detroit Free Press*, March 11, 1887, 5; and Edgar Kahn, "Albert Kahn," 25.

18 "The New Architecture," *Detroit News*, October 24, 1886, 8; Albert Kahn, "Thirty Minutes with American Architecture and Architects," typescript, presented to the Adcraft Club of Detroit, January 22, 1937, AK-BHL, box 1, file "Transcripts of Speeches, 1936–1939," 3. See the George D. Mason Collection in DPL-BHC for more examples.

19 Weeks and Edwards, *Walkerville* 113–34.

20 "Lake Front of Proposed Hotel at Kingsville, Ont.," *American Architect and Building News*, March 23, 1889, 25, plate; notation on riverside of photograph, "Mettawa [*sic*] Inn, Kingsville, Ontario," AKP-AAA, box 5, file 60; Bloomfield, "Albert Kahn and Canadian Industrial Architecture," 5–6; Brown, *Rails Across Ontario*, 88-89; Weeks and Edwards, *Walkerville*, 164.

21 "On the Sixth of December . . . ," *American Architect and Building News* 31 (January 3, 1891), 1; and Albert Kahn, "Industrial Architecture—Its Problems and Obligations," transcript of an address for the Boston Society of Architects, November 12, 1940, AKA-BHL, box 1, file "Transcripts of Speeches, 1940–1942," 1.

22 "On the Sixth of December . . . ," *American Architect and Building News*, 1; Bennett, "You Can't Build Skyscrapers," 122; Pearson, "The Power That Erring Men Call Chance," *Detroit Free Press*, February 25, 1940, pt. 1, p. 7; Ferry, "Representative Detroit Buildings," 53; Sawyer, *Albert Kahn*, 11, 29.

23 "Henry Bacon," *Pencil Points*, 74; and Sawyer, *Albert Kahn*, 27.

24 "Henry Bacon," *Pencil Points*, 74; "On the Sixth of December . . . ," *American Architect and Building News*, 1; Bennett, "You Can't Build Skyscrapers," 122; Albert Kahn, "Industrial Architecture," 2; "Henry Bacon, 1856–1924," 193; Pearson, "The Power That Erring Men Call Chance," *Detroit Free Press*, February 25, 1940, pt. 1, p. 7; Davies, "Million-Dollar 'Office Boy,'" 15; King, *Creative-Responsive-Pragmatic*, 11; Hildebrand, *Designing for Industry*, 7, 9.

25 Swales, "Henry Bacon as a Draftsman," *Pencil Points*, 43; King, *Creative-Responsive-Pragmatic*, 11.

26 Albert Kahn, "Our Traveling Scholar," 39–41; Bennett, "You Can't Build Skyscrapers," 122.

27 Swales, "Master Draftsmen," pt. 12, p. 58.

28 "Among the Artists," *Detroit Evening News*, January 17, 1872, 16; "The Coming Art Loan," *Detroit Free Press*, May 13, 1895, 5; Swales, "Master Draftsmen," pt. 5, p. 39; Swales, "Master Draftsmen," pt. 12, p. 43.

29 George D. Mason's *Diary* for 1893, entry for July 18, MS/Mason, George D., box one: diaries, BHC DPL; and Ferry, "Albert Kahn 1869–1942," 9. Ferry likely drew this information directly from Kahn or Mason.

30 "New Belle Isle Police Station," *Detroit Free Press*, February 18, 1892, 8; and "Parks and Boulevards," *Detroit Free Press*, March 22, 1893, 9.

31 State Board (Michigan), *World's Columbian Exposition*, 30; Albert Kahn, "Thirty Minutes with American Architecture and Architects," typescript, 5.

32 "Ford Inspects a Monument to His Genius at World Fair," *Detroit Free Press*, May 16, 1934, 3.

33 Kahn, "Thirty Minutes with American Architecture and Architects," typescript, presented to the Adcraft Club of Detroit, January 22, 1937, AK-BHL, box 1, file "Transcripts of Speeches, 1936–1939," 3–5. See also Tallmadge, *Story of Architecture in America*.

34 "Fisheries," *Detroit News*, May 1, 1893, 7; S. A. Forbes, "The Aquarium of the United States Fish Commission at the World's Columbian Exposition," *Bulletin of the United States Fish Commission* 13 (Washington, DC: United States Government Printing Office, 1894), 143.

35 "The Fisheries Building," *Detroit News*, July 3, 1893, 3; advertisement for Evening News World's Fair Excursion, *Detroit News*, September 3, 1893, 11; *Handbook of the World's Columbian Exposition with Special Descriptive Articles*, 144–46; Tarleton H. Bean, *Report of the Representative of the United States Fish Commission at the World's Columbian Exposition* (Washington: Government Printing Office, 1896), 177.

36 Van Brunt, *Architecture and Society*, 270–71.

37 "The City in Brief," *Detroit News-Tribune*, January 7, 1894, 5; "Current News of the Fine Arts," *New York Times*, January 14, 1894; *Seventeenth Annual Report of the Board of Trustees of the Public Library of the City of Milwaukee* (Milwaukee: Board of Trustees, 1894), 9–11; and *Historic American Building Survey No. WIS-270* (Milwaukee, WI: Milwaukee Public Library and Museum), 9–10; unidentified newspaper clipping, [December 14, 1900], AKP-AAA, microfilm roll 1114, frame 64; Kahn, "Tribute to George D. Mason 1923 [1926]," AKA-BHL, box 1. The Milwaukee firm of Ferry & Clas won the competition.

38 Stark, *City of Destiny* 421; "Death of Hazen S. Pingree," *Literary Digest*, 778.

39 Malcolm W. Bingay, *Of Me I Sing*, 175; Holli, *Reform in Detroit*, 133, 138, 140.

40 "Architects' Doings," *Detroit News*, May 6, 1894, 22; "Will Be an Ornament," *Detroit Free Press*, July 11, 1895, 4; "Boston Architectural Exhibition," 72, 76; Holli, *Reform in Detroit*, 68–69.

Chapter 3

1 "Goes to Cornell," *Detroit Evening News* May 5, 1897, 5; Ross and Catlin, *Landmarks of Wayne County and Detroit*, pt. 2, p. 95; Leake, *History of Detroit*, 1125–28; "College of Architecture," 5.

2 1893 Diary, George D. Mason Papers, DPL-BHC MS / Mason, George D., box 1; "As He Is Known," 127; Albert Kahn, "Architect Pioneers in Development of

Industrial Building," 376; and "His Masterpiece," *Detroit News*, December 7, 1926, 14.

3 Undated correspondence, A. B. Trowbridge to A. Kahn, AKP-AAA, microfilm roll 1111, frames 1367–69; Bellinger, *Cornell Era*, vol. 30, 87; Homes, *Who's Who in New York*, 1268.

4 Undated correspondence, A. B. Trowbridge to A. Kahn, AKP-AAA, microfilm roll 1111, frames 1367–69.

5 "Architects' Doings," *Detroit News-Tribune*, August 18, 1895.

6 "Architects' Doings," *Detroit Evening News-Tribune*, August 25, 1895, 4; "Architects' Doings," *Detroit Evening News-Tribune*, September 1, 1895, 4; "Architects' Plans," *Detroit Evening News-Tribune*, October 6, 1895, 4; Ross and Catlin, *Landmarks of Wayne County and Detroit*, 843.

7 An 1896 newspaper notice suggests the formation within the week from December 29, 1895, and January 4, 1896. An 1897 biographical sketch of Trowbridge sets the date at January 1, while Hildebrand, citing Mason's notes, identifies the date as January 4. (Mason's 1895 diary makes no mention of the formation and his diary for 1896 is not included among others in the DPL-BHC.) In the absence of further, similarly credible information to break the tie or establish another date, I opted for recognizing the first week of January 1896 as the start of the firm. "Architects' Doings," *Detroit Evening News-Tribune*, January 5, 1896, 4; "Marx Comes Off," *Detroit News*, September 18, 1900, 9; Ross and Catlin, *Landmarks of Wayne County and Detroit*, pt. 2, p. 95; Hildebrand, *Designing for Industry*, 18.

8 "Realty and Building," *Detroit Free Press*, May 3, 1896, 12; "Detroit," *Brickbuilder*, 93; "Architects' Doings," *Detroit Evening News-Tribune*, January 5, 1896, 4; "Architects' Doings," *Detroit News-Tribune*, January 19, 1896, 4; "Harbor Springs Hotel," *Detroit News-Tribune*, June 21, 1896, 8; "Architects' Doings," *Detroit News*, August 23, 1896, 11; "Beats Last Year," *Detroit News-Tribune*, October 23, 1898, pt. 1, p. 12; *U.S. Census Records for Detroit, 1900*, entries for George W. and Nellie M. Nettleton; Dwight G. Baird, "Does Utility Forbid Beauty?" *Industry Illustrated* (April 1925), 48; Albert Kahn, "Architect Pioneers in Development of Industrial Building," 376. Trowbridge married Gertrude M. Sherman August 17, 1896, at Great Neck, New York. The year of Nettleton's marriage is assumed from his moving from a boarding house to a residence, as noted in the *Detroit City Directory for 1889*, 182. The ranking of the Grand and Harbor Springs Hotels is based upon Inglis, *Northern Michigan Handbook for Travelers*, 170.

9 Albert Kahn, "Architect Pioneers in Development of Industrial Building," 376.

10 "Damaged by Fire," *Detroit Free Press*, December 18, 1896, 7; "New School Buildings," *American School Board Journal*, n.p.; " 'Twill Cost $20,000," *Detroit Evening News*, April 8, 1897, 5.

11 "New Bethany Chapel," *Detroit Free Press*, August 9, 1896, 8; "Annual Church Meeting," *Detroit Free Press*, April 14, 1897, 3; "Bethany Memorial Church," *American Architect and Building News*; Albert Kahn, "Architect Pioneers in Development of Industrial Building," 376; Hildebrand, *Designing for Industry*, 25.

12 Grant Hildebrand blazed the trail for the resurgence of Kahn studies with his 1974 volume, *Designing for Industry*. It remains a go-to resource for scholars, but in his discussion of this period he mentions Children's Hospital as one of the firm's first commissions. He notes that it was a sizable building, "but it was not a moneymaker." According to a *Detroit Free Press* report, however, the Children's Free Hospital was designed by Rantoul & Andrews of Boston and the construction contract was let in June 1895 for the significant sum of $125,000. With most of the work complete before Kahn left Mason & Rice, it seems Nettleton, Kahn & Trowbridge had no involvement in the construction of the hospital. "Children's Free Hospital," *Detroit Free Press*, June 30, 1895, 18; "Is Nearly Completed," *Detroit Free Press*, December 29, 1895, 13; Hildebrand, *Designing for Industry*, 25.

13 "Register of Alumni, Engineering and Architecture, 1860–1913," University [of Michigan] *Bulletin, Department of Engineering: General Announcement, 1908–1909*, 230; Bennett, "You Can't Build Skyscrapers," 124. For more on Julius, see Michael Smith, *Concrete Century*.

14 Ross and Catlin, *Landmarks of Wayne County and Detroit*, 95; "Correspondence / Alexander Buel Trowbridge to the Editor," *Architectural Review* 6 (May 1899), 67.

15 Correspondence, George W. Nettleton to Stephen Keyes Stanton, January 19, 1898, MS / Stanton Family, 1898, Jan. 19, DPL-BHC. Kahn partnership drawings are in the Detroit Institute of Arts Department of Prints, Drawings and Photographs collection, where I examined them in January 2017.

16 "Synopsis of Building News," *Inland Architect and News Record* 32 (October 1898): 30; "Building in 1898," *Detroit Free Press*, January 1, 1899, pt. 1, p. 7; Leck, "Helen Newberry Nurses Home," 264; Kahn, "Architect Pioneers in Development of Industrial Building," 376; Ferry, "Albert Kahn 1869–1942," 10. Nettleton & Kahn–designed homes appear in the October and November 1898 numbers of *Inland Architect and News Record* 32. A record of exhibitions of the Nurses' Home design includes *Catalogue of the Twelfth Annual Exhibition by the Chicago Architectural Club at the Art Institute* (March 30 to April 16, 1898), 41; *Catalogue: Annual Exhibition of the Saint Louis Architectural Club* (April 20 to May 2, 1899), 18; *Catalogue of the First Annual Exhibition of the Detroit Architectural Club* (April 28 to May 12, 1900), n.p. In addition, the design was featured in the Fourteenth Annual Exhibition of the Architectural League of New York. "League and T Square Club Exhibitions," *Brickbuilder*, 23–24.

17 "Beats Last Year," *Detroit News-Tribune*, October 23, 1898, pt. 1, p. 12; "Building in Detroit in 1898," *Detroit Free Press*, January 1, 1899, 7; "His New Library," *Detroit News*, January 24, 1900.

18 "News of the Architects," *Detroit Free Press*, May 14, 1899, pt. 1, p.11; "Building in 1899," *Detroit Free Press*, December 32, 1899, pt. 1, p. 9; "News of the Architects," *Detroit Free Press*, December 24, 1899.

19 Albert Kahn, "Architect Pioneers in Development of Industrial Building," 376.

Chapter 4

1 Holli, *Reform in Detroit*, 203.

2 William Livingston, *Livingston's History of the Republican Party*, vol. 2, 216–17; Holli, *Reform in Detroit*, 21, 29–30, 53–54; Cyril and Marjorie Player, "The Life Story of Hazen S. Pingree, Part Two," *Detroit News*, January 28, 1932, 15; "Virtual Jewish World, Michigan, United States," Jewish Virtual Library, accessed January 15, 2024, www.jewishvirtuallibrary.org/michigan-jewish-history#google_vignette.

3 "He Wears No Collar," *Detroit Free Press*, October 15, 1898, 3; *Detroit Journal*, June 27, 1899, DEH-BHL, box 1, scrapbook 1, 54; unidentified clipping, vertical file Heineman, David E., DPL-BHC; Livingston, *Livingston's History of the Republican Party*, 217; Louis L. Richards, "Biographical Sketches," MS / Catlin, G.B., George B. Catlin Papers, vol. ZR3, F-K, DPL-BHC, 69; Holli, *Reform in Detroit*, 219.

4 Livingston, *Livingston's History of the Republican Party*, 217; "Detroit's Fine Aquarium," *Detroit Free Press*, December 4, 1904, illustrated supplement, 3; De Bont, *Stations in the Field*, 51, 59–60.

5 "More Money for Belle Isle Park," *Detroit Journal*, August 21, 1899, DEH-BHL, box 1, scrapbook 1, 56; *Journal of the House of Representatives of the State of Michigan, 1899*, vol. 1 (Lansing, MI: Rupert Smith, 1899), 2106.

6 *Journal of the House of Representatives of the State of Michigan, 1899*, vol. 1, 2106; *Detroit News*, October 29, 1899, DEH-BHL, box 1, scrapbook 1, 58; "An Aquarium on Belle Isle," *Detroit Free Press*, November 9, 1899, 4; "Town Talk," *Detroit News*, November 10, 1899, 5.

7 Lloyd, "Crystal Palace Aquarium," 473; "Please the People," *Detroit Free Press*, November 9, 1899, 5.

8 "Plans for Aquarium," *Detroit News*, January 26, 1900, 1; "Mum's the Word," *Detroit News*, October 11, 1900, pt. 1, p. 10.

9 "Town Talk," *Detroit News*, January 2, 1899, 4; Diary, 1899, MS / George D. Mason Papers, DPL-BHC, box 2, file 2:1; "Zach Rice Better," *Detroit News*, November 18, 1902, 5; "Last Rites Monday for Zachariah Rice," *Detroit News*, October 5, 1929, 13.

10 Diary, 1899, MS / George D. Mason Papers, DPL-BHC, box 2, file 2:1; *Record Minutes of the Meetings of the Commissioners of Parks and Boulevards*, MS / Detroit Parks and Boulevards Commission, M6 1899–1900, DPL-BHC, vol. 9, 115 (November 27, 1899); Hale, "New York Aquarium," 845; Blackford, "Dr. Tarleton Hoffman Bean," 190–93.

11 Lloyd, "Proposed Channel Islands' Zoological Station," 144; William P. Seal, "Observations on the Aquaria of the U.S. Fish Commission at Central Station, Washington, D.C.," *Bulletin of the United States Fish Commission* 10 (Washington, DC: United States Government Printing Office, 1892), 1–2; Allen, *Naturalist in Britain*, 179–83; Stickney, *Aquaculture of the United States*, 92–93. Piecemeal information on the commission's participation in expositions can be found in its annual reports.

12 Notebook, Zoological Aquarium, 1899–1900, n.p., MS / George D. Mason Papers, DPL-BHC, box 4, file 4:12; and Diary, 1899, MS / George D. Mason Papers, DPL-BHC, box 2, file 2:1.

13 Diary, 1899, MS / George D. Mason Papers, BHC, box 2, file 2:1; *Chapin Book of Genealogical Data*, 1598.

14 Notebook, Zoological Aquarium, 1899–1900, n.p., MS / George D. Mason Papers, DPL-BHC, box 4, file 4:12.

15 "New Aquarium Building," *Detroit Free Press*, December 23, 1899, 10; "City News," *Detroit News*, February 22, 1900, 5.

16 "Building," *Detroit News*, February 11, 1900, 8.

17 Correspondence, Julius Kahn to Albert Kahn, January 14, 1900, AKF-BHL, box 1; unidentified newspaper clipping [December 14, 1900], AKP-AAA, microfilm roll 1114, frame 64. A plate of Nettleton's residence appeared in *Inland Architect and News Record* 28 (1896).

18 Death certificate for George W. Nettleton; "Toiled Too Hard," *Detroit News*, December 14, 1900, 3.

19 Albert Kahn, "Architect Pioneers in Development of Industrial Building," 377. Roland Gies worked for the firm during this time; there were likely others. "New Architect in Field," *Detroit News*, May 24, 1903, pt. 1, p. 27.

20 "Science Hall for the M.M. Academy," *Detroit Free Press*, July 15, 1900, 7; "News of the Architects," *Detroit Free Press*, September 16, 1900, pt. 2, p. 8; "News of the Architects," *Detroit Free Press*, October 21, 1900, pt. 2, p. 10; "Sigma Phi House Opening," *Detroit Free Press*, October 21, 1900, 4; Seeley, *History of Oakland County, Michigan*, vol. 1, 285.

21 Kahn reminisced that he designed an addition to Joseph Boyer's house prior to providing the same service for Henry B. Joy, which would put the work somewhere between January 1900 and July 1901, but documentation remains elusive. "News of the Architects," *Detroit Free Press*, July 21, 1901, pt. 1, p. 1; Albert Kahn, "Architect Pioneers in Development of Industrial Building," 377. For more on the misattribution of the Boyer Machine Company Shop, see Meister, "Albert Kahn's Partners in Industrial Architecture," 80, 84.

22 Correspondence, George W. Nettleton to Albert Kahn, June 8, 1900, AKP-AAA, microfilm roll 1111, frames 1432–34; Albert Kahn, "Architect Pioneers in Development of Industrial Building," 377.

23 Correspondence, Edwin P. Baron to Nettleton & Kahn, July 25, 1900, AKP-AAA, microfilm roll 1111, frames 1436–39; unidentified newspaper clipping [December 14, 1900], AKP-AAA, microfilm roll 1114, frame 64.

24 *Record Minutes*, vol. 9, 197 (February 21, 1900). "Beacon to the Commerce of the Great West," *Detroit Free Press*, February 23, 1900, 2; "Will Attract Visitors," *Detroit Free Press*, February 28, 1900; "Who Caused the Delay?" *Detroit Free Press*, July 8, 1900, 2; "Bicentennial Memorial Project Abandoned," *Detroit Free Press*, July 14, 1900, 2; Mathewson, "Detroit Bicentennial Memorial," 709–10.

25 *Record Minutes*, vol. 10, 22 (July 30, 1900); "Aquarium Will Now Be Built," *Detroit Free Press*, July 31, 1900, 4.

26 *Detroit News*, August 12, 1900. The architects expressing initial interest in the contest were: W. D. Butterfield, T. B. Coughlin, A. B. Crans, Joy & Bancroft, Malcomson & Higginbotham, George D. Mason, Mueller & Mildner, John Natus & Co., Nettleton & Kahn, F. Carl Pollmar, Edward A. Schilling, John G. Scott & Co., Mortimer L. Smith & Son, Stratton & Baldwin, Francis S. Swales, R. E. Raseman, Zachariah Rice, and George H. Ropes.

27 "Marx Comes Off," *Detroit News*, September 18, 1900, 9; "Monumental News," *Stone*, 270.

28 "That Aquarium," *To-Day* (Detroit), October 10, 1900, 4; *Detroit Free Press*, October 14, 1900.

29 "Realty and Building," *Detroit Free Press*, June 12, 1898, pt. 2, p. 7; "That Aquarium," *To-Day* (Detroit), October 10, 1900, 4; *Record Minutes*, vol. 10, 55 (September 19), 62 (October 1), and 65 (October 15, 1900).

30 Diary, 1900, MS / George D. Mason Papers, DPL-BHC, box 2, file 2:2 (Oct. 1, Oct. 2, 1900); *Record Minutes*, MS / Detroit Parks and Boulevards Commission, M6 1899–1900, DPL-BHC, vol. 10, 65 (October 15, 1900).

31 *Record Minutes*, vol. 10, 71 (October 15, 1900); *Detroit News*, October 15, 1900; *Twelfth Annual Report of the Commissioner of Parks and Boulevards, City of Detroit, Michigan* (Detroit: Raynor & Taylor, 1901), 19–23; "Municipal Notes," *Detroit News*, November 13, 1900, 5. Those submitting designs in the Detroit competition were: A. B. Crans, John Natus & Co., Nettleton & Kahn (submitting two designs), F. Carl Pollmar, Edward A. Schilling, Mortimer L. Smith & Son, George H. Ropes. *Record Minutes*, vol. 10, 74 (October 22, 1900). The three runners-up, collectively considered the "next best" and receiving $200 each, were Pollmar, Schilling, and Ropes. "Award Is Made," *Detroit News*, October 22, 1900, 1.

Chapter 5

1 Entrants understood that the judges would include two architects from a group consisting of Robert D. Andrews (of Boston), Cass Gilbert (New York), Frank Miles Day (Philadelphia), Edward B. Green (Buffalo), John G. Howard (New York), William B. Mundie (Chicago), and Charles F. Schweinfurth (Cleveland). The aquarial expert would either be Tarleton Bean (New York) or William de C. Ravenel (Washington, DC) and the conservatory expert would be either John F. Cowell (Buffalo), Fred Kantz (Chicago), or Levi R. Taft (Michigan Agricultural College, now Michigan State University). "Aquarium Designs," *Detroit News*, August 9, 1890, 5.

2 *Record Minutes of the Meetings of the Commissioners of Parks and Boulevards*, MS / Detroit Parks and Boulevards Commission, M6 1899–1900, DPL-BHC, vol. 10, 75 (October 22, 1900); Britton, "John Francis Cowell," 191–93.

3 Archibald Alison, *Essays on the Nature and Principles of Taste*; Sullivan, "Tall Office Building Artistically Considered," 408; Albert Kahn, "Architectural Trend,"

AKA-BHL, box 1, file "Transcripts of Speeches, 1930–1935," 7; Hersey, *High Victorian Gothic*, 10–12, 14–16.

4 Hersey, "J. C. Loudon and Architectural Associationalism," 89.

5 Loudon, *Remarks on the Construction of Hothouses.*

6 The dimensions of the Belle Isle Aquarium & Horticultural Building are drawn from surviving blueprints from the 1901 Mason & Kahn drawings, which appear faithful to the competition entry where the botanical portion is visible.

7 "European Ideas," *Detroit News*, November 28, 1899, 2.

8 Edward Newman, "Notices of New Books," 3747–52.

9 "Marine Aquaria," *Journal of the Society of Arts*, 518; "Fish Shows as Pecuniary Speculations," *The Spectator*, 45.

10 H. Dorner, "The Hamburg Aquarium," 195; "Award Is Made," *Detroit News*, October 22, 1900, 1.

11 "Marine Aquaria," *Journal of the Society of Arts*, 518.

12 Draper, "Howard, John Galen," vol. 2, 431; Blodgett, "Politics of Public Architecture," 64–68.

13 *Detroit City Directory for 1882*, 980; *Detroit City Directory for 1883* (Detroit: J. W. Weeks, 1883), 1043; *Record Minutes*, vol. 10, 74 (October 22, 1900); Albert Kahn, "Tribute to George D. Mason 1923 [1926]," AKA-BHL, n.p.

14 "Award Is Made," *Detroit News*, October 22, 1900, 1; "Smoothed Over," *Detroit News*, November 5, 1900, 5.

15 Correspondence, Gustav "Gus" Kahn to Albert Kahn, October. 27, 1900, AKP-AAA, microfilm roll 1111, frame 166. Gus Kahn & Co., a plumbing and gas fitting business, was chartered in 1899, *Metal Worker* 52 (November 11, 1899), 47.

16 "Little Grafts," *To-Day* (Detroit), October 26, 1900, 1; "A Family Matter," *Detroit News*, November 16, 1900, 12; "Baisley Was Quite Nettled," *To-Day* (Detroit), November 16, 1900, 1; "Balsley Was Nettled by the Questioning," *Detroit Free Press*, November 17, 1900, 5.

17 *Detroit Journal*, October 15, 1900, DEH-BHL, box 1, scrapbook 1, 150; Holli, *Reform in Detroit*, 214–15.

18 "Only One Point," *Detroit News*, July 10, 1899, 5; Bryce, "Discussion of 'The Open Shop,'" 1; Holli, *Reform in Detroit*, 7; Richard Jules Oestreicher, *Solidarity and Fragmentation*, 233, 235. The Debate Handbook Series collection, *Selected Articles on the Open Versus Closed Shop*, offers insight into the often biased arguments, pro and con, on the subject in the early twentieth century.

19 Oestreicher, *Solidarity and Fragmentation*, 236, 244–45; Michigan State Administrative Board, *Michigan: A Guide to the Wolverine State*, 241 (it should be noted this source presents an arguably faulty characterization of open shops); Kennedy, *The Automobile Industry*, 250–51; "Are Leaving Chicago," *Detroit Free Press*, November 6, 1905, 7.

20 "Loses Health, Gains an Idea," *Detroit News*, March 29, 1930, 2. For other factors contributing to automobile manufacturers, particularly, locating in the Detroit area, see Rubenstein, *Changing US Auto Industry*, chapters 1 and 2.

21 *Record Minutes*, vol. 10, 96–98 (November 26, 1900); *Record Minutes*, vol. 10, 101 (December 3, 1900); *Record Minutes*, vol. 10, 118 (January 7, 1901); "Plans Revised," *Detroit Free Press*, January 8, 1901, 3; "$1,000,000 in New Buildings in Detroit," *Detroit News-Tribune*, January 13, 1901, 18. The division between the aquarium and conservatory became more pronounced when exhibit hall access between the two was closed to the public. An early (ca. 1910) photograph shows another set of doors added near the foot of the stairs. Research suggests the division was made permanent between 1918, when a newspaper account still mentions the flight of stairs between the two, and 1922, when another refers to the aquarium balcony that replaced it. The balcony was obliterated with the installation of a large display tank in 1981. Over the years, many came to think of the structure as two separate buildings built at different times. "Flower Show Blaze of Color," *Detroit News*, March 31, 1918, pt. 2, p. 9; "Fairest Posies at Isle Shows," *Detroit News*, November 11, 1922, 5.

22 Unidentified newspaper clipping [December 14, 1900], AKP-AAA, microfilm roll 1114, frame 64.

23 Death certificate for George W. Nettleton; "Funeral of Architect George W. Nettleton," *Detroit Free Press*, December 19, 1900. The other pallbearers were Frank C. Baldwin, Alpheus W. Chittenden, Henry J. Meier, Richard Mildner, and Charles Kotting. My July 2018 inquiry at Woodmere Cemetery revealed that George Nettleton was interred in section B, lot 169, on December 18, 1900. There is no grave marker, perhaps reflecting the architect's impoverished circumstances. I would like to express my appreciation to the counselors and grounds crew of Woodmere Cemetery, Detroit, Michigan for their efforts on behalf of George Nettleton's memory.

24 Unidentified newspaper clipping, [December 14, 1900], AKP-AAA, microfilm roll 1114, frame 64.

25 Albert Kahn, "Architect Pioneers in Development of Industrial Building," 377.

Chapter 6

1 Albert Kahn, "Architect Pioneers in Development of Industrial Building," 377.

2 Nellie M. Nettleton to Albert Kahn, June 17, 1902, AKP-AAA, microfilm roll 1111, frame 478; "New Architect in Field," *Detroit News*, May 24, 1903, pt. 1, p. 27. In Nellie's letter, written from Colorado Springs, she thanks Kahn for his letter and check. The check may have represented residual income from the Nettleton & Kahn partnership or a charitable offering. Kahn made residual payments to Trowbridge following the latter's departure in 1897. Alexander Buel Trowbridge to Albert Kahn, October 17, 1898, AKA-BHL, box 1, file "Correspondence-Albert Kahn-Letters to Kahn 1898–1900."

3 While many sources credit Nettleton & Kahn, Mason & Kahn, or Kahn for the Belle Isle structure, research for this volume only found one instance where the architect personally took credit for, or even acknowledged, the design after Mason took over the construction. *The Book of Detroiters* is a collection of brief

sketches promoting the merits of Detroit civic leaders relying on information supplied by the subjects. In the 1908 edition Kahn (or someone responding on his behalf) provided a list of significant structures by the architect as: "Detroit Aquarium and Horticultural Bldg., Burroughs Adding Machine Plant, Temple Beth El, Packard Motor Car plant, Palms Apartment Bldg., etc." Albert Marquis, *Book of Detroiters*, 5–6, 259. By the next edition of this publication in 1914, containing updates and revisions again supplied by the subjects, Kahn's list reads, "Burroughs Adding Machine Plant, Temple Beth El, Packard Motor Car plant, Hudson, Chalmers, Lozier and Ford Motor plants, Detroit Free Press Bldg., etc." Albert Marquis, *Book of Detroiters*, 7, 273.

4 "Plans Revised"; and "Wanted-Help-Male," *Detroit Free Press*, January 31, 1901, 6.

5 Alexander B. Trowbridge to Albert Kahn, January 9, 1901, AKP-AAA, microfilm roll 1111, frame 363. Trowbridge left his position at Cornell in 1902 and returned to Europe for advanced studies. In 1904 he established a private practice in New York City, partnering with Frederick J. Ackerman. In 1918 Trowbridge was employed as consulting architect for York & Sawyer's Federal Reserve Bank of New York, which led to longer engagement with the Federal Reserve Board in Washington, DC. Trowbridge & Ackerman dissolved in 1921 as Trowbridge concentrated on consulting. He served as consulting architect for two prominent library structures in the nation's capital: Paul Cret's 1932 Folger Shakespeare Library (which he appears to have secured through family connections) and Pierson & Wilson's 1939 Annex to the Library of Congress (now known as the Adams Building). Trowbridge died in retirement in 1950. Clearly established in Washington, his grandson, Alexander Buel Trowbridge III, would later serve as President Lyndon Baines Johnson's Secretary of Commerce. Trowbridge, *Trowbridge Genealogy*, 664; *Eighth Annual Report of the Federal Reserve Board: Covering Operations for the Year 1921* (Washington DC: United States Government Printing Office, 1922), 363–64; Stephen H. Grant, *Collecting Shakespeare: The Story of Henry and Emily Folger* (Baltimore: Johns Hopkins University Press, 2014), 145; and "Architect of the Capitol: John Adams Building," Architect of the Capitol, accessed October 10, 2018, www.aoc.gov/capitol-buildings/john-adams-building.

6 "Engaged Dr. Armstrong," *Detroit Free Press*, January 22, 1901, 5; *Record Minutes of the Meetings of the Commissioners of Parks and Boulevards*, MS / Detroit Parks and Boulevards Commission, M6 1899–1900, DPL-BHC, vol. 10, 140, (February 4, 1901); "Addition to Clark Park," *Detroit Free Press*, February 5, 1901, 5; and "Bolger's Plans," *Detroit News*, May 16, 1901, 5.

7 For a seminal study of technology's effect on architecture between the nineteenth and twentieth centuries, see Banham, *Architecture of the Well-Tempered Environment*.

8 "News of the Architects," *Detroit Free Press*, February 10, 1901, 10; "Personal," *Detroit Free Press*, March 23, 1902, 6.

9 "Helps Detroit," *Detroit Free Press*, March 9, 1901, 4; "An Aquarium Expert," *Detroit Evening News*, March 8, 1901, 12.

10 *Detroit News-Tribune*, March 31, 1901; *Detroit News-Tribune*, April 17, 1901.
11 *Detroit Evening News*, April 16, 1901; Franklin, Freund, and Sloman, *History of Congregation Beth El*, 21.
12 "New Temple Beth El Will Be a Handsome Edifice and Richly Fitted Up," *Detroit Free Press*, November 30, 1901, pt. 1, p. 11; "New Temple Beth El Which Will Be Built at Woodward Avenue and Erskine Street," *Detroit News*, November 30, 1901, 11; Franklin, Freund, and Sloman, *History of Congregation Beth El*, 26. For an example crediting Kahn for the break with architectural tradition, see Goldman, "Albert Kahn," 4.
13 *Record Minutes*, vol. 11, 59 (October 28, 1901).
14 Arthur Alexander Stoughton to Albert Kahn, January 19, 1902, AKP-AAA, microfilm roll 1111, frame 482; James B. Nettleton to Albert Kahn, February 27, 1902, AKP-AAA, microfilm roll 1111, frame 493.
15 Diary, 1902, MS / George D. Mason Papers, BHC-DPL, box 2, file 2:3; *Detroit News-Tribune*, February 23, 1902, pt. 2, p. 2; "News of the Architects," *Detroit Free Press*, March 23, 1902, pt. 1, p. 6.
16 "New Engineering Building for the University of Michigan," *The Technic*, 3; "Will Do Extra Work," *Detroit Free Press*, March 15, 1902, 3; "News of the Architects," *Detroit Free Press*, April 27, 1902, pt. 1, p. 11; "News of the Architects," *Detroit Free Press*, May 18, 1902, pt. 2, p. 2; Professor Dennison, and "In Six Months," *Detroit News*, December 27, 1903, pt. 1, p. 5.
17 "News of the Architects," *Detroit Free Press*, March 23, 1902, pt. 2, p. 6; "Partnership Dissolution," *Detroit News*, March 23, 1902, pt. 1, p. 15; "New Architect in Field," pt. 1, p. 27.

Chapter 7

1 "Bolger's Plans," *Detroit News*, May 16, 1901, 5; *Detroit Tribune*, June 1, 1901.
2 "Town Talk," *Detroit News*, May 6, 1902, 5; "Five Thousand Men Quit Work," *Detroit News*, May 7, 1902, 1; "Work on the New Horticultural Building," *Detroit News*, August 26, 1902, 5; "A Scarcity of Help Delays Building," *Detroit News*, August 28, 1902, 5; "Belle Isle's New Buildings," *Detroit Free Press*, September 14, 1902, pt. 4, p. 8.; Diary, 1902, MS/George D. Mason Papers, BHC-DPL, box 2, ff 2:3.

There has been some controversy as to whether these frames were actual bronze or painted cypress wood. It seems, however, that cypress may have only been used as gasket frames intended to swell with moisture, providing an effective seal in an era before epoxy sealants. Metal frames would be needed to brace against the swelling, and a letter by Mason to the commission establishes they were bronze. *Record Minutes of the Meetings of the Commissioners of Parks and Boulevards*, MS / Detroit Parks and Boulevards Commission, M6 1899–1900, DPL-BHC, vol. 12, 34 (September 2, 1902).
3 "A Due Sense of Fitness," *Detroit News*, August 21, 1901, 2; "Worthy Measure," *Shooting and Fishing*, 483; Bean, "Detroit Aquarium," 165; "Belle Isle's New Buildings," *Detroit Free Press*, September 14, 1902, pt. 3, p. 8. While the *Free Press*

account does not identify Bean by name, based on the date and other details in the article he was surely the expert in question.

4 "To Please the People," *Detroit Free Press*, February 2, 1903, 5; "Made Experts Laugh," *Detroit Free Press*, May 11, 1903, 5; "To Hold Salt Water," *Detroit News*, May 11, 1903, 3; "Got Pointers in the East," *Detroit Free Press*, September 5, 1903, 3; and *Fifteenth Annual Report of the Commissioner of Parks and Boulevards, Detroit, Michigan*, 34.

5 "Homes for the Fish," *Detroit Tribune*, September 21, 1903; *Fourteenth Annual Report of the Commissioner of Parks and Boulevards, Detroit, Michigan* (Detroit: Raynor & Taylor, 1903), 15; "Sayings and Doings," *Detroit Free Press*, June 30, 1905, 5; *Fifteenth Annual Report of the Commissioner of Parks and Boulevards*, 14–15, 34.

6 "On Cold Winter Days, Belle Isle Is Being Put in Shape for the Summer Season," *Detroit News*, December 23, 1902, 3; "Torrid Session and Hot Shot for Fowle," *Detroit News*, March 22, 1904, 3; Sherman, "Third Largest Aquarium in the World," 405.

7 *Fifteenth Annual Report of the Commissioner of Parks and Boulevards*, 34.

8 J. Jungwirth & Company, to Mason & Kahn, June 8, 1901, AKP-AAA, box 3, file 54. Born in Austria in 1858 (or perhaps 1860) and educated in Viennese art schools, Jungwirth immigrated in 1882 and settled in Detroit in 1884 after a stint making cabinets in Grand Rapids. Jungwirth employed a carving machine for roughing out duplicate work, to be finished by hand, and modeled ornament to be executed in other material, such as terra-cotta and bronze. "Woodwork in Detroit," *Detroit News*, February 17, 1918, pt. 4, p. 7; Burton and Burton, *History of Wayne County and the City of Detroit, Michigan*, vol. 5, 183–84; "J. Jungwirth Services Set," *Detroit News*, September 23, 1940, 9.

9 "Belle Isle's New Beauty Spot—The Horticultural Building," *Detroit Free Press*, November 13, 1904, pt. 2, p. 1; and *Fifteenth Annual Report of the Commissioner of Parks and Boulevards*, 34.

10 "Detroit's Fine Aquarium," *Detroit Free Press*, December 4, 1904, supplement 4, 3.

11 *Fifteenth Annual Report of the Commissioner of Parks and Boulevards*, 35; Kohlmaier and on Sartory, *Houses of Glass*, 55; and Hix, *Glasshouse*, 31–33.

12 Lloyd, "Aquaria," 621.

13 *Fifteenth Annual Report of the Commissioner of Parks and Boulevards*, 35; "Detroit's Finc Aquarium," *Detroit Free Press*, December 4, 1904, supplement 4, 3; *Sixteenth Annual Report of the Commissioner of Parks and Boulevards, Detroit, Michigan*, 19; Busch, "Model Aquarium of Detroit," 31.

14 "Will Beat All Former Years," *Detroit Free Press*, April 24, 1905, 5; "The Parks and Boulevards of Detroit," 211; Conway, "Detroit Aquarium," 67.

15 "Improvement of the Aquarium," *Zoological Society Bulletin*, 73–76; "Progress of the Improvements at the Aquarium," *Zoological Society Bulletin*, 141; "More Public Aquariums for America," *Zoological Society Bulletin*, 149; "Further Improvements at the Aquarium," *Zoological Society Bulletin*, 205–6; "Final Stages in the Remodeling of the Aquarium," *Zoological Society Bulletin*, 276.

16 Townsend, *Public Aquarium*, 328–31; Chappell, *Architecture and Planning*, 231; Furnweger, *Shedd Aquarium*, 12, 24.
17 "Growing Ferns and Other Plants in Glass Cases," *Gardener's Magazine*, 162; *First Report of the Commissioners*, 41–45; "Influence of Light on Health," *London Lancet*, 452; Allen, *Naturalist in Britain*, 133–36.
18 "Influence of Light on Health," *London Lancet*, 452.
19 "Visiting Day at St. Thomas Hospital," *Graphic*, 1; Verderber, *Innovations in Hospital Architecture*, 21–23.
20 "Greenhouse in an Engine Room," *Gardening Illustrated*, 353.
21 Kohlmaier, *Houses of Glass*, 305–7.
22 Borth, *Masters of Mass Production*, 111.

Chapter 8

1 "The Romantic Rise of Two Brothers Whose Achievements Have Worked a Revolution in the Constructive World," *Detroit News-Tribune*, September 20, 1908, pt. 1, p. 20.
2 Borth, *Masters of Mass Production*, 101.
3 "News of the Architects," *Detroit Free Press*, May 26, 1901, pt. 2, p. 7; "News of the Architects," *Detroit Free Press*, July 7, 1901, pt. 2, p. 3; "News of the Architects," *Detroit Free Press*, July 21, 1901, pt. 1, p. 10; "News of the Architects," *Detroit Free Press*, August 18, 1901, pt. 3, p. 8; Albert Kahn, "Architect Pioneers in Development of Industrial Building," 377; Meister, "Albert Kahn's Partners," 80.
4 Meister, "Albert Kahn's Partners," 92–93.
5 "Illness Is Fatal to Joseph Boyer," *Detroit Free Press*, October 25, 1930, 2; Simmons, " 'Continuous Clatter,' " 9; Meister, "Albert Kahn's Partners," 80.
6 Simmons, " 'Continuous Clatter,' " 13; Meister, "Albert Kahn's Partners," 80
7 Robert Campbell, "Boyer 'Made Good'—Because He Worked," *Detroit Times*, pt. 5, p. 4.
8 Leland and Millbrook, *Master of Precision*, 51–52, 57, 267–68, n1. Like Kahn's reminiscences, the manuscript relied upon by Leland and Millbrook as a source of insight was at times faulty on dates and other details. Henry Leland would go on to found the Cadillac and Lincoln Motor Car Companies.
9 "Real Estate Outlook," *Detroit Free Press*, January 28, 1900, pt. 1, p. 10; "Real Estate," *Detroit Free Press*, July 23, 1900, pt. 2, p. 8; Robert Campbell, "Boyer 'Made Good'—Because He Worked," *Detroit Times*, November 12, 1922, pt. 5, p. 4.
10 Russell Barnes, "Urges Land Tax Increase to Reduce Other Levies," *Detroit News*, September 5, 1932, 6; Meister, "Albert Kahn's Partners," 80. Boyer purchased a house on Dawson Street prior to February 1901 and expected to move his family into it by the first of May, suggesting alterations were involved during the two-and-a-half-month interval. Although Kahn is not mentioned by this source, this is surely the work he recalled in "Architect Pioneers," and would have come to him while Nettleton & Kahn was still in operation. "Brevities," *Detroit News*, February 16, 1901, 4.

11 Robert Campbell, "Boyer 'Made Good'—Because He Worked," *Detroit Times*, November 12, 1922, pt. 5, p. 4; "A Revival," *Detroit News-Tribune*, November 4, 1900, 19.

12 John Hubert Gruesel, "Joseph Boyer, Inventor," *Detroit Free Press*, January 14, 1906, pt. 4, p. 3; "Illness Is Fatal to Joseph Boyer," *Detroit Free Press*, October 25, 1930, 2; Meister, "Albert Kahn's Partners," 81.

13 "Real Estate Field," *Detroit Free Press*, September 30, 1900, pt. 3 p. 10; "New Shops of the Boyer Machine Company," 248–50; Meister, "Albert Kahn's Partners," 81.

14 "An Example to Emulate," *Detroit Free Press*, October 27, 1930, 6; "County Has Been Hogged," *Detroit Free Press*, October 5, 1900, 2 (this headline was mismatched to the article, the proper headline, "Employer Who Looks After His Men," appeared on p. 5 of the newspaper); "Real Estate Field," *Detroit Free Press*, September 30, 1900, pt. 3 p. 10; Robert Campbell, "Boyer 'Made Good'—Because He Worked," *Detroit Times*, November 12, 1922, pt. 3, p. 4; H. Der Garabedyan, M.D., "Memory of Boyer Accorded Tribute" *Detroit Free Press*, October 28, 1930, 6; "Detroit Machinists Made Good Again," *Detroit Free Press*, May 24, 1901, 1.

15 "Detroit Plant Is a Model," *Detroit Free Press*, October 15, 1902, 9.

16 Drawings: Job No. 181, Factory for the Consolidated Pneumatic Tool Co., Scotland, Albert Kahn, Architect, AKA-BHL. I would like to thank Michael G. Smith for bringing these drawings to my attention; "The Fraserburgh Steel Works," *Fraserburgh Herald and Northern Counties Advertiser*, March 17, 1903, 8. This source credits Brebner & Jenkins with the design, but that concern seems to have been a local contractor and a desire to foster local civic pride may have motivated the attribution. Mullgardt is identified as the architect of the Fraserburgh Consolidated Pneumatic Tool Company shop, along with Boyer's St. Louis and Detroit shops, in the entry under his name in *Press Reference Library*, 99. I would like to thank Mr. Robert Henderson of the Fraserburgh Heritage Society for his efforts and assistance regarding this intriguing building.

17 "Workingmen's Condition," *Detroit Free Press*, June 3, 1903, 12.

18 "Human Element in the Architect's Organization," 43.

19 "News of the Architects," *Detroit Free Press*, May 26, 1901, pt. 2, p. 7; "News of the Architects," *Detroit Free Press*, July 7, 1901, pt. 2, p. 3; "News of the Architects," *Detroit Free Press*, August 18, 1901, pt. 3, p. 8.

20 "Apartment Building for Dr. J. B. Book," drawing, AKA-BHL.

21 "News of the Architects," *Detroit Free Press*, May 26, 1902, pt. 2, p. 7: "The 'Woodward' Apartments," classified advertisement, *Detroit News*, January 25, 1902, 10.

22 "News of the Architects," *Detroit Free Press*, March 16, 1902, pt. 1, p. 7; Michael Smith, *Concrete Century*, 13.

23 *Calendar of the University of Michigan, 1896–97*, 273; Julius Kahn, "Coal Hoists," 392; Julius Kahn to Albert Kahn, January 14, 1900, AKF-BHL, box 1; *General Catalogue of Faculty and Students, 1837–1901*, 152; *University* [of Michigan] *Bulletin, Department of Engineering*, 230; Irwin, "Julius Kahn," 1, 742.

24 "News of the Architects," *Detroit Free Press*, March 16, 1902, pt. 1, p. 7; "News of the Architects," *Detroit Free Press*, March 30, 1902, pt. 2, p. 6.

25 "Among the Architects," *Detroit Free Press*, September 20, 1903, pt. 1, p. 11.

26 Edgar Kahn, "Albert Kahn," 26.

27 Original drawings in AKP-BHL; "News of the Architects," *Detroit Free Press*, April 21, 1901, pt. 2 p. 2; "News of the Architects," *Detroit Free Press*, August 18, 1901, pt. 3 p. 8; "Sayings and Doings," *Detroit Free Press*, August 29, 1901, 5; "Those Floors in 'The Palms,'" *Detroit News-Tribune*, April 20, 1902, 23. Sources identify this project as apartments for D. James B. Book previous to February 1902, when "The Palms" was adopted as the building's name. "Local Brevities," *Detroit Free Press*, February 27, 1902, 10.

28 Borth, "Masters of Mass Production," 106; Beasley and Stark, *Made in Detroit*, 78.

29 The story of the Palms load test was resurrected in Meister, "Albert Kahn's Partners," 82.

30 Blueprint drawing, "Belle Isle Aquarium & Horticultural Building," AKA-BHL; "Office of the Commissioner of Parks and Boulevards," classified advertisement, *To-Day* (Detroit), September 10, 1901, 8; "Architects Say Little," *Detroit News-Tribune*, June 29, 1902, pt. 1, p. 23. The Gearing Brothers Company won the contract for the apartment building mason work while the contract for the fireproofing and concrete work of the Belle Isle structure went to the Schillinger Brothers Company. "News of the Architects," *Detroit Free Press*, August 18, 1901, pt. 3, p. 8; *Thirteenth Annual Report of the Commissioner of Parks and Boulevards, City of Detroit, Michigan* (Detroit: Raynor & Taylor, 1902), 19.

31 "Metzger's Automobile Store," *Detroit News-Tribune*, April 27, 1902, pt. 1, p. 23. The first mention of this project in the press appears to have been a month earlier as a two-story building with Mason & Kahn identified as the architect. "News of the Architects," *Detroit Free Press*, March 23, 1902, pt. 2, p. 6.

32 "Complete in All Appointments," *Detroit Free Press*, August 17, 1903, pt. 1, p. 7; Metzger, "Good Advice from a Successful Man," 36–37.

33 "Retail Trade and Garages," *Automobile*, 619.

34 "Complete in All Appointments," *Detroit Free Press*, August 17, 1903, pt. 1, p. 7.

35 "Metzger's Automobile Store," *Detroit News-Tribune*, April 27, 1902, 23; "Complete in All Appointments," *Detroit Free Press*, August 17, 1903, pt. 1, p. 7; "New Store for Wm. E. Metzger at Jefferson Ave. and Brush St." *Detroit News-Tribune*, February 15, 1903, 23; "Retail Trade and Garages," *Automobile*, 619. See also "Metzger's New Quarters," *Motor World*, 4 (September 4, 1902), 658.

36 Metzger, "Good Advice from a Successful Man," 36; "Complete in All Appointments," *Detroit Free Press*, August 17, 1903, pt. 1, p. 7; Woodford, *We Never Drive Alone*, 7–8, 15. Metzger, also Detroit's leading bicycle merchant, was initially attracted to the sales and service of automobiles but in time found his way into manufacturing, perhaps most famously as the M in the E-M-F Company, which was later acquired by the Studebaker Corporation. The newspaper article lists Truman H. Newberry as the Detroit Automobile Club's president, Joy as

first vice-president, Russel A. Alger Jr. as second vice-president, Dexter Mason Ferry Jr. as secretary and treasurer. Founding members included Fred M. Alger, Charles A. Ducharme, Philip McMillan. All invested in Packard. "Detroit Auto Club," *Detroit Free Press*, July 3, 1902, 3.

37 "Metzger Is Climbing," *Detroit Free Press*, June 11, 1905, pt. 5, p. 6.

Chapter 9

1 Adrian Fuller, "The Story of Defense's Architect," *Detroit Free Press*, November 30, 1941, pt. 5, p. 2.

2 Meister, "Albert Kahn's Partners," 93.

3 "Plant of the Superior Match Co.," *Detroit News-Tribune*, March 8, 1903, pt. 3, p. 18; "Will Buck Match Trust," *Detroit Free Press*, December 6, 1903, pt. 3, p. 8; Mills, "Perpetual Inventory Forms," 36–39; Bradley, *The Works*, 28–29.

4 "Superior Match Co. Has Filed Articles," *Detroit Free Press*, December 17, 1902, 9; "A Large Match Factory," *Detroit Free Press*, February 22, 1903, pt. 1, p. 11; "Plant of the Superior Match Co.," *Detroit News-Tribune*, March 8, 1903, pt. 3, p. 18; "Canton Hollow Block," *Brick and Clay Record*, 16; Mills, "Perpetual Inventory Forms," 36 A; 1910 photograph showing a portion of the exterior of the Superior Match Company factory, DPL-BHC, file "SD/Industries & Business Houses—Hoskins Manufacturing Co., Inc." (a later occupant of the works).

5 Mills, "Perpetual Inventory Forms," 36; "Plant of the Superior Match Co.," *Detroit News-Tribune*, March 8, 1903, pt. 3, p. 18; "Superior Match Co. Closes Plant," *Wooden and Willow-Ware Trade Review*, 54. The description of the Superior Match Plant is based upon an illustration accompanying this source, and the original drawings.

6 Meister, "Albert Kahn's Partners," 83–84. In addition to Boyer and Joy, the initial investors were Fred M. and Russell A. Alger Jr., sons of a lumber mogul who was also Michigan governor; Richard P. Joy, who, with his brother Henry, were sons of a railroad magnate; Philip H. and William O. McMillan, sons of a U.S. senator and grandsons to the founder of the Great Western Railroad; John S. and Truman Newberry, sons of a rail car manufacturer and U.S. representative; and Charles A. Ducharme, son of a hardware merchant and founder of the Michigan Stove Works. "Detroit Men Buy Autoworks," *Detroit News*, October 8, 1902, 8.

7 "Formally Organized," *Detroit News*, January 15, 1901, 2; "Boom the City," *To-Day* (Detroit), January 8, 1901, 4; John Hubert Gruesel, "Joseph Boyer, Inventor," *Detroit Free Press*, January 14, 1906, pt. 4, p. 3.

8 "Huge Auto Factory," *Detroit News*, May 26, 1903, 4; Albert Kahn, "Architect Pioneers," 377.

9 "Real Estate Budget," *Detroit Free Press*, August 2, 1903, 9; Meister, "Albert Kahn's Partners," 85.

10 "Real Estate Budget," *Detroit Free Press*, August 2, 1903, 9; "New Packard Works," *Automobile*, 612; "Packard Dealers Celebrate," *Motor Record*, 95; Meister, "Albert Kahn's Partners," 85.

11 "News of the Architects," *Detroit Free Press*, June 14, 1903, pt. 1, p. 3; "Another Big Automobile Factory," *Detroit News-Tribune*, June 14, 1903, pt. 3, p. 27; "Summer Lethargy," *Detroit News*, August 2, 1903, 23; Baird, "Does Utility Forbid Beauty?" 45. For more discussion on Kahn's emphasis on Joy's role in his success, see Meister, "Albert Kahn's Partners," 92–93. It should be noted that the *Free Press* article attributes the specialization announcement to Albert and Louis Kahn, but this is surely an error as the Packard work is clearly attributed to Albert and Julius.

12 "News of the Architects," *Detroit Free Press*, July 12, 1903, pt. 2, p. 9.

13 Albert Kahn, "Architect in Industrial Building," 13–15; "Architect Honored," *Detroit News*, April 18, 1943, pt. 2, p. 10; "Rites Set for Wilby Tomorrow," *Detroit News*, December 12, 1957, 61. Whether Wilby's contributions to the architectural side of the business outweighed contributions in engineering is a matter of speculation that may be impossible to resolve at this point. At a 1941 tribute that Kahn attended, Wilby was credited as originating engineering aspects of the Ford Highland Park Plant. Based on evidence such as signatures on office drawings, however, later Kahn employees believed him to have been more concerned with the decorative. At any rate, it seems Wilby's contribution was significant, meriting the associate designation and Kahn's praise. "Honored by Architects," *Detroit News*, May 25, 1941, pt. 1, p. 16; Hildebrand, *Designing for Industry*, 59.

14 Albert Kahn, "Architect in Industrial Building," 13.

15 Wight, "Use of Burned Clay Products," 76; Meister, "Albert Kahn's Partners," 86–88.

16 "Among the Architects," *Detroit Free Press*, September 20, 1903, pt. 1, p. 11; Meister, "Albert Kahn's Partners," 88.

17 "The Trussed Concrete Steel Co. Organized," *Detroit Free Press*, October 8, 1903, 9; "Company to Push Kahn's Inventions," *Detroit Times*, October 8, 1903, 1; "The Open Hearth," *Blast Furnace and Steel Plant* 8 (April 1920), 265; Burton, *The City of Detroit, Michigan, 1701–1922*, 20. The company's first treasurer and secretary were Herman Krolik and Ralph M. Dyar, respectively.

18 "The Trussed Concrete Steel Co. Organized," *Detroit Free Press*, October 8, 1903, 9; "Company to Push Kahn's Inventions," *Detroit Times*, October 8, 1903, 1; "Work for the Builders," *Ohio Architect and Builder*, 44; Meister, "Albert Kahn's Partners," 86–88.

19 "News of the Architects," *Detroit Free Press*, March 20, 1904, 8; advertisement for Trussed Concrete Steel Co., *American* 76 (July 1913), 82. Other competitors included Donaldson & Meier and Rogers & Macfarlane of Detroit, J. C. Lewellyn of Chicago, and two Battle Creek participants unnamed in the newspaper account.

20 "The Age of Concrete," *Detroit Free Press*, November 17, 1907, pt. 4, p. 4; "National Gallery Extension," *Builder*, 464; "Moritz Kahn," *Weekly Bulletin of the Michigan Society of Architects*, 3; Cody, *American Architects Abroad, 1870–2000*, 38; Darley, *Factory*, 82.

Chapter 10

1 "Another Factory," *Detroit Free Press*, March 29, 1904, 1.

2 "Business Notes," *Detroit News*, July 20, 1904, 4; Burton, *The City of Detroit, Michigan, 1701–1922*, 557–58; Russell Barnes, "Urges Land Tax Increase to Reduce Other Levies," *Detroit News*, September 5, 1932, 6.

3 Burton, ed., *The City of Detroit, Michigan, 1701–1922*, 558 (quotation); and Meister, "Albert Kahn's Partners," 88.

4 "Factory of the American Arithmometer Co.," *American Architect and Building News*, 107–8.

5 "Another Husky Addition to Detroit's Splendid Industries," *Detroit News-Tribune*, July 24, 1904, pt. 3 p. 2.

6 "Another Husky Addition"; "An Army of Men at Work on Arithmometer Plant," *Detroit Free Press*, October 23, 1904; "Factory of the American Arithmometer Co.," *American Architect and Building News*, 108; Ferry, "Albert Kahn 1869–1942," 22. Historians have largely overlooked this key structure in the Kahn opus, perhaps because the phenomenal success of its owners led to multiple alterations that quickly obliterated the merits of the original 70,304-square-foot design. Additions and new structures on the site added 257,422 square feet to the plant by 1910, with more planned. "History of the Burroughs Adding Machine Company," *Michigan Manufacturer and Financial Record*, 35.

7 Burton, *The City of Detroit*, 558.

8 "The Concrete Steel and Tile," *Detroit Times*, October 29, 1904, 1; "New Construction Co.," *Detroit News-Tribune*, October 30, 1904, 22; "Industrial," *Iron and Machinery World*; MacManus and Beasley, *Men, Money and Motors*, 52; "An Example to Emulate," *Detroit Free Press*, October 27, 1930, 6; Langworth and Weber, "Alvan Macauley and the Dominant Six," 131.

9 "Cement Floor Stood Test," *Detroit Free Press*, August 13, 1905, pt. 1, p. 7; "Cadillac and Packard Automobile Shops," *Engineering Record*, 545–46; "Digest of Current Concrete and Cement Literature," *Concrete Engineering*, 151; Hyde, "Assembly-Line Architecture," 7; and Michael Smith, "First Concrete Auto Factory," 442–44. Although Concrete Steel & Tile was responsible for the design and construction of many projects that stand solidly today, the company dissolved in 1909 following a tragic November 21, 1906, worksite accident in Rochester, New York, in which four workers died and many were injured. A detailed discussion of this incident can be found in Michael Smith, *Concrete Century*, 132–40.

10 Meister, "Albert Kahn's Partners," 92.

11 Albert Kahn, "Architect Pioneers," 377–78; and Ray Peterson, "'The Power That Erring Men Call Chance,'" *Detroit Free Press*, February 25, 1940, pt. 1, p. 7.

12 Bennett, "You Can't Build Skyscrapers," 124.

13 Bennett, "You Can't Build Skyscrapers," 121; Borth, *Masters of Mass Production*, 122, 127; Magaziner, "Working for a Genius," 62.

14 "Cadillac and Packard Automobile Shops," *Engineering Record*, 545; Bennett, "You Can't Build Skyscrapers," 124; Hyde and Abbot, *Lower Peninsula of Michigan*, 50; Michael Smith, "First Concrete Auto Factory," 447–48.
15 "The Cadillac and Packard Automobile Shops," *Engineering Record*, 545.
16 *Reinforced Concrete in Factory Construction*, 243. For more discussion on Number Ten's proper place in architectural history, see Meister, "Albert Kahn's Partners," 90–93, and Smith, "First Concrete Auto Factory," 447–50.
17 "Packard Company Is Enlarging," *Detroit Free Press*, October 18, 1908, pt. 1, p. 20; Bennett, "You Can't Build Skyscrapers," 124.
18 "Automobile Industry and Trade in Detroit," *Automobile*, 37.
19 Pierce Building Committee to Lockwood, Greene & Co., April 16, 1906, AKP-AAA, microfilm roll 1111, frame 501; Knowlton, "New Manufacturing Plant," 263; "Digest of Current Concrete and Cement Literature," *Concrete Engineering*, 151; Hildebrandt, *Designing for Industry*, 34–35.
20 Knowlton, "New Manufacturing Plant," 263; Hildebrandt, *Designing for Industry*, 35.
21 Knowlton, "New Manufacturing Plant," 263–65; Hildebrandt, *Designing for Industry*, 38.
22 "Bright Outlook in Building for Incoming 1906," *Detroit Free Press*, December 31, 1905, pt. 1, p. 15.
23 "News of the Architects," *Detroit Free Press*, July 19, 1903, pt. 2, p. 9; "Among the Architects," *Detroit Free Press*, September 20, 1903, 11; "Detroiter Makes Concrete Plans," *Detroit News*, November 11, 1906, pt. 2, p. 1; "'Come On In'—Cement Is Fine," *Detroit Free Press*, July 23, 1908, pt. 2, pp. 14–16.
24 "Eight-Story Office Structure Figures in 10-Year Lease," *Detroit Free Press*, April 22, 1917, pt. 4, p. 10; Michael Smith, *Concrete Century*, 175–77.
25 "Palmer Bldg. to Be Ready Sept. 1," *Detroit Free Press*, January 23, 1910, pt. 1, p. 9; "Kahn System Economy Construction" advertisement, 940.
26 "New Tower Block to Overlook Park," *Detroit Free Press*, July 27, 1913, pt. 4, p. 1; "The Cleanliness of Glazed Atlantic Terra Cotta," *Atlantic Terra Cotta*, 1; "Architectural Department," *Michigan Technic*, 246.
27 Aymar Embury II, "Impressions of Three Cities," 78.
28 Seymour, "Trussed Concrete Building," 323.
29 "Points to Remember in Building a New Store," *Trade*, 20; E. L. Elliot, "Light and Truth," 588; "Gas Company," *Midwestern*, 31.
30 "Six Story Music House to be Built on Woodward Ave. for Grinnell Bros.," *Detroit Free Press*, April 21, 1907, pt. 1, p. 12; "Grinnell Bros. New Building a Veritable Temple of Music," *Detroit Free Press*, April 26, 1908, pt. 1, p. 8.
31 "Enter New Building," *Detroit Free Press*, March 31, 1908, 3; "Grinnell Bros. New Building a Veritable Temple of Music."
32 "Owen & Co. Will Have Nine-Story Building," *Detroit Free Press*, January 5, 1909, 5; "Building Being Erected at Gratiot Ave. and Brush St. for Owen & Co.," *Detroit Free Press*, May 23, 1909, pt. 2, p. 9.

33 "Building New Quarters," *Detroit Free Press*, December 5, 1909; "Daylight Store Is Now Open," *Detroit Free Press*, February 4, 1910, 5.

34 "Half of Building Is for Newsboys," *Saginaw News*, April 7, 1905, 12; "One of the Most Unique and Artistic Buildings Solely for Newspaper Use," *Grand Rapids Press*, January 1, 1907, 2; "New Home of the Grand Rapids Press Which Is Opened to the Public Today," *Detroit News*, January 1, 1907, 2; DiGirolamo, *Crying the News*, 282, 285–86.

35 "Around the Town," *Detroit Free Press*, August 13, 1931, 5; Borth, *Masters of Mass Production*, 127; Wittkopp, "Cranbrook House," 90.

36 Borth, *Masters of Mass Production*, 126; and Conn, *Divided Mind*, 217, 219.

37 "Old D.A.C. Men Grow Enthusiastic Over Plans for Its Rejuvenation" *Detroit News*, December 1, 1912, pt. 6, p. 4; "Old Bows to New in Athletic Club," *Detroit Free Press*, December 14, 1912, 5; "Athletic Club is Dissolved by Directors," *Detroit Free Press*, January 10, 1913, 12; Borth, *Masters of Mass Production*, 128; Bingay, *Detroit Is My Hometown*, 308, 23.

38 "Expert Gives Good Advice to D.A.C. Men," *Detroit Free Press*, January 12, 1913, 10; "Plans Ready for Detroit Athletic Club's New Home," *Detroit Free Press*, November 23, 1913, 1; and Albert Kahn, "Detroit Athletic Club Building," 174.

39 "Dynamic Detroit Pays Tribute to New Club Rooms," *Detroit Free Press*, April 18, 1915, pt. 3, p. 11; "Gymnasium Voted Best in Land," *Detroit Free Press*, April 18, 1915, pt. 3, p. 10; Albert Kahn, "Detroit Athletic Club Building," 175–76; and "Architectural Types," *Detroit News-Tribune*, February 6, 1916, pt. 5, p.13.

40 Magaziner, "Working for a Genius," 62–63.

41 "D.A.C. Plans are Reality; Home Surety," *Detroit News*, January 5, 1913, pt. 1, p. 1; "Mr. Roosevelt and the D.A.C.," *Jewish Chronicle*, March 3, 1916, 4; "Mr. Roosevelt and the D.A.C.," *Jewish Chronicle*, May 26, 1916, 6. Accusation of anti-Semitism attended the earlier D.A.C. as well, see Philip Slomovitz, "Purely Commentary," *Detroit Jewish News*, January 16, 1987, 24.

42 "D.A.C. Plans are Reality" pt. 1, p. 1; and Correspondence, Henry B. Joy to Hugh Chalmers, February 13, 1913 (AKP-AAA, microfilm roll 1111, frames 517–19).

43 Correspondence, Henry B. Joy to Hugh Chalmers, February 13, 1913 (frame 519); Correspondence, Henry B. Joy to Albert Kahn, May 27, 1915 (AKP-AAA, microfilm roll 1111, frame 520). The presence of a copy of Joy's letter to Chalmers in this archive and the timing of his note to Kahn, suggests he sent the former to the architect only after the D.A.C.'s completion. By sending to Kahn only the copy of his letter to Chalmers, and not the recipient's reply, Joy did not betray any protocol regarding confidentiality.

44 "D.A.C. Plans to Flash on Screen," *Detroit News*, December 14, 1913, pt. 5, p. 5; "Detroit Athletic Club Completes $1,100,000 Fund at Enthusiastic Meeting," *Detroit Free Press*, December 17, 1913, 1–2.

45 Charles A Hughes, "Come and Take a Trip through the New D.A.C. with Secretary Hughes," *Detroit News*, January 31, 1915, pt. 3, p. 6; and "Co-Operation Big Factor in Building New Home of D.A.C.," *Detroit News*, April 17, 1915, 2.

46 "Detroit Athletic Club Now is Sure of Long Waiting List," *Detroit Free Press*, February 7, 1915, 17; Hodges, *Building the Modern World*, 72.
47 Paul Conrad, "Knudsen Honored by Industry and Family on 60th Birthday," *Detroit News*, March 26, 1939, pt. 1, p. 4.

Chapter 11

1 "Ford Company to Help Get Sewer," *Detroit Free Press*, May 16, 1914, 9; Ford and Crowther, *My Life and Work*, 71; Beasley and Stark, *Made in Detroit*; Biggs, *Rational Factory*, 101.
2 "Ford Motor Company," *Cycle and Automobile Trade Journal*, 126–28; Ford and Crowther, *My Life and Work*, 24, 30, 50–51, 71–75; Link, *Forging Global Fordism*, 29.
3 Borth, *Masters of Mass Production*, 108; Bingay, *Detroit Is My Hometown*, 306–7. See also Biggs, *Rational Factory*, 101.
4 "Ford Motor Company to Erect New Factory," *Horseless Age*, 59; "Builders' News," *Detroit Free Press*, July 4, 1909, 9.
5 "New Factory at Kansas City," *Ford Times*, 5; Biggs, *Rational Factory*, 100. The *Ford Times* misidentifies the architect as "Mr. Alfred Kahn," but notes his traveling to Kansas City while planning the company's first assembly plant (see below in text). Biggs notes that only vague references remain concerning the design process of the Ford Highland Park Plant, but concludes Ford engineers designed the layout, "and turned the basic plans over to the Kahns to enclose." In quoting the Ford engineer, George Thompson, she adds his appraisal that, "Mr. Kahn was a wonderful architect but he didn't know anything about [the industry]" (brackets in source). Ford Chief Construction Engineer Edward Gray claimed his team developed plans and specifications while Kahn merely coordinated construction. Hyde, "Assembly-Line Architecture," 14. While these engineers certainly laid down the parameters for Ford plants, this sort of marginalization of Kahn's role challenges credibility. Future Ford production manager William Knudsen is likely more accurate in describing the process as a collaboration, with Kahn being remarkably perceptive in designing to production needs.
6 Ford and Crowther, *My Life and Work*, 113.
7 "Ground Broken for New Factory," *Detroit News*, August 9, 1908, 1; "Daylight for American Factories," *Michigan Manufacturer and Financial Record*, 42; "Detroit Steel Products," advertisement for Fenestra, 9. "Ford Motor Co. Will Have the Largest Building Under One Roof in Michigan," *Detroit News*, July 5, 1908, pt. 2, p. 1; "New Ford Factory Building Is One Sixth of Mile Long: More Than Six Acres of Floor Space," *Detroit Free Press*, July 4, 1909, 9.
8 "Ford Motor Co. Will Have the Largest Building," *Detroit News*, July 5, 1908, pt. 2, p. 1; "Extensive Construction Work in Progress Back of Big Ford Plant on Woodward Ave," *Detroit Free Press*, October 24, 1909, pt. 3, p. 11; "Ford Offices in New Quarters," *Detroit Free Press*, February 5, 1911, 23; Arnold, *Ford Methods and the Ford Shops*, 23.

9 “Ford Offices in New Quarters,” 23; *Ford Factory Facts*, 9, 13–14, 51, 53.

10 “Marvelous Story of Ford Motor Company Told to Adcrafters,” *Detroit Free Press*, February 23, 1913, 1, 2; Arnold, *Ford Methods and the Ford Shops*, 23; Nevins, *Ford*, 452–53.

11 “Ford Company to Build Additions to Great Plant,” *Detroit Free Press*, May 16, 1913, 6; *Ford Factory Facts*, 25.

12 “Highland Park’s Total $1,056,570,” *Detroit Free Press*, July 6, 1913, pt. 5, p. 2; “Ford Power Plant Will Set Record,” *Detroit Free Press*, December 29, 1913, 1; Benson, “What Ford Wages Have Done?,” 262; “Ford Factory to Resume Today,” *Detroit Free Press*, August 7, 1915, 5; “Doubled Ford Plant Part of Big Plan,” *Detroit News*, January 27, 1916, 1, 15.

13 “Daylight Illumination for Manufacturing Buildings,” *American Architect*, 238–39.

14 “Plans and Contracts,” *Detroit News*, June 3, 1906, pt. 3, p. 1; “Building Permits,” *Detroit News-Tribune*, July 4, 1909, pt. 2, p. 1; “Lozier Plant Is Rising,” *Detroit Free Press*, June 26, 1910, pt. 3, p. 8; “Real Estate and Building,” *Detroit Free Press*, July 31, 1910, pt. 3, p. 8.

15 Davies, “Million-Dollar ‘Office Boy,’ ” 15.

16 “750,000 Plant for Auto Parts,” *Detroit Free Press*, June 3, 1910, 6; “Main Building Has 6 Acres Floor Space,” *Detroit News*, June 29, 1910, 2; “Dodge Brothers’ New Automobile Parts Manufactory,” *Detroit Free Press*, January 15, 1911, pt. 4, p. 8; Hyde, *Dodge Brothers*, 23, 31, 42–43, 47–49.

17 “Master Builders of Modern Era,” *Detroit Free Press*, May 1, 1913, pt. 2, p. 3; and Hyde, *Dodge Brothers*, 49–51.

18 “Dodge Brothers to Build Autos,” *Detroit Free Press*, May 27, 1912, 10; Hyde, *Dodge Brothers*, 50–51.

Chapter 12

1 Tallmadge, *Story of Architecture in America*, 214–15. Among his other accomplishments, Tallmadge designed the 1929 memorial monument for Louis Sullivan in Chicago’s Graceland Cemetery. Sullivan died in poverty five years earlier with his grave only identified with a simple marker.

2 Tallmadge, *Story of Architecture in America*, 286.

3 Albert Kahn, “Packard Garage,” 110; “Genesis,” *Packard*, 5.

4 “New Packard Service Building,” *Motor Age*, 37; “Dignity of Service,” *Packard*, 4; “Good Show Windows,” *Packard*, 19; “The Long Island Service Building,” *Packard*, back cover; Albert Kahn, “Thirty Minutes with American Architecture and Architects,” typescript of a speech presented to the Adcraft Club of Detroit, January 22, 1937, AKA-BHL, box 1, file “Transcripts of Speeches, 1936–39,” 10.

5 “Business Briefs,” *Motor Age*, 38; “On Your Right—,”*Packard*, 16.

6 Tallmadge, “ ‘Chicago School,’ ” 69–74, 78; “Chicago’s Packard Place,” *Packard*, 12.

7 “Motor Car News,” *Detroit News*, March 19, 1910, 23; “New Ford Branch Completed,” *Motor Age*, 35.

8 "Detroit Again Makes New Building Record," *Detroit Free Press*, December 14, 1913; "Large Motor Parts Center for Detroit," *Automotive Industries*, 741; "Remodeling to Make Office Building," *Detroit Free Press*, November 22, 1925, pt. 5. p. 5; Ferry, "Representative Detroit Buildings," 56.

9 Borth, "This Is Knudsen," 159, 161; and Nevins, *Ford*, 458–59.

10 "Ford Buys Big Plant," *Detroit Free Press*, February 4, 1919, 1; "Ford Motor Company Acquires Pressed Steel Plant," *Automobile*, 313; "Buffalo Steel Mills Purchase," *Michigan Manufacturer and Financial Record*, 5; Borth, "This Is Knudsen," 159; "William Knudsen Dies at Age of 69," *New York Times*, April 28, 1948, 28.

11 "Buffalo Steel Mills Purchase," *Michigan Manufacturer and Financial Record*, 5; and Nevins, *Ford*, 460–61.

12 Beasley, *Knudsen*, 54; Rubenstein, *Changing US Auto Industry*, 53–56, 60–68, 78; Bryan, *Henry's Lieutenants*, 155.

13 Beasley, *Knudsen*, 53–55.

14 Paul Conrad, "Knudsen Honored by Industry and Family on 60th Birthday," *Detroit News*, March 26, 1939, pt. 1, p. 4; Albert Kahn, "Address of Mr. Albert Kahn, F.A.I.A.," 7; Beasley, *Knudsen*, 54, 138, 361. Although a journalist of note and competent researcher, Beasley's biography of Knudsen falls short of the sort of treatment such a historic figure is due. Knudsen's health was in decline as it was being written and, in my opinion, Beasley was reliant on his compromised memory in some sections. This granted, the biography is still a valuable record, but either Knudsen did not share many memories of his association with Kahn or Beasley omitted them as not critical to the narrative.

15 Swales, "Master Draftsmen," pt. 12, p. 43.

16 Bennett, "You Can't Build Skyscrapers," 121; "It Is Not Too Late for Dues," *Weekly Bulletin of the Michigan Society of Architects*, 1; Ferry, "Albert Kahn 1869–1942," 27.

17 Rowland, "Architecture and the Automobile Industry," 206.

18 Hitchcock, *Architecture*, 403; Albert Kahn, "Architectural Trend," typescript, AKA-BHL, box 1, file "Transcripts of Speeches, 1930–1935," 1.

19 Kahn, "Architectural Trend," 3.

20 Granger, "Some Impressions of Modern German Architecture," 197, 199.

21 "Studio-Talk, Berlin," *International Studio*, 152; Kimball and Edgell, *History of Architecture*, 515.

22 Shiner, "Embodying the Spirit of the Metropolis," 97.

23 George G. Booth to Charles Moore, January 31, 1905, Archives, Smithsonian, records unit 81, box 17, item 49: Nettleton, Nellie M. 1905.

24 Marlen Pew, "Detroit News Building," iii; "Detroit News Building Photo in Paris Exhibit," *Detroit News*, May 19, 1921, 1; Baird, "Does Utility Forbid Beauty?" 46.

25 Rowland, "Milestone in American Architecture," 3; Leonard L. Cline, "Imposing Buildings Newly Constructed Show Forward Step," *Detroit News*, November 10, 1917, pt. 5, p. 7; Edgell, *American Architecture of To-Day*, 291, 294.

26 "Detroit News Building," *Architectural Forum*, 27–28.

27 Rowland, "Milestone in American Architecture," 3; "Detroit News Building," *Architectural Forum*, plate 4; "Detroit News Building," *Architectural Forum*, 27–28; "Detroit News Published from New Home," *Editor and Publisher*, i–ii.
28 Malcolm W. Bingay, "Our Town," *Detroit Free Press*, June 13, 1948, pt. 2, p. 1.
29 Embury, "Impressions of Three Cities," 79.
30 Albert Kahn, "Architectural Trend," typescript, AKA-BHL, box 1, file "Transcripts of Speeches, 1930–1939," 2.

Chapter 13

1 "Work Started on $1,000,000 Aviation Field," *Detroit News*, May 24, 1917, 1, 2.
2 "Old Murphy Power Building Is Made into Business Block," *Detroit Free Press*, March 23, 1917, 9; "Personal," *American Contractor*, 20; Baldwin, "Offices of Albert Kahn," 125; Hildebrand, *Designing for Industry*, 60; Hyde, "Assembly-Line Architecture," 20; Michael Smith, *Designing Detroit*, 84. After leaving Kahn's office, Wilby taught at the University of Michigan College of Architecture and Design from 1922 to 1943. He died at his home in Windsor, Ontario, in 1957, at age eighty-nine. Donnelly, *The University of Michigan*, 1303.
3 Baldwin, "Offices of Albert Kahn," 126–29; Borth, *Masters of Mass Production*, 127.
4 Granger, "Architect of Tomorrow," 91–92.
5 "Work Started on $1,000,000 Aviation Field," *Detroit News*, May 24, 1917, 2. "Aviation School Will Be Speeded," *Detroit Free Press*, May 25, 1917, 26; "U.S. Aviation Field at Mt. Clemens," 11; and "Aviation School Will Open July 5," *Detroit Free Press*, June 18, 1917, 5.
6 "Work Started on $1,000,000 Aviation Field," *Detroit News*, May 24, 1917, 1; Hendrick, "Teaching American Boys to Fly," 524–25; Sweetser, *American Air Service*, 106–8; Goldberg, *History of the United States Air Force*, 19; Maurer, *U.S. Air Service in World War I*, 93–94; Hyde, "Assembly-Line Architecture," 21.
7 Wilson, *Destructive Creation*, 9–10.
8 U.S. Senate, *Hearing Before Committee on Naval Affairs on Eagle Boats*, 65th Cong., 3rd sess. (1919), 5–8.
9 U.S. Senate, *Hearing Before Committee on Naval Affairs on Eagle Boats*, 13–25; "Building the 'Eagle' Class of Submarine Destroyer," *Motorship*, 5.
10 Hendee, "Building 'Eagle' Boats," 324–26; "Building the 'Eagle' Class of Submarine Destroyer," *Motorship*, 5; "Remarkable Speed," *Modern Building*, 13, 15–16.
11 Naval History Division, *Dictionary of American Naval Fighting Ships*, 744–45.
12 Saint, *Image of the Architect*, 72.
13 "Notes Concerning Federal Government Building," *Architectural Forum*, 220; "Fifty-First Convention," *American Architect*, 554.
14 Albert Kahn, "Architect in Industrial Building," 12–16.
15 "The Fifty-First Convention," *American Architect*, 554.
16 Kahn, "Architect in Industrial Building," 15, 19.
17 Kahn, "Architect in Industrial Building," 30.

18 George C. Nimmons, "Modern Industrial Plants," pt. 1, p. 414. The second part of Nimmons's essay includes photographs of industrial work by Kahn and others but does not discuss any individuals in the text. Nimmons, "Modern Industrial Plants," pt. 2, pp. 533–49.

19 "City Leads in War Activity," *Detroit News*, June 29, 1918, 12; Wilson, *Destructive Creation*, 18–19.

20 Kennedy, *The Automobile Industry*, 98, 102; Wilson, *Destructive Creation*, 35–36.

21 "Senate Inquiry Absolves Ford," *Detroit Free Press*, April 28, 1919, 12; W. K. Kelsey, "Paul King Sprung That Eagle Boat 'Leak,'" *Detroit News*, January 22, 1919, 1.

22 "Shows U.S. Lost Money on Eagles," *Grand Rapids Press*, January 15, 1919, 2.

23 Hildebrand, "Albert Kahn," 34.

Chapter 14

1 "Review of Building Activity in 1919," *Architectural Forum*, 6; Ferry, "Representative Detroit Buildings," 56.

2 "New Buildings Vast Project," *Detroit News*, May 12, 1919, 1. For accounts of Durant's opposition to the building and the motivations of GM's board, see Gustin, *Billy Durant*, 199; Arculus, *Durant's Right-Hand Man*, 205.

3 Matte, "Construction Details," 624; "General Motors Building at Detroit," *Contractor's Atlas*, 5–16; "General Motors Building, Detroit, Michigan," *Architecture and Building*, 88; Chappell, "Reconsideration of the Equitable Building in New York," 90; Abrahamson, "'Actual Center of Detroit,'" 63.

4 Matte, "Construction Details," 624; "General Motors Building, Detroit, Michigan," *Architecture and Building*, 88.

5 Ferry, "Representative Detroit Buildings," 56.

6 "Inches Finds City's Police Rank High," *Detroit Free Press*, September 13, 1919, 11.

7 In 1919 Kahn prepared preliminary plans for a two-story, stone-faced reinforced concrete headquarters building estimated to cost about $300,000. When the City Council named Kahn as the architect it had grown to six stories costing an estimated $1,500,000. "Iron and Steel Construction News," *Bridgemen's Magazine*, 479; "Kahn to Plan New Police Building," *Detroit Free Press*, January 8, 1921, 16.

8 "Kahn to Plan New Police Building," *Detroit Free Press*, January 8, 1921, 16; "Detroit Police Quarters to Be the Best in Nation," *Detroit Free Press*, January 8, 1921, pt. 4, p. 1; Knight, "Detroit Has Fine New Police Headquarters," 32; "Joy to Be Arrested in New Headquarters," *Detroit News*, October 1, 1922, pt. 1, p. 10.

9 "Pontchartrain to House Bank," *Detroit News*, March 26, 1919, 23; "Modern 24-Story Bank Structure to Rise on Site of Pontchartrain," *Detroit Free Press*, February 1, 1920, pt. 1, p. 2; "Loss of Hotel Benefits City," *Detroit Free Press*, March 13, 1920, 2; "Builder Take Site of Bank," *Detroit Free Press*, June 20, 1920, pt. 1, p. 1.

10 "The First National Bank of Detroit," *Through the Ages*, 4; "First National Bank, Detroit Mich.," *Architecture and Building*, 60.

11 "Important Industrial Group Is Started on West Side," *Detroit Free Press*, October 12, 1919, 14; "Paige to Double Present Output," *Detroit Free Press*, June 15, 1919, pt. 4, p. 8.

12 "Ford to Sell Big Plant, Is Rumored," *Detroit Free Press*, November 23, 1918, 1; Nevins and Hill, *Ford*, 207, 209–10; "Industry Giant Is Rouge Plant," *Detroit Free Press*, January 20, 1924, pt. 6, p. 7; Hildebrand, *Designing for Industry*, 101–8.

13 Samuel Marquis, *Henry Ford*, 42, 118, 125–26; "Knudsen's Life Fitting Prelude to Gigantic Job," *Detroit Free Press*, May 29, 1940, 4; Beasley, *Knudsen*, 92, 105–13.

14 "Knudsen, Ford Manager, Goes to Chevrolet Co.," *Detroit News*, March 26, 1922, pt. 1, p. 2; "Knudsen Takes Charge of Chevrolet," *Automotive Industries*, 723; Beasley, *Knudsen*, 117, 122–23; Patton, "Assembly Line," 100.

15 "Body Firm Incorporates," *Detroit News*, July 25, 1908, 5; Ed L. Ways, "Mother of the Fisher Brothers Builds Shrine on Site of Ancient Church," *Detroit News*, July 24, 1927, pt. 2, p. 5; Malcolm Bingay, "The Life Story of Frederic J. Fisher, an Epic of Great Family Fidelity," *Detroit Free Press*, July 15, 1941, 5.

16 "Architects Plan Large Apartment," *Detroit Free Press*, December 14, 1919, pt. 4, p. 12; "Body Business Growth Is Told," *Detroit News*, January 18, 1925, pt. 10, p. 15; Glasscock, *Gasoline Age*, 173.

17 "Rush Buildings for Chevrolet," *Detroit Free Press*, September 28, 1922, pt. 2, p. 1; "Ohio," *American Contractor*, 52; "New York," *American Contractor*, 42; "Ohio," *American Contractor*, 54; "Ohio," *American Contractor*, 52.

18 Samuel Marquis, *Henry Ford*, 164.

19 Baldwin, *Henry Ford and the Jews*, 199, 235–36; Bingay, *Detroit Is My Hometown*, 307–8.

20 Baird, "Does Utility Forbid Beauty?" 46, 48; Baldwin, *Henry Ford and the Jews*, 199.

21 Baldwin, *Henry Ford and the Jews*, 235–36; Malcolm W. Bingay, "Good Morning," *Detroit Free Press*, April 30, 1948, 6.

22 Cheney, *New World Architecture*, 166; Lane, *Architecture and Politics in Germany, 1918–1945*, 121–24; Mallgrave, Introduction to *Modern Architecture*, 3–4, 43.

23 "Engineering Laboratory at Dearborn Completed," *Ford News*, 1. Administration offices remained at the Highland Park Plant until a separate, Kahn-designed building for those operations opened in Dearborn (in an area sometimes called Fordson, in recognition of the property's ownership) in 1928. In addition to its function as an incubator for company innovation and site of the top executive offices, the building accommodated Henry's personal pursuits: a dance floor where he and his wife provided instruction, storage of artifacts he was collecting for his future museum, and the presses of the *Ford News* and the infamous *Dearborn Independent* and other corporate publishing concerns. "Ford Engineering Laboratory Layout," The Henry Ford.

24 "New and Enlarged Shops," *American Machinist*, 596g; "Work Started on Laboratory," *Detroit Free Press*, April 8, 1923, pt. 1, p. 5.

25 "Well Known Firm Adopts New Title," *Detroit News*, March 9, 1918, 20; "Engineering Laboratory at Dearborn Completed," *Ford News*, 5; Nimmons, "Industrial Buildings," 19; Hildebrand, *Designing for Industry*, 124–25; "Bradley," *Works*, 194, 196. In the article cited above, Nimmons seems to have become closer to Kahn in his opinion regarding the lack of architect involvement in industrial construction in the eleven years since he penned his "Modern Industrial Plants" articles for *Architectural Record*. In the present article he notes that few of his colleagues have made inroads into this important area of building and "there is no one to blame for it but the architects themselves" (15–16).

26 "Work Started on Laboratory," *Detroit Free Press*, April 8, 1923, pt. 1, p. 5.

27 Nimmons, "Industrial Buildings," 19; Wright, *Frank Lloyd Wright on Architecture*, 143. Wright does not identify the building but places it in the context of a visit to "Henry Ford's plant." Later in his address, Wright mentions seeing old glass chandeliers hanging "in the engineering building" that were destined for Ford's museum. Clearly, Wright was inside the Ford Engineering Laboratory at some point and what little description he provides strongly points to it as the Kahn building he found beautiful and a "fine thing" (143–44).

Chapter 15

1 "New Michigan Corporations," *Michigan Manufacturer and Financial Record*, 28; U.S. House of Representatives, *Report of the Committee on Naval Affairs, Pursuant to H. Res. 30, a Resolution Authorizing and Directing an Investigation of the Progress of the War Effort*, 78th Cong., 2nd sess., 1944, 226; Correspondence, December 12, 1942, Mrs. Henry (Laura P.) Bacon to Mrs. Albert (Ernestine) Kahn, AKP-AAA, microfilm roll 1111, frame 480; King, *Creative-Responsive-Pragmatic*, 18. King places the year of incorporation as 1922, but this appears incorrect.

2 "Moritz Kahn Dies on Train," *Detroit News*, January 16, 1939, 1; U.S. House of Representatives, *Investigations of the Progress of the War Effort, Report of the Committee on Naval Affairs*, 79th Cong., 2nd sess., December 11, 1944. House Report No. 2056, 225; "Head of Famous Firm, Louis Kahn, Dies at 60," *Detroit Free Press*, September 2, 1945, pt. 1, p. 3; King, *Creative-Responsive-Pragmatic*, 18.

3 Baird, "Does Utility Forbid Beauty?," 52.

4 Harold J. Wilcox, "Fords Building Aviation Field," *The Detroit News*, July 6, 1924, pt. 1, p. 1.

5 "Detroit Aspires to Air Supremacy" *Air Transportation*, 61–64. Also see O'Callaghan, *Henry Ford's Airport and Other Aviation Interests, 1909–1954*.

6 "Ford Air Transport Reports Favorable Year," *Aviation*, 622.

7 "Detroit Aspires to Air Supremacy," *Air Transportation*, 64; "Chance Vought Aircraft to Build Factory at Hartford," *Air Transportation*, 10; "Dearborn Inn Opening Set for Late in June," *Detroit News*, March 4, 1931, 38.

8 "Architect Flies over Buildings He Designed," *Detroit Free Press*, August 16, 1928, 12.

9 "Detroit Free Press Building," *Contractors' and Engineers' Monthly*, 52; "There Is No Finer Office Building," advertisement, *Detroit Free Press*, February 22, 1925, pt. 6, p. 6; "Detroit Free Press Building, Detroit, Mich.," *American Architect*, 26.

10 "In and Out of Town," *Town and Country*, 42.

11 "Temple for Maccabees in Yankee Architecture," *Detroit News*, May 24, 1925, pt. 11, p. 1.

12 "The Maccabees Building," *Buildings and Building Management*, 37, 39.

13 "Temple for Maccabees in Yankee Architecture," *Detroit News*, May 24, 1925, pt. 11, p. 1; "Ground Broken by Maccabees," *Detroit Free Press*, December 30, 1925, 7.

14 Albert Kahn, "Thirty Minutes with American Architecture and Architects," typescript of a speech presented to the Adcraft Club of Detroit, January 22, 1937, AKA-BHL, box 1, file "Transcripts of Speeches, 1936–39," 10.

15 "Site of Huge Fisher Building Dedicated," *Detroit Free Press*, August 26, 1927, 1, 3.

16 "Site of Huge Fisher Building Dedicated," 3; "Fisher Tower Nearly Ready," *Detroit News*, October 7, 1928, pt. 1, p. 2; Ansel, "New Fisher Building," 7.

17 "Moving the Mountains to Town," *Evening Star* (Washington, DC), February 16, 1930, pt. 7, p. 5; "Fisher Tower Nearly Completed," *Detroit News*, October 7, 1921, pt. 1, p.1; "Editorial Comment," *American Architect*, 253; Ferriss, *Metropolis of Tomorrow*, 44.

18 Albert Kahn, "Fisher Building," 212, 220.

19 *Fisher Building*, 7, 11, 17; "New Era Is Opened by Fisher Building," *Detroit Free Press*, May 20, 1928, pt. 6, p. 10; "Building for Beauty," *Grand Rapids Press*, November 5, 1928, 6; "Moving the Mountains to Town," *Evening Star*, (Washington, DC), February 16, 1930, pt. 7, p. 5. More on this fine building, and color photographs, can be found in Hodges, *Building the Modern World*, 104–11.

20 "Beauty and Efficiency Mark Kresge Building," *Detroit Free Press*, May 18, 1930, pt. 7, p. 2.

21 "New Building Seen Great Credit to City," *Detroit Free Press*, May 18, 1930, pt. 7, p. 2; and "Beauty and Efficiency Mark Kresge Building," *Detroit Free Press*, May 18, 1930, pt. 7, p. 2.

22 "Beauty and Efficiency Mark Kresge Building," pt. 7, p. 2; "Kresge Employees Have Exceptional Comforts," *Detroit Free Press*, May 18, 1930, pt. 7, p. 1; and personal observation.

23 "Mr. Hearst and Party Arrive for Fete," *Detroit Times*, December 6, 1929, 2.

24 "Mr. Hearst and Party Arrive for Fete," 2.

25 Kahn, "Architect Pioneers," 378. Bennet supports this number, while a decade later Nelson stated the number of employees as "about 400" in pre-Depression "normal times." A numeric tally of Nelson's description of the individual departments supports Kahn's number of 350, however. This included some 40 in administrative positions, 15 accountants, 30 specification writers and estimators, around 90 mechanical and electrical engineers, and some 175 architectural designers and draftspersons. Bennett, "You Can't Build Skyscrapers," 121; "Organization of Albert Kahn, Inc." *Architectural Forum*, 91.

26 Baird, "Does Utility Forbid Beauty?" 46; *Dedication of the Detroit Times New Building*, December 6, 1929, 23.

27 Robertson, "Factories of Henry Ford," 439.

28 Bennett, "You Can't Build Skyscrapers," 121; Hyde, "Assembly-Line Architecture," 21.

29 "It Is Not Too Late for Dues," *Weekly Bulletin of the Michigan Society of Architects*, 1; Smith, *Designing Detroit*, 30, 40, 119.

30 Examples of attempts to share the firm's "secrets" of organizational success are Baldwin, "Offices of Albert Kahn" and George Nelson's "Organization" published in *Architectural Forum* (November 1918 and August 1938, respectively). The latter was reprinted in Nelson's *Industrial Architecture of Albert Kahn, Inc.*

Chapter 16

1 Banham, *Concrete Atlantis*, 11, 15

2 For more in-depth study, one might start with Hitchcock, *Modern Architecture*. In this volume, Hitchcock writes of New Pioneers of a New Tradition in architecture. Within a few years he characterized their work as the International Style, as discussed below.

3 Lane, *Architecture and Politics in Germany, 1918–1945*, 41.

4 Brashear, *Albert Kahn and His Family in Peace and War*, 62.

5 Kahn-Mahomedov, "Creative Trends," 9–11; Kentgens-Craig, *Bauhaus and America*, 85. A collection of salient manifestos are conveniently collected in Conrads, *Programs and Manifestoes on 20th-Century Architecture*. Some architects, notably Frank Lloyd Wright, may have objected to being represented therein.

6 Grady, *Seeing Red*, 91–92; Lissitzky, *Russia*, 27–30.

7 Schneider, *Making the Fascist State*, 244, 361–62; Newcomb, *History of Modern Architecture*, 67.

8 Patric, "Imperial Rome Reborn," 284, 293. For a discussion of early receptions of the ideological forces that would have global impact in the 1930s, see Schivelbusch, *Three New Deals*.

9 For more on the political upheaval surrounding the Bauhaus, see Lane, *Architecture and Politics in Germany*, 79–86, 171–72; Elaine S. Hochman, *Architects of Fortune: Mies van der Rohe and the Third Reich* (New York: Weidenfeld & Nicolson, 1989), 87–102; and Reginald Issacs, *Gropius: An Illustrated Biography of the Creator of the Bauhaus* (Boston: Bulfinch Press, 1991), chapters 3 and 4.

10 S. Frederick Starr, "OSA: The Union of Contemporary Architects," in *Russian Modernism: Culture and the Avant-Garde, 1900–1930*, ed. Gibian, George and H. W. Tjalsma, (Ithaca, New York: Cornell University Press, 1976), 196.

11 "Precedents Upset in Home Designing," *Detroit Free Press*, April 29, 1928, pt 6. P 4; and Issacs, *Gropius*, 143, 227.

12 Lane, *Architecture and Politics in Germany*, 119–23; and Issacs, *Gropius*, 149.

13 Lane, *Architecture and Politics in Germany*, 121.

14 "Soviet Engineers Here," *New York Times*, November 5, 1928, 35; Sutton, *Western Technology and Soviet Economic Development, 1917 to 1930*, 183, 344–45.

15 William C. Richards, "Kahn Will Build for Soviets," *Detroit Free Press*, May 5, 1929, pt. 1, p. 1; Kravchenko, *I Chose Freedom*, 460.

16 "Soviet Engineers Here," *New York Times*, November 5, 1928, 35; Ivanov, "Life of a Leader," 28–35.

17 William Henry Chamberlin, *World's Iron Age*, 112–13, 124–26; Bingay, *Detroit Is My Hometown*, 308; Beasley, *Knudsen*, 165; Brashear, *Albert Kahn and His Family in Peace and War*, 97.

18 Bingay, *Detroit Is My Hometown*, 308. Pulitzer Prize–winning *New York Times* correspondent William Duranty and renowned performer Paul Robeson are well-documented examples of those who knowingly praised the Soviet government while hiding its oppressive nature. For one firsthand account of how this massive deceit was achieved, see Beal, *Proletarian Journey*.

19 Gitlow, *I Confess*, 301–2; Leonard, *Secret Soldiers of the Revolution*, 109; Melnikova-Raich, "Soviet Problem with Two 'Unknowns,'" pt. 1, pp. 60–61.

20 "That Russian Contract," *Detroit Free Press*, May 15, 1929, 6; Knickerbocker, *Red Trade Menace*, 97; and *Dzerzhinsky Tractor Plant at Stalingrad*, 21, 35.

21 Rodney Dutcher, "Reflections on Life in Washington Circles," *Bay City Times*, September 27, 1929, 4; H. R. Knickerbocker, "Trains, Telegrams Work Moving Slowly in Red Russia Despite Foreign Aid," *Detroit Free Press*, December 15, 1930, 13; Philip A. Adler, "Success for Russia's 5-Year Plan Seen by Detroiter," *Detroit News*, January 3, 1932, pt. 2, p. 7; Kravchenko, *I Chose Freedom*, 51; and Melnikova-Raich, "Soviet Problem with Two 'Unknowns,'" pt. 1, p. 61. Adler as quoted here is a later and more concise restatement, surely from notes, of observations he made in a 1929 report from Stalingrad. See Philip Adler, "Russia 'Arming' with Tractors," *Detroit News*, December 15, 1929, pt. 2, p. 3.

22 Adler, "Russia 'Arming' with Tractors," pt. 2, p. 3; *Dzerzhinsky Tractor Plant at Stalingrad*, 21, 35.

23 William C. Richards, "Kahn Will Build for Soviets," *Detroit Free Press*, May 5, 1929, pt. 1, p. 1; *Dzerzhinsky Tractor Plant at Stalingrad*, 21, 35 (quotations); Melnikova-Raich, "Soviet Problem with Two 'Unknowns,'" pt. 1, pp. 61, 62, 65.

24 Kopp, "Foreign Architects in the Soviet Union," 18–38; Leder, *My Life in Stalinist Russia*, 116 (regarding *partiinost'*); Melnikova-Raich, "The Soviet Problem with Two 'Unknowns,'" pt. 1, p. 62. For a more expansive discussion of American involvement in the Five-Year Plan, including Kahn's Soviet contracts, see Cohen, Crawford, and Zimmerman, *Detroit-Moscow-Detroit*.

25 Beal, *Proletarian Journey*, 280. Beal was in the USSR while his murder conviction related to a labor strike was on appeal. (He traveled with a CPUSA-supplied forged passport.) He became a fugitive after the Soviets kept him there following the loss in the appeal process. Beal was so disillusioned by his experience that he managed to return to the United States in 1933, determined to educate the

public about the reality of the Soviet Union. He eventually turned himself into authorities to serve his sentence. Beal, *Proletarian Journey*, chap. 24.

26 Beal, *Proletarian Journey*, 293, 298, 304, 313–17; Filene, *Americans and the Soviet Experiment, 1917–1933*, 241.

27 "Fleeing Russians Shot Down, Report," *Detroit Free Press*, September 14, 1930, pt. 1, p. 1; Brashear, *Albert Kahn and His Family in Peace and War*, 62.

28 "Detroiters Reds' Slaves," *Detroit Free Press*, September 21, 1930, pt. 1, p. 12; "Fear for Safety of Detroit Workers in Soviet Plant," *Detroit Times*, September 22, 1930, 3; "Red Slave Charge Unverified Here," *Detroit Free Press*, September 22, 1930, 7.

29 Melnikova-Raich, "Soviet Problem with Two 'Unknowns,'" pt. 1, 65–66; "Detroiter Says Soviet Plan Is Due to Fail," *Detroit Free Press*, October 27, 1931, 10; Crawford, "Closing the Loop," 242–43.

30 Robeson, *Undiscovered Paul Robeson*, 281, 296.

31 Many of the manifestos are collected in Conrads, *Programs and Manifestoes*.

32 Hitchcock, *Modern Architecture*, 200; Vidler, *Histories of the Immediate Present*, 6.

33 Hitchcock, *Modern Architecture*, 216. One could assume that "Finnish influence" is a reference to Eliel Saarinen, who became a visiting professor at the University of Michigan in 1924 before moving to Cranbrook Academy of Art. While he had some impact, including inspiring the design of Kahn's Fisher Building, it is difficult to find support for Hitchcock's assertion of Finnish influence becoming "dominant in Michigan."

34 "Architecture Authority at Art Institute Tonight," *Detroit News*, January 13, 1931, 16; E. P. Richardson, "Will Discuss Architecture," *Detroit Free Press*, January 11, 1931, pt. 4, p. 4.

35 Hitchcock, *Modern Architecture*, 110, 189; "Recent Art Books at the Public Library," *Detroit News*, August 24, 1930, pt. 10, p. 5.

36 Albert Kahn, "Architectural Trend," *Journal of the Maryland Academy of Sciences*, 106–14; Maryland Science Center, "Mission and History." For discussion of multinational efforts to target the general public in advancing ideology through the arts, see Marquardt, *Art and Journals on the Political Front, 1910–1940*, 270–72.

37 Kahn, "Architectural Trend," typescript of a speech presented to the Maryland Academy of Sciences, April 15, 1931, AKA-BHL, box 1, file "Transcripts of Speeches, 1930–1935," 1.

38 Kahn, "Architectural Trend" typescript, 1–3.

39 Kahn, "Architectural Trend" typescript, 18–20.

40 Kahn, "Architectural Trend" typescript, 14, 17.

41 Filene, *Americans and the Soviet Experiment, 1917–1933*, 256–59.

42 This presumption is based on congressional investigation testimony regarding similarly assigned trainees at the FMC Rouge Plant at the same time and the reminisces of Victor Kravchenko, a Soviet engineer assigned to the U.S. in 1942. "Ford Co. Fears No Communists," *Detroit Free Press*, July 27, 1930, pt. 1, p. 5; Kravchenko, *I Chose Freedom*, 443–45.

43 "Fears Amtorg Agent Was Slain by Soviet," *New York Times*, April 4, 1931, pt. 1, p. 2; "Amtorg Denial in Death," *New York Times*, April 5, 1931, pt. 1, p. 15; Tony Weitzel, "Of Cabbages . . . and Kings," *Detroit News*, August 16, 1948, 30.

44 "Behind the Scenes," *Scribner's Magazine*, 90 (July 1931), 117; Gitlow, *Whole of Their Lives*, 223–24; and Menand, "Historical Romance," 78.

45 Edmund Wilson, "Despot of Dearborn," 24, 33. Within his essay, Wilson referenced a March 1931 article appearing in *Atlantic Monthly* (26), making it possible he was influenced by Kahn's "Architectural Trend," presented before its April publication.

Chapter 17

1 For examples, see "State Buildings to be Hastened," *Flint Journal*, February 21, 1930, 8; "News Plans Additions to Present Buildings," *Detroit News*, March 7, 1930, 1. For an account on the experience of Americans in Kahn's Moscow office, see Sonia Melnikova-Raich, "Two Contracts," 182–92.

2 "Fishers to Build 10-Story Edifice at Once," *Detroit Free Press*, September 28, 1930, pt. 1, pp. 1, 3; "Citizens Laud Fisher Move," *Detroit Free Press*, September 28, 1930, pt. 1, p. 3.

3 "Fishers to Build 10-Story Edifice at Once"; "City Helps to Speed New Fisher Building," *Detroit Free Press*, October 10, 1930, 9; "Work on New Building Begun," *Detroit Free Press*, October 16, 1930, 3.

4 J. D. M. White, "Motor City Investor's Roundtable," *Detroit Free Press*, June 6, 1931, 17.

5 "Building Here Called Symbol of Faith in Detroit," *Detroit Free Press*, September 24, 1931, 15.

6 "Building Here Called Symbol of Faith in Detroit"; "Downtown's New Emporium," *Detroit News*, September 27, 1931, pt. 6, p. 3; Hitchcock and Johnson, *The International Style*, 86.

7 Albert Kahn, "Reinforced Concrete Architecture These Past Twenty Years," 132.

8 Frank D. Webb, "The Auto World," *Detroit Free Press*, July 18, 1931, 12; "Moto Giants Fighting Foes of Individualism," *Detroit Free Press*, May 20, 1934, pt. 1, p. 8; Lohr, *Fair Management*, 60; Sorenson, *Ford Shows*, 105, 108; and Ganz, *1933 Chicago World's Fair*, 1–2, 71–73.

9 Arthur Pound, *Turning Wheel*, 453–54; Ganz, *1933 Chicago World's Fair*, 79–80.

10 "Kahn Sees New Russia Banish Old Architecture," *Detroit News*, November 1, 1931, pt. 10, p. 3; Kyrilov, "Golosov Brothers," 112.

11 Sketches, AKP-AAA, microfilm roll 1114, frames 131, 132; "Around the Town," *Detroit Free Press*, August 19, 1931, 10.

12 "Reds Seen Advancing" *Detroit Free Press*, August 24, 1931, 7; "Kahn Predicts Soviet Success," *Detroit Free Press*, October 27, 1931, 1. Newspaper accounts of Kahn employees who worked in the Soviet Union are rare but document one-year stints.

13 Tim Tzouliadis, *Forsaken*, 98, 120.

14 "Charges Communist Censors Color Soviet News," *Border Cities Star* (Windsor, Ontario), November 5, 1931, 5; "Kahn Firm Gives Reply," *Border Cities Star*, November 5, 1931; email correspondence, Sonia Melnikova-Raich to the author, November 8, 2021.

In *Albert Kahn*, Bucci writes that in the Windsor Library presentation Bruss claimed that Kahn's Soviet contracts "included a clause regarding the promotion of Communism in the United States" (95). This may be an error in transcription or translation, but what Bruss was actually quoted as saying is recorded in the text of this chapter. This is a significant difference, but Kahn nevertheless certainly argued for normalized diplomatic relations, which would ease credit issues. Kahn's motivation may have been heartfelt compassion for the Soviet people as well as the desire to grow employment in the U.S., as he stated more than once. Bucci deserves recognition for bringing this easy-to-overlook article on Bruss and Moritz's response (below) to light.

15 "Sponsors U.S., Soviet Trade," *Detroit Free Press*, January 25, 1932, 4; "Cites U.S. Loss in Soviet Trade," *Detroit News*, January 25, 1932, 13.

16 "Kahn on Way Back to Russia," *Detroit News*, March 4, 1932, 47; "Kahns Break with Soviet on Payment for Services," *Detroit Free Press*, March 29, 1932, 7; "Kahn Quits Job Helping Soviets," *Flint Journal*, March 29, 1932, 5; Philip A. Adler, "Albert Kahn Has Faith in Soviet Trade Future," *Detroit News*, April 24, 1932, 11; "Albert Kahn Believes United States Ought to Recognize Russia," *Saginaw News*, April 26, 1932, 4; Sonia Melnikova-Raich, "Two Contracts," 193. While many sources mention the number of employees in the Moscow office at the time of its closing as twenty-four, an Associated Press report in the *Flint Journal* noted twenty-one returning. Per an Associated Press report in the *Saginaw News*, Kahn stated on his return that "all but a few of the 24" were back in the U.S. Melnikova-Raich quotes one of the returning employees as writing that "only two agreed" to stay.

17 Alfred H. Barr Jr., preface to the original 1932 edition, Hitchcock and Johnson, *The International Style*, 27; Riley, *The International Style: Exhibit 15*, 213.

18 Hitchcock and Johnson, *The International Style*, 42–43, 101.

19 Henry-Russell Hitchcock Jr. and Philip Johnson, "The Extent of Modern Architecture," 22; Terry Smith, *Making the Modern*, 83; Riley, *The International Style: Exhibit 15*, 63. For discussions of historians' reaction to "Architectural Trend," see Terry Smith, "Albert Kahn," 31; and Hodges, *Building the Modern World*, 167–68.

20 Albert Kahn, "Approach to Design," *Pencil Points*, May 1932, 299.

21 Kahn, "Approach to Design," 299–300; and Hartman and Cigliano, *Pencil Points Reader*, xiii.

22 Kahn, "Approach to Design," 300.

23 Kahn, "Approach to Design," 300.

24 Kahn, "Approach to Design," 300–301.

25 Kathryn Smith, *Wright on Exhibit*, 82–83. For full texts of two correspondences from Wright to Johnson on this matter, see Wright, *Letters to Architects*, 89–91.

26 Riley, *The International Style: Exhibit 15*, 87–88; Wright, *Collected Writings*, vol. 3, 146; Kathryn Smith, *Wright on Exhibit*, 82–83.
27 Wright, *Collected Writings*, vol. 3, 113–15, 146.
28 Borth, *Masters of Mass Production*, 127.
29 Florence Davies, "Thoughts About Style," *Detroit News*, December 4, 1932, pt. 3, p. 16.
30 Davies, "Thoughts About Style."
31 Davies, "Thoughts About Style."

Chapter 18

1 Kahn-Mahomedov, "Creative Trends," 18; Hochman, *Architects of Fortune*, 101–3; and Painter, *Mussolini's Rome*, 59–60.
2 Lyon et al., *National Recovery Administration*, 3; Thomas Smith, "New Deal as a Cultural Phenomenon," 214–17.
3 One example is found in Bucci, *Albert Kahn*, 97.
4 "Facts About the General Motors Exhibit," typescript, 1933, CPL-COPC, box 8, file 16, 1; "General Motors Building," promotional brochure, 1934; Pound, *Turning Wheel*, 453; Ganz, *1933 Chicago World's Fair*, 81, 453–54.
5 Albert Kahn, "Pageant of Beauty," 26.
6 "Architecture," typescript, CPL-COPC, box 8, file 12, p. 2; Lohr, *Fair Management*, 48.
7 "Greatest of Automobile Shows to Be Staged at World's Fair in Chicago," *Detroit Free Press*, April 30, 1933, pt. 1, p. 12; Ganz, *1933 Chicago World's Fair*, 81.
8 "World Fair Spirit Reflected in New De Soto Building," *Grand Rapids Press*, November 4, 1933, 13.
9 "Chrysler Plans Office Building," *Detroit Free Press*, September 3, 1933, pt. 2, p. 10; "New Chrysler Offices Started," *Detroit Free Press*, September 7, 1933, 16; Albert Kahn, "Office and Display Building," 1, 3; and Kahn, "Thirty Minutes with American Architecture and Architects," typescript of a speech presented to the Adcraft Club of Detroit, January 22, 1937, AKA-BHL, box 1, file "Transcripts of Speeches, 1936–1939," 14.
10 Ganz, *1933 Chicago World's Fair*, 81.
11 "Address of Albert Kahn, Architect of the Ford Motor Company's Exhibit at a Century of Progress Exposition, Chicago Institute of Architects, March 20, 1934," typescript, CPL-COPC, box 8, file 12.
12 "Address of Albert Kahn," CPL-COPC; "Ford Inspects a Monument to His Genius at World Fair," *Detroit Free Press*, May 16, 1934, 1; Thomas Burke, *History of the Ford Rotunda*, 10; Ganz, *1933 Chicago World's Fair*, 81.
13 Lohr, *Fair Management*, 49.
14 "Motor Giant Fighting Foes of Individualism," *Detroit Free Press*, May 20, 1934, 1.
15 "Buildings at World's Fair Stir Up Furor Among U.S. Architects," *Detroit Free Press*, July 23, 1933, pt. 1, p. 10; Voyce, *Russian Architecture*, 134, 205; Hudson, *Blueprints and Blood*, 159–60, 165, 209.

16 "*Bauhaus* Man," *Time*, 32; Lane, *Architecture and Politics in Germany, 1918–1945*, 152–53, 171–72; Hochman, *Architects of Fortune*, 97–99, 148–52; George Nelson, *Building a New Europe*, 141.

17 *Nation Builds*, 19, 131; and Hochman, *Architects of Fortune*, 162.

18 Henry-Russell Hitchcock, foreword to 1966 edition, Hitchcock and Johnson, *The International Style*, 20–21; Philip Johnson, foreword to 1995 edition, Hitchcock and Johnson, *The International Style*, 15.

19 Tallmadge, *The Story of Architecture in America*, 302, 309.

20 "World Fair Spirit Reflected in New De Soto Building," *Grand Rapids Press*, November 4, 1933, 13.

21 Wright, *Letters to Architects*, 107.

22 Albert Kahn, "Architectural Trend," 13–14.

23 Albert Kahn, "Thirty Minutes with American Architecture," typescript, presented to the Adcraft Club of Detroit, January 22, 1937, AKC-BHL, box 1, file "Transcripts of Speeches, 1936–1939," 15.

24 Stoddard White, "All Decked Out in a New Building, WWJ Steps Out," *Detroit News*, September 13, 1936, pt. 3, p. 9.

25 "Architect's Drawing . . . ," *American Aviation*, 15; "Dodge Starts Its New Plant," *Detroit Free Press*, October 28, 1938, 16; Mock, *Built in the USA*, 95.

26 Albert Kahn, "Industrial Architecture," 5.

27 Letter of condolence, Eric Mendelsohn, New York, to Ernestine Kahn, Detroit, December 11, 1942, AKP-AAA, pdf of microfilm roll 1111, frame 1033; Eric Mendelsohn, New York, to Ernestine Kahn, Detroit, March 27, 1943, AKP-AAA, pdf of microfilm roll 1111, frame 1034; "Eric Mendelsohn," Guggenheim Memorial Foundation.

28 Kahn, "Thirty Minutes with American Architecture," typescript, presented to the Adcraft Club of Detroit, January 22, 1937, AKC-BHL, box 1, file "Transcripts of Speeches, 1936–1939," 16; Cret, "Albert Kahn," 15.

29 Helen C. Bower, "Architecture Talk Given by Expert," *Detroit Free Press*, October 20, 1938, 11.

30 Wright, "Address of Frank Lloyd Wright," 7; "Industry's Architect," *Time*, 42.

31 "The Taliesen Fellowship," facsimile reprint of 1933 brochure; Alexander, *Insufficient Funds*, 112.

32 "With the Lecturers," *Detroit Free Press*, October 16, 1938, pt. 3, p. 18; "Architect Lectures Town Hall Group," *Detroit News*, October 20, 1938, 20; Helen C. Bower, "Architecture Talk Given by Expert," *Detroit Free Press*, October 20, 1938, 11.

33 Bower, "Architecture Talk Given by Expert," 11; Abercrombie, *George Nelson*, 17.

34 "Albert Kahn," *Architectural Forum* 69 (August 1938). Coverage of the firm runs from page 87 to 142 (quotation from 89); Abercrombie, *George Nelson*, 15.

35 "Albert Kahn," *Architectural Forum* 69 (August 1938), 87–90. As an example of Nelson's style, he wrote of Mies following a 1935 interview, "He likes his food and knows his wines, and with a sufficient quantity of both inside him he can become a charming and mellow conversationalist." Nelson, *Building a New Europe*, 82.

36 Abercrombie, *George Nelson*, 15–16.
37 Newcomb, *History of Modern Architecture*, 132–33, 137–38.
38 McAndrew and Mock, *What Is Modern Architecture?*.
39 "Windowless Factory Building," *Western Architect*, 25; "—And Now I Always Use Simonds," *Popular Science Monthly*, 109; Wilkinson, *Supersheds*, 50.
40 Albert Kahn, "Industrial Architecture," 8.

Chapter 19

1 Roland Marchand, "Designers Go to the Fair," pt. 1, pp. 90–91, 97–99; Marchand, "Designers Go to the Fair," pt. 2, 103–4.
2 Russell Barnes, "Aerial Plant Sets Record," *Detroit News*, April 14, 1939, 27; Hildebrand, *Designing for Industry*, 183
3 Barnes, "Aerial Plant Sets Record."
4 Barnes, "Aerial Plant Sets Record."
5 The military aspect of the Five-Year Plan was well known throughout the Soviet Union and a report suggesting the intention of converting Kahn-designed tractor plant plans to tank production appeared in a Detroit newspaper in late 1930. H. R. Knickerbocker, "Reds Build Convertible Tractor-or-Tank Plant," *Detroit Free Press*, December 14, 1930, 1, 3. Also see Dunn, *Soviet Economy and the Red Army*, 20.
6 Malcolm W. Bingay, "Good Morning," *Detroit Free Press*, July 16, 1942, 6. Kahn biographers sometimes quote the slightly different version of the same interview appearing in Bingay, *Detroit Is My Hometown*, 309–310.
7 Melnikova-Raich, "Two Contracts, Girls in Socks, and the Great Turning Point," 192; Meerovich, "Albert Kahn in the History of Soviet Industrialization," 214–15.
8 "Detroit Architect Draws Plans for New Navy Bases," *Detroit News*, February 19, 1940, 25; Albert Kahn, "Architecture in the National Defense Program," transcript of speech given to the Society of Automotive Engineers, Detroit, April 28, 1941, AKA-BHL, box 1, 2–3; Woodbury, *Builders for Battle*, 75–76.
9 Kahn, "Architecture in the National Defense Program," typescript 3.
10 Woodbury, *Builders for Battle*, 130, 227, 271–72; Herman, *Freedom's Forge*, 172.
11 Borth, *Masters of Mass Production*, 128; and, for more on Knudsen and the Arsenal of Democracy, see Herman, *Freedom's Forge*. It is my intention to follow this volume with one focused on the relationship between Kahn and Knudsen and its historic impact.
12 "Kahn Forms New Firm," *Detroit Free Press*, July 30, 1940, 15; Borth, *Masters of Mass Production*, 123; Donald Nelson, *Arsenal of Democracy*, 123; Herman, *Freedom's Forge*, 66–71, 96.
13 "Head of Famous Firm, Louis Kahn, Dies at 60," *Detroit Free Press*, September 2, 1945, pt. 1, p. 3; and Walton, *Miracle of World War II*, 211.
14 "Their Combined Wealth Is 'Some' Change," *Detroit News*, May 7, 1922, pt. 9, p. 8; Robert S. Ball, "First Tank Received by Army," *Detroit News*, April 24, 1941, 1; "Chrysler Gets 53 Million Job," *Detroit News*, August 16, 1940, 1, 2.

15 "Army Gets First Tank at Chrysler's," *Detroit Free Press*, April 25, 1941, 1, 4; Albert Kahn, "Chrysler Tank Arsenal," 15.
16 "Ford Bomber Plant," *Michigan Society of Architects Weekly Bulletin*, 81; Hyde, *Arsenal of Democracy*, 90–91; Peterson, *Planning the Home Front*, 26.
17 Borth, *Masters of Mass Production*, 125; Stout, *Great Engines and Great Planes*, 12–16; Young, *Building Engines for War*, 236–37.
18 "Albert Kahn—Master Builder," *Detroit Free Press*, December 9, 1942, 6; Borth, *Masters of Mass Production*, 122; Beasley, *Politics Has No Morals*, 130–31.
19 "Tribute to Albert Kahn," *Octagon*, 32.
20 Michigan Department of Health Death Certificate file 300275: Albert Kahn, December 8, 1942; Hodges, *Building the Modern World*, 176.
21 Franklin, "Tribute to Albert Kahn," 13.
22 Email correspondence, Michael Skinner to the author, July 5, 2023. In the 1980s, Mr. Skinner was able to make a copy of the original photograph (which I have seen in digital form) before its being sold in a private transaction. He was told by a credible source that it hung in Kahn's office at the time of his death. I would like to thank Mr. Skinner for making and keeping a record of this remarkable artifact and Levi Smith for bringing it to my attention. Its present status is unknown.
23 Albert Kahn, "Industrial Plants for Defense," 63.

Epilogue

1 "Weds 'Other Woman' on Heels of Divorce," *Detroit Free Press*, August 27, 1928, 1.
2 Williamson, *American Architects and the Mechanics of Fame*, 13, 19, 239n21.
3 "Albert Kahn," *Detroit Times*, December 9, 1942, 22.
4 Cret, "Albert Kahn," 16.
5 "Conversation with Frank Lloyd Wright," (Filmways, 1958).
6 Zimmerman, "Labor of Albert Kahn." A directory of Kahn's extant work in the metropolitan Detroit area alone runs some three hundred entries. See Carlson, *Kahn's Detroit*.
7 For instance, Messel was not one of the over twenty-four hundred architects treated with biographical entries in the four-volume *Macmillan Encyclopedia of Architects*, edited by Adolf K. Placzek (New York: Free Press, 1982).
8 Mock, *Built in the USA Since 1932*, 94–95; "Hitchcock to Talk at Architects' Meet," *Detroit Free Press*, October 14, 1945, 10; Hitchcock, "Architecture of the Mid-Twentieth Century," 1.
9 Hitchcock, "Architecture of the Mid-Twentieth Century," 2–3; Hitchcock, "Architecture of Bureaucracy," 4.
10 Hitchcock, "Architecture of Bureaucracy," 6.
11 Hitchcock, "Architecture of Bureaucracy," 4–5.
12 Paul Heyer, *Architects on Architecture*, 290; Jordy, *American Buildings and Their Architects*, 311–37; Hyde, *Arsenal of Democracy*, 65–69.
13 Sargeant, "Frank Lloyd Wright," 87; Hitchcock, "Architecture of Bureaucracy," 6; Heyer, *Architects on Architecture*, 280–81; and Lambert, *Building Seagram*, 134.

14 Martin Weil, *Pretty Good Club*, 101–2; Schivelbusch, *Three New Deals*, 80–81; Legislative Reference Service of the Library of Congress, *Trends in Russian Foreign Policy Since World War I*, 21. For an unambiguous, 1939 example identifying the left and right wings of the socialist movement as communist and fascist, respectively, see the memoir by Benjamin Gitlow, a former national executive director of Communist Party USA: *I Confess*, 25, 41.

15 Rauschning, *Hitler Speaks*, 9, 137, 179–80; Leach, "Righteous Path of Least Resistance," 5–9.

16 Rauschning, *Hitler Speaks*, 185–87, 248–49; Fest, *Hitler*, 780.

17 "Text of Address by Secretary Ickes on 'It Is Happening Here,'" *New York Times*, December 31, 1937, 6.

18 Zimmerman, "After," 210; Zimmerman, "Building the World Capitalist System," 231–56.

19 Bernstein, *Perilous Progress*, 75; Vidler, *Histories of the Immediate Present*, 6–7; De la Vega, "Historical Legacy," 73–78. While Bernstein's focus is on economics, he makes the point that the New Deal need for specialists benefited doctoral programs, and this had a longstanding ripple-effect throughout higher learning.

20 Melnikova-Raich, "Soviet Problem with Two 'Unknowns,'" pt. 1, p. 76, and pt. 2, pp. 18–20.

21 For more discussion of Kahn's past exclusion from architectural histories, see Terry Smith, *Making the Modern*, 80–86; Hodges, *Building the Modern World*, 166–70.

22 Zimmerman, "Albert Kahn's Territories," 119.

23 Cret, "Albert Kahn," 15. I use the qualifier "professional" as the undeniably consequential Thomas Jefferson, while the designer of noteworthy structures, did not make architecture his career. Albert Speer, architect for the Third Reich, had historic impact that lives in infamy, but mostly through his role as Hitler's armaments and war production minister.

Bibliography

Archival Sources

The listed archives are troves of particular interest to Kahn scholarship and many of the published sources in the articles and books sections below were found in their collections. Called out under this heading are the unique and invaluable holdings I heavily consulted.

AKA-BHL: Albert Kahn Associates Records. Bentley Historical Library, University of Michigan, Ann Arbor.

AKF-BHL: Albert Kahn Family Papers. Bentley Historical Library, University of Michigan, Ann Arbor.

AKP-AAA: Albert Kahn Papers. Archives of American Art. Smithsonian Institution, Washington, DC.

Archives, Records Unit 81, Correspondence. Smithsonian Institution, Washington, DC.

BHC-DPL: Burton Historical Collection. Detroit Public Library.

COPC-CPL: Century Of Progress Collection. Chicago Public Library.

DEH-BHL: David E. Heineman Collection. Bentley Historical Library, University of Michigan, Ann Arbor.

NAHC-DPL: National Automotive History Collection. Detroit Public Library.

University of Michigan Museum of Art. University of Michigan, Ann Arbor.

Published Sources

Articles

Abrahamson, Michael. "'Actual Center of Detroit': Method, Management and Decentralization in Albert Kahn's General Motors Building." *Journal of the Society of Architectural Historians* (March 2018): 56–76.

"Albert Kahn." *Architectural Forum* (August 1938): 87–90.

Alexander, Bob. "Parlour Aquariums." Accessed May 31, 2021. www.parlouraquariums.or.uk. It is hoped that this great source of information on Victorian-era aquaria remains accessible for future scholarship. It was the passion of Bob Alexander

who, with the assistance of his wife, pursued the subject with zeal and generosity fitting of a British naturalist before his passing in 2018.
"American Workingmen's Expedition to the Paris Exhibition." *Engineering and Building Record* (July 6, 1889): 72.
"—And Now I Always Use Simonds 'Red End' Hacksaw Blades." Advertisement. *Popular Science Monthly* (June 1931): 109.
Ansel, L. Verne. "The New Fisher Building." *Michigan Technic* (February 1929): 7, 20.
"Architect's Drawing . . ." *American Aviation* (December 1, 1937): 15.
"Architectural Department." *Michigan Technic* (December 1914): 246–47.
"As He Is Known, Being Brief Sketches of Contemporary Members of the Architectural Profession." *Brickbuilder* (May 1915): 127.
"Automobile Industry and Trade in Detroit." *Automobile* 9 (December 12, 1903): 609–12.
Baird, Dwight G. "Does Utility Forbid Beauty?" *Industry Illustrated* (April 1925): 32–52.
Baldwin, George C. "The Offices of Albert Kahn, Architect, Detroit, Michigan." *Architectural Forum* (November 1918): 125–30.
"*Bauhaus* Man." *Time* (February 8, 1937): 32.
Bean, Tarleton H. "The Detroit Aquarium." *Forest and Stream* (August 30, 1902): 165.
"Behind the Scenes." *Scribner's Magazine* (July 1931): 117.
Bennett, Helen Christine. "You Can't Build Skyscrapers with Your Head in the Sky." *American Magazine* 108 (December 1929): 16–17, 121–24.
Benson, Allan L. "What Ford Wages Have Done?" *Pearson's Magazine* (March 1915): 259–68.
"Bethany Memorial Church, Detroit, Mich." *American Architect and Building News* (December 13, 1897), plate.
Blackford, Charles Minor. "Dr. Tarleton Hoffman Bean." *Transactions of the American Fisheries Society* (June 1917): 189–93.
Bloomfield, Gerald T. "Albert Kahn and Canadian Industrial Architecture." *Society for the Study of Architecture in Canada Bulletin* (December 1985): 4–10.
Borth, Christy. "This Is Knudsen." *Forum* (March 1939): 159–63.
"The Boston Architectural Exhibition." *Architectural Review* (May 1899): 72, 76.
Britton, N. L. "John Francis Cowell." *Journal of the New York Botanical Garden* (September 1915): 191–93.
Bryce, Joseph W. "A Discussion of 'The Open Shop.'" *Michigan Manufacturer and Financial Record* (May 24, 1913): 1, 3.
"Buffalo Steel Mills Purchase." *Michigan Manufacturer and Financial Record* (February 19, 1910): 5.
"Building the 'Eagle' Class of Submarine Destroyer." *Motorship* (May 1918): 5.
"Building Intelligence." *Engineering Record* (April 4, 1891).
Busch, Henry W. "The Model Aquarium of Detroit." *Parks and Recreation* (April 1920): 30–35.
"Business Briefs/Philadelphia, Pa." *Motor Age* (December 1, 1910): 38.
"The Cadillac and Packard Automobile Shops of Reinforced Concrete." *Engineering Record* (November 17, 1906): 545–46.

"Canton Hollow Block." *Brick and Clay Record* (July 1, 1912): 16.
"Chance Vought Aircraft to Build Factory at Hartford." *Air Transportation* (August 10, 1929): 10.
Chappell, Sally A. Kitt. "A Reconsideration of the Equitable Building in New York." *Journal of the Society of Architectural Historians* (March 1990): 90–95.
"Chicago's Packard Place." *Packard* (July 1, 1910): 12.
"The Cleanliness of Glazed Atlantic Terra Cotta." *Atlantic Terra Cotta* (October 1914): 1.
"College of Architecture." *Cornell Alumni News* (April 5, 1899): 5.
"A Conversation with Frank Lloyd Wright." Filmways Corporation: 1958. YouTube. Accessed May 1, 2023. www.youtube.com/watch?v=5OKtdh7TX5k.
Conway, Richard J. "The Detroit Aquarium." *Aquarium* (December 1913): 66–67.
Crawford, Christina E. "Closing the Loop: Soviet Memoirs of American Technical Consultants, 1928–1934." In *Detroit-Moscow-Detroit: An Architecture for Industrialization, 1917–1945*, edited by Jean-Louis Cohen, Christina E. Crawford, and Claire Zimmerman, 225–51. Cambridge, MA: MIT Press, 2023.
Cret, Paul. "Albert Kahn." *Octagon* (February 1943): 14–15.
Davies, Donald M. "Million-Dollar 'Office Boy.'" *This Week* (May 5, 1940): 6, 15.
"Daylight for American Factories." *Michigan Manufacturer and Financial Record* (September 21, 1912): 42.
"Daylight Illumination for Manufacturing Buildings." *American Architect* (June 14, 1911): 238–39.
"Death of Hazen S. Pingree." *Literary Digest* (June 29, 1901): 778.
De la Vega, Macarena. "A Historical Legacy: Henry-Russell Hitchcock and Early Modernism." *Cuaderno de Notas* (2015): 73–78.
"Detroit." *Brickbuilder* (May 1896): 93.
"Detroit Aspires to Air Supremacy in $20,000,000 Airport Program." *Air Transportation* (June 15, 1929): 61–67.
"The Detroit Free Press Building." *Contractors' and Engineers' Monthly* (December 1924): 52–53.
"Detroit Free Press Building, Detroit, Mich." *American Architect* (January 5, 1926): 26.
"The Detroit News Building." *Architectural Forum* (January 1918): 27–28.
"Detroit News Published from New Home." *Editor and Publisher* (October 20, 1919): i–ii.
"Detroit Steel Products." Advertisement for Fenestra. *American Architect* 103 (April 23, 1913): 9.
"Digest of Current Concrete and Cement Literature." *Concrete Engineering* (October 1907): 151–55.
"The Dignity of Service." *The Packard* (January 7, 1911): 4.
Dorner, H. "The Hamburg Aquarium." *Forest and Stream* (November 2, 1876): 195.
Draper, Joanne E. "Howard, John Galen." In *Macmillan Encyclopedia of Architects*, edited by Adolf K. Placzek, vol. 2, 431. New York: Free Press, 1982.
"Editorial Comment." *American Architect* (February 20, 1929): 253.

Elliot, E. L. "Light and Truth." *Illuminating Engineer* (January 1909): 588.

Embury, Aymar, II. "Impressions of Three Cities, II: Detroit." *Architecture* (March 1915): 77–80.

"Eminent Detroit Architect Dead." *Michigan Architect and Engineer* (January 1929): 4.

"Engineering Laboratory at Dearborn Completed." *Ford News* (December 8, 1924): 1, 5.

"Eric Mendelsohn." Guggenheim Memorial Foundation. Accessed February 7, 2023. www.gf.org/fellows/eric-mendelsohn/.

"Factory of the American Arithmometer Co., Detroit, Mich." *American Architect and Building News* (April 1, 1905): 107–8.

"Failures in Reinforced Concrete and Their Lessons." *Concrete and Constructional Engineering* (March 1907): 30–38.

"A Famous 'Reform Mayor.'" *Munsey's Magazine* (December 1896): 325–26.

"'Fenestra' Steel Window Sash." *Railway Master Mechanic* (December 1911): 567–68.

Ferry, W. Hawkins. "Albert Kahn 1869–1942." In *The Legacy of Albert Kahn*, 8–27. Detroit: Detroit Institute of Arts, 1970.

———. "Representative Detroit Buildings: A Cross Section of Architecture, 1823–1943." *Bulletin of the Detroit Institute of Arts* (March 1943): 46–60.

"The Fifty-First Convention of The American Institute of Architects." *American Architect* (May 8, 1918): 552–54.

"Final Stages in the Remodeling of the Aquarium." *Zoological Society Bulletin* 21 (April 1906): 276.

"First National Bank, Detroit Mich." *Architecture and Building* (June 1922): 60–61.

"The First National Bank of Detroit." *Through the Ages* 3 (May 1925): 3–8.

"Fish Shows as Pecuniary Speculations." *Spectator* 48 (January 9, 1875): 45.

"Ford Air Transport Reports Favorable Year." *Aviation* (May 3, 1926): 622.

"Ford Bomber Plant." *Michigan Society of Architects Weekly Bulletin* (December 30, 1941): 75–81.

"Ford Engineering Laboratory Layout, Dearborn, Michigan, Circa 1924." The Henry Ford. Accessed May 29, 2019. www.thehenryford.org/collections-and-research/digital-collections/artifact/254102.

"Ford Lets Contract for Glass Plant." *Automotive Industries* (March 1923): 30.

"The Ford Motor Company." *Cycle and Automobile Trade Journal* (December 1, 1909): 126–28.

"Ford Motor Company Acquires Pressed Steel Plant." *Automobile* (February 19, 1910): 313.

"Ford Motor Company to Erect New Factory." *Horseless Age* (July 8, 1908): 59.

Franklin, Leo M. "A Tribute to Albert Kahn" *Michigan Society of Architects Weekly Bulletin* (March 30, 1943): 13.

"Further Improvements at the Aquarium." *Zoological Society Bulletin* (April 1905): 205–6.

"The Gas Company." *Midwestern* (May 1909): 31.

"General Motors Building at Detroit the Largest Office Building in the World." *Contractor's Atlas* (September 1921): 15–16.

"General Motors Building, Detroit, Michigan." *Architecture and Building* (November 1921).
"Genesis." *The Packard* (January 7, 1911): 5.
Goldman, Norma. "Albert Kahn: Architect, Artist, Humanist." *Michigan Jewish History* (Winter 1993): 2–16.
"Good Show Windows." *The Packard* (January 7, 1911): 19.
Granger, Alfred Hoyt. "The Architect of Tomorrow." *American Architect* (January 15, 1919): 91–93.
———. "Some Impressions of Modern German Architecture." *Architectural Record* (September 1909): 197–203.
"A Greenhouse in an Engine Room." *Gardening Illustrated* (August 16, 1879): 353.
"Growing Ferns and Other Plants in Glass Cases." *Gardener's Magazine* (April 1834): 162–63.
Hale, W. H. "The New York Aquarium." *Outlook* (November 7, 1896): 845.
Hendee, Searle. "Building 'Eagle' Boats in Vast Conservatory." *Popular Mechanics* (September 1910): 324–27.
Hendrick, Burton J. "Teaching American Boys to Fly." *The World's Work* (September 1917): 522–27.
"Henry Bacon." *Pencil Points* (March 1924).
"Henry Bacon, 1856–1924," *American Magazine of Art* (April 1924): 190–93.
G. L. Hersey, "J. C. Loudon and Architectural Associationalism," *Architectural Review* (London) 144 (August 1968): 89.
Hildebrand, Grant. "Albert Kahn: The Second Industrial Revolution." *Prospecta* (1975): 31–40.
"The History of the Burroughs Adding Machine Company." *Michigan Manufacturer and Financial Record* (January 4, 1913): 35.
Hitchcock, Henry-Russell. "The Architecture of Bureaucracy and the Architecture of Genius." *Architectural Review* (January 1947): 3–6.
———. "Architecture of the Mid-Twentieth Century." *Michigan Society of Architects Weekly Bulletin* (November 6, 1945): 1–4.
Hitchcock, Henry-Russell, and Philip Johnson. "The Extent of Modern Architecture." In *Modern Architecture—International Exhibition*, edited by Henry-Russell Hitchcock, Philip Johnson, and Lewis Mumford, 21–24. New York: Museum of Modern Art, 1932.
"The Human Element in the Architect's Organization." *Pencil Points* (April 1924): 43–47.
Hyde, Charles K. "Assembly-Line Architecture: Albert Kahn and the Evolution of the U.S. Auto Factory, 1905–1940." *IA: The Journal of the Society for Industrial Archeology* (1996): 5–24.
"The Improvement of the Aquarium." *Zoological Society Bulletin* (April 1903): 73–76.
"In and Out of Town." *Town and Country* (March 1, 1928): 42.
"Industrial." *Iron and Machinery World* 96 (November 5, 1904): 25.
"Industry's Architect." *Time* (June 29, 1942): 40–42.

"Influence of Light on Health." *London Lancet* (February 1845): 451–52.
"Iron and Steel Construction News-Michigan." *Bridgemen's Magazine* (September 1919): 479.
Irwin, O. W. "Julius Kahn, M. Am. Soc. C. E." *Transactions of the Society of American Civil Engineers* (1945): 1, 742.
"It Is Not Too Late for Dues, Photos, Bios." *Weekly Bulletin of the Michigan Society of Architects* (January 17, 1931): 1.
Ivanov, Vassily. "The Life of a Leader." In *Those Who Built Stalingrad as Told by Themselves*, edited by Y. Ilyin and B. Galin, 15–74. Moscow: Co-Operative Publishing Society for Foreign Workers in the USSR, 1934.
"John Scott & Company Reorganize." *Michigan Architect and Engineer* (April 1926): 72.
Kahn, Albert. "Address of Mr. Albert Kahn, F.A.I.A." *Michigan Society of Architects Weekly Bulletin* (July 14, 1942): 7.
———. "The Approach to Design." *Pencil Points* (May 1932): 299–301.
———. "The Architect in Industrial Building." *Modern Building* (May–June 1918): 12–30.
———. "Architect Pioneers in Development of Industrial Building." *The Anchora of Delta Gamma* (May 1937): 376–78.
———. "Architectural Trend." *Journal of the Maryland Academy of Sciences* (April 1931): 106–14.
———. "Chrysler Tank Arsenal." *Michigan Society of Architects Weekly Bulletin* (December 30, 1941): 15–16.
———. "Detroit Athletic Club Building." *Architecture* (July 1915): 174–76.
———. "The Fisher Building." *American Architect* 135 (February 20, 1929): 211–20.
———. "Industrial Architecture." *Michigan Society of Architects Weekly Bulletin* (December 27, 1939): 5–10.
———. "Industrial Plants for Defense (A Talk Before the Adcraft Club of Detroit, November 28, 1941)." *Michigan Society of Architects Weekly Bulletin* (December 30, 1941): 61–63.
———. "Office and Display Building for Chrysler Corporation." *Michigan Society of Architects Weekly Bulletin* (October 2, 1934): 1, 3.
———. "Our Traveling Scholar." *American Architect and Building News* (July 18, 1891): 39–41.
———. "The Packard Garage, New York." *Architects' and Builders' Magazine*, n.s., 9 (December 1907): 110–12.
———. "A Pageant of Beauty." *Architectural Forum* (July 1933): 26.
———. "Reinforced Concrete Architecture These Past Twenty Years." *Concrete* (April 1924): 129–34.
Kahn, Edgar. "Albert Kahn: His Son Remembers." *Michigan History* (July/August 1985): 24–31.
Kahn, Julius. "Coal Hoists." *Mines and Minerals* (April 1899): 392–95.
Kahn-Mahomedov, S. O. "Creative Trends." In *Building in the USSR, 1917–1932*, edited by O. A. Shividkovsky, 9–17. New York: Praeger, 1971.

"Kahn System Economy Construction." Advertisement. *McClure's* (April 1911): 940.
Knight, John G. "Detroit Has Fine New Police Headquarters." *American City* (July 27, 1922): 32.
Knowlton, Howard S. "New Manufacturing Plant for the George N. Pierce Co., Buffalo, N.Y." *Engineering Record* (September 7, 1907): 263–67.
"Knudsen Takes Charge of Chevrolet." *Automotive Industries* (March 30, 1922): 723.
Kopp, Anatole. "Foreign Architects in the Soviet Union During the First Two Five-Year Plans." In *Architecture and the New Urban Environment: Western Influences on Modernism in Russia and the USSR*, 18–50. Washington, DC: Smithsonian Institution, 1988.
Kyrilov, V. V. "The Golosov Brothers." In *Building in the USSR, 1917–1932*, edited by O. A. Shvidkovsky, 106–14. New York: Praeger Publishers, 1971.
"Large Motor Parts Center for Detroit." *Automotive Industries* (October 9, 1919): 741.
Leach, David Patrick. "The Righteous Path of Least Resistance: Hermann Rauschning's Warning to the World." Report, master's thesis, Kansas State University, 2022. Accessed October 10, 2024. krex.k-state.edu/server/api/core/bitstreams/31463cc5-e24c-496c-8c5c-2f0c0a60f487/content.
"League and T Square Club Exhibitions." *Brickbuilder* (February 1899): 23–25.
Leck, Harriet. "The Helen Newberry Nurses Home." *Modern Hospital* (April 1918): 264–66.
Lloyd, William Alford. "Aquaria: Their Past, Present and Future." *American Naturalist* (October 1876): 611–21.
———. "Crystal Palace Aquarium." *Nature* (October 12, 1871): 469–73.
———. "The Proposed Channel Islands' Zoological Station, Aquarium and Piscicultural Institute." *Nature* (December 20, 1877): 143–44.
"The Long Island Service Building." *The Packard* (January 1917): back cover.
"The Maccabees Building, Detroit." *Buildings and Building Management* (September 13, 1926): 35–39.
Magaziner, Henry Jonas. "Working for a Genius: My Time with Albert Kahn." *APT Bulletin* (2001): 59–64.
Mallgrave, Harry Francis. Introduction to Otto Wagner, *Modern Architecture* (1902), translated by Harry F. Mallgrave, 1–51. Santa Monica, CA: Getty Center for the History of Art and the Humanities, 1988.
Marchand, Roland. "Designers Go to the Fair." Part 1, "Walter Dorwin Teague and Professionalization of Corporate Exhibits, 1933–1940." In *Design History: An Anthology*, edited by Dennis P. Doordan, 89–102. Cambridge, MA: MIT Press, 2000.
———. "Designers Go to the Fair." Part 2, "Norman Bel Geddes, The General Motors 'Futurama,' and the Visit to the Factory Transformed." In *Design History: An Anthology*, edited Dennis P. Doordan, 103–21. Cambridge, MA: MIT Press, 2000.
"Marine Aquaria." *Journal of the Society of Arts* (May 3, 1872): 517–18.
Maryland Science Center. "Mission and History." Accessed August 18, 2024. www.mdsci.org/about/mission-history/.
Mason, George D. "A Few Facts of the Early Architectural Development of Detroit." *Weekly Bulletin of the Michigan Society of Architects* (April 19, 1948): 1, 5.

Mathewson, Anna. "The Detroit Bicentennial Memorial." *Century Magazine* (September 1900): 706–10.
Matte, Joseph, Jr. "Construction Details of General Motors Office Building." *Engineering News-Record* (April 14, 1921): 624–30.
McLean, Robert Craik. "Albert Kahn Signs Contract with Russians." *Western Architect* (March 1930): 39.
Meerovich, Mark G. "Albert Kahn in the History of Soviet Industrialization." Translated by Ariadne Arendt. In *Detroit-Moscow-Detroit: An Architecture for Industrialization, 1917–1945*, edited by Jean-Louis Cohen, Christina E. Crawford, and Claire Zimmerman, 199–221. Cambridge, MA: MIT Press, 2023.
Meister, Chris. "Albert Kahn's Partners in Industrial Architecture." *Journal of the Society of Architectural Historians* (March 2013): 78–95.
Melnikova-Raich, Sonia. "The Soviet Problem with Two 'Unknowns': How an American Architect and a Soviet Negotiator Jump-Started the Industrialization of Russia." Part 1: Albert Kahn. *IA: The Journal of the Society for Industrial Archeology* (2010): 57–80.
———. "The Soviet Problem with Two 'Unknowns': How an American Architect and a Soviet Negotiator Jump-Started the Industrialization of Russia." Part 2: Saul G. Bron. *IA: The Journal of the Society for Industrial Archeology* (2011): 5–28.
———. "Two Contracts, Girls in Socks, and the Great Turning Point." In *Detroit-Moscow-Detroit: An Architecture for Industrialization, 1917–1945*, edited by Jean-Louis Cohen, Christina E. Crawford, and Claire Zimmerman, 173–97. Cambridge, MA: MIT Press, 2023.
Menand, Louis. "The Historical Romance: Edmund Wilson's Adventures with Communism." *New Yorker* (March 24, 2003): 78–82.
Metzger, W. E. "Good Advice from a Successful Man." *Cycle and Automobile Trade Journal* (May 1, 1903): 36–37.
"Metzger's New Quarters." *Motor World* (September 4, 1902): 658.
"Michigan Chapter." *American Institute of Architects Quarterly Bulletin* (April 1908): 29.
Mills, James Cooke. "Perpetual Inventory Forms." *Business Man's Magazine* (October 1907): 35–40.
"Monumental News," *Stone* 21 (September 1900): 270.
"More Public Aquariums for America." *Zoological Society Bulletin* (April 1904): 149.
"Moritz Kahn." *Weekly Bulletin of the Michigan Society of Architects* (January 24, 1939): 3.
"The National Gallery Extension." *The Builder* (April 17, 1909): 464.
"National Terra Cotta Society." Advertisement in "Automobiles and Architecture." *Motor Age* (May 19, 1921): 88.
"New and Enlarged Shops." *American Machinist* (October 12, 1922): 596g.
"The New Engineering Building for the University of Michigan," *The Technic* (Engineering Society of the University of Michigan) (1902): 3.
"New Factory at Kansas City." *Ford Times* (August 15, 1909): 5.

"New Ford Branch Completed." *Motor Age* (December 29, 1910): 35.

Newman, Edward. "Notices of New Books." *The Zoologist* (November 1873): 3741–59.

"New Michigan Corporations." *Michigan Manufacturer and Financial Record* (November 10, 1923): 28.

"New Packard Service Building." *Motor Age* (December 24, 1910): 37.

"The New Packard Works." *Automobile* (December 12, 1903): 612–14.

"New School Buildings." *American School Board Journal* (January 1897): n.p.

"The New Shops of the Boyer Machine Company." *American Machinist* (March 7, 1901): 248–54.

"New York." *American Contractor* (October 21, 1922): 42.

Nimmons, George C. "Industrial Buildings." *American Architect* (January 5, 1926): 15–27.

———. "Modern Industrial Plants." Part 1. *Architectural Record* (November 1918): 414–21.

———. "Modern Industrial Plants." Part 2. *Architectural Record* (December 1918): 433–49.

"Northern MFG. Co.'s Success." *Cycle and Automobile Trade Journal* (June 1, 1903): 60–61.

"Notes Concerning Federal Government Building." *Architectural Forum* (June 1918): 219–22.

"Ohio." *American Contractor* (October 14, 1922): 52.

———.*American Contractor* (October 21, 1922): 54.

———.*American Contractor* (November 11, 1922): 52.

"On the Sixth of December. . . ." *American Architect and Building News* (January 3, 1891): 1.

"On Your Right—." *The Packard* (January 7, 1911): 16.

"Organization of Albert Kahn, Inc." *Architectural Forum* (August 1938): 91–96.

"Packard Dealers Celebrate 23rd Anniversary of Company." *Motor Record* (December 1922): 95.

"The Parks and Boulevards of Detroit." *Municipal Journal and Engineer* (March 7, 1906): 210–11.

Patric, John. "Imperial Rome Reborn." *National Geographic* (March 1937): 269–325.

Patton, Walter G. "Assembly Line." *Iron Age* (May 13, 1948): 100–102.

"Personal." *American Contractor* (May 26, 1917): 20.

"Personal and Club News: The Series of Five Discourses." *Brickbuilder* (May 1898): 93.

Pew, Marlen. "Detroit News Building Marks Milestone in Magical Growth of a City of Wonders." *Editor and Publisher* (October 20, 1911): iii, xi.

"Points to Remember in Building a New Store." *Trade* (December 7, 1904): 20.

"A Premiated Design for Aquarium and Horticultural Building in Belle Isle Park, Detroit, Mich." *American Architect and Building News* (July 20, 1901): plate.

"The Progress of the Improvements at the Aquarium." *Zoological Society Bulletin* (April 1904): 141–42.

"Retail Trade and Garages." *Automobile* (December 12, 1903): 619.

"Review of Building Activity in 1919." *Architectural Forum* (January 1920): 3–8.

Robertson, Howard. "The Factories of Henry Ford." *Architect and Building News* (March 11, 1927): 438–40.

Rose, Marc A. "Architect of the Colossal." Condensed from original publication in *Who* magazine. *Readers Digest* (February 1942): 22–26.

Rowland, Wirt C. "Architecture and the Automobile Industry." *Architectural Forum* (June 1921): 199–206.

———. "Heigh Ho! I Go to 'The Fair.'" *Weekly Bulletin of the Michigan Society of Architects* (October 23, 1934): 1, 4–6.

———. "A Milestone in American Architecture." *Modern Building* (September–October 1917). 1–5.

Sargeant, Winthrop. "Frank Lloyd Wright." *Life* (August 12, 1946): 84–96.

Schrenk, Lisa D. "Fordism, Corporate Display, and the American Expositions of the 1930s." In *Meet Me at the Fair: A World's Fair Reader*, edited by Laura Hollengreen et al., 181–95. Pittsburgh, PA: ETC Press, 2014.

Seymour, George J. "The Trussed Concrete Building." *Industrial Magazine* (April 1907): 323.

Sherman, Pruella Janet. "Third Largest Aquarium in the World." *World To-Day* (March 1904): 403–6.

Shiner, Helen. "Embodying the Spirit of the Metropolis: The Warenhaus Wertheim, Berlin, 1896–1904." In *Modernism and the Spirit of the City*, edited by Iain Boyd Whyte, 97–118. New York: Routledge, 2003.

Simmons, David A. "'The Continuous Clatter': Practical Field Riveting." *IA: The Journal of the Society for Industrial Archeology* (November 2, 1997): 5–20.

Smith, Michael G. "The First Concrete Auto Factory: An Error in the Historic Record." *Journal of the Society of Architectural Historians* (December 2019): 442–53.

Smith, Terry. "Albert Kahn: High Modernism and Actual Functionalism." In *Albert Kahn: Inspiration for the Modern*, edited by Brian Carter, 29–40. Ann Arbor: University of Michigan Museum of Art, 2001.

Smith, Thomas Vernor. "The New Deal as a Cultural Phenomenon." In *Ideological Differences in World Order: Studies in the Philosophies and Science of the World's Cultures*, edited by F. S. C. Northrop. New Haven, CT: Yale University Press, 1949.

Starr, S. Frederick. "OSA: The Union of Contemporary Architects." In *Russian Modernism: Culture and the Avant-Garde, 1900–1930*, edited by George Gibian and H. W. Tjalsma, 188–208. Ithaca, NY: Cornell University Press, 1976.

Stockbridge, Frank Parker. "How Ford Builds Submarine-Chasers in a Factory." *Popular Science Monthly* (October 1918): 71–74.

"Studio-Talk, Berlin." *The International Studio* (August 1909): 150–52.

Sullivan, Louis H. "The Chicago Tribune Competition." *Architectural Record* (February 1923): 151–57.

———. "The Tall Office Building Artistically Considered." *Lippincott's Monthly Magazine* (March 1896): 403–9.

"Superior Match Co. Closes Plant." *Wooden and Willow-Ware Trade Review* (December 12, 1907): 54.

Swales, Francis S. "Henry Bacon as a Draftsman." *Pencil Points* (May 1924): 43–62.
———. "Master Draftsmen." Part 5: Francis H. Bacon. *Pencil Points* (August 1924): 39.
———. "Master Draftsmen." Part 12: Albert Kahn. *Pencil Points* (June 1925): 43–58, 84.
Tallmadge, Thomas E. "The 'Chicago School.'" *Architectural Review* (April 1908): 69–74, 78.
"Through the Death of Dankmar Adler. . . ." *American Architect and Building News* (April 21, 1900): 17.
"Trade Notes." *Carpentry and Building* (August 1899): 170.
"Tribute to Albert Kahn." *Octagon* (July 1942): 32.
"U.S. Aviation Field at Mt. Clemens Result of Joy's Efforts." *Michigan Manufacturer and Financial Record* (June 9, 1917): 11.
"Visiting Day at St. Thomas Hospital, Surrey Gardens." *The Graphic* (June 24, 1871): 1.
Wight, Peter B. "The Use of Burned Clay Products in the Fire Proofing of Buildings." Part 2. *American Architect and Building News* (September 8, 1906): 67–69.
Wilson, Edmund. "The Despot of Dearborn." *Scribner's Magazine* (July 1931): 24–35.
"Windowless Factory Building." *Western Architect* (January 1931): 25.
Wittkopp, Gregory. "Cranbrook House." In *The Art of Collaboration and Innovation: Albert Kahn Associates*, edited by Caitlin Wunderlich, 90–91. New York: Visual Profile Books, 2022.
"Work for the Builders." *Ohio Architect and Builder* (March 1904): 44.
"The Workingmen's Expedition to Europe." *Engineer* (August 3, 1889): 32.
"A Worthy Measure." *Shooting and Fishing* (March 27, 1902): 483.
Wright, Frank Lloyd. "Address of Frank Lloyd Wright." *Michigan Association of Architects Weekly Bulletin* (July 14, 1931): 1–8.
———. "Frank Lloyd Wright Speaks Up." *House Beautiful* (July 1953): 86–88, 90.
Zieman, Irving. "Albert Kahn." *Michigan Architect and Engineer* (December 1954): 29–33, 40–41.
Zimmerman, Claire. "After." In *Albert Kahn's Industrial Architecture: Form Follows Performance*, edited by Thorsten Bürklin and Jürgen Reichardt, 210–20. Basel, Switzerland: Birkhäuser Verlag, 2019.
———. "Albert Kahn in the Second Industrial Revolution." *AA Files* 75 (2017): 28–44.
———. "Albert Kahn's Territories." In *Office US: Agendas*, edited Eva Franch i Gilabert, Amanda Reeser Lawrence, Ana Miljacki, and Ashley Schafer, 117–27. Zürich: Lars Müller, 2014.
———. "Building the World Capitalist System: The 'Invisible Architecture' of Albert Kahn Associates of Detroit, 1900–1961." *Fabrications* 29 (2019): 231–56. doi.org/10.1080/10331867.2019.1603134.
———. "The Labor of Albert Kahn." *Aggregate* 2 (December 12, 2014). www.we-aggregate.org/piece/the-labor-of-albert-kahn.

Books

Abercrombie, Stanley. *George Nelson: The Design of Modern Design*. Cambridge, MA: MIT Press, 1995.

Alexander, Peter C. *Insufficient Funds: The Financial Life of Frank Lloyd Wright*. Pittsburgh: Dorrance Publishing, 2021.

Alison, Archibald. *Essays on the Nature and Principles of Taste*. Edinburgh: Bell and Bradfute, 1790.

Allen, David Elliston. *The Naturalist in Britain: A Social History*. London: Allen Lane, 1976.

Arculus, Paul. *Durant's Right-Hand Man*. Victoria, British Columbia: Friesen Press, 2011.

Arnold, Horace Lucien, and Fay Leone Faurote. *Ford Methods and the Ford Shops*. New York: Engineering Magazine Company, 1915.

Baldasty, Gerald J. *E. W. Scripps and the Business of Newspapers*. Chicago: University of Illinois Press, 1999.

Baldwin, Neil. *Henry Ford and the Jews: The Mass Production of Hate*. New York: Public Affairs, 2001.

Banham, Reyner. *The Architecture of the Well-Tempered Environment*. Chicago: University of Chicago Press, 1969.

———. *A Concrete Atlantis: U.S. Industrial Building and European Modern Architecture, 1900–1925*. Cambridge, MA: MIT Press, 1986.

Beal, Fred E. *Proletarian Journey*. 1937. Reprint, New York: Da Capo Press, 1971.

Beasley, Norman. *Knudsen: A Biography*. New York: McGraw-Hill, 1947.

———. *Politics Has No Morals*. New York: Charles Scribner's Sons, 1949.

Beasley, Norman, and George W. Stark. *Made in Detroit*. New York: G. P. Putnam's Sons. 1957.

Bellinger, Henry Myers, Jr., ed. *The Cornell Era*, vol. 30. Ithaca, NY: Andrus & Church, 1898.

Bernstein, Michael A. *A Perilous Progress: Economists and Public Purpose in Twentieth-Century America*. Princeton, NJ: Princeton University Press, 2001.

Biggs, Lindy. *The Rational Factory: Architecture, Technology, and Work in America's Age of Mass Production*. Baltimore, MD: Johns Hopkins University Press, 1996.

Bingay, Malcolm W. *Detroit Is My Hometown*. New York: Bobbs-Merrill, 1946.

———. *Of Me I Sing*. New York: Bobbs-Merrill, 1949.

Blodgett, Geoffrey. "The Politics of Public Architecture." In *Cass Gilbert, Life and Work: Architect of the Public Domain*, edited by Barbara S. Christen and Steven Flanders, 62–72. New York: W. W. Norton, 2001.

Borth, Christy. *Masters of Mass Production*. New York: Bobbs-Merrill, 1945.

Bradley, Betsy Hunter. *The Works: The Industrial Architecture of the United States*. New York: Oxford University Press, 1999.

Brashear, William R. *Albert Kahn and His Family in Peace and War*. Ann Arbor: Bentley Historical Library, University of Michigan, 2008.

Brown, Ron. *Rails Across Ontario*. Toronto: Dundurn, 2013.

Bryan, Ford R. *Henry's Lieutenants*. Detroit: Wayne State University Press, 1993.
Bucci, Federico. *Albert Kahn: Architect of Ford*. Translated by Carmen DiCinque. New York: Princeton Architectural Press, 1993.
Burke, Thomas. *The History of the Ford Rotunda: 1934–1962*. Hicksville, NY: Exposition Press, 1976.
Burton, Clarence Monroe, ed. *The City of Detroit, Michigan, 1701–1922*. Detroit: S. J. Clarke, 1922.
Burton, Clarence M., and A. Agnes Burton, eds. *History of Wayne County and the City of Detroit, Michigan*. Detroit: S. J. Clarke, 1930.
Calendar of the University of Michigan, 1896–97. Ann Arbor: University of Michigan, 1897.
Carlson, Dale A. *Kahn's Detroit: A Field Guide to Albert Kahn Designs of the Metro Area*. Berkley, MI: Dale Carlson, 2022.
Carter, Brian, ed. *Albert Kahn: Inspiration for the Modern*. Ann Arbor: University of Michigan Museum of Art, 2001.
Chamberlin, William Henry. *The World's Iron Age*. New York: Macmillan, 1941.
The Chapin Book of Genealogical Data. Vol. 2. Chapin Family Association: Hartford, CT, 1924.
Chappell, Sally A. Kitt. *Architecture and Planning of Graham, Anderson, Probst and White, 1912–1936: Transforming Tradition*. Chicago: University of Chicago Press, 1992.
Cheney, Shelden. *The New World Architecture*. London: Longman, Green, 1930.
Christensen, Lars K. *Between Denmark and Detroit*. Aarhus, Denmark: Aarhus University Press, 2021.
Cody, Jeffry W. *American Architects Abroad, 1870–2000*. London: Routledge, 2003.
Cohen, Jean-Louis, Christina E. Crawford, and Clair Zimmerman, eds. *Detroit-Moscow-Detroit: An Architecture for Industrialization, 1917–1945*. Cambridge, MA: MIT Press, 2023.
Conn, Peter. *The Divided Mind, Ideology and Imagination in America, 1898–1917*. Cambridge: Cambridge University Press, 1983.
Conrads, Ulrich, ed. *Programs and Manifestoes on 20th-Century Architecture*. Translated by Michael Bullock. Cambridge, MA: MIT Press, 1970.
Le Corbusier. *Vers une architecture*. Paris: G. Crès, 1924.
Darley, Gillian. *Factory*. London: Reaktion Books, 2003.
De Bont, Raf. *Stations in the Field: A History of Place-Based Animal Research, 1870–1930*. Chicago: University of Chicago Press, 2015.
DiGirolamo, Vincent. *Crying the News: A History of America's Newsboys*. Oxford: Oxford University Press, 2019.
Donnelly, Walter A., ed. *The University of Michigan: An Encyclopedic Survey*. Part 7. Ann Arbor: University of Michigan Press, 1953.
Dunn, Walter S., Jr. *The Soviet Economy and the Red Army, 1930–1945*. Westport, CT: Praeger, 1995.
The Dzerzhinsky Tractor Plant at Stalingrad: A Sketch of Its Construction. Moscow: Co-Operative Publishing Society of Foreign Workers in the USSR, 1932.

Edgell, E. H. *The American Architecture of To-Day*. New York: Charles Scribner's Sons, 1928.

Esperdy, Gabrielle. *Modernizing Main Street: Architectural and Consumer Culture in the New Deal*. Chicago: University of Chicago Press, 2008.

Ferriss, Hugh. *The Metropolis of Tomorrow*. 1929. Reprint, Dover Publications, Mineola, NY: 2005.

Ferry, W. Hawkins. *The Buildings of Detroit*. Detroit: Wayne State University Press, 1968.

Fest, Joachim C. *Hitler*. Translated by Richard and Clara Winston. New York: Harcourt Brace Jovanovich, 1974.

Filene, Peter C. *Americans and the Soviet Experiment, 1917–1933*. Cambridge, MA: Harvard University Press, 1967.

Ford Factory Facts. Detroit: Ford Motor Company, n.d. (1915).

Ford, Henry, and Samuel Crowther. *My Life and Work*. Garden City, NY: Doubleday, Page, 1923.

Franklin, Rabbi Leo M., Adolph Freund, and Adolph Sloman. *A History of Congregation Beth El, Detroit, Mich., 1900–1910*. Vol. 2. Detroit: Winn & Hammond, 1910.

Furnweger, Karen. *Shedd Aquarium: The First 75 Years*. San Diego, CA: Tehabi Books, 2005.

Ganz, Cheryl R. *The 1933 Chicago World's Fair: A Century of Progress*. Chicago: University of Illinois Press, 2008.

General Catalogue of Faculty and Students, 1837–1901. Ann Arbor: University of Michigan, 1902.

Gitlow, Benjamin. *I Confess: The Truth About American Communism*. New York: E. P. Dutton, 1939.

———. *The Whole of Their Lives: Communism in America and an Intimate Portrayal of Its Leaders*. New York: Charles Scribner's Sons, 1948.

Glasscock, C. B. *The Gasoline Age: The Story of the Men Who Made It*. New York: Bobbs-Merrill, 1937.

Goldberg, Alfred, ed. *A History of the United States Air Force, 1907–1957*. Princeton, NJ: D. Van Nostrand, 1957.

Gosse, Edmund. *The Life of Philip Henry Gosse, F.R.S.* London: Kegan Paul, Trench, Trübner, 1890.

Grady, Eve Garrette. *Seeing Red: Behind the Scenes in Russia Today*. New York: Brewer, Warren & Putnam, 1931.

Gregersen, Charles E., and Joan W. Saltztein. *Dankmar Adler: His Theatres and Auditoriums*. Athens, OH: Swallow Press, 1990.

Gustin, Lawrence R. *Billy Durant: Creator of General Motors*. Ann Arbor: University of Michigan Press, 2008.

Handbook of the World's Columbian Exposition with Special Descriptive Articles. Chicago: Rand McNally, 1893.

Hartman, George E., and Jan Cigliano, eds. *Pencil Points Reader: A Journal for the Draft Room, 1920–1943*. New York: Princeton University Press, 2004.

Herman, Arthur. *Freedom's Forge: How American Business Produced Victory in World War II*. New York: Random House, 2012.

Hersey, George L., *High Victorian Gothic: A Study in Associationism*. Baltimore, MD: Johns Hopkins University, 1972.

Heyer, Paul. *Architects on Architecture: New Directions in America*. New York: Walker, 1966.

Hildebrand, Grant. *Albert Kahn: An American Architect Abroad*. Ann Arbor: University of Michigan Press, 1972.

———. *Designing for Industry: The Architecture of Albert Kahn*. Cambridge, MA: MIT Press, 1974.

Hitchcock, Henry-Russell. *Architecture: Nineteenth and Twentieth Centuries*. Baltimore, MD: Penguin Books, 1958.

———. *Modern Architecture: Romanticism and Reintegration*. New York: Rayson & Clark, 1929.

Hitchcock, Henry-Russell, and Philip Johnson. *The International Style*. New York: W. W. Norton, 1932.

Hix, John. *The Glasshouse*. London: Phaidon, 1996.

Hochman, Elaine S. *Architects of Fortune: Mies van der Rohe and the Third Reich*. New York: Weidenfeld & Nicolson, 1989.

Hodges, Michael H. *Building the Modern World: Albert Kahn in Detroit*. Detroit: Wayne State University Press, 2018.

Holleman, Thomas J., and James P. Gallagher. *Smith, Hinchman & Grylls: 125 Years of Architecture and Engineering, 1853–1978*. Detroit: Wayne State University Press, 1978.

Holli, Melvin C. *Reform in Detroit: Hazen S. Pingree and Urban Politics*. New York: Oxford University Press, 1969.

Homes, Frank R., ed. *Who's Who in New York (City and State)*. 8th ed. New York: Who's Who Publications, 1924.

Hooker, Clarence. *Life in the Shadows of the Crystal Palace, 1910–1927: Ford Workers in the Model T Era*. Bowling Green, OH: Bowling Green State University Popular Press, 1997.

Hudson, Hugh D., Jr. *Blueprints and Blood: The Stalinization of Soviet Architecture, 1917–1937*. Princeton, NJ: Princeton University Press, 1994.

Hyde, Charles K. *Arsenal of Democracy: The American Automobile Industry in World War II*. Detroit: Wayne State University Press, 2013.

———. *The Dodge Brothers: The Men, the Motor Cars, and Their Legacy*. Detroit: Wayne State University Press, 2005.

Hyde, Charles K., and Diane B. Abbot, ed. *The Lower Peninsula of Michigan: An Inventory of Historic Engineering and Industrial Sites*. Washington, DC: Historic American Engineering Record, Office of Archeology and Historic Preservation, U.S. Department of the Interior, 1976.

Inglis, J. G. *Northern Michigan Handbook for Travelers*. Petosky, MI: Geo. E. Sprang, 1898.

Isaacs, Reginald. *Gropius: An Illustrated Biography of the Creator of the Bauhaus*. Boston: Bulfinch Press, 1991.

Jordy, William H. *American Buildings and Their Architects: The Impact of European Modernism in the Mid-Twentieth Century*. Vol. 4. Garden City, NY: Doubleday, 1972.

Kennedy, E. D. *The Automobile Industry: The Coming of Age of Capitalism's Favorite Child*. New York: Reynal & Hitchcock, 1941.

Kentgens-Craig, Margret. *The Bauhaus and America: First Contacts 1919–1936*. Translated by Lynette Widder. Cambridge, MA: MIT Press, 2001.

Kimball, Fiske, and George Harald Edgell. *A History of Architecture*. New York: Harper & Row, 1918.

King, Sol. *Creative-Responsive-Pragmatic: 75 Years of Professional Practice, Albert Kahn & Associates, Architects-Engineers*. New York: Newcomen Society in North America, 1970.

Knickerbocker, H. R. *The Red Trade Menace: Progress of the Soviet Five-Year Plan*. New York: Dodd, Mead, 1931.

Kohlmaier, Georg, and von Sartory, Barna. *Houses of Glass: A Nineteenth Century Building Type*. Translated by John C. Harvey. Cambridge, MA: MIT Press, 1986.

Kravchenko, Victor A. *I Chose Freedom: The Personal and Political Life of a Soviet Official*. New York: Charles Scribner's Sons, 1946.

Lambert, Phyllis. *Building Seagram*. New Haven, CT: Yale University Press, 2013.

Lane, Barbara Miller. *Architecture and Politics in Germany, 1918–1945*. Cambridge, MA: Harvard University Press, 1968.

Langmead, Donald, and Donald Leslie Johnson. *Architectural Excursions: Frank Lloyd Wright, Holland and Europe*. Westport, CT: Greenwood Press, 2000.

Langworth, Richard M., and Don E. Weber. "Alvan Macauley and the Dominant Six." In *Packard: A History of the Motor Car and the Company*, edited by Beverly Rae Kimes, 128–51. Princeton, NJ: Princeton Institute for Historical Research, 1978.

Leake, Paul. *History of Detroit*. Chicago: Lewis Publishing, 1912.

Leder, Mary M. *My Life in Stalinist Russia: An American Woman Looks Back*. Bloomington: Indiana University Press, 2001.

Leland, Mrs. Wilfred C., and Minne Dubbs Millbrook. *Master of Precision: Henry M. Leland*. Detroit: Wayne State University Press, 1966.

Leonard, Raymond W. *Secret Soldiers of the Revolution: Soviet Military Intelligence, 1919–1933*. Westport, CT: Greenwood Press, 1999.

Lewis-Hind, Henriette. *Gari Melchers: Painter*. New York: William Edwin Rudge, 1928.

Link, Stefan J. *Forging Global Fordism: Nazi Germany, Soviet Russia and the Contest over the Industrial Order*. Princeton, NJ: Princeton University Press, 2020.

Lissitzky, El. *Russia: An Architecture for World Revolution*. [In Russian.] 1930. Translated by Eric Dluhosch. Cambridge, MA: MIT Press, 1970.

Livingston, William. *Livingston's History of the Republican Party*. Detroit: Wm. Livingston, 1900.

Lodge, John C., and M. M. Quaife. *I Remember Detroit*. Detroit: Wayne State University Press, 1949.

Lohr, Lennox R. *Fair Management: The Story of A Century of Progress Exposition*. Chicago: Cuneo Press, 1952.

Loudon, J. C. *Remarks on the Construction of Hothouses*. London: J. Taylor, 1817.

Lyon, Leverett S., Paul T. Homan, Lewis L. Lorwin, George Terborgh, Charles L. Dearing, and Leon C. Marshall. *The National Recovery Administration: An Analysis and Appraisal*. Washington, DC: Brookings Institution, 1935.

MacManus, Theodore F., and Norman Beasley. *Men, Money and Motors: The Drama of the Automobile*. New York: Harper & Brothers, 1929.

Marquardt, Virginia Hagelstein, ed. *Art and Journals on the Political Front, 1910–1940*. Gainesville: University Press of Florida, 1997.

Marquis, Albert Nelson, ed. *The Book of Detroiters: A Biographical Dictionary of Leading Living Men of the City of Detroit*. 2nd ed. Chicago: A. N. Marquis, 1914.

Marquis, Samuel S. *Henry Ford: An Interpretation*. Boston: Little, Brown, 1923.

Maurer, Maurer, ed. *The U.S. Air Service in World War I*. Vol. 1. Washington: Office of Air Force History, 1978.

May, George S., ed. *Encyclopedia of American Business History and Biography: The Automobile Industry, 1920–1980*. New York: Facts on File, 1989.

McAndrew, John, and Elizabeth Mock. *What Is Modern Architecture?* New York: Museum of Modern Art, 1942.

Michigan State Administrative Board of the Writers' Program of the Work Projects Administration. *Michigan: A Guide to the Wolverine State*. New York: Oxford University Press, 1941.

Mock, Elizabeth, ed. *Built in the USA Since 1932*. New York: Museum of Modern Art, 1945.

Morrison, Jeff. *Guardians of Detroit: Architectural Sculpture in the Motor City*. Detroit: Wayne State University Press, 2019.

A Nation Builds: Contemporary German Architecture. New York: German Library of Information, 1940.

Naval History Division. *Dictionary of American Naval Fighting Ships*. Washington, DC: Department of the Navy, 1976.

Nelson, Donald M. *Arsenal of Democracy: The Story of American War Production*. New York: Harcourt, Brace, 1946.

Nelson, George. *Building a New Europe: Portraits of Modern Architects*. New Haven, CT: Yale University Press, 2007.

———. *Industrial Architecture of Albert Kahn, Inc.* New York: Architectural Book Publishing, 1939.

Nevins, Allan. *Ford: The Times, the Man, the Company*. New York: Charles Scribner's Sons, 1954.

Nevins, Allan, and Frank Ernest Hill. *Ford: Expansion and Challenge, 1915–1933*. New York: Charles Scribner's Sons, 1957.

Newcomb, Rexford. *History of Modern Architecture*. Scranton, PA: International Textbook, 1942.

Nyhan, Miriam. *Are You Still Below? The Ford Marina Plant, Cork, 1917–19*. Cork, Ireland: Collins Press, 2007.

O'Callaghan, Timothy J. *Henry Ford's Airport and Other Aviation Interests, 1909–1954*. Ann Arbor, MI: privately printed, 1995.
Oestreicher, Richard Jules. *Solidarity and Fragmentation: Working People and Class Consciousness in Detroit, 1875–1900*. Chicago: University of Illinois Press, 1986.
Painter, Borden W., Jr. *Mussolini's Rome: Rebuilding the Eternal City*. New York: Palgrave Macmillan, 2005.
Peterson, Sarah Jo. *Planning the Home Front: Building Bombers and Communities at Willow Run*. Chicago: University of Chicago Press, 2013.
Pound, Arthur. *The Turning Wheel: The Story of General Motors through Twenty-Five Years, 1908–1933*. Garden City, NY: Doubleday, Doran, 1934.
Press Reference Library: Notables of the West. Western Edition, vol. 2. New York: International News Service, 1915.
Rauschning, Hermann. *Hitler Speaks: A Series of Political Conversations with Adolf Hitler on His Real Aims*. London: Thornton Butterworth, 1939.
Reinforced Concrete in Factory Construction. New York: Atlas Portland Cement Company, 1907.
Riley, Terence. *The International Style: Exhibit 15 and the Museum of Modern Art*. New York: Rizzoli, 1992.
Robbins, E. Clyde, comp. *Selected Articles on the Open Versus Closed Shop*. Debate Handbook Series. Minneapolis, MN: H. W. Wilson, 1911.
Robeson, Paul Jr. *The Undiscovered Paul Robeson: An Artist's Journey 1898–1939*. New York: John Wiley & Sons, 2001.
Ross, Robert B., and George B. Catlin. *Landmarks of Wayne County and Detroit*. Revised by Clarence W. Burton. Detroit: Evening News Association, 1898.
Rubenstein, James M. *The Changing US Auto Industry: A Geographical Analysis*. New York: Routledge, 1992.
Russell, John Andrew. *The Germanic Influence in the Making of Michigan*. Detroit: University of Detroit, 1927.
Saint, Andrew. *Architect and Engineer: A Study in Sibling Rivalry*. New Haven, CT: Yale University Press, 2007.
———. *The Image of the Architect*. New Haven, CT: Yale University Press, 1983.
Schivelbusch, Wolfgang. *Three New Deals: Reflections on Roosevelt's America, Mussolini's Italy, and Hitler's Germany*. Translated by Jefferson Chase. New York: Metropolitan Books, 2006.
Schneider, Herbert W. *Making the Fascist State*. New York: Oxford University Press, 1928.
Schrenk, Lisa D. *Building a Century of Progress: The Architecture of Chicago's 1933–34 World's Fair*. Minneapolis: University of Minnesota Press, 2007.
Scripps, James E. *A Genealogical History of the Scripps Family and Its Various Alliances*. Detroit: privately printed, 1903.
Seeley, Thaddeus D., comp. *History of Oakland County, Michigan: A Narrative Account of Its Historical Progress, Its People, and Its Principal Interests*. Chicago: Lewis Publishing, 1912.

Slayton, Amy E. *Reinforced Concrete and the Modernization of American Building, 1900–1930*. Baltimore, MD: Johns Hopkins University Press, 2001.

Smith, Kathryn. *Wright on Exhibit: Frank Lloyd Wright's Architectural Exhibitions*. Princeton, NJ: Princeton University Press, 2017.

Smith, Michael G. *Concrete Century: Julius Kahn and the Construction Revolution*. Ann Arbor: University of Michigan Press, 2024.

———. *Designing Detroit: Wirt Rowland and the Rise of Modern American Architecture*. Detroit: Wayne State University Press, 2017.

Smith, Terry. *Making the Modern: Industry, Art and Design in America*. Chicago: University of Chicago Press, 1993.

Sorenson, Lorin. *The Ford Shows*. Osceola, WI: Motorbooks International, 1991.

Stark, George W. *City of Destiny: The Story of Detroit*. Detroit: Arnold-Powers, 1943.

———. *Detroit: An Industrial Miracle*. Detroit: Detroit Directory of Business and Industry, 1951.

Stickney, Robert R. *Aquaculture of the United States: A Historical Survey*. New York: John Wiley & Sons, 1996.

Stout, Wesley W. *Great Engines and Great Planes*. Detroit: Chrysler Corporation, 1947.

Sutton, Antony C. *Western Technology and Soviet Economic Development, 1917 to 1930*. Stanford, CA: Hoover Institution, 1968.

Sweetser, Arthur. *The American Air Service: A Record of Its Problems, Its Difficulties, Its Failures, and Its Final Achievements*. New York: D. Appleton, 1919.

Tallmadge, Thomas E. *The Story of Architecture in America*. 1927. Rev. ed. New York: W. W. Norton, 1936.

The Ten Year Book of Cornell University, 1868–1908. Vol. 9. Ithaca, NY: Cornell University, 1908.

Townsend, Charles Haskins. *The Public Aquarium: Its Construction, Equipment, and Maintenance*. Washington, DC: Department of Commerce, 1928.

Trowbridge, Francis Bacon, comp. *The Trowbridge Genealogy: History of the Trowbridge Family in America*. New Haven, CT: private printing, 1908.

Tzouliadis, Tim. *The Forsaken: An American Tragedy in Stalin's Russia*. New York: Penguin Press, 2008.

University Bulletin, Department of Engineering: General Announcement, 1908–1909. Ann Arbor: University of Michigan, 1908.

Van Brunt, Henry. *Architecture and Society: Selected Essays of Henry Van Brunt*. Edited by William A. Coles. Cambridge, MA: Belknap Press, 1969.

Verderber, Stephen. *Innovations in Hospital Architecture*. New York: Routeledge, 2010.

Vidler, Anthony. *Histories of the Immediate Present: Inventing Architectural Modernism*. Cambridge, MA: MIT Press, 2008.

Voyce, Arthur. *Russian Architecture: Trends in Nationalism and Modernism*. New York: Philosophical Library, 1948.

Walton, Francis. *Miracle of World War II: How American Industry Made Victory Possible*. New York: MacMillan, 1956.

Weeks, Elaine, and Chris Edwards. *Walkerville: Whiskey Town Extraordinaire*. Windsor, Ontario: Walkerville Publishing, 2015.
Weil, Martin. *A Pretty Good Club: The Founding Fathers of the U.S. Foreign Service*. New York: W. W. Norton, 1978.
Wilkinson, Chris. *Supersheds: The Architecture of Long-Span, Large Volume Buildings*. Oxford: Butterworth Architecture, 1991.
Williamson, Roxanne Kuter. *American Architects and the Mechanics of Fame*. Austin: University of Texas Press, 1991.
Wilson, Mark R. *Destructive Creation: American Business and the Winning of World War II*. Philadelphia: University of Pennsylvania Press, 2016.
Woodbury, David O. *Builders for Battle: How the Pacific Naval Air Bases Were Constructed*. New York: E. P. Dutton, 1946.
Woodford, Frank B. *We Never Drive Alone: The Story of the Automobile Club of Michigan*. Detroit: Automobile Club of Michigan, 1958.
Wright, Frank Lloyd. *Collected Writings*. Edited by Bruce Pfeiffer. Vol. 3. New York: Rizzoli, 1993.
———. *Frank Lloyd Wright on Architecture: Selected Writings*. Edited by Frederick Gutheim. New York: Grosset & Dunlap, 1941.
———. *Letters to Architects*. Edited by Bruce Brooks Pfeiffer. Fresno, CA: The Press at California State University, 1984.
Young, Edward M. *Building Engines for War: Air-Cooled Radial Aircraft Engine Production in Britain and America in World War II*. Warrendale, PA: SAE International, 2024.

Governmental Sources

Annual Report of the Commissioner of Parks and Boulevards, City of Detroit, Michigan. Reports 12–15, Detroit: Raynor & Taylor, 1901–4. Report 16, Detroit: Franklin Press, 1905.
Bean, Tarleton H. *Report of the Representative of the United States Fish Commission at the World's Columbian Exposition*. Washington: Government Printing Office, 1896.
Bulletin of the United States Fish Commission. Vols. 10, 13. Washington, DC: United States Government Printing Office, 1892, 1894.
City of Detroit Journal of the Common Council from January 13, 1903, to January 12, 1904. Detroit: Thomas Smith, 1904.
Detroit City Directory for 1882 [and subsequent years]. Detroit: J. W. Weeks, 1882, 1883; Detroit: R. L. Polk, 1887, 1889.
Fifteenth Annual Report of the Commissioner of Parks and Boulevards, Detroit, Michigan. Detroit: Raynor & Taylor, 1903.
First Report of the Commissioners for Inquiring into the State of Large Towns and Populous Districts, Great Britain. Vol. 1. London: W. Clowes & Sons, 1844.
Historic American Building Survey No. WIS-270. Milwaukee, WI: Milwaukee Public Library and Museum.

Journal of the House of Representatives of the State of Michigan, 1899. Vol. 1. Lansing, MI: Rupert Smith, 1899.

Legislative Reference Service of the Library of Congress. *Trends in Russian Foreign Policy Since World War I*. Washington, DC: United States Government Printing Service, 1947.

Michigan Department of Health Death Certificate. File 300275: Albert Kahn, December 8, 1942.

Nash, Donna M., comp. *Report of the Michigan Century of Progress Commission on the Michigan Exhibit, a Century of Progress Exposition, Chicago, 1933*.

National Register of Historic Places Registration Form: Omaha Ford Motor Company Assembly Plant, November 15, 2004. Form prepared by Jennifer Honebrink, AIA. Lawrence Sommer, director, Nebraska State Historical Society. preservation .cityofomaha.org/wp-content/uploads/2023/06/BD-127-N_Ford-Motor-Co_NR.pdf.

Sixteenth Annual Report of the Commissioner of Parks and Boulevards, Detroit, Michigan. Detroit: Raynor & Taylor, 1905.

Seventeenth Annual Report of the Board of Trustees of the Public Library of the City of Milwaukee. Milwaukee: Board of Trustees, 1894.

State Board (Michigan). *World's Columbian Exposition: State of Michigan*. Flint: W. H. Werkeiser & Sons, 1892.

U.S. House of Representatives. *Report of the Committee on Naval Affairs, Pursuant to H. Res. 30, a Resolution Authorizing and Directing an Investigation of the Progress of the War Effort*. 78th Cong., 2nd sess. 1944.

U.S. Senate. *Hearing Before Committee on Naval Affairs on Eagle Boats, Pursuant to S. Res. 404*. 65th Cong., 3rd sess. 1919.

Exhibit Catalogues and Ephemera

Albert Kahn: Architect Abroad. Charles H. Sawyer, director. Ann Arbor: University of Michigan Museum of Art, 1972.

Burroughs, Clyde H. *Retrospective Exhibition of Paintings by Gari Melchers*. Detroit: Detroit Institute of Arts, 1927.

Catalogue: Annual Exhibition of the Saint Louis Architectural Club. 1899. Google Books. books.google.com/books?id=DaMaAAAAYAAJ&printsec.

Catalogue of the First Annual Exhibition of the Detroit Architectural Club. 1900. Google Books. books.google.com/books?id=IS0-AQAAMAAJ&printsec.

Catalogue of the Twelfth Annual Exhibition by the Chicago Architectural Club at the Art Institute (March 30 to April 16, 1899). Google Books. books.google.com/books ?id=1J8aAAAAYAAJ&pg.

Dedication of the Detroit Times New Building. December 6, 1929. Hathi Trust. babel .hathitrust.org/cgi/pt?id=mdp.39015071536554&seq=1.

The Fisher Building. Detroit: New Center Development, 1928. Hathi Trust. babel .hathitrust.org/cgi/pt?id=mdp.39015071312923&seq=1.

"General Motors Building: A Century of Progress." Promotional brochure. 1934. Collection of the author.

Hitchcock, Henry-Russell, Jr., Philip Johnson, and Lewis Mumford. *Modern Architecture—International Exhibition.* New York: Museum of Modern Art, 1932.
Meister, Chris. *Albert Kahn at the Crossroads: The "Lost" Belle Isle Aquarium & Horticultural Building Blueprints.* Exhibit catalogue. Southfield, MI: Lawrence Technological University, 2017. Collection of the author.
Mock, Elizabeth, ed. *Built in the USA: A Survey of Contemporary American Architecture.* New York: Museum of Modern Architecture, 1945.
Scripps, James E. *Descriptive Account of the New Edifice Erected for Trinity Church, Detroit.* Detroit: Ladies Aid Society of Trinity Church, 1892.
"The Taliesen Fellowship." Facsimile reprint of 1933 brochure. Scottsdale, AZ: Frank Lloyd Wright Foundation, 2003. Collection of the author.

Index

Note: Page numbers in italics refer to figures.

About the Author

Chris Meister is an independent scholar and the author of *James Riely Gordon: His Courthouses and Other Public Architecture*, which was honored with the Victorian Society in America's Ruth Emery Award and the Conservation Society of San Antonio Publication Award. His articles have appeared in the *Journal of the Society of Architectural Historians* and *Southwestern Historical Quarterly*. He lives in Royal Oak, Michigan, with his wife, Katie.